Multilingualism and Education

For decades, international researchers and educators have sought to understand how to address cultural and linguistic diversity in education. This book
offers the keys to doing so: it brings together short biographies of thirty-six
scholars, representing a wide range of universities and countries. These
biographies reflect on the scholars' personal life paths and how their individual life experiences have led to and informed their research. This approach
highlights how theories and concepts have evolved in different contexts while
opening up pedagogical possibilities from diverse backgrounds and being
enriched by the life experiences of leading researchers in the field. Beyond
these questions, the book also explores the dynamic relationships among
languages, power, and identities, as well as how these relationships raise
broader societal issues that permeate both global and local language practices.
It is essential reading for students, teacher educators, and researchers interested in the impact of multilingualism on education.

GAIL PRASAD'S research examines social representations of plurilingualism
and approaches to teaching for critical multilingual language awareness.
She received the 2016 Pat Clifford Award for Early Career Research in
Education from the Canadian Education Association and the 2016 AERA
Second Language Research SIG Dissertation Award from the American
Educational Research Association.

NATHALIE AUGER is a full professor at the University of Montpellier. She
leads international research in linguistics and didactics. She won a European
Commission prize for innovation regarding language teaching in multilingual
contexts. She has edited a dozen books, and various websites including
videos, on the subject for more than fifteen years.

EMMANUELLE LE PICHON-VORSTMAN is a faculty member at the Ontario
Institute for Studies in Education at the University of Toronto, and head of the
Centre de Recherches en Éducation Franco-Ontarienne (CRÉFO). Since
2009, she has led several international research projects on the inclusion of
minority students in education. She works as a consultant, researcher, evalu-
ator, and reviewer for several international organizations.

Multilingualism and Education

Researchers' Pathways and Perspectives

Edited by

Gail Prasad
York University

Nathalie Auger
University of Montpellier

Emmanuelle Le Pichon-Vorstman
University of Toronto

Shaftesbury Road, Cambridge CB2 8EA, United Kingdom

One Liberty Plaza, 20th Floor, New York, NY 10006, USA

477 Williamstown Road, Port Melbourne, VIC 3207, Australia

314–321, 3rd Floor, Plot 3, Splendor Forum, Jasola District Centre, New Delhi – 110025, India

103 Penang Road, #05–06/07, Visioncrest Commercial, Singapore 238467

Cambridge University Press is part of Cambridge University Press & Assessment, a department of the University of Cambridge.

We share the University's mission to contribute to society through the pursuit of education, learning and research at the highest international levels of excellence.

www.cambridge.org
Information on this title: www.cambridge.org/9781009017053

DOI: 10.1017/9781009037075

First published 2022
First paperback edition 2024

A catalogue record for this publication is available from the British Library

Library of Congress Cataloging-in-Publication data
Names: Prasad, Gail, editor. | Auger, Nathalie, 1973- editor. | Le Pichon-Vorstman, Emmanuelle, 1972- editor.
Title: Multilingualism and education : researchers' pathways and perspectives / edited by Gail Prasad, Nathalie Auger, Emmanuelle Le Pichon Vorstman.
Description: Cambridge, United Kingdom ; New York, NY: Cambridge University Press, 2022. | Contributions that were originally in French have been translated into English for publication. | Includes bibliographical references and index.
Identifiers: LCCN 2021039262 (print) | LCCN 2021039263 (ebook) | ISBN 9781316517079 (hardback) | ISBN 9781009017053 (paperback) | ISBN 9781009037075 (epub)
Subjects: LCSH: Linguists–Biography. | Language teachers–Biography. | Language and education. | Multilingual education. | Multilingualism–Research. | Multiculturalism in education. | Language teachers–Training of. | BISAC: LANGUAGE ARTS & DISCIPLINES / Linguistics / General | LCGFT: Autobiographies. | Essays.
Classification: LCC P83 .M85 2022 (print) | LCC P83 (ebook) | DDC 404/.2072–dc23/eng/20211118
LC record available at https://lccn.loc.gov/2021039262
LC ebook record available at https://lccn.loc.gov/2021039263

ISBN   978-1-316-51707-9   Hardback
ISBN   978-1-009-01705-3   Paperback

Contents

Figures

List of Contributors

MEHMET-ALI AKINCI, University of Rouen

NATHALIE AUGER, University of Montpellier

THERESA AUSTIN, University of Massachusetts Amherst

FRANCIS BANGOU, University of Ottawa

DAT BAO, Monash University

JEAN-CLAUDE BEACCO, University of the New Sorbonne

MERCÈ BERNAUS, Autonomous University of Barcelona

MARISA CAVALLI, European Centre for the Modern Languages (ECML) of the Council of Europe

VIKTORIJA L. A. ČEGINSKAS, University of Jyväskylä

DANIEL COSTE, ENSL, emeritus

DIANE DAGENAIS, Simon Fraser University

ESTER DE JONG, University of Florida

PIERRE ESCUDÉ, INSPE Bordeaux, ESPE Aquitaine

CAROLE FLEURET, University of Ottawa

GILLES FORLOT, INALCO Paris

LAURENT GAJO, Geneva University

OFELIA GARCÍA, City University of New York

CÉCILE GOÏ, University of Tours

MAUREEN KENDRICK, University of British Columbia

KENDALL A. KING, University of Minnesota

CLAIRE KRAMSCH, University of California–Berkeley

PHAN LE HA, Universiti Brunei Darussalam and University of Hawaii at Manoa

EMMANUELLE LE PICHON-VORSTMAN, University of Toronto

DAVID LITTLE, Trinity College Dublin

MARIE-PAULE LORY, University of Toronto Mississauga

JEFF MACSWAN, University of Maryland

EMILEE MOORE, Autonomous University of Barcelona

ENRICA PICCARDO, University of Toronto

GAIL PRASAD, York University

ELATIANA RAZAFIMANDIMBIMANANA, University of New Caledonia

SVEN SIERENS, Ghent University

NIKOLAY SLAVKOV, University of Ottawa

HEATHER JANE SMITH, Newcastle University

SHELLEY K. TAYLOR, University of Western Ontario

KELLEEN TOOHEY, Simon Fraser University

PIET VAN AVERMAET, Ghent University

RAHAT ZAIDI (NAQVI), University of Calgary

1   Humanizing Research(ers) and Understanding How Concepts Evolve in Context

Gail Prasad, Nathalie Auger and Emmanuelle Le Pichon-Vorstman

Educational linguistics has many faces, embodied by thousands of researchers around the world. Whether scholars use similar or divergent terminology, it can be difficult to discern the contours of how concepts are taken up across and even sometimes within contexts. The interpretation of theoretical constructs requires a contextual articulation in relation to history: Where have theoretical constructs come from? How do they manifest? And, where might they lead us? This book aims to bring to life issues and perspectives regarding multilingualism and education that have emerged in specific contexts and through varied lived experiences. Taking a biographical approach, through the individual trajectories of contributing researchers, allows us to better understand how our epistemologies shape the way we mobilize concepts.

Although language biographies have been theorized as a key component of language learning and teaching, they have rarely been used as the basis of reflection for researchers about their own research. This book offers readers the opportunity to encounter scholars more personally. Research can too easily become disembodied and decontextualized through academic reporting. One of the limits with decontextualized scientific reports is that they obscure the fact that they are based on interpretations of concepts and practices from one context to another. Gradually, contextual processes of interpretation can produce alternative conceptualizations that can at times appear to be in conflict with their origins.

While it is expected that researchers may reference concepts in different ways and for different purposes, as we come to know researchers' biographies and trajectories, it becomes easier to understand how different nuances and meanings may have evolved. Based on this knowledge, the reinterpretation and reinvestment of concepts and practices create the opportunity to expand research opportunities on a more solid foundation. To this end, we invited scholars working at the intersections of language and education to share their language biographies and research trajectories. Accordingly, the objective was to paint a picture of how their work takes up concepts and practices related to multilingualism. Scholars across various career stages reflected on how personal and lived experiences contributed to their sensibility towards language(s) and how theories have evolved out of practice and vice versa.

Readers will discover how diverse experiences have led researchers to adopt different terminologies to describe language teaching and learning, their positionalities and their connections across domains (Second Language Acquisition, sociolinguistics, anthropology, education, sociology, linguistics, etc.). While such differences are likely to produce division within the field of educational linguistics, they can also lead to productive intramural discussions to further our thinking and to contribute to the collaborative production of knowledge and complex ways of seeing, doing and being. Readers will also discover how scholars' reflections on their research have led to innovation in theory and in practice. Beyond these epistemic questions, the scholars will further explore the dynamic relationships among languages, powers and identities and how these relationships raise broader societal issues that permeate both global and local language practices.

Individual perspectives that are shared herein are woven across multiple life worlds: families, schools, academic positions and society. Transgressions across these different spheres have led academics to make choices in their personal and academic lives. Their experiences (whether they choose them or not) invariably mark them in different ways: speaking a language at home and another at school; witnessing or experiencing exclusion (symbolic or real violence); and falling in love with countries, languages and people.

Since the Multilingual Turn, we have seen a veritable explosion of terms that have tried to capture shifting perspectives on language(s) and their users. A way forward cannot be designed without or apart from language(s). In the Post-Multilingual Turn, we leave a paradigm of opposition or complementarity proposed by binary models such as 'bilingual', 'dual language education', 'compartmentalization' and 'two solitudes'. To go beyond inter-models ('interculturality', 'interlanguage') progressively opens up complex 'trans', 'hybrid', 'multi' and 'pluri' possibilities. In each contribution, concepts have been operationalized in different ways. Rather than seeing these differences in opposition, in this book, readers are invited to seek understanding of how plural meanings can advance their own understanding of language(s) in education and research. Emergent terminology reflects that languages, variations and modes co-exist. This reality must be taken into account as we embrace evolving critical perspectives.

Indeed, it seems vital at this point in history that we develop the academic practice of embodied dialogue. Involving scholars who work in the same field across different contexts and in different languages, this book stresses the value of cultivating a practice of sustained listening across different generations, genders, countries and continents.

We begin by recounting how our own research trajectories first brought us together and how our professional and personal experiences have further been enriched through collaboration. Our work together within and across contexts and languages allows us to reflect on how concepts and practices change, adapt and necessarily evolve as they are taken up in different ways with different audiences.

1.1   From Our Own Experiences of Variability Regarding Concepts

The vision for this book began to take shape when Gail Prasad and Nathalie Auger started working together first in France and then across the Atlantic between France and Canada and the United States. As they compared their own academic references, they did not necessarily share the same visions of similar concepts in English and French, and noticed that, in the end, they often used different notions to refer to similar experiences. They soon became aware that concepts that might appear at first to be in conflict were not necessarily so. Their relationship as colleagues and friends, however, encouraged them to persist in linguistic and cultural collaboration to work through perceived conflicts to build understanding of one another and their respective and shared work.

As three co-editors, our trajectories and work have raised many questions. It was first in 2013 that Gail Prasad's and Nathalie Auger's paths crossed virtually and then in real time and space. Gail Prasad had become invested in research in Canada's minority French-language schools through her graduate work at the Ontario Institute for Studies in Education at the University of Toronto (OISE/UT) and the Centre de Recherche en Éducation Franco-Ontarienne (CRÉFO). At the time, as a self-professed monolingual Anglophone, she suffered from extreme linguistic insecurity and wanted to improve her French. She was also interested in multilingual/plurilingual approaches to teaching and learning in Europe that she had been introduced to in part through Nathalie Auger's work in France. When Gail was awarded a Weston doctoral fellowship to pursue international research at the University of Montpellier 3, she and Nathalie started to think about what it actually meant to collaborate as two researchers with common interests but different languages.

During that year-long collaboration, they came to see many commonalities in their interests. Translanguaging was a relatively new concept at the time, rising from New York in North America, whereas plurilingualism had become a key lens for European language research and institutions. In discussing scholarship in English and in French, their collaboration perhaps made it easier to build on commonalities rather than to focus on potential conflicts. They were both focused on linguistically minoritized populations even though the contexts and the particularities of their study populations differed. This is not to say that generalization across contexts and populations is always suitable but rather that in investing in understanding one another, they were better able to go deeper in their reflections and to move beyond their comfort zones.

Emmanuelle Le Pichon and Nathalie Auger met in 2016 when they were both working with newcomer students in their respective contexts. They were interested in how the different countries in which they lived – the Netherlands, Canada and France – could ask the same questions about the integration of these students into education but treat the answers very differently. In the meantime, they met in London at a conference on Roma students (Romtels), where different concepts such as translingualism or plurilingualism were intensively discussed. No book at the time dealt with these transnational aspects. In 2019, Gail moved back to Canada from the United States and Emmanuelle Le Pichon joined the editorial team for this book. In coming together, their experiences allowed them as co-editors, colleagues and friends to realize the richness of collective work across contexts, languages and epistemologies.

The volume is organized into three sections:

1 The introduction outlines the methodology for the book with particular emphasis on the need for a synergistic vision for multilingual research and practice in education animated by the thinking of researchers from different generations, countries and continents.
2 Individual contributions from researchers make up the body of this collection. Authors share their language biography and, in particular, the elements that have influenced their interest in the issue of multilingualism in the education system and for each of the following three sets of concepts (multilingualism/plurilingualism/heteroglossia, intercultural/pluricultural/ multicultural education, linguistic repertoire/communicative repertoire, awareness of language and language awareness, intercomprehension and education for cross linguistic transfer, translanguaging) to reflect on the evolution of the concepts in their own contexts, explaining their use of or reluctance towards these notions. Where they drew other concepts and practices related to multilingualism, they were asked to explain how and why they had come to propose, adopt and apply said alternatives. While each contribution was written by scholars themselves in first person in English and/or French, the editors also gave them the opportunity to write in the language of their choice or to use different languages to enrich the meaning they wanted to give to their thoughts. Contributions that were originally in French have been translated into English for publication. However, the editors have tried to respect authors' choices to move between languages in their texts. For example, at times, English translations are

provided alongside the original text for quotations. All together this collection includes contributions from thirty-six authors.

3 The conclusion then offers a meta-reflection on three recurrent themes and questions for further study.

As scholars we all know the shock of discovering the name of a renowned scientist on his or her badge at a conference and linking it to all the publications of the individual in question. As this book has taken shape, we have also come to reflect on the contribution of this collection for scholars and graduate students who read extensively but do not always have the advantage of knowing authors personally and the complex histories of various concepts and practices. While we appreciate the productive nature of constructive debate and scholarly discussion, we recognize the need today more than ever to overcome binary thinking and move towards complex, embodied ways of engaging in critique of theories, concepts and practices rather than individuals. In a highly mobile world, concepts, practices and authors routinely cross boundaries, giving rise to different meanings within different contexts. This book aims to elaborate on how such crossing can move our field forward.

This book then can also be read as a story of a discovery: the discovery of life courses that all converge towards a reconceptualization of language and education in the Post-Multilingual Turn. Individual contributions bring to light the contingencies of genetics, history, mobility, migration, power and vulnerability in relationships between and among people. Or put differently, these stories of mobility and migration told through the subjectivity of their respective narrators allow each author to put forward their own histories, perspectives and concepts as they have followed an advanced academic path.

We bring together scholars from a wide range of universities across four continents and various disciplines (linguistics, ethnology, anthropology, pedagogy). Browsing through the memories of these authors will allow readers to discover how the sometimes happy, often unhappy experiences have enriched their thinking about languages and contexts, including concepts of minoritization, racism, glottophobia and stigmatization. From the outset, we wish to underscore that experiences of minoritization are not always visible: in this book, the reader will discover that racial origin is not always indicated by name; that systemic racism is everywhere, but its many manifestations vary according to context; that academic norms and values are not homogeneous either but often depend on the geographical areas in which the universities are located; that a prestigious origin in one country is not necessarily prestigious in the other; racism, exclusion and discrimination, namely, on the basis of language persist everywhere. Taken together, the resulting work makes visible both the incredible range of concepts that authors are discussing across contexts (see index) and the theoretical depth of discussion related to these concepts. For the presentation of the biographies, we have chosen to adopt an alphabetical order based on the surnames of the authors.

Mehmet-Ali Akinci begins by reminding us how schools in France at the beginning of the twentieth century punished students caught speaking a dialect by forcing them to clean the toilets because they 'had shit in their mouths!'. Coming from a family of traditional immigrants from Turkey, he shows how 'immigrant origin' often appears in the common imagination as a factor explaining their failure at school. His psycholinguistic background is marked by his fight against discrimination and *glottophobia* at school.

Nathalie Auger, who grew up between and within languages, pleads for a plural and inclusive 'hospitable' pedagogy, a pedagogy *of* and *for* diversity. Through the encounter and study of social representations of plurilingualism and linguistic diversity within urban multilingualism, she has examined social and linguistic fractures that generate verbal and symbolic violence, multilingual walls and stigmatization. These experiences naturally led her to address these fractures in her work through a linguistically sensitive pedagogy.

Theresa Austin is the daughter of Japanese immigrants by her mother and African-Americans by her father. Her history has led her to navigate between languages and identities that were attributed to her as she learned and developed the concept of a 'wholistic imagined identity'. She explains how the monolingual ideology in the United States has impacted her family life, preventing her from becoming a full member of the cultural groups of her choice.

Francis Bangou chose to fight social injustice by advocating for the empowerment of marginalized groups of learners. His social and academic background, made of geographical and institutional patchworks of language norms and habits, has led him to reject binary explanations, such as nature versus nurture and speaker versus language, in order 'to recognize that speaker, language, and matter are perpetually becoming other in creative relational and ever changing entanglements'.

The work of **Jean-Claude Beacco** brought him to the Council of Europe. There he became interested in the management of cultural Otherness, shedding new light on questions of legitimacy of certain languages in relation to others. For him, 'the stakes are being played at the pedagogical level, [. . .], but also at the structural level, through the indispensable coming together of at least language coursework and language(s) of schooling coursework'.

Mercè Bernaus grew up in Spain, in a language imposed by the oppressor, and reminds us that school is a political instrument manipulated by the official language. **Emilee Moore,** daughter of Italian migrants in Australia, explores the stigma surrounding the indigenous communities in Australia and their right to live and learn in their languages. Together, they explore how gesture, ways of dressing and dance movements can contribute to learning, in the context of different sociocultural dynamics and through collaborative and activist approaches that include the whole semiotic repertoire of students.

Marisa Cavalli discovered at a very young age that her family's dialect put her in a marginal position, under the symbolic domination of the tourists who invaded her Italian village every year. This situation led her to fight for the rights of minorities from an inclusive pedagogical perspective. She promotes the maintenance of languages, shedding light on the social-political power relations and, in turn, on the pedagogical aspects.

The story of **Viktorija Ceginskas** is a story of interactions between different ethnicities, cultures and languages on the borders of the Baltic States. She shows how stateless refugees may compensate for their loss of identity by strong emotional bonds with families, native countries and languages. She shows how 'language use and practices help to determine a person's self- and externally ascribed identification by others, and provide orientation in everyday social interactions, including the recognition as a valid and represented group member with specific rights'.

Daniel Coste, the father of what has been coined 'plurilingual competence', demonstrates 'the intricacy of the historical, territorial, patrimonial, migratory, even ethnic and religious, and always economic, social, and political aspects that, depending on various configurations, affect the representations and positionings of social actors with regard to linguistic plurality'. He helps us to tease apart 'chosen plurilingualisms from forced plurilingualisms', and to remember that there are 'unfortunate, insecure, perhaps handicapping plurilingualisms'.

Diane Dagenais highlights her parents' resistance to linguistic assimilation and her own path between alternating and mixing languages. She quickly became aware of the boundaries between languages and of artificial and oppressive school policies. Her research has led her to explore children's linguistic practices, stereotypical representations and to fight against social inequalities by supporting multilingual pedagogies against unfair and oppressive practices.

Ester de Jong traces her development of a bilingual/multilingual stance through her personal and professional experiences. These began in the Netherlands and involved crossing back and forth from Europe to the United States and a variety of international contexts, investigating bilingual education systems, teacher development and practices. Her research has led her to affirm 'bilinguals are bilinguals' as a starting place for principled decision-making concerning equitable policy and practice with bi/multilinguals.

Pierre Escudé's text begins with a reminder of the history of dialects across France, and particularly Occitan. He draws our attention back to the nineteenth century and France's systemic repression of minority languages. Against this tide, he gradually became the ambassador of these so-called dialect languages and developed the field of intercomprehension, actively challenging the adage:

'One country, one language'. On the contrary, he describes how linguistic diversity may reinforce national identity, surprisingly, through its most recent immigrants: 'If my little one speaks Occitan, he will really be French'.

Carole Fleuret offers a vision of social injustice and racism in France during the 1980s by recounting her experience of the denial of the languages of migration at school, including the language of her grandfather. Through her research, she fights against the loss of the linguistic capital using children's literature, pluriliteracy repertoires and invented spelling to rethink school programmes.

Gilles Forlot also denounces French monolingualism and a homogenizing view of the Republic. He advocates fighting off these 'zombies', as he describes them, by dealing with 'the attention to exceptions in language systems, the illegitimacy of all forms of language contact, [and] a supposedly necessary balanced set of skills when one learns/speaks a language'.

Laurent Gajo offers a Swiss perspective from a mixed Italo-French family in a time when only men could transmit their nationality. Very soon convinced he was more than two passports, his research led him to education and specifically to the conceptualization of plurilingualism and the 'didactization of alternation that could respond to the complexity of classrooms'.

'I have learned these words when I first went to school in La Habana, Cuba'. This is how **Ofelia Garcia** introduces the reader to an in-depth discussion of the concepts of translanguaging, multilingualism, plurilingualism, heteroglossia, xenophobia and discrimination. She explains how well-intentioned educational programmes can carry the stigma of Otherness and discrimination. She strongly advocates the use of the full semiotic repertoires of students, moving away from monolingual ideologies and neo-liberal economics, curricula and pedagogy.

In France, **Cécile Goï** questions the notion of cultural otherness while mocking the times when she played with the Gypsies in her small village as a child. This experience was the seed of her first 'gesture of indignation' in response to ostracism related to cultural and linguistic diversity. Making sense of such experiences produced a profound reflection on social cohesion, equal opportunities and educational success, in particular for newly arrived students.

As for **Maureen Kendrick**, her Ukrainian family experiences in Canada inspired her to develop reciprocal teaching with migrant students. Through her work, she mobilizes not only languages but also multimodal semiotic resources to create access to new knowledge and opportunities for students.

Through the perspectives of raciolinguistics, language ideology, power and identity, **Kendall King** explores the tectonics of theoretical changes in applied linguistics over the last thirty years. She challenges the concepts of the native speaker, motivation and even the notion of language itself. From the study of language loss, maintenance and revitalization, she moved to superdiverse contexts. She discovered the hybridity and fluidity of languages and cultures, and shifted towards a more holistic view of bilingualism and bilinguals.

Claire Kramsch grew up between four different languages, French, English, German and Yiddish. She shares how beyond the differences in languages, it is the misunderstandings between the speakers of these languages that have always fascinated her and that have guided her research. Literature and discourse analysis led her to develop the concept of symbolic competence.

Through her own trajectory, as well as her daughter's, **Emmanuelle Le Pichon** describes their experiences of 'languages belonging' and legitimacy from France to Canada via Italy, the Netherlands and the United States. Emmanuelle Le Pichon shows her concern with categorizing and reductive terms such as foreign language or L1, L2, L3 and proposes alternative ways for a proactive celebration of diversity in the classroom.

David Little learned French and German in the UK in a monolingual environment. His research quickly focused on the agency of the learners. Having worked with refugees and then with multilingual schools, involving many languages in the classroom, he rejects translanguaging. Rather, he suggests that collaborative learning tasks should be carried out with different languages in mind.

As a new immigrant to Canada, **Marie-Paule Lory** lived the popular 'Canadian experience', including learning and working with English-speaking researchers. Her vision of multilingualism in Ontario is to address the 'threat' to the sustainability of the French language while taking the risk of changing teacher practices in multilingual classrooms.

Jeff MacSwan describes himself as an 'incorrigible' child of the working class in the United States. His work continues to be devoted to disadvantaged children. From the 'opportunity room' to the university, MacSwan deals with commitment, understanding, respect in his pedagogical approach to fighting ideology about natural limitations and socio-economic reproduction.

Phan le Ha 's childhood in Hanoi, Vietnam, brought her into contact with words, expressions and songs in Russian, French, Chinese and English in turn: languages that were designated as the enemy's language, 'alongside her mother tongue Vietnamese'. In a duet with **Bao Dat**, they venture into a reflection on the hybridity and intertextuality of memories and languages rejecting colonial categorizations anchored in discourses of self and others.

From Italy to France and then Canada, **Enrica Piccardo** experienced a multifaceted journey with Italian, French, English, classical languages and dialects which nourished a holistic and complex approach of language learning that focuses on 'the ensemble of linguistic, cultural and semiotic means that allows students to find their place in the world'.

Gail Prasad, daughter of an inter-racial, -cultural, -linguistic and -religious couple, grew up with only one language, 'the language of opportunity'. At an early age, she experienced systemic racism and exclusion, while navigating multilingual interactions as an act of resistance. Creativity and criticality are at the heart of her research investigating the coercive power relations among majoritarian and minoritized language users. She sees school as 'a protected space for imagining and building more equitable societies'.

Elatiana Razafimandimbimanana explains how, during her childhood, from Canada, Madagascar and Kenya to France, she experienced multilingualism, which in turn led her to co-construct pluri-artistic practices with students from New Caledonia. Deeply affected by being 'impure' in her own linguistic practices, she defines an ideology of purity spread around the world and how she turns to art to empower her plurilingual students.

Nikolay Slavkov experienced learning the languages of the Soviet bloc in Bulgaria. Beyond the Iron Curtain of the Cold War, he developed a passion for English and immigrated to China and then to Canada. Initially reticent about plurilingualism and translanguaging, he slowly opened up to multilingual classes and his own plurilingual children to propose a reflection on the destigmatization of bilingual and multilingual practices.

Heather Jane Smith experienced isolation in her early childhood in the United Kingdom because of her Canadian accent. She then decided to work in Zimbabwe, and back in Newcastle, she focused on the negative prejudices that prevailed regarding multiculturalism in education, taking into account British values and national security, and the growing racist nativist discourse in the English media.

Shelley K. Taylor recounts her impression, growing up in a multilingual city in Canada with multilingual parents, that everyone had their own 'secret' languages. While she has been a lifelong learner of languages, her journey reflects a blurring of boundaries between naturalistic and instructed Second Language Acquisition. Through her research on multilingual education navigating across different language families and global contexts, she challenges educators' monolingual mindsets to promote students' academic achievement and multilingual development.

Kelleen Toohey went to school on the Canadian prairies with Ukrainian-Canadian and Cree classmates. Strongly influenced by the civil rights movement, she continued to document diverse cultural practices to give students 'voice'. Using video cameras, tripods, storyboards and video editing software, she continues to enhance enaction in classrooms, including both human and non-human actors.

In Belgium, **Piet Van Avermaet** and **Sven Sierens** offer a joint biography where 'Dutch' and local dialects were their norm. Both of them grew up in a multilingual environment with migrant classmates. As researchers, they turned to a critical sociolinguistic perspective to propose functional multilingual learning to give multilingual students a chance to use their linguistic repertoires.

Rahat Zaidi shapes her reflection on her experiences in Iran, North America and Europe and on the lives of her own daughters in Canada to develop specific multilingual practices that can foster transculturation and strengthen the hybrid identities of newly arrived students.

The heart of this book is the personal linguistic biographies and critical reflections of thirty-six contributing authors, who wrote these chapters separately or in pairs. While we sought to include a range of perspectives in this collection, some of our invitations to contribute were declined. We recognize that it is not always easy, comfortable or even safe to expose one's own life. We are grateful to each author for stepping out of their comfort zones and for revealing a part of their lives that they may not be accustomed to sharing within and beyond the Academy. Indeed, many contributing authors noted in their correspondence with us how unconventional autobiographical writing felt for them.

All the authors are active in academia and are linked to the field of education through the prism of language. Each of their contributions addresses at least some of the six concepts presented in this chapter. In addition to concrete examples, they take the reader on a journey across four continents, as well as many different academic and sociolinguistic contexts. At the end of the book, readers will find a glossary of the terms explicitly treated by each author. For example, a graduate seminar focused on raciolinguistics can easily refer to chapters that deal explicitly with this concept.

The purpose of this book is to open up a broader discussion on the issues raised at the beginning of this introduction: where have theoretical constructs come from? How do they manifest? Where might they lead us? For this reason, in lieu of offering a conclusion, we offer a final chapter in which we open the discussion of avenues for future research and development in the field of language and education. We offer our special thanks to Valerie Dailly from the Centre de Récherche en Éducation Franco-Ontarienne (CRÉFO), who helped to coordinate the preparation of the final manuscript. We wish readers much pleasure in discovering the many stories that make up this book and the people behind rich scientific work. Finally, we invite you to reflect on your own biographies and trajectories as dynamic language users, learners, teachers and researchers.

2   Become a Teacher-Researcher to Find Your Turkish

Mehmet-Ali Akinci

2.1   By Way of Introduction

On the occasion of the publication of his book *Discriminations: Combating Glottophobia* in 2016, Philippe Blanchet gave an interview to a weekly newspaper in which he recalled the structural elements of an inclusive school that the newspapers found difficult to question,

How did you come to be interested in this subject?

Probably because my grandmother told me about her childhood. In her school in Marseille, at the beginning of the 20th century, little girls who were caught speaking Provençal had to clean the toilets. And repeat offenders were forced to lick them *"puisqu'elles avaient de la merde dans la bouche !"* This seemed intolerable to me. But, nowadays, teachers no longer use this kind of method ... No, but glottophobia takes other forms. I'm thinking of this young pupil newly arrived in France, who was asked by the teacher what his name was. He answered "Ahmed", pronouncing the 'h' strongly. Do you know what he was told?

"No."

In France, we don't pronounce the 'h'. Your name is Amed. Repeat: Amed!

The teacher was probably not aware of this, but by refusing his first name, he was rejecting the child himself, his parents, his language and his culture. The pupil broke down in tears. (Blanchet 2016 in Escudé (2018: 206)

It goes without saying that this story is not unique, and all those who have grandparents who attended the École de la République at the beginning of the twentieth century can tell identical stories in all regions of France. But what about the school of the twenty-first century? Is it so different when it comes to the reception and integration of allophone pupils, second and even third generation pupils from immigrant families?

Based on my language biography, I will try to argue how, personally, I arrived at bi-plurilingualism and bilingual education and, above all, show how I have turned a language identity that might have seemed disabling into an advantage.

Figure 2.1 Mehmet-Ali Akinci in secondary school in France

2.2 Some Elements of My Language Biography

I was born and raised in a small village in the Aegean region of Turkey (Çivril, Denizli). At the beginning of January 1981, I sadly learned that my father, an immigrant worker in France, wanted to bring his family to France. I was twelve years old and was in the first year of secondary school. When I arrived in France at the end of January, I was immediately integrated into an initiation class (CLIN at the time) in a primary school. It was a big surprise because the class was made up of pupils aged six to fourteen years old from several countries, some of them not yet knowing how to read and write, and others, like me, having already been schooled in their countries of origin. If I wanted to directly integrate into a sixth-grade class in a general education college at the beginning of the September school year, I had to put the maximum effort into achieving a minimum mastery of French.

As I came from a traditional immigrant family – a father who dropped out of school at primary school, a mother who was illiterate, living in a neighbour-hood with a majority of Portuguese and North African inhabitants – I had to work hard not only to learn French but also to continue my normal schooling. On the other hand, while my parents had not been able to go to school, their goal was always that I should go all the way to university!

Fate sometimes does things well! If my father had chosen not France but Germany, his original dream, as his destination country, my life would have been quite different, as I would not have been able to follow a general path because of the very selective German education system at a very early age. The richness of the French education system lies in its ability to allow as many people as possible to go as far as possible: a journey that would have been just as unlikely without the continuous support of my parents and the sacrifice of my adolescence entirely devoted to my studies. At the end of my secondary education, they were certainly very proud of me because I was one of the first young Turkish immigrants in the Grenoble area to obtain the Baccalauréat.

Although my parents had grand hopes that I would pursue my studies for a long time, like many immigrant parents, they had no idea about bilingualism. For them, I didn't need to go to Turkish classes as I had already attended primary school in Turkey. I could have attended a class on Teaching Languages and Cultures of Origin (ELCO). In fact, it was the first Turkish class available at the time. In retrospect, I think my parents would have enrolled me in these classes if only they had taken place in my neighbourhood and not more than 10 kilometres away, as was the case. When I arrived in the final year of high school, I knew that Turkish could be taken as an elective in the Baccalaureate. In spite of my limited knowledge of Turkish, I courageously chose this option. From then, with a certain maturity, I contacted the Turkish ELCO teacher in the area in order to take his courses for secondary school students. He kindly welcomed me and offered me individualized work. What a memory looking back! Without doubt I learned some words, but I can't say if it really helped me to get a good grade in Turkish!

At the beginning of September 1988, I enrolled in the Modern Literature course of study in Linguistics at the University Stendhal Grenoble 3. After reading a lot of novels in order to constantly improve my French, I had fallen in love with French literature since middle school. On the other hand, the fact that I had never studied Latin was an obstacle to pursuing studies in French literature. So it was both by default and out of interest that I chose Linguistics option, as it was the one that led to the Master's diploma in French as a Foreign Language (Français Langue Étrangère (FLE)), which would one day allow me, eventually, to go back to my home country, Turkey, to teach French.

For my third-year Licence, I was enrolled in Sciences du Langage (a general course) and Sciences du Langage (FLE course). One was for research and the other for professional purposes: a pragmatic choice, in short. This pivotal year was a turning point for the rest of my studies in that, on the one hand, I was taking this double degree and, on the other hand, my French-Turkish bilingualism enabled me to find a 'job' alongside my studies. Indeed, an association in Grenoble recruited me as a certified interpreter-translator in

Turkish and as a linguistic and cultural facilitator for children of Turkish origin. These two jobs, for which I had no experience, introduced me to the Turkish language that I had been practicing until then without really knowing it in a formal, academic way. In the summer, I went to Turkey to look for reference books on Turkish grammar, methods of Turkish as a foreign language and classical Turkish novels.

This was a key moment for me in the pursuit of my studies, my research and my involvement in the field. Once again, my future would probably have been quite different if I had not had this opportunity to work with Turkish children. I would have remained, like many children from immigrant families, at a limited language level, speaking the oral Turkish language of my home village! I learned in one year much more than I had learned in my entire life.

Once again, I had to make a choice for my Master's degree. Should I continue in sociolinguistics of language contact by choosing the language practices of young people from Turkish immigrant backgrounds as the research subject of my dissertation or should I enrol in formal linguistics in order to deepen my meagre knowledge of the Turkish language? As I did not have enough knowledge of Turkish, it was difficult for me to invest myself on the first subject. So I decided to work on the Turkish language. I had no idea about Turkish grammatical metalanguage! I was strongly attracted to comparative linguistics courses on verbs and to the research group Metagram (Grammatical Metalanguage), which had been initiated by Denis Creissels and Michel Maillard, and I turned to them.

Regarding the teaching of Turkish, as I had the opportunity to take part in workshops within community associations and having conducted a comparative research study of French with Turkish during my DEA (Master's equivalent), the Department of Linguistics gave me the opportunity to teach Turkish in the French as a Foreign Language Education training as an unknown language. This experience of teaching Turkish was once again an opportunity for me to deepen my knowledge of Turkish.

2.3   From a Community Interpreter to a Researcher on French-Turkish Bilingualism in France and in Europe

My life as a teenager from an immigrant family from Turkey has certainly also allowed me to deepen my knowledge of the Turkish language while progressing in French, because from the very first years in France I had taken on, as the oldest member of the family, the role that a head of family should in principle play: taking care of the 'paperwork'. Not only did I serve as an interpreter for my parents but also, little by little, for the whole Turkish community in Grenoble. I unconsciously became an intermediary between the Turkish community and the surrounding community.

At the end of my Master's, one of my co-directors informed me that one of his colleagues from the University Lumière Lyon 2 was looking for a PhD student to work on the acquisition and development of narrative skills in bilingual Turkish children in France. Leaving comparative linguistics for psycholinguistics was my new challenge! At the beginning of September 1993, there I was, a doctoral student in a new university and, above all, engaged in a completely new scientific orientation.

During my doctoral years, my readings, which had been mostly French, gradually became predominantly English. The Lyon-based team that Harriet Jisa headed at the time in the new Laboratoire Dynamique du Langage (UMR CNRS, created in 1994) was part of an international network working on the narrative skills of monolingual and bilingual children. My progressive insertion into this team and the collective work carried out allowed me to appropriate new notions. Then my PhD thesis aimed to describe the development of narrative skills of bilingual Turkish immigrant children aged five to ten years old in France in a comparative perspective (comparison with Turkish and French monolingual and Turkish-Dutch bilingual children).

2.4   From Theories on Bilingualism to the Language Practices of Children from Immigrant Families

As explained in previous sections, during my formative years, the teacher-researchers whose paths I have crossed have contributed profoundly to my training. Some of them helped me to discover the advantages of comparative linguistics and others helped me with the study of bilingualism in contexts of language contacts such as those of immigrant populations. Bilingualism was still a little-studied concept in France in the 1990s. However, there was abundant literature from countries such as Canada (Hamers and Blanc, 1983), Switzerland (Grosjean, 1982; Lüdi and Py, 1986) and Belgium (Baetens-Beardsmore, 1986).

Since the early work of Skutnabb-Kangas and Toukomaa (1976), which had shown the direct relationship between the child's competence in the L1 and competence in the L2, research has multiplied to confirm this result. The work of Cummins (1979, 1991, among others), the precursor of the language interdependence hypothesis, shows that the L1 and L2 competence of a bilingual individual is common and interdependent.

It is common in the sense that two or more languages that are used by an individual, although apparently using separate mechanisms, function through the same central cognitive system. This commonality between the two languages is also referred to as 'underlying common competence' (Cummins, 1980, 1991).

It is interdependent in the sense that the level of proficiency in L1 may influence the acquisition of L2. Knowledge acquired in L1 can be positively transferred during the acquisition of L2. The knowledge and skills that a child possesses in his or her L1 can greatly contribute to the development of the same knowledge and skills in his or her L2. However, according to Cummins (1991, 2014), there are some prerequisites for transfer to occur: the first is in the L1. It must be sufficiently developed prior to intense exposure to the L2, for example, in the school setting. The other conditions concern the L2. First, the child must have sufficient exposure to the L2, both at school and in the community, and second, the child must be sufficiently motivated to learn it. Cummins (2014) points out that transfer will not take place if these conditions are not met.

If I superimpose this hypothesis of interdependence on children from immigrant families, their L1 level at the time of schooling and their conditions of exposure to L2 from that point on should be taken into account. For the majority of these children, schooling in kindergarten is the place of first contact with the L2, as it corresponds to the beginning of intense exposure to this language. According to Cummins' hypothesis, the conditions for L2 are not met until the child is in school, that is, when the child is 'submerged' in the L2. This is when the child will be sufficiently exposed to the L2 and motivated to learn it, as they have no other choice if they wish to communicate within the school.

Cummins (2008) emphasizes the diversity of language proficiency levels. He distinguishes the level of proficiency required for contextualized communication from that required for decontextualized communication. The first, entitled Basic Interpersonal Communicative Skills (BICS), is low cognitive demand, while the second, entitled Cognitive Academic Language Proficiency (CALP), is high cognitive demand. This is the difference, for example, between a daily conversation in which the interlocutors are in a shared context and referential communication, which consists of transmitting precise information to an interlocutor. The first case corresponds more to communication situations that children may be exposed to in the home environment, that is, only in L1, while the second case corresponds more to communication situations that they may be exposed to in the school environment, that is, only in L2. This means that children from migrant families have a basic level of competence in L1 (and in L2 for some) when they start to acquire an academic level of competence in L2. The development of CALP requires special adaptations and adjustments to the classroom environment and teaching strategies for minority children.

Therefore, for children from immigrant families, the failure to transfer skills from L1 to L2, where appropriate, is likely to be based on the L1 level at the time of intense exposure to L2 rather than on insufficient exposure to L2 in the home environment and lack of motivation for its acquisition, which are often cited as the main reasons for difficulties or even academic failure for these children in France.

2.5   In Conclusion

I must stress the essential roles of parents and teachers. The former should not only maintain the child's motivation to maintain his or her language and culture of origin but also engage in more dialogue with the child, follow the child's schooling (even if only to ask the child every day if the homework is done, for example) and, if he or she is old enough to understand, make him or her aware of the family's migratory history. The latter have the onerous task of teaching these children, known since the early 2000s as 'allophone children', the language of the school by combating prejudices insofar as the variable 'immigrant background' often emerges in the common imagination as an explanatory factor for their failure at school. In fact, in practice, these children are not given the chance in France to develop their bilingualism to the full. Teachers are sometimes victims of the paradox that restrains bilingualism when it comes to the children of migrants and encourages it for the elite.

If the Turkish language and culture are not nurtured, reinforced by formal learning, and if they are not valued to a greater extent within the family, one can be sure that in the long run the children will not develop bilingualism but will experience what is usually referred to as subtractive bilingualism and an attrition of the language and culture of origin. As Bensekhar-Bennabi (2010) reminds us, the transmission of the family language to children is not only a guarantee of maintaining intergenerational ties but also of integration and academic success.

REFERENCES

Baetens-Beardsmore, H. (1986). *Bilingualism: Basic Principles*. Clevedon: Multilingual Matters.

Bensekhar-Bennabi, M. (2010). La bilingualité des enfants de migrants face aux enjeux de la transmission familiale. *Enfances & Psy* 47(2), 55–65.

Blanchet, P. (2016). *Discriminations: combattre la glottophobie*. Paris : Éditions Textuel.

Cummins, J. (1979). Linguistic interdependence and the educational development of bilingual children. *Review of Educational Research* 49(2), 222–251.

   (1980). The construct of language proficiency in bilingual education. In G. E. Alatis (ed.), *Georgetown Round Table on Languages and Linguistics*. Washington: Georgetown University Press, pp. 76–93.

   (1991). Interdependence of first and second language proficiency in bilingual children. In E. Bialystok (ed.), *Language Processing in Bilingual Children*. Cambridge: Cambridge University Press, pp. 70–89.

   (2008). BICS and CALP: Empirical and Theoretical status of the distinction. In B. Street and N.H. Hornberger (eds.), *Encyclopedia of Language and Education, Volume 2: Literacy*. New York, NY: Springer Science + Business Media LLC, pp. 71–83.

(2014). L'éducation bilingue. Qu'avons-nous appris de cinquante ans de recherche ? In I. Nocus, J. Vernaudon, and P. Mirose (eds.), *L'école plurilingue en outre-mer. Apprendre plusieurs langues*. Rennes: Presses Universitaires de Rennes, pp. 41–63.

Escudé, E. (2018). L'apprentissage par les langues, une évidence scolaire à réaliser. In K. Komur-Thilloy and S. Djordjevic (eds.), *L'école, ses enfants et ses langues*. Mulhouse: Editions Orizons, pp. 199–217.

Grosjean, F. (1982). *Life with Two Languages: An Introduction to Bilingualism*. Cambridge, MA: Cambridge University Press.

Hamers, J. F. and Blanc, M. (1983). *Bilinguisme et bilingualité*. Bruxelles: Mardaga.

Lüdi, G. and Py, B. (1986). *Être bilingue*. Bern: Peter Lang.

Skutnabb-Kangas, T. and Toukomaa, P. (1976). *Teaching Migrant Children's Mother tongue and Learning the Language of the Host Country in the Context of the Socio-cultural Situation of the Migrant Family*. Tampere: Tukimuksia Research Reports.

3   Between Languages, Norms and Social Variations

Nathalie Auger

3.1   Elements of a (Socio-)Linguistic Biography: Between Sociolinguistic Norms and Variation

In retrospect, it has not simply been by chance that my research has focused on representations of plurilingualism and linguistic diversity. I was born in a city which could be translated from French as 'word': Meaux ('mot'), a suburb of Paris. Was this a premonition for a linguist? I've lived between social and linguistic fractures since my childhood: my mother was a primary teacher who was educated in Paris and, according to French urban sociolinguistics, she was considered to be from the 'Centre' socially and linguistically; whereas, my dad was from the working class and he left school at the age of fourteen. He was from the social periphery and used varieties of French that differed from the norm.

Questions of fidelity and 'treachery' that are dear to the Sociolinguistics department at the University of Montpellier where I completed my PhD immediately offered a conceptual framework for my banal journey. Living between linguistic and social variations provoked strong symbolic violence as a result of the clash of not being from the same milieu. My interest was naturally drawn to the equitable treatment of languages and variations, as well as in issues of verbal violence at school, where language is at the heart of all interactions.

3.2   Within the Multilingual Walls of the 20th Arrondissement of Paris

We eventually moved to a multilingual working class neighbourhood (20th arrondissement) in Paris, where hearing and speaking different languages was the norm, mainly because of the presence of immigrants, as in the Palme d'Or-awarded movie 'Entre les murs' (translated into 'The Class' in English). I lived between these walls for more than twenty years, and went to school from kindergarten to high school in the popular areas of

Figure 3.1 Photo de classe : The silent languages of the School of the Republic in Paris in the 1980s: Arabic, Creole, Spanish, Hindi, Portuguese, Serbo-Croatian, Vietnamese... (not to mention, probably, those that I had not identified at the time)

Belleville and Ménilmontant. We lived urban multilingualism before it had been theorized (Bulot and Messaoudi 2003). Multilingualism and multiculturalism became our norm: my neighbour was from overseas territories; my school friend from Tunisia; and, my best friend from ex-Yugoslavia (long before the war). The area mixed humble Jewish, Muslim and, of course, Catholic communities. We never discussed the use of French as a norm among us, especially at school where other languages became silent. Meanwhile, we continued bathing in a pool of language mixing. When I entered middle school, languages were used to classify students via opportunities to learn English, German or Russian. Even then, it struck me as odd that certain students (from the periphery) who were already bilingual and multilingual could not gain access to these additional language learning experiences. Friends had been separated according to their relationships with high-ranking languages. These initial experiences planted the grain for my interest in Content and Language Integrated Learning (CLIL) classrooms and classrooms for allophone learners where content was taught through a foreign language.

3.3   In the Multilingualism of the Middle-School Elite

Here I was for the first time among the elite, in grade 6 in what the curriculum called 'bilingual English' even though we had never learnt English through content. We had around six to seven hours of English per week. This door to be part of the academic elite was opened to me as a result of my honourable results and to my mother, a teacher who knew the principal of the college. My mother's family was a generation ahead of my father's regarding educational achievement: Thanks to the career path of my maternal grandfather, a figure of transition after my father's departure, who had unexpectedly integrated both the linguistic and social norm by obtaining a law degree at the age of twenty. His own father, a shepherd at La Villette (long before the new Cité des Sciences district), could not read and his mother made corsets. She had, however, obtained a certificate of studies, a very rare diploma for a woman before 1900.The value of her certificate, however, was never fully recognized. The issue of gender is yet another story of stigmatization, which I have addressed timidly in a recent chapter (Auger and Fracchiolla 2011).

My maternal grandfather's language integration did not take place without stigma. Even today, in my Master's level Sociolinguistics and Didactics core curriculum course, I still use my grandfather's French textbooks, the titles of which, 'Use Good French, Free yourself from your bad habits', speak directly to the stigmatization of informal varieties of French (Gadet 1992). Climbing up the social ladder took our family from the Villette slaughterhouses of the 19th to the 20th arrondissement, a long way from the 16th and the privileged Left Bank of the Seine River, which we would have never been able to reach. I also retain, in addition to the various language expressions of my 20th, a popular Parisian 'accent' that my 'r's sometimes betray.

3.4   The Mediterranean Area: Opening Up to a Plural
and Reconciled Identity

In the summer, with my grandfather, we would go to the 'South', to the langue d'Oc region and to Auvergne near Montpellier, by the sea. The Mediterranean gradually became synonymous with holidays, exoticism and freedom during my youth.

My father's family was also devoted to the real cult of the Mediterranean: my maternal grandmother had lived in Algeria during the Second World War, while her sister travelled through Africa. After the war, my great-aunt and godmother decided to settle on the Mediterranean coast, this time on the European side, and she welcomed my father on every holiday. My father, who was a great swimmer, swore only by the palm trees and the Mediterranean Sea.

The Mediterranean evokes this positive otherness: the possibility of entering into a renewed dialectic of the same and the other, where the other, migrant students, whether Arabic-speaking or Berber-speaking in my class as a child and then as a teacher and a researcher, becomes the same on the other side of the sea, which leads to the acceptance of a plural identity. Thus, I joined the Maison des Sciences Humaines (MSH) of Montpellier, which was largely dedicated to the dynamics of identities in the Mediterranean era, and then I took over the leadership of the south/southwest pole of the École Doctorale Algéro-Française du français (EDAF) in 2009.

3.5   Plural, Hidden, Chosen Identities

The question of 'plural identities' (Lahire 1998) was obvious to me from childhood. I came very quickly to the awareness that hidden or claimed identities always arise at some point or another.

To illustrate the hidden identities in my family, I recall my father's half-sister who was born in 1944, after several years of forced labour when my grandfather was obliged to work on a German farm. My learning of German is like this moment of history: a third language, an added language, a language I didn't know what to do with, a language not really learned, not really understood. In fact, I learned about this aunt only a few years ago ...

Hidden identities if I think of my grandmother's Algerian love affair in Algeria during that same period ...

My research has also been inspired by claimed identity and linguistic variation in the family, especially on the side of my maternal grandmother: a woman without complex, of modest origin, with a more than temperamental character. She assumed her Picardy childhood and sang me the rhymes of the Ch'Nord with humour. Her origins in the North then go back to Belgium and Germany. I spent all my free time with her: noon, weekends and school holidays included. She was an unlikely couple with my maternal grandfather, a precursor in English and an advocate of the social and linguistic norm. However, my maternal grandparents' relationship had a strong unifying principle, which I saw at work on my school grounds: meritocracy. They became the educational watchwords for my sister and I. Sitting at our small desks, we worked constantly with vigour. We were girls, so we had to join the public service for job security as women. My grandparents believed in merit and told us how my grandfather had earned his law degree without being able to buy any books, spending hours memorizing legal articles in the icy Parisian St. Genevieve Library in the middle of winter at the top of the mountain. 'This order, which reconciles the demands of culture with those of a social ascent based on merit and work' (Bertucci 2007) was supposed to motivate me, but internally it revolted me and always pushed me to be interested in the margin, in variation, to participate in the change of representations in this field.

I spent my schooling going through the norm, manipulating it, using it without always recognizing myself in it. For me, the only reason for learning was what allowed expression and the possibility of being alive: French, other languages, the arts (singing, visual arts, dance) and biology. In my research path, I went back over these disciplines, and I analyzed and linked them to understand the interactional modes they can offer for teaching and learning French as a second and, recently, as a first language. These analyses may offer didactic avenues.

During my schooling, I also realized that I liked these disciplines not only because they enable self-expression but also because they were rooted in a to-and-fro with reflection. The exercise that gave me the most satisfaction was the written essay. This discursive exercise requires the writer to navigate the complex interplay of words and feelings, which may be seen as a raw or rudimentary introduction to linguistics.

Language has always seemed to me to be an inseparable whole: literature with linguistics, teaching-learning with the practices of norms and variations.

For me, plurilingualism and pluri-normalism have always presented similar issues. As Py (2006) has noted, researchers in linguistics and language teaching and learning increasingly share the idea that monolingualism is but one example of plurilingualism. Ultimately, when someone passes from one register to another they are also practising a kind of plurilingualism. Consequently, plurilingualism to me is less a topic of study onto itself or a specific practice than an active reflection about variation in languages in general and their pedagogical implications of variation. I bring this lens on variation to my work in the training of French teachers and to my research regarding students with migrant backgrounds.

3.6   School, Languages and Representations in the Face of a Plurilingualism/ Plurilinormalism

My biography set the framework for research in relation to my personal and professional itinerary as it facilitated my sensitivity to languages and variations, as well as a certain form of incomprehension in the face of the antinomic representations that they can give rise to, especially at school. Discourse analysis and sociolinguistics offered conceptual tools to study these phenomena, to distance oneself from them and to objectify them. From classes for migrant children to CLIL, and Canadian French immersion, my research programme has been constructed to respond, through an attempt to 'connect' (Billiez et al. 2003), to the pedagogic 'disjunctions' in language teaching and learning. The social and school representations that I have sought to identify, notably also through family surveys, have made it possible to explain and shed light on a certain number of ethnographic observations at school. Research has revealed that languages and variations are a major issue for schools, and they can be used both to construct verbal violence or to help develop the plurilingual and pluricultural skills of pupils. Advocacy and action in favour of a sociolinguistic approach to variation is not the research agenda per se. Rather, it is intended to characterize, on the one hand, the type of sociolinguistic focus that I have been able to apply to field study and, on the other hand, the pedagogical innovations that I have attempted to implement.

3.7   Difficulties in Implementing Actions for Variation at School: A Question of Representations of Language

Although variation, a commonplace phenomenon that is inherent in language activity, has finally become the crux of the problematic, this notion still often clashes with the standard conception of language, of which the language of schooling is the reference. However,

[t]he observation of diversity makes it necessary to consider language productions in their historical and social context, outside of which many speakers' attitudes are not understood (thus, the norm, a product of ideology, has ordinary everyday effects). French is obviously a language like any other, but the sociolinguistic peculiarity of its strong adherence to the ideology of the standard makes it somewhat singular, explains. Gadet (2003: 22–23)

It follows that trying to ensure that schools adopt linguistically responsive pedagogies that take into account the language(s) that a student has acquired through family and social experience can be very difficult. One of the difficulties of 'awakening to the variation of language practices consists in moving from value judgements, assertions and explanations of phenomena' (Treignier and Meray 1985: 38) to explore the use of migrant languages to support learning in mainstream classrooms in France (Auger 2014).

The idea of conceiving 'plurilingual resources as a space for variation' has often been discussed (Py 2006: 169). 'Relativizing models and functionalizing variation, even beyond the limits of the dominant norm, means questioning the evaluative norms of almost an entire society. It therefore comes up against powerful opposition, including among those who would have an interest in such an operation' (Vargas 1991: 18).

3.8   Paths for the Future

Many proposed language pedagogies are based on ethnographic and sociolinguistic research methods: corpus observation, discourse analysis, work on representations and language practices. The implementation of these approaches can help to develop a plurilingual conception of pupils, in particular by taking into account variation: variation which helps to move from one language to another, to the language of schooling, to a foreign language, to language useful to achieve competencies in various disciplines. These activities can therefore play on the normative nature of some teachers' profiles. Gadet (2003: 43–45), in drawing up 'a list of the features at play in variation in French', shows that these are ultimately 'few in number, since the variational material of a language, where everything cannot vary, is necessarily limited'. This should reassure the various actors in the school and would make it possible to 'stop seeing a language as an encapsulated, impermeable entity, closed in on itself and fixed in the form of prescriptive norms' (Py 2006: 169). The challenge remains, however, that 'all language teachers, beyond the specificity of their own discipline, have to face in common the task of proposing a norm, which is inevitable because it is socially indispensable, while managing the diversity of individual or collective repertoires' (Dabène 1994: 172).

By considering the notion of variation as the crux of the problem of social representations of language in schools, I remain centred on the speaker and his or her learning without succumbing to the temptation of didactic categories (French as a first, second language, language of schooling, language for contents etc.) as a way to develop competences for French as a foreign language within a plurilingual paradigm (Auger 2017). Perhaps there is in this choice some possibility of the emergence of tracks inscribed on the side of the learner and not of the homogeneous class, of variation and not of enclosed varieties? Variational activities are practices of inter- (between languages, within languages) that seek to implement the hospitality of a 'host language' (Pochard 2002). Helping to raise awareness of the language demands of schooling, while welcoming variations, would perhaps be one of the keys to an integrated, plural and inclusive 'hospitable' pedagogy (Auger 2008), a pedagogy of and for diversity (Auger 2021).

REFERENCES

Auger, N. (2008). Les arts du langage, des pratiques de l'inter pour mettre en œuvre l'hospitalité. *Diversité Ville-École-Intégration, accueillir les élèves nouveaux arrivants, L'Ecole et le principe d'hospitalité* C. Cortier, 153, Paris: CNDP, pp. 161–165.

(2014). Exploring the use of migrant languages to support learning in mainstream classrooms in France. In C. Leung, D. Little and P. Van Avermaet, eds., *Managing Diversity*. Bristol: Multilingual Matters, pp. 223–242.

(2017) Developing competence for French as a foreign language within a plurilingual paradigm. In S. Coffey and U. Wingate, eds., *New Directions in Foreign Language Education Research*. London: Routledge (Taylor and Francis), pp. 151–164.

(2021). Examining the nature and potential of plurilingual language education: Toward a seven-step plurilingual language education framework. In E. Piccardo, A. Germain-Rutherford and G. Lawrence, eds., *The Routledge Handbook of Plurilingual Language Education*, pp. 465–484.

Auger, N. and Fleuret, C. (2018). Where is diversity in classrooms welcoming newcomers? *Language Awareness Journal*.

Auger, N. and Fracchiolla, B. (2011). Interculturality and the cultural construction of gender categories in the reception classroom. In A. Duchêne, A. and C. Moïse, eds., *Language, Gender and Sexuality*. Éditions Nota Bene, Language and Discourse Practices, Quebec, pp. 229–252.

Bertucci, M-M. (2007). *Enseignement du français et plurilinguisme*, revue en ligne ADEB-Université de Tours, www.adeb.asso.fr/tours2007/

Billiez, J., Candelier, M., Costa-Galligani, S., Lambert, P., Sabatier, C. and Trimaille, C. (2003). Contacts de langues à l'école : disjonctions et tentative de raccordement. In J. Billiez and M. Rispail, eds., *Contacts de langues: Modèles, typologies, interventions*. Paris: L'Harmattan, pp. 301–315.

Bulot, T. and Messaoudi, L. (2003). *Urban Sociolinguistics*. Proximity series, EME.

Dabène, L. (1994). *Repères sociolinguistiques pour l'enseignement des langues*. Paris: Hachette, coll. Références.

Gadet, F. (1992). *Le français populaire*. Paris: PUF.

(2003). *La variation sociale en français*. Paris : Ophrys.

Lahire, B. (1998). *L'homme pluriel*. Paris: Nathan.

Pochard, J.-C. (1996). Le Français Langue Seconde hôte: Un cas limite de FLS. In P. Martinez, ed., *Le Français langue seconde. Apprentissage et curriculum*. Paris: Maisonneuve et Larose, pp. 101–131.

(2002). French as a second language host: A borderline FSL case. In P. Martinez, ed., *French as a Second Language*. Paris: Maisonneuve et Larose, pp. 101–131.

Py, B., (2006). Bilingual education and plurilingualism, the case of the Aosta Valley. *Swiss Bulletin of Applied Linguistics* 49(2), 169–171.

Treignier, J. and Meray, A. (1985). 'They don't speak French well, the Arabs!' Evaluative norms of children and teachers in preschool. Benchmarks. For the renewal of the teaching of French: 'They speak differently' for a pedagogy of language variation. 67, pp. 33–50.

Vargas, C. (1991). Normes sociolinguistiques, didactique du français et politique de la langue. In R. Delamotte-Legrand, ed., *Cahiers de linguistique sociale, sociolinguistique et didactique*. Rouen: CNRS, Presses universitaires de Rouen, pp. 9–20.

4   Learning to Language, Learning to Live:
An Essay on Literacies of Language Learning

Theresa Austin

As a language teacher, educator and researcher, I am both a subject and object in my lifelong project to examine how language learning impacts our social interactions and thinking. Clearly, as a social being, context matters with its attendant power relations and changing social value systems, as well as our own bodily and emotional states: dispositions and aging process. In my language biography, I chose to present a re-storying of my lived experiences in becoming aware of language and learning to live with diversity across my life in different geographic spaces. I present selected vignettes of my language learning history, as its complexities represent vivid moments of learning that may not be accounted for in the research that narrowly defines language development through controlled experiments that are conducted on structural language features.

4.1   US Ideology of Monolingualism: Impact on Multilingual Family Life

In the United States, my father was raised to believe that speaking another language hindered learning a second language, English. So while living in the still-segregated South post–World War II, he convinced my mother not to speak her second language, Japanese, but rather to use her third, English. His concern about language ideology and potential anti-Japanese sentiment seemed to be stronger than his concern about the ever-present racism he faced as an African American and our family's biracial makeup. Though members of my paternal side of the family continued to have a range of abilities to use or understand Creole French and English, my father maintained his position on English. My mother acquiesced to my father's demands despite the irony of the necessity to use her recently acquired third language to raise all of my siblings, as she, herself, was a second language learner of Japanese. There were exceptions though, when moments afforded her spontaneous Rykyuu language to express her emotions toward us and when on occasion she sought to meet and create friendships with those who spoke Japanese.

Figure 4.1 Elementary desires to belong and succeed as a multilingual learner

4.2   Growing Up to Be an English Learner

My paternal aunt tells a story about my budding English language development as a four year old. She was a tired and hungry teenager returning home to eat when she caught my brother, sister, and me playing with the containers of stored food in the refrigerator. So, very agitated, she demanded, "Tell me who did this," and I responded, "Who did this." As an early English language learner, the pragmatics of the embedded clause were not yet understood, but rather the need to be obedient and the fear of punishment were understood emotionally and socially. My aunt struggled to keep from laughing as she was fighting off her hunger pains.

4.3   Moving across Linguistic Boundaries

In my early schooling, my family moved to Panama, where I attended a private school at which I was immersed in another multilingual setting, Spanish-English. I clearly saw how much Spanish was valued and very useful not only for making friends on the playground but learning in class. I remember how eager I was to participate in my Spanish-medium class. As I took up the performances of a "good student," I would raise my hand whenever the teacher asked a question. One day I watched how each student went to the chalkboard and wrote their name. When finally I was called on to go to the chalkboard, I did exactly what each student had done before, and wrote my name. However, the question that the teacher had asked was different and my answer was to the previous question. As I was eagerly wanting to participate, I hadn't understood the question but assumed that it was the same question. As I was embarrassed by my mistake, I sheepishly sat down and started watching again how others responded. I also remember repeating in my head over and over the questions the teacher asked. My listening to Spanish commands and questions improved over time, so that I could participate and answer well enough to eventually be able to win the "prize" of writing on the board.

As I moved into the middle grades, my family returned to the southern United States, where only a few people in my school had the experience of learning another language. The only other speaker was a nun, who coincidently was also from Panama. When my teacher learned that I had lived in Panama and had learned Spanish, I was taken immediately to visit that nun. I was encouraged to converse with her. However, no one had wondered or even thought to ask if I could hold a conversation in Spanish. The assumption was that I had "learned Spanish" and that signaled a wholistic imagined identity as a Spanish user. Yet, I had only interacted as a student with peers in a classroom where Spanish was the medium of communication and where on the play yard I learned to play games with rhymes for jumping rope, counting who would be "it," and *rayuela*, also known as hopscotch. I had not learned to engage or manage a conversation with an adult of such high stature, who was interested in getting to know me. With a few answers and nods, my interlocutor realized that I was an emerging bilingual and very much a beginner at that. She kindly kept me engaged over the semester and I had the privilege of being her classroom assistant and occasionally speaking short phrases in Spanish

4.4   Initiation into High Schooling: Merging across Raciolinguistic Boundaries

By the time I reached high school, I had experienced crisscrossing the United States from the south west to the east and finally settling on the west coast. The English accents and social practices in many of the states became an intriguing guessing game, which I was very eager to play, enabling me to locate people by their English accents. My ear paid attention to the vowels, short phrases, and intonation patterns that became cues to locate my interlocutors' origins.

Yet despite the different neighborhoods in which I grew up, all were populated by diverse multilingual families whose children, like me, had used English throughout schooling but were well accustomed to a variety of accents from bilinguals. In fact, I had come to expect diversity wherever my father chose to transplant us, whether it was racial, cultural, linguistic, or ethnic.

De facto segregated housing practices, which were created through realtors' refusals to represent or sell to African Americans, affected the location of the high school that my family was designated to attend. In my high school experience, while a diverse student body was ever present, there was a distinctive raciolinguistic boundary between groups of Chicanos, Blacks, and Whites. Asian Americans were so few that they could be counted on one hand. As academic tracking placed me in the university-bound cohort, my classmates were primarily White when taking subjects such as math, English and Spanish languages, and science. My classmates were more diverse in other subject matter such as social studies, home economics, arts, and physical education. I remember how my initial friendships emerged based on connections to other students whose families had migrated from the south and were not based on my affiliations with Spanish or Japanese. As such, southern African American English, in particular creole-style English, was our shared heritage langaculture, a safe place for bonding through shared language and culture.

As my repertoire expanded to include formal learning of Spanish, I became more aware of the Mexican varieties of Spanish in my high school through interactions with peers and teachers whose language features represented varieties that contrasted with our textbook's use of peninsular Spanish. My ears could detect differences that were rarely acknowledged in the classroom. I enjoyed continuing the accent guessing game and developed a fondness and fluency in Spanish through afterschool activities in our Spanish Club and the new friendships that were forged there.

4.5 University Expanding Horizons: Orienting toward Language Specialization

All college students face choosing a direction in which to anchor their studies. For me it was clear: I enjoyed the experiences of learning Spanish and my relationships with teachers and peers, so I majored in Spanish language and linguistics and minored in Japanese. I encountered my first challenge when my major courses were instructed through the medium of Spanish. While the orality was familiar, the academic register and the accompanying reading and writing requirements were absolutely daunting. I was floored that I was expected to be as fluent in Spanish when interpreting literature and linguistics as well as in literary criticism and structural linguistic analysis.

My only recourse to maintaining my major was to seek tutoring from both peers and university support services. However, working fulltime to support my studies strained my efforts to acquire an academic register. I distinctly remember my Cuban tutor telling me, "You'll never amount to much if you don't stop working and dedicate yourself to your studies."

With the help of student loans, I was able to secure a place in a study abroad program in Spain and spent a year once again in a Spanish-using cultural environment in the Basque country and Madrid. However, this learning experience was astonishingly different, yet so intriguing. Apart from the linguistic differences from my prior life experiences, the cultural lessons throughout the year whetted my appetite for understanding youth, social norms, and language. This was not the language of my textbooks but an experience of learning about social hierarchies in another cultural world, where language use and becoming a language user were salient through interactions with social class, host family relationships, and friendships cultivated in particular spaces. Activities with a variety of members from diverse social groups, from working class youth to those who served in the military and university students, transformed my own awareness of language learning and I adopted a peninsular-style Spanish, not only with the use of vosotros, ceseo, and lexis, but also with the attendant paralinguistic and extralinguistic features that I learned there. I became good at imitating the staccato and more guttural intonation of a Madrileña and using corporal movements (with my head, hands, and body stance), as a sojourner in Spain. It was hard for those listening to me to take up the complexity of my identities as an Afro-Okinawan American exchange student. So I begrudgingly had to accept that I was often misidentified as a Filipina.

4.6   Theorizing Learning and Becoming a Language Educator

After completing my BA and working, I returned to complete my MA and Doctoral studies. What is striking about this period for most who return is the change that one needs to make as a learner to becoming a producer of new knowledge. The further I progressed after my master's, the more I had to face the fear of not knowing and the challenge of demonstrating my search to seek answers. This transition to theorize my own learning and to grapple with theories that could explain second language and language learning changed my thinking dramatically. I began to see theories of language as different worldviews about what I once thought was uniform, structured, and rule-governed.

As I continued to teach language courses inside and outside of the university, I could see how the populations I taught, adolescents, university students, teachers, and even sexagenarians, all brought different life experiences and their own ideas about how languages should be taught and learned. My ideas about a universal and uniform way to structure learning were inadequate to work with such diverse populations. I came to value more the way culture influenced what each population expected and what knowledge they used in learning a second language.

My journey to find the best way to teach and learn opened me up to theories beyond the psycholinguistic ones that I had become familiar with in my early days of researching language acquisition. My bookshelves changed authors from Krashen, Lightbown, Scovel, Ellis, Larsen-Freeman, and Doherty to replacements by Agar, Duff, Lantolf, Wiley, Wong, and Pavelenko. I embraced the variation in languages and cultures with a big Ah hah! Pragmatics, sociolinguistics/ social linguistics, and anthropological linguistics became the fields to which I turned to help me shape my applied linguistic background to serve matters of education, pedagogy, and teacher education (Austin 1998).

Attending and presenting at professional conferences as a newly minted doctor of philosophy brought excitement and challenges. Encountering con-flicting views about the nature of language and learning was part of the introduction to becoming a professional. Learning where to present what types of research to seek further supportive feedback was a particularly daunting search for community. I remember after one presentation at a professional conference, I was approached by a renowned scholar and asked, "So how do you define interaction." Confident that I could answer without trembling, I rattled off my definition and the source, "I am using Susan Gass, Allison MacKey and Teresa Pica's definition" and I cited the reference from my reference list (Gass, MacKey, Pica 1998). The response I received startled me, "Oh, so that's your definition," and the researcher walked away. I could see that my definition was not suitable to this representative of the community that I was trying to enter.

After I picked up my bruised self-image, this conflict helped me to look closer into the competing worlds of language research and the overlapping of similar terms signaling different meanings. I set out to understand the assump-tions that underpinned my questions and the theories that supported my research. I realized that, rather than being devoted to a particular theory, I was more committed to understanding particular problems in trying to educate in and for multilingual societies.

4.7   Developing Research and Assuming Responsibility as a Language Teacher Educator/Researcher

As my research spanned diverse contexts across time, diversity and social justice became central to my probing and questioning. What were historically shaped opportunities to learn languages? How did policies affect these choices? Why did ideologies about language have such an influence on what the average person thought about learning? How do we learn about these ideologies through discourses? My questions became honed in educational settings and fostered developing tools to conduct research as a transformative humanizing practice to respond to the intersections of racism, linguicism, and classicism in particular. I use historical case research to bring to light struggles against the inequities that deprived populations of access to language education or robbed them of their native tongues (Austin 2009b: Austin, Stillwell, and Rondeau 2013). I engaged in ethnographic research to explore how particularities in language education create affordances and constraints to learning, privileging some and disadvantaging others (Pirbhai-Illich, Turner, and Austin 2009). I turned to narratives and self studies to help me understand the lives of others and my own in a way that could share insights about the identities and knowledges that were shaped through language learning (Austin 2009a, 2019; Pirbhai-Illich et al. 2011) In this way, I became and still am becoming a teacher educator and researcher.

In this process, I have become more active in challenging my own long-held beliefs about theories and praxis, a practice informed by theory. I am willing to question these as a way to open myself up to alternative theories and concepts. Once, in a small professional gathering of researchers at all stages of their careers, I asked a question of the presenter about the population that was being described as "subjects." I wondered aloud,"What relations of power existed between the participants and the researcher," and "how might this have exerted some influence on conducting research with Black participants?" The researcher who had reported that her subjects had refused to answer certain questions was White. However, the researcher had not considered racial relations as having much to do with the face-to-face interviewing process and declared that "it was something difficult to ascertain." After the talk, as I was leaving, other people had similar thoughts and thanked me for raising the questions. I headed for the door and the researcher called out to me to see if I had a moment to talk. We discussed several ways in which the researcher could take into account the relationship of the interviewee and interviewer in producing the data gathered in the context of the interview. We exchanged business cards and the researcher mentioned that in future the representations that were drawn from the data would be modified. This exchange affirmed that I was on the right road and could help others to take into account how social identities and our performances as researchers affect our contributions to knowledge.

4.8   Arriving at a Beginning

The vignettes I have shared speak to the very social, political, and emotional nature of learning multiple languages. The prevailing politics of any given time impact a family's and individuals' ideologies and aspirations. Geographic locations and movement in and out of these provide affordances and obstacles. A learner's desire to become a member of a cultural group, even of the "writing on the chalkboard privileged group," impacts decisions about learning to participate and, finally, expectations that knowing a language means knowing how to use it in many contexts, yet this knowing is never complete and is constantly developing if one is given the support to continue. These are the lessons I learned early and they inspired me to continue my struggle to build my multilingualism and professional identity. I wonder how much further I could have achieved had I been encouraged and supported all along. I imagine how many others in my family could also have developed these beautiful tools of multilingual communication and multicultural perspectives if they had resisted the societal messages that influenced each of us in different ways and extents. I vow to use the insights and inspiration I have learned along the way with others to support their journeys along the path.

REFERENCES

Austin, T. (1998). Crosscultural pragmatics-building in analysis of communication across cultures and languages: Examples from Japanese. *Foreign Language Annals* 31(3), 1–21.

(2009a). Conflicting discourses in language teacher education: Reclaiming voice in the struggle. *Educational Foundations*, Summer-Fall, 23(3–4), 41–60.

(2009b). Linguicism and race in the United States: Impact on teacher education from past to present. In R. Kubota and A. Lin, eds., *Race, Culture, and Identities in Second Language Education: Exploring Critically Engaged Practice*. New York: Routledge, pp. 252–270.

(2019). Sites of struggle: Heritage language teacher education, instruction and learning. In D. Macedo, ed., *Decolonizing Foreign Language Education*. New York: Routledge, pp. 131–151.

Austin, T., Stillwell, K., and Rondeau, S. (2013). (Dis)appearance of deficit: How teachers struggle to serve multilingual students under "English Only." In P. Orelus, ed., *Affirming Language Diversity in Schools and Society: Beyond Linguistic Apartheid*. NewYork: Taylor & Francis Publishers.

Gass, S., MacKey, A., and Pica,T. (1998). The role of input and interaction in second language acquisition: Introduction to the special issue. *The Modern Language Journal* 82(3), 299–307.

Pirbhai-Illich, F., Turner, N., and Austin, T. (2009). Using digital technologies to address Aboriginal adolescents' education: An alternative school intervention. *Multicultural Education & Technology Journal* 3(2), 144–162.

Pirbhai-Illich, F., Austin, T., Paugh, P. and Fariño, Y. (2011). Responding to "innocent" racism: Educating teachers in politically reflexive and dialogic engagement in local communities. *Journal of Urban Learning, Teaching, and Research* 7, 27–40.

5 A Retrospective Look at Multi/Pluri/ Linguistic Transformations

Francis Bangou

5.1 Introduction

During my career, I have had the pleasure and privilege of working as a researcher and educator in a variety of scientific and educational environments (United States, France and Canada) that have nourished my reflection on my multi/pluri/linguistic educational and scientific practices. It was therefore quite early on that I came to terms with the idea that nothing is set in stone and that everything is constantly changing according to circumstances. This contribution recounts how multilingual and plurilingual concepts and practices have evolved in relation to my academic and linguistic trajectories.

5.2 The United States and Multicultural Education

I moved to the United States in the late 1990s to teach French as a foreign language and pursue a Master of Arts in French and Pedagogy as part of a one-year exchange program between a French university and an American state university. My first semester in the United States was probably one of the most difficult periods of my life, because suddenly I found myself immersed in a language and new educational practices that I did not master and which sometimes conflicted with what I knew best. For example, one of the courses I had to take as an international student was to learn how to write a research paper. In this course, I learned that a good introduction should clearly state the main thesis of the text and then present the main lines of the argument. In the French educational system, it was the opposite; the thesis closed the argument. It therefore seemed illogical to me to reveal the fruit of my thoughts beforehand, because in my opinion this was detrimental to the text. Beyond language and editorial conventions, it was my way of reasoning that was called into question. So, I failed my first paper, and my confidence, which had already been shaken, simply collapsed. Unfortunately, this feeling of helplessness was exacerbated by the lack of support from the teacher, who one day said, 'You French people we never know exactly what your papers are about, you just talk, talk ... '

Figure 5.1 Master of Arts Graduation Ceremony, Kent State University, Ohio

It was these experiences that attracted me to Multicultural Education (ME). This area of study was intended to combat social injustices, to contribute to the empowerment of marginalized learners and to challenge the institutional policies, practices, discourses and prejudices that perpetuate social and educational inequalities (Banks and Banks 1995; Nieto 2017). For example, Cummins' (1996, 2000) work in language acquisition and bilingual education has, among other things, addressed educational practices that lead bilingual students to abandon their heritage language(s).

As a young teacher-researcher, it was important to me to make my research and teaching culturally relevant (Ladson-Billings 1994) with the aim of establishing fertile educational and scientific environments without loss of cultural integrity. In addition, it became crucial to promote additive bilingualism by valuing students' prior knowledge and sensitizing teachers to the needs of students from linguistic minorities (Nieto 2004).

At the same time, all bilingual programmes in the area where I was had been abolished as a result of the aggressive lobbying of nationalist movements. This left many teachers feeling helpless in the face of the influx of Spanish-speaking students into their classrooms. It was important to raise their language awareness so that they could help all students acquire the required academic literacies. To do this, I drew on the work of Halliday and Matthiessen (2004) and Schleppegrell (2004) to explain the specificities of the predominant discursive genres in various school subjects. This training was part of a large-scale research project, one of the objectives of which was to collect data enabling teachers to demonstrate to their superiors that allophone learners in their classrooms were not 'deficient'.

All in all, ME allowed me to assert myself personally and professionally. However, ethnic and cultural issues tended to dominate the work in the field, to the detriment of other aspects of diversity that I felt were equally important. Moreover, at the time, most of the work associated with allophone learners was concerned with bilingualism, and in an increasingly mobile and connected world it seemed important to me to go beyond this concept.

5.3   France and the Didactique du Plurilinguisme

After a long period in the United States, I returned to France in 2005, where I worked in the field of French as a Foreign Language (FLE). Until then, my academic socialization had mainly taken place in English and my adaptation on my return was not easy. Among other things, I had to relearn how to write in French in a sustained register, because over the years English had taken over. In fact, I was experiencing what was an ever-evolving multilingual and multicultural competence (Coste, Moore and Zarate 2009).

At that time, the concept of plurilingualism in an American academic setting remained marginal. Having said that, I had to make this concept my own quite quickly, because in France it was ME that was not very present. Didactique du plurilinguisme (DP) and ME had in common that they considered learners as social actors and valued taking into account their identity and prior knowledge to help them appropriate new knowledge. However, the specificities of the socio-cultural, political and academic contexts associated with the origins of these two fields of study meant that there were also fundamental differences between DP and ME.

In my view, DP differed in part from ME in its strong interest in the development of proficiency in several languages. Work in the field has thus made it possible to challenge traditional and compartmentalized conceptions of language learning and use, which were now seen as part of a plural and integrated competence (Candelier and Castelotti 2013). From this perspective, subtractive and additive conceptions of language skills were no longer appropriate

In the same period, I was coordinating the Bachelor's course in FLE, where students started learning an unknown language and at the same time wrote a reflective dossier on their learning. I was interested in the role that this teaching/learning mechanism could play in the development of plurilingual awareness among these students (Bangou and Omer 2008). The data from this study revealed that most participants had little awareness that plurilingualism could contribute to the development of their teaching profile. We therefore felt that it was important to better guide the reflective process to enable students to become aware of the role that plurilingual repertoires could play in learning.

At this point in my academic and language career, I felt better equipped conceptually and methodologically to prepare learners and educators to live in a plural society by drawing on language repertoires. However, in order to achieve this objective in the best possible way, I felt it was important to go beyond language and to use other elements of the learners' 'funds of knowledge' as well (Moll et al. 1992).

5.4   Canada and Complexity

When my contract came to an end, I moved to Canada to work in a bilingual university setting (French and English). I've been there for fourteen years now and throughout my days English and French intertwine in a dance led by one or the other of these languages depending on the activities. This could be associated with the concept of translanguaging (Garcia and Wei 2014), which in recent years has grown in popularity.

Since my arrival in Canada, in my research, I have been using knowledge acquired in ME and DP to break down the language representations of teachers working with newcomer learners in Ontario's French-language schools. These representations are deeply rooted in the struggle of Francophone minority communities to preserve the French language and culture. In such a setting, teachers are often reluctant to integrate the learners' heritage languages into their teaching for fear that this would be detrimental to learning French (Fleuret, Bangou and Ibrahim 2013; Fleuret, Bangou and Berger 2015; Fleuret, Bangou and Fournier 2018). It is then important to show them that learners' heritage languages are resources they can draw on to support learning French. Power relations also come into play in the ties between schools and parents of immigrant students. Although parents appreciate the support offered to them, the challenges they face every day as newcomers mean that they cannot always get involved in their children's schooling as much as they would like. This results in frustration for parents and teachers. It is therefore crucial to document the experiences of these families in order to implement targeted strategies and facilitate their inclusion in schools (Fleuret, Bangou and Fournier 2018).

What emerges very clearly from research in Language Education is that teaching/learning languages is a dynamic and complex phenomenon. As a result, in recent years, many researchers have moved away from traditional disciplinary fields of reference in Language Education (i.e. linguistics, psychology and social sciences) to find new theoretical and methodological frameworks that enable them to conceptualize and study the complexity of teaching/learning languages. In part, this is how dynamic systems theory entered the field (Larsen-Freeman 2012). Indeed, some researchers have used this theory to view translanguaging as a creative adaptation process of bi/plurilingual speakers that involves the use of a dynamic and complex network of multiple language practices and semiotic signs depending on the communicative tasks to be performed (Garcia and Wei 2014). To some extent, this could be reminiscent of plurilingual competence. Perhaps for this reason, in the CEFR supplementary volume (Council of Europe, 2018), translanguaging is included in the term plurilingualism. In this respect, Piccardo (2016) considers that the concept of plurilingualism is also in line with the theories of complexity, as it incorporates the notions of imbalance, targeted use of different language resources and dynamism in specific contexts.

More recently, other theoretical frameworks based on the ontology of Gilles Deleuze and Félix Guattari (1987) have also emerged to provide another perspective on the complexity of teaching/learning languages. My current research is part of this movement (Bangou, Waterhouse and Fleming 2019). Deleuzo-Guattarian theorizing in Language Education is part of a broader transdisciplinary onto-epistemological shift that has become collectively known as new materialism (Dolphijn and Van der Tuin 2012). In my view, what makes this line of thinking promising is that it rejects all binaries such as nature/culture, mind/matter, text/context, speaker/language, and recognizes that speaker, language and matter are perpetually becoming other in creative relational and ever-changing entanglements (Pennycook 2018; Toohey et al. 2015). As a result, the focus has shifted from the linguistic, human, cognitive and social to the material. It is in this spirit that Canagarajah (2018) uses the concept of assemblage (Deleuze and Guattari 1987) to problematize the privileged status generally accorded to speakers and language in communication and meaning construction. Drawing on observational data associated with the communicative performance of international researchers, Canagarajah argues that language proficiency and language learning are constantly shaped in sociomaterial assemblages where speakers and language are decentralized. Dagenais et al. (2019), for their part, propose the concept of *agencement plurilitératié* to experiment with the creativity of social and material tangles in multimodal and multilingual communicative events. Similarly, Toohey (2018) sees languaging as the assemblage of movements, bodies, objects and languages. It thus differs from translanguaging, which focuses more on how speakers creatively use a network of semiotic resources to communicate.

5.5   Conclusion

Within this nearly twenty-year-long linguistic and academic journey, multilingual and plurilingual concepts and practices have emerged and have been transformed into a tangle of connections among scientific advances, socio-academic contexts, personal experiences, individuals, languages, texts, emotions, etc. The transformations expressed in this text are therefore singular and cannot be reproduced. Thus, the concepts and practices associated with teaching/learning in languages in multi/plurilingual contexts are constantly becoming other within multiple entanglements, some of which will be materialized in this book and will, I hope, contribute to maintaining the vitality of Language Education.

REFERENCES

Bangou, F. (2019). Experimenting with creativity, immigration, language, power, and technology: A research agencement. *Qualitative Research Journal* 19(2), 92–92. https://doi.org/10.1108/QRJ-D-18-00015

Bangou, F. and Omer, D. (2008). L'émergence d'une conscience plurilingue par l'initiation à la posture réflexive. In M. Candelier, G. Ioannitou, D. Omer and M. T, Vasseur, eds., *Conscience du plurilinguistique: Pratiques, représentations et interventions*. Rennes: Presses Universitaires de Rennes, pp. 51–63.

Bangou, F., Ibrahim, A. and Fleuret, C. (2015). 'C'est la clé du succès': Thinking through the parental experience of a new support program for newcomer students in minority French-speaking schools in Canada. *International Journal of Society, Culture and Language* 3(2), 35–46.

Bangou, F, Waterhouse, M. and Fleming, D. (2019). *Deterritorializing Language, Teaching, and Learning: Deleuzo-Guattarian Perspectives on Second Language Education*. Leiden: Brill/Sense.

Banks, J. A. and Banks, C. A. M. (1995). *Handbook of Research on Multicultural Education*. New York: Simon & Schuster Macmillan.

Canagarajah, S. (2018). Materializing 'competence': Perspectives from international STEM scholars. *The Modern Language Journal* 102(2), 268–291. https://doi.org/10.1111/modl.12464

Candelier, M. and Castelotti, V. (2013). Didactique(s) du (des) plurilinguisme (s). In J. Simonin and S. Wharton, eds., *Sociolinguistique du contact: Dictionnaire des termes et concepts*. Lyon: ENS Éditions, pp. 179–221. DOI : 10.4000/books .enseditions.12435

Coste, D., Moore, D. and Zarate, G. (2009). *Compétence plurilingue et pluriculturelle*. Council of Europe, Language Policy Division. https://rm.coe.int/168069d29c

Council of Europe (2018). Common European Framework of Reference on Languages: Teaching, Learning, Assessment – Companion volume with new descriptors. Accessed 22 November 2019 from https://rm.coe.int/cecr-volume-complementaire-avec-de-nouveauxdescripteurs/16807875d5

Cummins, J. (1996). *Negotiating Identities: Education for Empowerment in a Diverse Society*. Los Angeles: California Association for Bilingual Education.
    (2000). *Language, Power, and Pedagogy: Bilingual Children in the Crossfire*. Clevedon: Multilingual Matters.

Dagenais, D., Brisson, G., Forte, M. and André, G. (2019, March). Story production assemblages at home. In Expanding the Applied Linguistics Lens on Multiliteracies: Sociomaterial Assemblages. Symposium presented at *Annual Meeting of the American Association of Applied Linguistics*, Atlanta, Georgia.

Deleuze, G. and Guattari, F. (1987). *A Thousand Plateaus: Capitalism and Schizophrenia*. (B. Massumi, trans.). Minneapolis: University of Minnesota Press (Original work published 1980).

Dolphijn, R. and van der Tuin, I. (2012). *New Materialism: Interviews & Cartographies* [Open access E-book]. Ann Arbor, MI: Open Humanities Press. Freely available online at http://hdl.handle.net/2027/spo.11515701.0001.001

Fleuret, C., Bangou, F. and Berger, M.-J. (2015). *Le programme d'appui aux nouveaux arrivants: Un regard sur les pratiques pédagogiques mises en œuvre dans les écoles élémentaires francophones de l'Ontario*. Ottawa, ON: Centre franco–ontarien de ressources pédagogiques, pp. 1–105. www.lecentrefranco.ca/catalogue/ressources/programme-dappui-aux-nouveaux-arrivants/

Fleuret, C., Bangou, F. and Fournier, C. (2018). Le point sur les services d'appui en français pour les nouveaux arrivants dans les écoles francophones de l'Ontario: Entre politiques, réalités et défis. In C. IsaBelle, ed., *Système scolaire franco-ontarien: D'hier à aujourd'hui: Pour le plein potentiel des élèves franco-ontariens. État des lieux : études et pratiques*. Québec: Canada Presses de l'Université du Québec, pp. 243–276.

Fleuret, C., Bangou, F. and Ibrahim, A. (2013). Langues et enjeux interculturels: Une exploration au cœur d'un programme d'appui à l'apprentissage du français de scolarisation pour les nouveaux arrivants. *Revue canadienne d'éducation* 36(4), 280–298.

Garcia, O. and Wei, L. (2014). *Translanguaging: Language, Bilingualism and Education*. New York: Palgrave MacMillan.

Halliday, M. and Matthiessen, C. (2004). *An Introduction to Functional Grammar* (2nd ed.). London: Arnold.

Ladson-Billings, G. (1994). *The Dreamkeepers: Successful Teachers of African American Children*. San Francisco: Jossey-Bass.

Larsen-Freeman, D. (2012). Complex, dynamic systems: A new transdisciplinary theme for applied linguistics? *Language Teaching* 45(2), 202–214.

Luke, A. (2005). Two takes on the critical. In B. Norton and K. Toohey, eds., *Critical Pedagogies and Language Learning*. Cambridge: Cambridge University Press, pp. 21–30.

MacLaren, P. (2000). *Che Guevara, Paolo Freire and the Pedagogy of Revolution*. Lanham, MD: Rowman & Littlefield.

Moll, L., Amanti, C., Neff, D. and Gonzales, N. (1992). Funds of knowledge for teaching: Using a qualitative approach to connect homes and classrooms. *Theory into Practice* 31(2), 132–141.

Nieto, S. (2004). *Affirming Diversity: The Sociopolitical Context of Multicultural Education*. New York: Longman.

(2017). Re-imagining multicultural education: New visions, new possibilities. *Multicultural Education Review* 9(1), 1–10. https://doi.org/10.1080/2005615X .2016.1276671

Pennycook, A. (2018). *Posthuman Applied Linguistics*. New York: Routledge.

Piccardo, E. (2016). Plurilingualism: Vision, conceptualization, and practices. In P. P. Trifonas and T. Aravossitas, eds., *Handbook of Research and Practice in Heritage Language Education*. Berlin: Springer International Handbooks of Education, pp. 2–17. DOI 10.1007/978-3-319-38893-9_47–11

Schleppegrell, M. J. (2004). *The Language of Schooling: A Functional Linguistics Perspective*. Mahwah, NJ: Lawrence Erlbaum Associates, Inc.

Toohey, K. (2018). *Learning English at School: Identity, Socio-material Relations and Classroom Practice* (2nd ed.). Bristol and Blue Ridge Summit: Multilingual Matters.

Toohey, K., Dagenais, D., Fodor, A., Hof, L., Nuñez, O., Singh, A. and Schulze, L. (2015). 'That sounds so cooool': Entanglements of children, digital tools, and literacy practices. *TESOL Quarterly* 49(3), 461–485. https://doi.org/10.1002/tesq .236

6 Multilingualism as Lived, Felt and Evolving through Dialogue and Melody of Life

Dat Bao and Phan Le Ha

6.1 Somewhat Provoking Introduction

Proficiency has been one key indicator around which scholarly understanding of multilingualism has been built. Indeed, what multilingualism means varies greatly according to how one perceives the question of proficiency (see, for example, Kemp 2009; Dewaele and Wei 2012; Cenoz 2013). Despite the academic consensus that multilingualism refers to the use of two, three, or more languages, there remains vast disagreement concerning whether a speaker is qualified as a multilingual or not, contingent on the degree of proficiency and functional capability against which that speaker is judged. It is, in fact, impossible to reach an absolute settlement of the concept. Instead, as language and teacher educators and scholars, we find it our intellectual call and responsibility to continue to enrich the understanding and enactment of multilingualism through empirical research, pedagogy, community service, academic discussion, life experiences, and exchanges of ideas. With this in mind, in this chapter, we choose to look beyond proficiency, which has been adequately discussed in the dominant discourse, and direct our reflections to less addressed facets of languages in the field. They include thought sharing, nuances, resources, bonding, emotions, challenges, and context, among others. We do not consciously select these ideas to build our themes, but simply identify them as they emerge from real-life multilingual experiences. In a way, we are looking into a range of verbal and nonverbal encounters that bring sociocultural meanings to multilingualism, without inspecting ability orientations.

In this chapter, we would like to echo the growing scholarship on translanguaging and bilingualism/multilingualism (Garcia and Wei 2014; Garcia and Kleyn 2018) and further argue that when a multilingual person is conversing or writing in a language, other languages do not switch off or disappear. Instead, the multilingual presence persists in a covert, saturated manner, in the same way as marination in the cooking process that might not be visible but delicately caters to the taste. The pinecone hand gesture, which is commonly used among many Italians, is an illustration of such dynamics:

Figure 6.1 "As toddlers in songwriting, we toy with lyrics and tunes in our playground. Music and lyrics become a roadmap of our thinking, whereby multilingual sensibilities unfold beyond words"

Although one is speaking English words, the backing of that utterance would arrive in the form of Italian nonverbal language. Such covert language gesturing occurs in many other cultures: A Japanese nod, a Vietnamese smile, the Indian head movement, among endless other instances. Being multilingual in this sense does not denote a movement from one language to the next; instead, the boundary or binary between languages simply do not exist anymore. Multilingualism takes on a flowing, effortless, and enjoyable nature, which brings people together, enhances the quality of ideas, and is free from judgments, as will be revealed in our discussion.

At the same time, scholarly understandings of multilingualism can both be elusive and constricted: Elusive owing to the lack of consensus of what the term means; constricted owing to the focus on the uttered word(s). We argue that the controversy of multilingualism is often confined within language itself: some emphasise the mastery of more than one language; others consider basic competence of different languages as a sufficient foundation for becoming a multilingual speaker. Whichever way the debate goes, both views at the two ends of the continuum choose to look at language per se, without indication of any other dimensions, such as politics, culture, and education. Moreover, scholarly mentions of multilingualism, and multi-competence to some extent, also tend to highlight *language* as the sole dimension of the concept. In one definition, for example, multi-competence is defined as the knowledge of several languages in the same mind (Cook 1994). That is, there is hardly any definition of multilingualism in the discourse as embracing, for instance, situated cultural nuances in it. Somehow, this unadventurous view makes it difficult for us to comprehend the complex dynamics of multilingualism with its social, historical, political, and contextual totality of all the interrelated and fluid elements shaping the concept. With this in mind, our chapter resists the conventional understanding of multilingualism by attempting to display the complex, dialogic, and ecological nature of what being multilingual means, in a context which moves us from Vietnam to Australia and beyond.

The chain of four vignettes illustrated in this chapter echoes the reality that there are far more multilingual speakers than monolinguals in the world's population (see, for example, Tucker 1999; Edwards 2004). In addition, these vignettes signify the understanding that someone who sees themselves as a multilingual not only knows languages but also inherits, embraces, and integrates nonverbal components underlying various languages into their social and linguistic whole.

6.2   Language Biography in Evolving Dialogues

The reflective account presented in this section is shared by Phan Le Ha, one of the two authors. It comprises four vignettes that are termed by their main contents: *Upbringing*, *Nurture*, *Interaction*, and *Life Appreciation*. Together they denote the flow of how multilingualism has been imbued in a person through a process of evolvement, from being a child in a sociable, memorable neighborhood to a supportive setting of advanced education; and from interactions with colleagues in varied social and professional contexts to a set of shared experiences as friends for life enjoyment. These stories are told by Le-Ha (given name), followed by comments on the accounts by both authors: Dat (given name) and Le-Ha.

6.2.1   Upbringing

Le-Ha was raised in a housing complex for teachers and professional staff working at the formerly named Teachers' College for Foreign Languages in Hanoi, Vietnam, and, like her childhood friends in those days, she heard words and expressions and songs in Russian, French, Chinese, and English alongside her mother tongue Vietnamese almost every day. Learning to count, greet, thank, and sing in these languages was just a way to socialize among our peers, as each child would pick up some foreign words and songs from their parents and siblings. Children sometimes even showed off by saying out loud how many foreign words they knew and would at times repeat without understanding many foreign words (sometimes of evil meaning) after grown-up children had spoken them. Le-Ha never thought of this environment as being multilingual at all, as perhaps children just enjoyed and absorbed everything instinctively. *Multilingual* and *multilingualism* as concepts or talked-about ideology simply did not exist in her language repertoire until she began her study for a Master's degree in Education in Australia.

Multilingualism in this scenario occurs in the child's early exposure to socialization. The historical, political, and economic context of Vietnam has left incontestable traces on the linguistic make-up and, to some extent, embedded sociocultural practices of everyday communication in the country. Very often, children might not be aware that they know words from more than one language until they are told that their frequently spoken words did not originate from the same root. Multilingualism, thus, is subconsciously experienced before it is educationally acquired. Despite this, natural use and schooling might not be sufficient in strengthening multi-competence but would need more support from the community of wherever one resides. Context, in many cases, does not necessarily refer to one single setting, such as a neighborhood, a city, or a country. Instead, context can be internalized in a mobile sense. Specifically, Le-Ha's early exposure to multiple language use began in one location and carried on in another, as characterized by a mentoring process. The evolution of the child's multilingual repertoire, in many cases, stretches beyond a linguistic matter and takes on a social significance, as will be verified by the subsequent vignette.

6.2.2   Nurture

Le-Ha's awareness for multilingualism was gradually ignited by many theoretical discussions and readings introduced in her MA program and later her PhD, while her appreciation for it was growing stronger, as she was working more closely with Rosemary Viete, her supervisor for her MA and PhD theses.

Le-Ha was inspired by Rosemary's life experiences, writings, and conversations in the presence of various languages. Rosemary not only wrote poetry and short stories in her multiple choices of English, German, and Spanish but was also curious about the languages that her students spoke. She loved how Le-Ha enjoyed writing academic English and Vietnamese with a touch of poetry and a sense of multi-tonguedness. This mentor would appreciate Le-Ha's style of writing and eagerly engaged with her writer voice and identity, as expressed in varied linguistic and sociocultural means, forms, and shapes. These inspiring and enriching conversations between Le-Ha and Rosemary somehow made such abstract concepts as *heteroglossia*, *third space*, *hybridity*, and *intertextuality* feel at home in Le-Ha's expanding multilingual dictionary. Multilingual and multilingualism then were no longer locked in far-removed theoretical debates and readings but became vivid, enjoyable, permeating, and close to her heart.

Multilingualism as such is well cultivated through the mentorship of a multilingual lecturer with decades' exposure to international humanities and rich experience with culturally diverse students. All of these build a compassionate bond between Rosemary and her students, which sustains inspiration in effortless ways. This logic matches the scholarly view that intercultural empathy is a common quality among mentors with intercultural acquaintance and background (see, for example, Garvey and Murray 2004). What counts the most in this scenario are not the resources pulled out from Rosemary's repertoire but, more importantly, it is her openness and appreciation toward students' very own linguistic, cultural, and educational resources, so that students know every nuance of their meaning will be nurtured. Such bonding occurs on such a deep-seated level as to be instinctively felt beyond formal, conscious pedagogy. We argue that the environment for multilingual competence to flourish in someone is more than just the setting but the synergy between the inspiring and the inspired on a sustainable and mutual respect basis, as is evident in Rosemary's and Le-Ha's joint-crafted piece on their journey of interactions (Viete and Phan 2007).

6.2.3   Interactions

As she became more and more interested in language and education and was working on her first authored book in 2006–2007, Le-Ha crossed path with Viv Edwards, one of the two founding editors of the journal *Language and Education* and editor of the *New Perspectives on Language and Education* book series, published by Multilingual Matters. Viv's sociolinguistic approach to multilingualism is both powerful in her scholarship and in her guidance of young scholars and her thoughtful and enriching engagement with speakers of other languages. Out of many correspondences between Viv and Le-Ha is one that teaches Le-Ha tremendously, and beyond theoretical knowledge, about the meaning of multilingual and multilingualism. Viv kindly agreed for Le-Ha to include the correspondence in our chapter.

A few years ago, while she was being treated in hospital, Viv found herself wondering, observing, and intrigued by the multilingual surroundings. "Multilingualism is normal condition," but "for the most part, taken for granted," as Viv later wrote in a blogpost in 2018.[1] The medical staff, caretakers, patients and their families, and the cleaning staff and technical support team: everyone there was multilingual and interested in learning a new language. English was just one of the languages that they all spoke and used to communicate. The sociolinguist (and perhaps also the anthropologist-linguist) inside Viv did not miss the opportunity to *do research* and write up a compelling piece on her experience in that multilingual hospital. When Viv shared the writing, Le-Ha promptly responded with what profoundly stirred up her multilingual memories that had been subconsciously accumulated from diverse settings.

Dear Viv,

How I love your multilingual spirit! You always live multilingually, breathe multilingually and sense multilingually. Not sure if I could ever capture this spirit in any way fully but I am trying :). The people in the clinic must have been so rejoiced with your presence and research :). I love it.

I read your blog piece and can't help thinking about so many small conversations I've had with friends and strangers in Melbourne. Many of them worked as interpreters for medical clinics and courts and immigration services there. They told me they often felt a lack of appreciation for multilingualism in places like that. They acknowledged that that very lack benefited them financially but worried them at the same time and made them forever feel like a stranger in their new home. There were times some relatives of the people whom they were helping even humiliated them because they didn't sound 'native speaker' enough when speaking English :(, thus questioning if their 'bilingual capabilities' were actually reliable. This lack of appreciation comes from all possible pockets of the population, at times totally unexpected.

I remember how delighted I was whenever I bumped into or came across a colleague (originally from Vietnam like me) in Australia and in the U.S who can also speak Vietnamese; but as strange as it may sound, some of them refused to speak Vietnamese in return. A few even told me "it's unprofessional to speak Vietnamese in an English-speaking environment", when at that very moment we were basically the only two people present :(. My kind of 'multilingual/bilingual excitement and innocence' has been crushed many times, but so what I walked my girls to school in Melbourne singing the Vietnamese anthem while they were singing the Australian anthem and switching . . . hahahaha . . . languages are here to stay. (Phan Le Ha's email to Viv, 2018)

---

[1] https://channelviewpublications.wordpress.com/2018/01/23/the-multilingual-hospital-confessions-of-a-sociolinguist/

Multilingualism in this context is expressed via shared contemplations between two academics. Echoing a similar ecological understanding as in the first vignette, personal exchanges between Le-Ha and Viv freeze a moment that our subconscious mind might overlook: We see a still frame representing how multilingual practices constantly yield empirical data. Quite often, multilingualism remains so deeply embedded in our experience that we might take it for granted and forget to observe its dynamic and significance on a frequent basis. Sometimes research can be as simple as observing and detailing life as it is naturally lived, rather than planning for events to be theatrically staged for data extraction. The former method is similar to enjoying an orange to the fullest by eating it; the latter resembles the manipulating act of squeezing juice out of the orange and throwing the fruit away after use. The marvel of Viv's experience is that she did not intend to conduct research while being treated in that multilingual hospital, but it was research that came to her. When the process of discovery offers itself to scientists without prearranged experimentation, that discovery is as fresh and genuine as life. Likewise, when a new experience joins us without an appointment, that moment exhibits a touch of authenticity that is liberated from formal institutional efforts. As can be drawn from the dialogue between Le-Ha and Viv and in Viv's blogpost, multilingual practice in this hospital context embraces the element of care, because when nurses use the language of their patients to ease out communication challenges, then bonding, voicing compassion, and service represent humanity at its best. We argue that such compassion as well as other layers of meanings, intentions, manners, and emotions embedded in interactions and communication are not in any way less important than proficiency or language competence per se. For a more holistic understanding of and approach to multilingualism, these very elements ought to be recognized and included theoretically and pedagogically.

6.2.4   Life Appreciation

For years, while we were colleagues at Monash University in Australia, our (Le-Ha's and Dat's) offices were opposite to each other. Besides collaborative academic projects, we composed songs on the guitar and performed them as teaching resources in our courses on language, culture, and curriculum. Le-Ha would write poems, often in Vietnamese and occasionally in English; Dat would strum the instrument, while both would attempt to sing them in melodies. In this way, our multilingual composition began. We have been writing and composing together since those days. One emerging theme from this collaboration is the conceptualization and theorization of silence as literacy and mobility with multilingual nuances, a literacy that is often undermined in classroom teaching and learning (Bao and Phan 2016). In our latest coauthored article titled "*Multiple Classrooms of Life: English, Ideology and Sparkle*

Moments" (Phan and Bao 2019), ideology is conceptualized in light of moments of weakness and vulnerability, only to sparkle as the authors traveled through languages and varied domains of language in our multiple life circumstances and incidents, both personally and professionally.

The multilingual element in the context of our life and work composition is unbound by languages or countries. For us, the meaning of multilingualism can be renewed and redefined as the interface between the languages of genres, academia, emotions, poetry, music, art, and philosophy. Multilingualism, therefore, takes on an innovative stance as installation art when one utilizes poetic words to flavorize an intellectual and/or academic flair. For instance, when giving a session on intercultural issues and the role of English, Le-Ha and Dat would sing,

> Reimagine the world
> with you and me
> In this space
> called English
>
> Reimagine speakers
> in all places
> without circles
>
> You speak your own way
> I speak mine
> You borrow
> my meaning
> and make it shine
>
> I wouldn't judge it
> being short or long
> weak or strong
> right or wrong

(Unpublished song lyrics by Le-Ha and Dat)

Scholarship on the cultural politics of English (Phillipson 1992; Pennycook 1998/2017) has demonstrated the vast destruction caused by the hegemony of English and the extent to which the language has divided people and communities through excessive judgments, categorization, and the colonial discourse of Self and Other. As multilingual educators at heart, we not only need to resist contributing further to this segregation but also need to resist attributing to the "myth of monolingualism," as Edwards (2004, p. 3) powerfully argues. Multilingualism is the norm even in countries and communities where English is the dominant language, reminded Edwards (2008). Language, in its wholesome practice, should be, to adopt Bon Jovi's words,"an open highway" (Crush 2000), which advocates a breakaway from restriction and boundary in the fulfillment of ideals and passions. Multiilingual practice does not need to divide users between cultural borders, nor should it be confined to judgment of skills or abilities. Instead, optimal productive practice of multilingualism happens when multilingual speakers act as their own critics in how well they reach the aims that they are inspired to achieve.

6.3   Open-Ended Conclusion

Some of the major conceptions that run through this chapter include creative self-resource, evolvement through nurture, empathy as synergy, multilingualism under challenge, intercultural interface, life appreciation, dialogic reflection, language as redefined, and the crescendos of multiple contexts. These ideas are not terminology borrowed or retrieved from the existing scholarship on multilingualism, but they emerged spontaneously through our vignettes and interpretations of multilingual realities. We feel that there is yet to be a framework in the literature that ties these constructs together. In a playful manner (and we beg forgiveness for being stubborn), we resist the idea of employing an intellectual framework to guide and explain life. Instead, we would like to attempt the reverse and form a dialogue from life itself, which might set us free from any predetermined model and which begs readers to tolerate the flow of a less structured discussion. This is because not everything in life can be settled in a well-ordered construction: Sometimes a complex sequence of experiences will continue to evolve beyond scholars' attempts to take control of its form. We (the authors) are included.

REFERENCES

Ansah, G. N. (2014). Re-examining the fluctuations in language in-education policies in post-independence Ghana. *Multilingual Education* 4(1), 12.

Bao, D. and Phan, L. H. (2016). Silence as literacy and silence as mobility. In S. Nichols and C. Snowden, eds., *Languages and Literacies as Mobile and Placed Resources*. Cornwall: Routledge, pp. 170–184.

Bon Jovi. "It's My Life." Crush (2000). AZLyrics. Retrieved from azlyrics.com/lyrics/bonjovi/itsmylife.html

Cenoz, J. (2013). Defining multilingualism. *Annual Review of Applied Linguistics* 33, 3–18.

  (2013). The influence of bilingualism on third language acquisition: Focus on multilingualism. *Language Teaching* 46(1), 71.

Cook, V. J. (1994). The metaphor of access to Universal Grammar. In N. Ellis, ed., *Implicit and Explicit Learning of Languages*. Cambridge, MA: Academic Press, pp. 477–502.

Dewaele, J. M. and Wei, L. (2012). Multilingualism, empathy and multicompetence. *International Journal of Multilingualism* 9(4), 352–366.

Edwards, V. (2004). *Multilingualism in the English-Speaking World: Pedigree of Nations*. Oxford: Wiley-Blackwell.

(2008). *Multilingualism in the English-speaking World: Pedigree of Nations* (Vol. 5). Hoboken, NJ: John Wiley & Sons.

Extra, G. and Yagmur, K. (2004). Language Rights Perspectives. *Urban Multilingualism in Europe: Immigrant Minority Languages at Home and School.* Bristol: Multilingual Matters, p. 73.

Garcia, O. and Kleyn, T. (2018). *Translanguaging with Multilingual Students: Learning from Classroom Moments.* New York: Routledge.

Garcia, O. and Wei, L. (2014). *Translanguaging: Language, Bilingualism and Education.* London: Palgrave MacMillan.

Garvey, E. and Murray, D. E. (2004). The multilingual teacher: Issues for teacher education. *Prospect* 19(2): 3–24.

Kemp, C. (2009). Defining multilingualism. In L. Aronin and B. Hufeisen, eds., *The Exploration of Multilingualism: Development of Research on L3, Multilingualism and Multiple Language Acquisition.* Amsterdam: John Benjamins Publishing Company, 6, pp. 11–26.

Pennycook, A. (1998). *English and the Discourses of Colonialism.* London and New York: Psychology Press.

(2017). *The Cultural Politics of English as an International Language.* London and New York: Taylor & Francis.

Phan, L. H. and Bao, D. (2019). Multiple classrooms of Life: English, ideology, and "sparkle" moments. *Changing English* 26(3), 238–252. Doi: www.tandfonline .com/doi/abs/10.1080/1358684X.2019.1590686

Phillipson, R. (1992). ELT: The native speaker's burden? *ELT Journal* 46(1), 1–18.

(2007). Linguistic imperialism: a conspiracy, or a conspiracy of silence? *Language Policy* 6(3–4), 377–383.

Tucker, G. R. (1999). A global perspective on bilingualism and bilingual education: Implications for New Jersey educators. *Journal of Iberian and Latin American Literary and Cultural Studies* 2(2), 332–340.

Viete, R. and Phan, L. H. (2007). The growth of voice: Expanding possibilities for representing self in research writing. *English Teaching: Practice and Critique* 6 (2), 39–57.

7 Revisiting the "Plurilingual-Intercultural" Orthodoxy

Jean-Claude Beacco

English Translation: Colleen Hamilton

La tua loquela ti fa manifesto
di quella nobil patria natio ...

Dante, Inferno X, 25-26.

7.1   Essay on my language autobiography

It is classic to try to account for the production activities of an intellectual, whatever his field of activity, through his personal trajectory and his private life. Since Barthes, there has been a lot of discussion, as far as literary production is concerned, about the relationship between "the man" and "the work". In France, language didactics has developed a response to these questions by importing the methodology of life stories (Ferrarotti, 1980; Poirier & Clapier-Valladon, 1980), considered as raw material for sociological studies. These have been focused on a speaker's relations with languages (Perregaux, 2002; Molinié, 2006) and have become the object of didactic studies, particularly regarding the construction of identities and relations to otherness.

Language biographies are much more rarely used by academics and researchers in language didactics. Their involvement in research on plurilingualism does not guarantee that their language practices, academic and personal, are indeed plurilingual. This personal reflection on my own language background is made of contacts with languages, as underlined in the Language Autobiography of the European Language Portfolio, but mostly, in my case, of encounters with people and, only later, in the middle of my trajectory, with ideas and values.

7.1.1   On first languages

I grew up in a multilingual family, which I realized many years later. As the son of Italian immigrants from Friuli (*provincia di Pordenone*), I was brought up in French, because my father refused, out of resentment, to use Italian, the language of a country that had not nurtured him, he said. There was no trace of

54

Figure 7.1 In the Jardins du Paradis (again!) at Shiraz

an accent in his French, except that of the purest Parigot, acquired on the building sites, since his arrival in France at the age of 16. My father's twin, whose life was in every way parallel to that of his brother, quietly displayed an Italian accent, which even prevented him from clearly pronouncing the first name of one of his sons: Alain. This is a good example for those who, like me, wish to underline the links between identity construction and a foreign accent.

My mother, who came from the same village in the Pre-Alps, also used only French, except for exchanges with her husband, that she did not want me to hear, and especially with my maternal grandmother, Lucia. She spoke only Friulian (one of the languages of the Rhaeto-Romanic group, along with Ladin and Romansh), her first language, and that of my parents, who had learned Italian at school. Lucia also knew her prayers in Latin (*Pater Noster*) whose recitation was always the last linguistic event before sleep. At the elementary school in the Hauts d'Ivry-sur-Seine, French was academic and common in its form. These forms were omnipresent, but I don't remember hearing other languages on the playground.

The first language I learned was Friulano *dal dilà del' ague* (from beyond the river, Tagliamento, i.e. western Friulian, influenced by Venetian), learned with friends in my village of origin, where I spent two or three months every summer until the age of 11. I never had the feeling of learning: I spoke Friulian, that's all. And it never occurred to me to mention it in class, not out of fear of marginalization, but out of happy linguistic schizophrenia. During those summers, I also learned Italian from my great-uncle, the abbot of the Benedictine abbey of Sesto al Reghena (Trame 2000), a man of great prestige and culture (Strasiotto 2012). He took me to celebrate compline with him in the dark crypt of the Romanesque church where the relics of St. Anastasia lie, from which came out of the shadows the mumbled prayers of the faithful dressed in black. There was nothing quite so reassuring as these first contacts with (church) Latin.

7.1.2   Languages of schooling

The world of childhood and Friulian (I still understand it a little) has gradually disappeared. But it decided my path. My great-uncle, who probably had some idea of what was behind it, had strongly recommended to my parents that I study Latin. At a time, the social selection at the college was between "the classics" literature classes and "the moderns" ones. After my success in the entrance exam in 6° at the lycée Henri IV, the closest to my home at the time, I found myself in section A, a potential royal road among classics literature which was so rewarding. The access to Latin was hard, but I got by with my Italian (*aquila* = eagle in Latin and in Italian). I don't remember much about learning English, except that it was taught in the same way as Latin, a school subject like any other. My curiosity for Antiquity, shared with some of my classmates, led me to learn Greek in grade 9, a complex language in which I did not excel but which still holds a great emotional place in my linguistic repertoire. I ended up taking an Italian course in second year university, thinking I would get some additional benefits, but I was not up to the level of Petrarch and Dante. I followed a university course in classics, the idea being to become a professor of literature. Travels were an opportunity to discover a bit of modern Greek and to read from the Iliad on the steps of the temple of Athena Nikè in the Parthenon. My master's thesis was on the homerisms in the Argonautics (Canto 3) of Apollonius of Rhodes, directed by P. Chantraine, member of the Institute, author of the Homeric Grammar (1958 and 1963). And then came the preparation for the agrégation in grammar, which was more reliable than that of literature, because it was based on falsifiable knowledge. It was a beautiful dive into Indo-European philology, that of the classical languages, in the history of French, with a little bit of ancient Provençal, a course chosen as an extra out of curiosity. From there, my encounter with the nascent linguistics: it is the Benveniste of Origins of the formation of names in Indo-European (1962) which gave me the desire to enter the Problems of general linguistics (1966). And I am still a fan of his Vocabulary of Indo-European Institutions (1969).

Languages as a profession, plurilingualism as a value

This linguistic prehistory led to a specialization: the teaching of French and languages. Appointed as a French teacher at the Ecole normale de Monastir (Tunisia; as part of the active national service), I was confronted with didactic problems in all their magnitude and I tried to accompany learners who had to study in a language not recognized by the school (Tunisian Arabic). Having then occupied a position in the Institutes of training of the teachers of French, in Buenos Aires, I discovered there the nascent didactics of French as a foreign language and tried myself to the analysis of the speech. It was also an opportunity to acquire a certain mastery of Spanish (via television) which has never left me. When I returned to France, I really began my career with my recruitment to the Bureau pour l'enseignement de la langue et de la civilisation françaises à l'étranger. Then, I found my Italian again during my stay in Rome (Cultural Service of the French Embassy) where I was in charge of the continuous training of French teachers. On my return, I was appointed to the University of Maine and the beginning of the university chapters in my history.

The diversity of languages is still my daily pleasure, those of French teachers all over the world, those of my colleagues at the Language Policy Unit of the Council of Europe, where my English has become presentable again, those of adult migrants and their children, whose importance for the cohesion of the European Union we are trying to show. I also speak English in the Paris metro, where all the languages of the world live, and I have met people on my many missions from Penang to Cochabamba, from Lovetch to Erbil. Additionally, I have spoken Italian and French in my family. And, as Daniel Coste finely points out in his Foreword to the volume of tributes dedicated to me: "Curious about languages and cultures in all their diversity, [J.-C. Beacco] has never denied his classical training and no doubt feels some nostalgia for it" (2013: 15). That's right: Tacitus and Virgule are on my table even if I don't frequent them much.

I was lucky enough to be able to build a happy linguistic repertoire: two co-identitarian languages, languages for feelings, work and travel, childhood languages never forgotten, no dead languages stifled by social pressure, languages acquired outside of school thanks to fellow travelers and a meta-discursive sensitivity, of professional origin, always alert to their variations and to the cultural forms of their uses. I did not encounter plurilingualism by chance: I fell into it when I was a child (not to quote Obelix), but it took me a long time to understand its value and to put my experience of languages at the service of my theoretical choices and of the values to which I adhere as a citizen.

7.1.3   Bibliographic Notes

My encounter with the "plurilingual-intercultural" conceptual complex did not result from my personal experience with languages, nor the diversity of cultural behaviors that I encountered through professional travels that took me (almost) everywhere in the world (from Hanoi in 1977 to Kyoto in 2014).

My reflection developed primarily on the intellectual level, when I came into contact with the Language Policy Unit of the Council of Europe. In fact, it has recently been renamed as such (previously, it was called the Modern Language Division) following a recommendation of the audit report that I was commissioned to write with Stephen Jones, then director of the CILT. This decisive "encounter" resulted in the production of the Guide: *From linguistic Diversity to Plurilingual Education: Guide for the Development of Language Education Policies in Europe* (Beacco and Byram 2007). The main ideas (plurilingualism, plurilingual education, language repertoire) have since undergone discursive modifications over the course of numerous related publications that I have produced, principally but not exclusively for the Council of Europe. This is not the place to reconstitute in detail the discursive avatars of these ideas.I instead propose a nonchronological synthesis.

My relationship with the "cultural-intercultural" dates further back, to my beginning as director of research in the Bureau for the Teaching of French Language and Civilization (BELC[1]) in 1976–1977: I was charged with completing a "language civilization" dossier, which remained unfinished, dedicated to the "salt marshes of Guérande" (the survival of which was in question).

7.2   On Foundational Concepts: Multilingualism, Plurilingualism

The term *multilingualism* seems to me to harken back to the field of sociolinguistics, where it is ordinarily (but not unanimously) used to designate the diversity of languages or language varieties that are present in a given territory, generally the territory of a political entity (country, region, etc.). It is also used to designate the diversity of languages or language varieties of a given speaker, in place of *polyglot*, which defines an exceptional speaker of languages, and *bilingual*, which is too narrow. It is in this sense that the word is exclusively employed in Council of Europe texts, distinguishable from the *multilingualism* that is associated with territories. The European Union texts employ only the world *multilingualism*, which in my opinion has the disadvantage of obscuring the individual dimension, that of the speaker and, in terms of

---

[1] Bureau pour l'enseignement de la langue et de la civilisation françaises à l'étranger, at this writing, specialized section of the Institut national de la recherche pédagogique (INRP, Paris).

teaching/learning, that of the learner: the focus is on languages but not those who employ them or who give them an existence. From this perspective, engaging oneself in plurilingualism means laboring over the definition and the spread of plurilingual and intercultural education. Its aim is to legitimize and develop the linguistic competence and language repertoire of speakers. The diversity of languages, which the speaker can leverage to communicate regardless of degree of mastery, and the competence to utilize them are shared across all speakers. It is the responsibility of educational systems to raise the awareness of all regarding their language resources and the nature of this competence, and to highlight this competence and develop it from the beginning of learning and throughout life. This is the near-standard definition of plurilingualism.

7.3 Interwoven Concepts: Competence, Repertoire

This classic characterization in Council of Europe texts distinguishes the language resources of a speaker, referred to metaphorically as *repertoire* (of an individual's languages), from the competence that allows for their acquisition and use.

Plurilingual competence is primarily understood as a *competence that can be acquired*,

All speakers are potentially plurilingual in that they are capable of acquiring several linguistic varieties to differing degrees, whether or not as a result of teaching. The aptitude for acquiring languages is natural and therefore within everyone's grasp. Plurilingual people are not exceptional speakers ... Plurilingualism is ordinary, even if the 'cost' and the psycholinguistic acquisition processes may differ according to whether it is the first or subsequent foreign language learned, or a variety close to or distant from the speaker's mother tongue (Beacco and Byram 2007, 2.3.3).

The language repertoire is characterized by its lack of homogeneity: Each language and language variety that constitute it, at a given moment in the language trajectory of a particular speaker, can be characterized by a competence profile (interacting, listening, writing, etc.) that can be specified by means of the reference levels of the Common European Framework of Reference (henceforward CEFR); these profiles are not identical across languages, in most cases. In addition, the repertoire is emergent, in the sense that each language's competence profile can be modified in light of its social uses but also because new languages can be incorporated and existing languages can become dormant through lack of use or self-censored repression in the case of stigmatized or less legitimized languages (regional language, migrant home language). The language varieties that constitute a repertoire can be assigned different functions: family use, work use, official/ordinary use, marking belonging in a community, etc. The distribution of uses of languages in a repertoire is not necessarily fixed. Additionally, in a given communicative context, speakers can use several varieties in succession or within the same utterance. This simultaneous use, traditionally referred to as *codeswitching*, allows the speaker great flexibility in communicating. From the teaching perspective, individual language repertoires can be used as a toolkit for metalinguistic activities examining forms, syntax, vocabulary, and the ethno-linguistic/anthropolinguistic organization of meaning making in communicative communities.

The definitions of these central concepts have been widely used and proven operational as a basis for educational policies with the goal of developing learners' plurilingualism. Yet some aspects remain to be clarified: Is plurilingual competence the same when it is activated for the acquisition of new languages and for the use of existing resources? In a general sense, a repertoire is a set of distinct elements joined together by a practice (e.g. a pianist's repertoire); languages in a repertoire are admittedly distinct linguistic systems, regardless of their internal variability, but is it a question of switching (even "internally," when several languages are used in the same utterance) or should we rather emphasize the continuum? And what effect does this all have on teaching?

7.4   Plurilingual *and* Intercultural Competence: A False Symmetry

This concept, proposed by Coste, Moore, and Zarate (1997 [2009]) in *Plurilingual and Pluricultural Competence*, was quickly disseminated as *plurilingual and intercultural competence*, where *inter-* highlights not only the diversity of "cultural" resources of the social actor but also the relational dimension. Since its publication, the two elements' symmetry, even their similarity (interpretable from the *and* that connects them), has been taken for granted. As can be seen from the treatment of the two concepts in numerous Council of Europe texts, "intercultural" is given prominence neither, for starters, in the CEFR, which does not propose descriptors for it, nor in the *Guide for the Development and Implementation of Curricula for Plurilingual and Intercultural Education* (Beacco et al. 2010, 2015). The case is the same in the *Framework of Reference for Plural Approaches to Languages and Culture*,[2] where this pair of words is used without any significant epistemological caution. The CEFR (Council of Europe, 2001) calls attention, clearly but doubtless too subtly, to this link, "The concept of plurilingual and pluricultural competence tends to ... stress the pluricultural dimensions of this multiple competence but without necessarily suggesting links between the development of abilities concerned with relating to other cultures and the

---

[2] http://carap.ecml.at/CARAP/tabid/2332/language/fr-FR/Default.aspx

development of linguistic communicative proficiency" (p. 168). Does this indicate that the two elements are identical, symmetrical, or correlated? In any case, this relationship is not sufficiently explored, which can lead to misunderstandings as teachers plan corresponding classroom activities.

Intercultural education can be conceptualized as educational measures in the teaching of languages and other subjects that aim to foster open, reflexive, and critical attitudes in order to enhance positive regard for contact with cultural others. Such education focuses on developing the curiosity of discovery and the careful and benevolent management of cultural alterity. It shares responsibility for intervening in attitudes, beliefs, and values. Activities that are intended to put these skills into practice focus on fostering encounters with alterity, eliciting verbal reactions to these discoveries, and seeking to guide students from spontaneous to controlled and reflexive reactions. If we accept this definition, intercultural education cannot be understood as a mirror of plurilingualism in the cultural domain, but rather as a specific process.

7.5   "Plurilingualism": Competence or Aptitude?

As stated previously, plurilingualism can in fact be considered a competence, as in the competence to communicate through the languages of one's repertoire and to leverage the language resources of every speaker. It is truly about competence, namely a capacity acquired through social experiences of communication, regularly occurring in an observable manner (as a skill) through activities that can be dissected into their component parts. Yet plurilingualism is also defined as "The intrinsic capacity…to use and learn, alone or through teaching, more than one language" (Beacco and Byram 2007, p. 17). In this sense, it is difficult to tell the difference between plurilingualism and the human language ability, which is (succinctly!) an innate disposition, developed in social contexts, resulting not from acquisition strictly speaking but rather from activation. In this way, the project of "plurilingualism" cannot be that of a competence to be acquired [since this confuses it with or bases it on a preexisting aptitude]. Plurilingual education's fundamental project is to allow each learner to leverage this aptitude, learning more than one required or chosen language, yet also to train learners in managing these languages. The definition of the *Guide for the Development and Implementation of Curricula for Plurilingual and Intercultural Education* (Beacco et al. 2010, 2015) highlights "the ability to use a plural repertoire of linguistic … resources to meet communication needs … and enrich that repertoire while doing so" (p. 8). But this text continues by highlighting that "Plurilingual competence refers to the repertoire of resources which individual learners acquire in all the languages they know or have learned" (p. 8), mixing competence and aptitude without further clarification.

If plurilingual competence, in the narrow sense, indicates the adequate management of languages in one's repertoire for communication, it begs the question of alternating or simultaneous use of different known languages. The ability to manage this alternation, which is mentioned in the earliest uses of the term *plurilingual competence*, would be primarily the ability to adapt to different situations and interlocutors by using more than one known language, for example when each person uses a first language (or X language and Y language) and is understood by the interlocutor. The other possible perspective on alternation encompasses its use in teaching, which has been termed *translanguaging*. Through strategic classroom language planning that combines two or more languages in a systematic way within the same learning activity, translanguaging seeks to assist multilingual speakers in making meaning, shaping experiences, and gaining deeper understandings and knowledge of the languages in use and even of the content that is being taught.

The reformulation of codeswitching as translanguaging (for example in the texts of Ofelia García) also [necessarily] draws attention to the position of the speaker: In their definition of translanguaging, García and Wei (2014) underscore the aspect of continuity, even unity, conferred to languages by virtue of their "contiguity" in an individual repertoire. The observable manifestations of alternation are the same and seem to obey complex "rules" that are not codified or reflexive, especially at the level of micro-alternation. Yet, where we see only switches or back-and-forths between languages (*shift or shuttle*), the authors posit "the speakers' construction and use of original and complex interrelated discursive practices that cannot be easily assigned to one or another traditional definition of language, but that make up the speakers' complete language repertoire" (p. 14). This construction has an evident aim, which is doubtless to mark, and moreover to claim, a language identity (and its affiliations), especially one that is built on multiple languages that include minority, foreign, stigmatized, and marginalized languages. Schools must welcome these *discursive practices* in order to foster the development of learners' repertoires, since learners also invest in this [language game].

The corresponding pedagogical practices, as described in English-language literature, are not fundamentally different from those used in bilingual instruction or Content-Language Integrated Learning (CLIL). Thus, in a study on the assessment of plurilingual competence, Lenz and Berthele (2010) proposed to evaluate plurilingual competence through *constructs* related to activities including mediation, text intercomprehension, and "polyglot dialogue."

However, if plurilingual competence indicates the ability to manage one's repertoire, we see that this definition can falter given that learners may already have developed their own identity-based discursive strategies. Moreover, when it concerns learning an unknown/foreign language, it is likely difficult to articulate *translanguaging* and interlanguage in such a way that the latter can be expected to increasingly approximate the target language. Finally, in terms of learning the language of school subjects (referred to as *rhétorique de la connaissance* or *academic discourse*), the diversity of languages brought to bear can of course contribute to knowledge construction through the multiple cognitive perspectives offered, yet science writing as taught at school is done in one language and [responds to] monolingual discursive rules that are beyond the learner.

7.6   Plurilingual Pedagogies: Between Diversity and Convergence

Plurilingual competence has become well-established and we will therefore continue to manage its ambiguities. This approach has been shown by the CEFR (Council of Europe, 2001) to target the convergence of foreign and other language teaching: "[the individual] does not keep these languages and cultures in strictly separated mental compartments, but rather builds up a communicative competence to which all knowledge and experience of language contributes and in which languages interrelate and interact" (p. 4). This competence is not the product of summing isolated or parallel monolingual competences. "This is not seen as the superposition or juxtaposition of distinct competences, but rather as the existence of a complex or even composite competence on which the social actor may draw" (Coste, Moore, and Zarate 1997, p. 11). Developing an individual competence involves fostering transversality across academic subjects that most often are unaware of each other: It is important to reestablish consistency between different teachings of language (national language, mother tongue, foreign language, classical language, etc.) and in languages, and therefore create convergence from the point of view of the speaker and organization of instruction.

But tension exists: Promoting diversity in foreign languages offered at school (which continues to be generally quite modest in Europe) is not necessarily paired with the promotion of accumulated convergences among language curricula. Teachers of less commonly taught languages in a given context (French, for example) campaign for diversity, but obviously because they count on the benefits to "their" language. They are not fundamentally motivated by the will to create "bridges" between different foreign language curricula, between programs and teaching [processes/practices], or even between forms of assessment for foreign languages and other subjects.

I feel that the stakes are being played at the pedagogical level, through active methods, collaborative activities, and class or school projects instigated by learners, but also at the structural level, through the indispensable coming together of at least language coursework and language(s) of schooling coursework. The path is long and winding, but I see no major inconvenience in continuing to be guided by *plurilingual and intercultural education*, old traveling companions whose strengths are known and whose weaknesses we can appreciate for what they are.

REFERENCES

Beacco, J.-C. and Byram, M. (2007). *De la diversité linguistique à l'éducation plurilingue: Guide pour l'élaboration des politiques linguistiques éducatives en Europe*. Strasbourg: Council of Europe.

Beacco, J.-C. and Lieutaud, S. (1981). *Mœurs et mythes. Lecture des civilisations et documents authentiques écrits*. Paris, France: Hachette-Larousse.

  (1985). *Tours de France: Travaux pratiques de civilisation*. Paris: Hachette.

Beacco, J.-C., Goullier, F., Fleming, M., Thürman, E., and Vollmer, H. (2015). *Les dimensions linguistiques de toutes les matières scolaires*. Strasbourg: Council of Europe.

Beacco, J.-C., Byram, M., Cavalli, M., Coste, D., Egli Cuenat, M., Goullier, F., and Panthier, J. (2015, nouvelle édition revue et augmentée de 2010). *Guide pour le développement et la mise en œuvre de curriculums pour une éducation plurilingue et interculturelle*. Strasbourg: Council of Europe. www.coe.int/t/dg4/linguistic/guide_curricula_FR.asp

Benveniste, E. (1962). *Origins of noun formation in Indo-European*. Paris: Maisonneuve.

  (1966). *Problèmes de linguistique générale*. Paris: Gallimard.

  (1969). *The vocabulary of Indo-European institutions*. Paris: Les Editions de Minuit.

Centre européen des langues vivantes (2012). *Cadre de 15pproache pour les 15pproaches plurielles des langues et des cultures*. Graz, CELV. https://carap.ecml.at/CARAP/tabid/2332/language/fr-FR/Default.aspx

Chantraine, P. (1958 and 1963). *Grammaire homérique, t. 1 et t. 2*. Paris: Klincksieck.

Council of Europe (2001). *European Language Portfolio*. Strasbourg: Council of Europe. https://www.coe.int/fr/web/portfolio/home

Coste, D. (2013). Foreword. In Stratilaki, S. & Fouillet, R. (Eds.). *Language education. Contexts and perspectives. Mélanges Jean-Claude Beacco*. Paris: Riveneuve.

Coste, D., Moore, D., and Zarate, G. (1997 [2009]). *Compétence plurilingue et pluriculturelle*. Strasbourg: Council of Europe.

Council of Europe (2001). *Cadre européen commun de référence pour les langues*. Strasbourg: Council of Europe.

  (2016). *Compétences pour une culture de la démocratie*. Strasbourg: Council of Europe. www.coe.int/t/dg4/education/Source/competences/competences-for-democratic-culture_fr.pdf

Ferrarotti, F. (1980). Les biographies comme instrument analytique et interprétatif. Cahiers internationaux de sociologie, 227–248.

García, O. and Wei, L. (2014). *Translanguaging: Language, Bilingualism and Education*. New York: Palgrave MacMillan.

Lenz, P. and Berthele, R. (2010). *Prise en compte des compétences plurilingues et interculturelles dans l'évaluation*. Strasbourg: Council of Europe.

Molinié, M. (2006). Language biography and plurilingual learning. Halshs.archives-ouvertes.fr

Morin, E. (2000). *Les sept savoirs nécessaires à l'éducation du futur*. Paris: Seuil.

Perregaux, C. (2002). Language (auto) biographies in training and school: for another understanding of the relationship to languages. Bulletin VALS-ASLA,76, 81–94.

Poirier, J. & Clapier-Valladon, S. (1980). The concept of ethnobiography and cross-cultural life stories. Cahiers internationaux de Sociologie, 351–358.

Strasioto, G. (2012): Tra Terra e Cielo. Vite di sacerdoti della Diocesi di Concordia-Pordenone vol. Ed. Il Popolo, settimanale diocesano. See p. 33–42: Mons. Tommaso Gerometta.

Trame, U. (2000). *L'abbazia di Santa Maria di Sesto al Reghena, Guida*. Milano, Skira.

8 The Languages That Started to Flourish in Our Childhood, Developed over Time into Beautiful Blooming Meadows

Mercè Bernaus and Emilee Moore

8.1 Mercè's Language Biography

I was born in Catalonia, a bilingual region in Spain, in 1945. My home language was Catalan and the official language imposed by Franco's dictatorship was Spanish/Castilian. At school we were taught in Spanish, and Catalan was forbidden, although outside the classroom the language we used to communicate with our friends and teachers was Catalan.

Probably because of that exceptional situation, I began to be interested in learning languages at a young age. When I was a child and I listened to the radio, the only language I could hear was Spanish, which was not my natural language; it was something exotic for me. I imagined that those people were foreigners and when we played games with other children we tried to imitate those people, inventing that strange language that we could only hear on the radio and that later on we learnt at school.

At the age of five, I went to school, where the only official language I was allowed to use in class was Spanish. When I was twelve, I started to learn Latin and French. Later on, classical Greek was introduced. Teachers never mentioned any similarities between Latin, Greek, Spanish or French, which were the languages we used and learnt at school.

I liked Latin and Greek, because deciphering the puzzle of texts in one of those languages was exciting and rewarding when I could place all the elements of the puzzle in the right place to clarify and explain what that text was about. Although that was an interesting exercise, what I most liked about languages was the fact that I could communicate and share my opinions and feelings with other people. However, in that regard, Latin and Greek were not the most appropriate languages to help me to achieve my goals.

At the age of fourteen, I had the opportunity to spend a month of my summer holidays in France, where I was able to put in practice my very elementary knowledge of French. I realised how quickly I could advance in my knowledge by being immersed in a place where the language used to communicate was one that I had only seen until then in grammar exercises that

Figure 8.1 Mercè (second on the right) in secondary school (Latin class)

Figure 8.2 Mercè (first on the left) in primary school

were not much help for holding a real communication. My interest in that language increased even more after that experience, which I repeated a year later.

At school, I started to attend a few English lessons as an extracurricular activity, which were taught in the same erroneous way as my curricular French lessons, and I dropped out after a few lessons.

It was time to decide what studies I wanted to continue onto at university. It was clear that I wanted to study languages, but what languages? Classical languages or modern languages? As I mentioned before, my main interest was to learn languages in order to communicate with other people who spoke those languages, and this helped me to decide in favour of a bachelor's degree in Romance Languages. For the first time in my education I was able to learn Catalan at university when it was still forbidden at schools. I also attended Spanish, French, Italian and Portuguese language lessons, and Spanish and French literature lectures.

My interest in the French language was growing, and I attended a summer course at the Catholic University in Paris when I was a student at the University of Barcelona. When I finished my bachelor's degree, I spent a whole academic year in Paris (1967–1968), where I improved my oral skills and learnt a lot about French culture during that famous May of '68.

Back home, I started to teach French in a primary and secondary school. I had to change my profile to become an English teacher after three years of preparation and taking summer courses for teachers in Great Britain, so I was studying at the same time as I was teaching. Later on, I completed my PhD thesis in the faculty of English and German Philology about motivation, attitudes and second language learning. When I finished with my doctoral thesis, I started to learn German, which I loved, although my knowledge is very basic. I do use it, however, whenever I have the occasion to do so.

My professional work has always been connected to teaching and learning second/foreign languages in schools and later on at university, in the Faculty of Education. At university, I taught second/foreign language teaching and learning methodology to student teachers and in-service language teachers.

8.2   Emilee's Language Biography

I was born in Australia in 1981 and was raised in a monolingual English-speaking family. However, my ancestors had not always been English speakers – while most had come to Australia from the British and Irish Isles, my great-great grandfather arrived in Sydney in 1890, after making the voyage from his native Lipari.

Of course, I never met my great-great grandfather, the last Italian-speaker in my family. I do remember the stories my grandfather and my mother have told me over the years, passed down to them, about life as an Italian migrant in Australia at the turn of the twentieth century. From these stories I learned that my great-great grandfather decided not to speak Italian on migrating to Australia, and not to teach Italian to his children, in order to assimilate.

I also heard stories of my grandfather's and my mother's own lives as Australians with Italian ancestry. My grandfather would tell me about the letters that Italian workers at the factory he managed would receive, written in Italian dialects that were not comprehensible to colleagues who spoke others. He would also tell me about how Italian workers would quickly learn Australian rhyming slang on the job. Or how in the war and post-war years, some Australians considered others of Italian ancestry to be enemies, leading the latter to chose anonymity to avoid ethnic slurs.

From my mother, I learned that in the 1970s, when she attended high school, having an Italian name still carried stigma, and her schoolmates would taunt her because of it. She, like her sisters, yearned to get married to change their surname to a more Anglo one.

Figure 8.3 Emilee's mother, Angela Moore (née de Luca), and grandfather, Angelo de Luca

As a young monolingual Australian, with an Anglo surname, pale skin and blue eyes, I longed to learn about other places, like the place my great-great grandfather had come from, and about people who were different from me. Times had changed, and Australia had started to embrace linguistic and cultural diversity as something positive. My ancestors' surname now conferred exoticism rather than stigma.

In primary school I took Indonesian, which was my first real contact with a language other than English. In high school I learned Spanish, and I remember crying to my father as a teenager, at a point in my life when I had to make decisions about what to do after school, telling him the only passion I had was language. I decided I wanted to be a humanitarian worker, either in an indigenous community in Australia or in Latin America, so that I could be among linguistically and culturally diverse people.

While I was at high school, in order to feed my thirst for other cultures and languages, my mother agreed to host three exchange students in our home, all of them from Spain. On finishing high school, I took up the invitation from one of the families whose son we had hosted to visit them in Barcelona. As a seventeen-year-old, I spent three months in the city, and not only realised that I still had a lot to learn beyond my high school Spanish but also experienced, more as an observer, what it meant to live in different languages – Catalan, Spanish and others – at the same time.

On returning to Australia, I continued my studies in Spanish at university, and also took Italian classes sporadically. I returned to Barcelona again as an exchange student in the final year of my undergraduate degree, began teaching English as a foreign language and also took basic Catalan classes. On returning to Australia at the end of this trip, I decided to become a teacher to allow me to continue to travel, and so completed a Graduate Certificate in TESOL and a Master's in Applied Linguistics. I also trained and registered as a volunteer in the Adult Migrant English Program.

On my second trip to Barcelona, I met the person who would eventually become my husband. On finishing my MA, I was granted a scholarship to continue my PhD studies in Catalonia, where I have lived ever since. On settling in Catalonia, I decided that being proficient not only in Spanish but also in Catalan was a priority for me for two reasons: on the one hand, I wanted to support the right of speakers of minority languages to live and learn in their languages; and on the other, I did not want language to be a barrier for my full participation in social and academic life. My work at the university has also meant I have learned some French and German.

I became a mother in 2017 and again in 2020, and am now raising trilingual children to be curious about and appreciative of the culturally and linguistically diverse world they are growing up in. Working as a teacher educator, I am conscious that while my children's three languages – English, Spanish and

Catalan – will all be part of their school curriculum, most of the over 300 languages spoken in Catalonia will not. I hope that those families, unlike my great-great grandfather, do not feel the need to surrender their languages in order to feel included in the place they are living.

8.3   Our Research and Teacher Education Practice

Our trajectories as researchers and as language teacher educators have followed separate yet complementary paths, which at times have crossed as we have worked on shared projects.

For both of us, the notion of *repertoire* has been central to our work. Gumperz was key in introducing the concept of the linguistic repertoire, within which he included the totality of the dialects, language varieties, styles, genres, speech acts and frames of interpretation used by people and groups (Gumperz 1982, p. 155). The concept of linguistic repertoire might be seen as expanding that of 'language' – in the sense of 'named language x', 'named language y', 'named language z' – for describing people's communicative knowledge and practices. Identifying, delimiting and describing languages has been a useful enterprise for linguists, and also for language teachers, but the categories used are not necessarily accurate ones for describing what language users actually know and do. The Italian workers on the factory floor that Emilee's grandfather spoke of, while supposedly all knowing 'Italian', had very different linguistic repertoires. While presumably sharing some similar features across their varieties and dialects of Italian, Emilee's grandfather noticed that the label 'Italian' was not really a useful one for describing his colleagues' linguistic resources. 'Spanish' would also not be the most useful category for describing how Mercè and her childhood friends mimicked the unfamiliar language they heard on the radio. Rather, they picked out both familiar and strange features of that language to create their own hybrid variety.

As both researchers and teacher educators, we have both primarily worked in the field of *plurilingual and pluricultural education* (Bernaus 2005; Moore and Nussbaum 2016). In this regard, the notion of repertoire has been fundamental for avoiding preconceived ideas about how speakers and learners should and do use and acquire linguistic resources, as well as cultural ones. Our approach to plurilingualism, and also to pluriculturalism, concurs with that put forward in the Common European Framework of Reference for Languages (Council of Europe 2001, 2018). This perspective differentiates between multilingualism and multiculturalism – which acknowledges the existence of different named languages in society, which are often uncritically linked to named cultures, so 'Spanish' and 'Italian' language and culture in the examples introduced earlier – and plurilingualism and pluriculturalism, which seek a more complex description of the resources that make up individuals' shared and at the same time unique, fluid and dynamic linguistic and cultural repertoires.

Some of our research on plurilingual and pluricultural education has included Mercè's coordination of the ECML's Language Educator Awareness (LEA) and Content Based Teaching + Plurilingual/Pluricultural Awareness (ConBaT+) projects. The former developed proposals for enriching language teacher education that included the competences required for promoting linguistic and cultural diversity, in order to build democratic citizenship, social cohesion and mutual understanding and respect in schools and beyond (Bernaus et al. 2007). The latter explored how to embed plurilingualism and pluriculturalism in content-based teaching (Bernaus et al. 2011). Similarly, Emilee has participated in projects such as the EU's 6th Framework Programme project Language Dynamics and Management of Diversity (DYLAN). Much of her work has been concerned with how the introduction of 'global' languages such as English across curricular subjects might be achieved in harmony with the linguistic and cultural diversity that characterises educational institutions and their students in this day and age (Moore 2016), and with how students' whole linguistic repertoires, including languages not taught at schools, might be included in educational practices (Moore and Vallejo 2018). We have both incorporated plural approaches to language and culture, inspired by our research and that of our colleagues (e.g. Candelier et al. 2012; Nussbaum 2013), in our work as teacher educators charged with helping to develop critical and creative (language) teachers who are able to accomplish inclusive educational practices in contexts of diversity. We are currently both involved in the Erasmus+ Key Action 3 project Linguistically Sensitive Teaching in all Classrooms.

Part of this research and practice as teacher educators has focussed on the notion of *intercomprehension* (e.g. Meißner et al. 2011). This has been the case in research by Emilee in international higher education settings, where scholars of Romance-language backgrounds, with heterogeneous linguistic repertoires, creatively find solutions to understand each other, without needing to recur to simultaneous interpreting services, or English as a lingua franca, two of the solutions available to them (Moore 2017). Intercomprehension might also refer to using one's full linguistic repertoire for making and testing hypotheses about the meaning of spoken or written texts in supposedly unknown languages. Thus, when reflecting on her language learning experiences, Mercè regrets that her teachers never encouraged students to draw on the other linguistic resources available to them when completing language exercises. In our work as teacher educators, inspired by complementary traditions such as *language awareness* (Bernaus et al. 2007), we have helped developed our students' knowledge of how their existing repertoires might support their access to, and acquisition of, new linguistic resources.

Our approach to plurilingualism and pluriculturalism is also similar to other notions that have been proposed for talking about repertoire. We have both recently engaged with the notion of *translanguaging* (García and Li 2014) to refer to resources and practices for communicating, learning and being similar to what we have already referred to as plurilingual and pluricultural repertoires. We have also engaged with translanguaging to designate a culturally and linguistically inclusive pedagogical practice that we understand as being almost synonymous to plurilingual and pluricultural education (Moore and Vallejo 2018). In Emilee's recent work (e.g. Moore and Bradley 2020), part of the Translation and Translanguaging: Investigating Linguistic and Cultural Transformations in Superdiverse Wards in Four UK Cities (TLANG) project, she has also used the notion of translanguaging as a way to talk about *multimodality*, or communicative resources beyond spoken and written language. In our work as researchers and teacher educators, and also as mothers and grandmother, we have been witness to how people, and children and young people in particular, communicate both through and beyond spoken and written codes, to incorporate semiotic resources that are not strictly linguistic: gesture, ways of dressing, references to mass media, dance moves, etc. Thus we, like other researchers and educators (e.g. Rymes 2014), are seeking ways to research, and teach our students about, how expanded semiotic repertoires contribute to semiosis and to learning.

Finally, both our research and teaching education practice have been intrinsically socially situated, and concerned with the role of different sociocultural dynamics in the educational process. Mercè has extensively researched the influence of students' and teachers' motivation and attitudes in language learning processes (e.g. Bernaus et al. 2004; Bernaus and Gardner 2008). The research framework that she has developed might help explain why Emilee's great-great grandfather found it necessary to abandon his use of Italian on arriving in Australia, or our own reasons for learning the languages we both know. It was this interest in attitudes and motivation that first brought us to work together, exploring the affective factors influencing plurilingual students' acquisition of Catalan in a linguistically and culturally diverse high school in downtown Barcelona (Bernaus, Moore and Cordeiro 2007). Much of Emilee's research has been ethnographic and sociolinguistic in nature, exploring linguistic and cultural diversity not just as phenomena in schools but also in society more generally, and asking how schools might both include that diversity and also impact on it. In this sense, she has incorporated critical, collaborative and activist approaches, both in her research and her teaching (e.g. Moore and Hawkins 2021; Moore and Vallejo 2018).

Both of us also volunteer in formal and non-formal educational programmes in contexts of diversity, in order to put into practice what we understand as sound plurilingual and pluricultural education, being education that is inclusive of students' whole semiotic repertoires.

REFERENCES

Bernaus, M. (2005). La coexistence de plusieurs langues et cultures: Un défi pour l'Union Européenne. *Les Langues Modernes* 4, 46–56.

Bernaus, M. and Gardner, R. C. (2008). Teacher motivation strategies, student perceptions, student motivation, and English achievement. *Modern Language Journal* 92(3), 387–401.

Bernaus, M., Moore, E. and Cordeiro, A. (2007). Affective factors influencing plurilingual students' acquisition of Catalan in a Catalan-Spanish bilingual context. *The Modern Language Journal* 91(2), 235–246.

Bernaus, M., Furlong, A., Jonckheere, S. and Kervran, M. (2011). *Plurilingualism and Pluriculturalism in Content-Based Teaching: A Training Kit*. Strasbourg/Graz: Council of Europe/European Centre for Modern Languages.

Bernaus, M., Masgoret, A. M., Gardner, R. C. and Reyes, E. (2004). Motivation and attitudes towards learning languages in multicultural classrooms. *International Journal of Multilingualism* 1(2), 75–89.

Bernaus, M., Andrade, A. I., Kervran, M., Murkowska, A. and Trujillo Sáez, F. (2007). *Plurilingual and Pluricultural Awareness in Language Teacher Education: A Training Kit*. Strasbourg/Graz: Council of Europe/European Centre for Modern Languages.

Candelier, M. et al. (2012). *Le CARAP: Compétences et Ressources*. Strasbourg: Council of Europe.

Council of Europe (2001). *Common European Framework of Reference for Languages: Learning, Teaching, Assessment*. Strasbourg: Council of Europe.

(2018). *Common European Framework of Reference for Languages: Learning, Teaching, Assessment*. Companion volume with new descriptors. Strasbourg: Council of Europe.

García, O. and Li, W. (2014). *Translanguaging: Language, Bilingualism and Education*. New York: Palgrave Macmillan.

Gumperz, J. J. (1982). *Discourse Strategies*. Cambridge: Cambridge University Press.

Meißner, F.-J., Capucho, F., Degache, C. H., Martins, A., Spita, D. and Tost, M. (2011). *Intercomprehension: Learning, Teaching, Research/Apprentissage, Enseignement, Recherche/Lernen, Lehren, Forschung*. Tübingen: Narr.

Moore, E. (2016). Conceptualising 'multilingual' higher education in policies and classroom practice. *Language Culture and Curriculum* 29(1), 22–39.

(2017). Doing understanding in transient, multilingual communities in higher education. *Journal of Linguistic Anthropology* 27(3), 289–307.

Moore, E. and Bradley, J. (2020). Resemiotisation from page to stage: The trajectory of a musilingual youth's poem. *Journal of Bilingual Education and Bilingualism* 23(1), 49–64.

Moore, E. & Hawkins, M. (2021). The affordances of an arts-based approach for building opportunities for young people's learning. In E. Moore & C. Vallejo, eds., *Learning English Out of School: An Inclusive Approach to Research and Action*. Berlin: Peter Lang, pp. 99–118. https://doi.org/10.3726/b18699

Moore, E. and Nussbaum, L. (2016). Plurilingüismo en la formación del alumnado de la ESO. In D. Masats and L. Nussbaum, eds., *Enseñanza y aprendizaje de las lenguas extranjeras en educación secundaria obligatoria*. Madrid: Síntesis, pp. 15–33.

Moore, E. and Vallejo, C. (2018). Practices of conformity and transgression in an out-of-school reading programme for 'at risk' children. *Linguistics and Education* 43, 25–38.

Nussbaum, L. (2013). Interrogations didactiques sur l'éducation plurilingue. In V. Bigot, A. Bretegnier and M. Vasseur, eds., *Vers le plurilinguisme ? 20 ans après*. Paris: Albin Michel, pp. 85–93.

Rymes, B. (2014). *Communicating beyond Language*. New York: Routledge.

9   On the Borderline between Languages and Knowledge

Marisa Cavalli

English Translation: Colleen Hamilton

The Val d'Aoste in Italy, which is located in the heart of the Alps, is the crossroads of diverse frontiers and a thoroughfare of people and languages, like every borderland. It belonged for centuries to the Francophone zone before tipping over to the Italian-speaking zone in 1861 during the unification of Italy. This small autonomous region is known for its language policy promoting French, which has become a minority language. This is where I was born.

My parents spoke to each other in "francoprovençal," after the war, when dialects symbolized peasantry and backwardness in a world that was changing (all too) fast. I did not learn to speak "francoprovençal," but, as with all cryptic family languages, I understand it. Italian was my first language, learned from both parents for whom it was a second language.

I do not remember the first time I encountered French at the age of six, at school, nor the precise moment when I realized that it was a different language. I understood very early that this language would allow me to cross the nearby borders and to communicate with people who had other ways of life.

Tourists began to invade our village. The invasion was also cultural, leading to feelings of shame about the dialect and the lower socioeconomic status of children in the village. Though I was fascinated by the world of city people, I was aware of my difference: I had another language. One and not two, since at the time I had entirely integrated in myself (compelled by symbolic domination) the dialect's shame and denial.

In middle school, I began learning Latin. In high school, Greek was added. The method used at the time for teaching language relied heavily on grammar and translation. Dictionaries were the most important tool. Of course, this teaching method pushed many students away from language learning, and school in general, especially patois- and dialect-speaking students from elsewhere in Italy.

At university, I chose modern languages and I studied English as well. My university courses in linguistics and Romance philology deepened my relationship to languages, giving me new tools for approaching them. At the same time, I began teaching French to middle school students, without any teaching or pedagogical training and I committed some true methodological . . . crimes.

76

Figure 9.1 1954: At the foot of the bell tower of Courmayeur built in the same granite of the surrounding mountains and merging into it. Traces of bilingualism regained just 7 years earlier after the Second World War

Fortunately, the students were there to help me and guide me through their success and failure, wishes and loathing, boredom and enthusiasm toward building an approach that was adapted to their needs. It was a long, very long, road. Continuing education supplemented my initial training (of which there was none), and teaching became a passion, an all-consuming interest, and especially a social mission.

My investigation of languages benefited from other dimensions and other questions of a historical and sociolinguistic nature, directly related to the status of different languages for my students. My reflection took into account more broadly the "linguistic niche" of the Val d'Aoste, the languages present and their relative power, the language policy decisions and their coherence when compared with the actual sociolinguistic situation of the society and circulating discourses. It was not simple to understand: The scientific, political, and common sense discourses had nothing in common. They constructed different, sometimes opposing images of reality. Take French as an example: In political discourse, it was THE "mother tongue" of those living in Val d'Aoste; in scientific discourse, it was a second language for some speakers; and in the discourse of common sense, it was a foreign language. How to account for this complexity? How to correctly formulate the minority question? How to get out of ideology?

After seventeen years of teaching in schools, I joined the Regional Institute for Education Research, where I was charged with in-service teacher training creation of teaching materials, documentation, and research for middle school French. From the beginning, my approach was interdisciplinary: When facing a "heavy" curriculum in languages, compartmentalized language teaching was unthinkable. My previous experiences of teaching French and collaborating closely with a colleague in Italian provided me with theoretical and practical arguments for integrated language teaching.

The research side became more important during the 1990s in parallel with the bilingual reform at the middle school level, which involved the transition from teaching French to teaching in French, via the use of two languages (Italian and French) in every subject area. Apart from investigations conducted on the implementation of the institutional aspects of bilingual reform, the research was primarily composed of numerous interinstitutional action research projects that were carried out in bilingual classes and in collaboration with teachers of diverse subjects.

The primary reason for my interest in plurilingualism as it relates to schooling systems lies in the fact that I lived immersed in a small, somewhat isolated universe where general language and language education policies as well as family language policies conditioned my relationship with languages, shaped my language and cultural repertoire, and piqued my curiosity regarding the diverse contradictions that I saw at work in my region.

9.1   Reflections on the Concepts

In the context of the Val d'Aoste, where I started out as a teacher of French, the very first conceptual question was to define, correctly and above circulating ideological discourses, the positioning or, if you will, the (affective, cognitive, psychological, cultural) status of this language as compared to the other language of schooling, Italian. The latter was spoken by the majority of students alongside dialects in everyday life. Skipping such a reflection seemed to be very dangerous, because language is not taught in the same way nor with the same representations or expectations if it is a first, second, or foreign language. The slightly altered definition of Cuq (1991) seemed fitting in my context and the appropriate teaching to apply (Cavalli 2002). The "minority" context of Val d'Aoste, in the ever-present controversy between defenders and detractors of French, added a strong ideological burden to this language that weighed down its teaching and learning: Another conditioning that had to be overcome or completely erased through stimulating language teaching grounded in the differentiation of motivations to learn, exchanges, love of reading, and among others, the intellectual pleasure of grammar and a structuring metalinguistic reflection.

As French had become the language of instruction, I stepped straight into the controversy surrounding "bilingualism," with all that implies in terms of normative and equilingual representations, presupposing the juxtaposition of two "perfect" monolingualisms. It was skewed from the beginning and reinforced by the co-officiality of Italian and French and by the widespread bilingual image of the region (Cavalli et al. 2003). The Val d'Aoste, in Council of Europe terms, is a multilingual territory where speakers are often plurilingual. It is a situation where language contact is frequent and where "markings" of one on the other are blatantly obvious. From the beginning, political choice resulted in language alternation in the curriculum: and not their separation, as then recommended by many models, often inspired by Canadian immersion. Already in the 1990s, Bernard Py and his team (Bourguignon et al. 1994) working to foster the appropriation of the second language in preschool, highlighted the didactic reason for this alternation. It was the early secondary level that, during its bilingual reform in the 1990s, tackled establishing and experimenting with a methodology of principled language alternation in academic subject areas.

The addition of English to the curriculum in the 1990s marked the transition from bi- to plurilingualism, but the decision was made by the Institute for Education Research not to subsume the bilingual dimension of disciplinary teaching in a more generic definition of "plurilingualism," which could easily result from the enrichment of language teaching, for we quickly saw the danger of a sort of dilution or thinning of the bilingual dimension of the concept of plurilingualism: Therefore it was decided to keep the idea of bi-/plurilingualism.

9.2   Integrated Language Teaching

Starting in the 1980s, following the 1977 national curricula inspired by the ten theses of GISCEL's *educazione linguistica* (Costanzo 2003), we began reflecting on integrated teaching for early secondary school in which equal time was spent on the two official languages. Whereas other Italian programs were limited to saying that the two language teachers (Italian and foreign language) should work together, the Regional Institute of Education Research implemented a common training program for all language teachers (Cavalli 1998). Later, in the 1990s, when a foreign language was introduced beginning in primary schools in the Val d'Aoste curriculum – first in pilot projects and then across schools – it seemed indispensable to include it in integrated language teaching. Thus, all of our training was designed for teachers of Italian and French, and later English. This training became more and more demanding over time: At the beginning, simply requiring participation in common courses, then the presence of groups of two or three language teachers in the same classroom, preparation of shared teaching materials, units, or experimental projects, coupled with action research, leading finally to a course for teacher educators that was directly related to bilingual reform.

The process of action research was the most productive means of training: Core groups of three language teachers planned concrete projects integrating the three languages; some of the class sessions were observed by teacher trainers and then discussed with teachers. This kind of demanding training distanced those teachers without available colleagues or sufficient time to dedicate to action research: and in some ways "cut them off" from continuing education.

This fieldwork between students and teachers, and the observations and discussions between trainers and teachers, allowed for the collective creation of an integrated language teaching methodology (Cavalli 1998), cognitive gain for students, and a (long-term) teaching gain for teachers (Cavalli 1993). It is worth noting that, at the time of these experiments, few projects accounted for students' own repertoires.

This type of methodology is not transferable wholesale from one context to another: It must be contextually based on the repertoires present in the classroom, the overall sociolinguistic context, and the language families involved. All of our reflection consisted of establishing a methodology and not creating ready-to-use teaching materials. Doubtless it is for this reason that integrated language teaching is often cited but rarely concretely exemplified in the domain of teaching. Nonetheless, this methodological option, in place of the creation of teaching materials, has the advantage of reaffirming teachers' autonomous role as emancipated, and moreover emancipatory, intellectuals (Giroux 1988).

9.3   The Bilingual Construction of Knowledge

Beginning in the 1990s, a decisive turn emerged for early secondary schools: bilingual reform envisaging the use of French throughout instruction. Methodologically, it brought up the question of how disciplinary content could be taught in two languages used by the same teacher – according to what can only be characterized as language alternation – and in an advantageous way for conceptualization in different disciplines. The technical expression that we used at the time was "language alternation" in class. It was not the spontaneous "bilingual speech" characteristic of the bilingual speaker, although it was inspired by it (Grosjean 1982, 2008, 2010, 2015; Lüdi and Py 2002) and was not yet considered *translanguaging* (García 2009; García and Wei 2014; García and Kleyn 2016). We wanted to choose a strong and realistic teaching option, intentionally and knowingly planned and executed so as to serve disciplinary conceptual acquisition. Let us say that, in light of current reflections on *translanguaging*, what we were collectively and interinstitutionally undertaking was not only about communication, its affective aspects, or taking up language as one's own, but rather our reflection was centered on the cognitive and discursive processes implemented in different subject areas (Coste and Pasquier 1992; Coste 1994, 2000; Py 1997, 2003; Gajo and Serra 1998, 2000).

This positioning was not frequently noted in research on the bilingual construction of knowledge, with few exceptions (e.g. Bange et al. 2005; Steffen 2013). It is obvious that this "bilingual" perspective on bilingual teaching could have been considered unorthodox at the time, since in the imaginary, including the scientific imaginary (or at least of some scientists), the paragon of this type of teaching was the "monolingual" model of language separation.

The action research represented the conceptual motor of bilingual reform: Having come together with methodologists and linguistic experts, teachers then experimented *in vivo* with the methodologies that allowed them to work on their subjects in two languages. With this bilingual reform, the crux of language teaching shifted: We pivoted from regarding our teaching as a simple school subject toward its use as a tool in the construction of knowledge in other subjects. A fertile, complex universe opened up: Through the interplay of the two languages, exposure to different materials, and discovery of the existence of different epistemologies within a single subject area, teachers were brought to deeply interrogate the epistemic challenges that confronted their students and themselves as professionals (Cavalli 2005).

Therefore, switching between languages was not only *translanguaging*, the passing of information from one code to another, but, as Bernard Py liked to say, it served as a magnifying glass for numerous aspects of disciplinary teaching. The texts and discourses could illustrate, as Daniel Coste imagined, an increasingly complex path at the heart of the subject, following the cognitive and affective development of the learner. Concepts were put into words (*languaging* as defined by Swain 2006) between two languages in order to deepen the construction of meanings. Bilingual reform was a beautiful interinstitutional adventure that rallied energies and galvanized the enthusiasm of many educational professionals, especially at the beginning when the innovative effervescence was strongest and the aspect of "knowledge construction" was the most original contribution of Val d'Aoste's schooling system to bi-/plurilingual education.

REFERENCES

Bange, P., Carol, R., and Griggs, P. (2005). *L'apprentissage d'une langue étrangère. Cognition et Interaction.* Paris: L'Harmattan.

Betemps, A., Bonis, G., Favre, V., Janin, B., Remacle, C., Rivolin, J. and Ronc, M.-C. (1994). *Espace, temps et culture en Vallée d'Aoste.* Aosta: IRRSAE-Vallée d'Aoste.

Bourguignon, C., Py, B. and Ragot, A.-M. (1994). Aspects psycholinguistiques. In R. Assuied et al., eds., *Recherche sur l'école maternelle bilingue en Vallée d'Aoste.* Aosta: IRRSAE-Vallée d'Aoste.

Cavalli, M. (1993). Tre lingue in Valle d'Aosta: l'insegnamento integrato di francese, italiano e inglese. In Italiano e oltre. 8(1). 31–35. https://giscel.it/wp-content/uploads/2018/07/Italiano-e-Oltre-1993_1.pdf

(ed.) (1998). *Pensare e parlare in più lingue – Esperienze di insegnamento e di formazione in Valle d'Aosta.* Aosta: IRRSAE-Valle d'Aosta.

(2002). Français langue seconde au Val d'Aoste : aspects curriculaires de l'enseignement bi-/plurilingue. In P. Martinez, ed., *Le français langue seconde - Apprentissage et curriculum.* Paris: Maisonneuve & Larose.

(2003). Discours bilingue et apprentissage des disciplines. Réflexions d'après les expériences du Val d'Aoste. In D.-L. Simon and C. Sabatier, eds., *Le plurilinguisme en construction dans le système éducatif: Contextes-Dispositifs-Acteurs.* Collection LIDIL, Grenoble: Université de Grenoble, pp. 32–46.

(2005). *Education bilingue et plurilinguisme: Le cas du Val d'Aoste.* Paris: Collection LAL, CREDIF, Didier, p. 370.

Cavalli, M., Coletta, D., Gajo, L., Matthey, M. and Serra, C. (2003). *Langues, bilinguisme et représentations sociales au Val d'Aoste – Rapport de recherche,* Aoste, Italy: IRRE-VDA.

Costanzo, E. (2003). *L'éducation linguistique (educazione linguistica) en Italie : une expérience pour l'Europe ?* Reference study. Strasbourg: Council of Europe, Language Policy Division (DGIV).

Coste, D. (1994). Conceptualisation et alternance des langues. In D. Coletta, E. Nicco and R. Tadiello, eds., *Pensare in due lingue, Atti del convegno regionale,* 16–17 settembre 1993. Aosta: IRRSAE-Val d'Aoste.

(2000). Immersion, enseignement bilingue et construction des connaissances. In J. Duverger, ed., *Actualité de l'enseignement bilingue,* Le français dans le monde – Numéro spécial. Paris: Hachette, pp. 86–94.

Coste, D. and Pasquier, A. (1992). *Langues et savoirs – Due lingue per sapere, Matériaux pour un apprentissage bilingue à l'école primaire. Principes et Méthodologie.* 1(14), 13–26.

Cuq, J.-P. (1991). *Le français langue seconde – Origines d'une notion et implications didactiques.* Paris: Hachette.

Gajo, L. and Serra, C. (1998). *De l'alternance des langues à un concept global de l'enseignement des disciplines (a.s. 1997/98).* Aosta: Assessorat de l'éducation et de la culture.

(2000). Enseignement bilingue, didactique des langues et des disciplines: une expérience valdôtaine. In P. Martinez and S. Pekarek, eds., *Didactique et contact de langues: Notions en question 2.* Paris: Hatier.

García, O. (2009). *Bilingual Education in the 21st Century: A Global Perspective*. New York: Blackwell/Wiley.

García, O. and Kleyn, T. (2016). *Translanguaging with Multilingual Students: Learning from Classroom Moments*. New York: Routledge.

García, O. and Li Wei (2014). *Translanguaging: Language, Bilingualism and Education*. New York: Palgrave Macmillan.

Giroux, H. A. (1988). *Teachers as Intellectuals: Toward a Critical Pedagogy of Learning*. Granby, MA: Praeger.

Grosjean, F. (1982). *Life with Two Languages: An Introduction to Bilingualism*. Cambridge, MA, and London: Harvard University Press.

  (2008). *Studying Bilinguals*. Oxford: Oxford University Press.

  (2010). *Bilingual – Life and Reality*. Cambridge, MA, and London: Harvard University Press.

  (2015). *Parler plusieurs langues – Le monde des bilingues*. Paris, Albin Michel.

Lüdi, G. and Py, B. (2002). *Etre bilingue*. Berne: Peter Lang (1st edition 1986).

Py, B. (1997). Education bilingue et alternance des langues: La négociation du code en contexte scolaire. *L'école valdôtaine* 36, 53–57.

  (2003). Introduction. In M. Cavalli et al., eds., *Langues, bilinguisme et représentations sociales au Val d'Aoste: Rapport final*. Aosta: IRRE-VDA, pp. 15–33.

Steffen, G. (2013). *Les disciplines dans l'enseignement bilingue: Apprentissage intégré des savoirs disciplinaires et linguistiques*. Frankfurt am Main: Peter Lang.

Swain, M. (2006). Languaging, agency and collaboration in advanced second language proficiency. In H. Byrnes, ed., *Advanced Language Learning: The Contribution of Halliday and Vygotsky*. London: Continuum, pp. 95–108.

10   Multilingualism as Part of Social Reality

Viktorija L. A. Čeginskas

Academically, I am an outsider to the fields of multilingualism and education as my background is in history and European ethnology. Practically, however, my personal experiences place me at the core of it. Based on my everyday experiences as a multilingual from birth and a mother of multilingual children, I will try to contribute to the discussion of multilingual practices in education from a personal angle that relates individual multilingualism and multilingual practices to sociopolitical issues.

10.1   A Multilingual Biography

My multilingual biography is inextricably linked with my mixed European family background. My parents were originally from the Baltic States, a region that historically constitutes a 'cultural borderland' (see Applebaum 2015) as regards the cross-interaction between different ethnicities, cultures and languages. Babylon became reality at home: we spoke and switched between Estonian, Lithuanian, French, Swedish and German, and later also included English in our discussions around the dining table, to which occasionally other languages were added in my parents' conversations with guests. Today my 'transnational, cross- and intercultural' family life and 'multilingual socialisation' continues: I am married to a Frenchman of Catalan origin who was born in Brazil. We met while working in the Netherlands, and we use English as our *lingua franca*. As we reside in Germany, our children are raised with Estonian, French, English and German.

My parents met at the University of Strasbourg in the early 1950s. Dating from their first encounter, French became my parents' adopted *lingua franca*. With the arrival of my oldest sister in the mid-1950s, our parents made a very uncommon and progressive decision at that time: they decided to raise us children in their mother tongues, Estonian and Lithuanian, while continuing to use French among themselves. My parents' decision was a rather remarkable act of resistance to macro geopolitical decisions and societal pressure

Figure 10.1 A happy, messy, multilingual childhood

to assimilate. They were stateless refugees, whose home countries were occupied by the Soviet Union, and, cut off from close family members by the Iron Curtain, they lacked practical and moral support for keeping up their languages in the everyday. My parents' determination to use their mother tongues with us children mirrored their political and intellectual mindset, and additionally reflected (and transmitted to us) the strong emotional bond they felt with their families, their native countries and languages.

My four siblings were born in France, Germany and Sweden, and I was welcomed as an unexpected late addition and as my family's first Swedish citizen by birth. It was normal for me to grow up with multiple languages at home. I spoke Estonian with my mother and grandmother, and Lithuanian with my father, French was spoken by my parents, German between my father and Estonian grandmother, and my four elder siblings and I used Estonian as a base with Swedish, and later also German, code-switching. Although French remained a passive language for many years, I had a selective understanding of the language from early days: very good in matters of direct personal interest (e.g. when my parents discussed Christmas presents), but I was also able to follow my parents' daily political discussions. Moreover, I found it normal that people spoke other languages inside and outside the family circle, which I did not understand. Actually, hearing these languages only aroused my curiosity and interest in them, and instilled some kind of 'multilingual awareness' (Jessner 2006). When I was not yet three years old, we moved from Sweden to Germany, where my father began working for the Lithuanian broadcasting service of Radio Liberty/Free Europe. Soon I was sent to kindergarten, where I tried to use Estonian, Lithuanian and Swedish with the other children (and staff) but they did not understand me. Far worse, they only answered in German. After my first days at kindergarten, I apparently declared that there was something 'seriously wrong!' with people who only spoke one language. It had never occurred to me that people would not speak or understand several languages.

Compared with my elder siblings, my set of languages changed after moving to Germany. German became my main institutional language (kindergarten, school), whereas the importance of Swedish was slowly reduced to passive understanding. As my Swedish language skills grew weaker, I gradually became aware that I shared more common cultural and social experiences with German than with Swedish peers. The older I grew, the more I became self-conscious of my language skills and pronunciation. A relatively banal incident was decisive for me to stop speaking Swedish from one day to another, approximately at the age of seven years (I felt deeply embarrassed because I could not remember the Swedish word for Wednesday in a conversation) but I continued understanding (and even reading) Swedish. Although I was still able to express myself in Swedish if needed, I increasingly preferred speaking English, a 'neutral' language, which I had picked up from one of my best friends and neighbours, an American boy.

I first learned reading and writing in German. I remember my surprise when I noticed that I could transfer these skills to my other languages. Soon I was easily reading in three languages, and less happily in two more, which seemed to pose bigger problems for either linking the spoken with the written language or motivating myself to read in it. At school, I noted one major difference between my classmates and myself in particular in foreign language classes: they would often get stuck when encountering unknown words, whereas my more efficient technique was to ignore such words as long as I still understood the context both in written exercises and in conversations. Furthermore, I was able to interrelate various linguistic and cultural resources (e.g. Ruíz 1984; Jessner 2006): I could deduct from certain languages, transfer ideas and terms, make associations and analogies between my various knowledge repertoires, which considerably helped me in foreign language classes and other school subjects (as well as outside school). While I was generally encouraged to speak and differentiate between multiple languages and to be able to negotiate cultural differences (i.e. to notice and bridge them) at home, a few schoolteachers and some other people (who usually had a monolingual and monocultural background) often considered the knowledge of other languages and cultural practices as a potential problem.

Owing to my background and the daily use of multiple languages, I felt transnational and transcultural long before I was aware of these terms. However, school and different forms of social interaction in 'monolingual contexts' contributed to making me feel 'different' (Ceginskas 2010), outside the norm, neither being represented nor acknowledged for who I was. Unlike most people I met, I had two homes: one in Germany, my actual 'base', and one in Sweden, where I would spend my holidays, where my siblings and my Estonian grandmother lived, and which therefore was associated with important emotions and memories. In a similar vein, from early days I began to categorise my language relationships in a specific way when introducing myself that was also telling about my complex construction of belonging and revealed the (im)balance between the needs and uses of my set of languages: Estonian was my 'mother tongue' and Lithuanian my 'father tongue'. While this emphasised their emotional qualities and significance for me, I was aware of limitations in my fluency. French was my 'parents' language', and hence a passive language, whereas German was my 'school language', which stressed its active use in the everyday. Finally, Swedish was my 'state language', which referred to its legal and political relevance in terms of citizenship and highlighted Sweden as my country of birth, both of which mattered before Sweden's accession to the European Union (1995) and the Schengen Agreement entering into force.

While I was quickly highly competent in German, it never felt like an emotionally meaningful language (it was, after all, my *school* language!), and I did not want to be German despite reluctantly beginning to acknowledge the role which language and socialisation played for me. Whenever my older siblings wanted to tease me, they called me 'German', or pointed out that I behaved in a 'typical German way', which considering our family history and our parents' and grandparents' experiences during Second World War was certainly not meant as a compliment. These comments did not help to form an emotional relationship with Germany or the German language. As 'Soviet' was reserved for political discussions, I only could call my siblings 'Swedish', which was a weak retort, and much less negative than being German, as we were Swedish citizens. Initially, I felt emotionally closer to the Swedish language and Sweden but, with time, the discrepancy between Sweden and Germany regarding the level of my language skills and socialisation became too obvious for me, and consequently I felt increasingly reluctant to introduce myself as a Swedish citizen or tick the box on the form. The fact that I had Estonian and Lithuanian parents, and sensed allegiance to their origins and linguistic identifications, added to my complex and plural linguistic, cultural and ethnic belonging but it also had a concrete impact on social practices and rights of membership.

The emotional component in my relationship to languages went beyond linguistic fluency, and it affected my decision of which language to use with my children. While my older siblings opted to speak (their school language) Swedish with their children for various reasons, I chose Estonian. Following my mother's early death, I was afraid of losing my language skills and, subsequently, my bonds with my mother, her past, her family and her country. When my children were born, my father was still alive and our interaction could initially ensure such vital ties to himself and Lithuania. However, my two sisters strongly criticised my choice, and for many years, we continued to have an argument about the fact that I did not use my 'best' language (German) for forming a relationship with my children, which they claimed deprived my children of a good linguistic basis. The conflict ebbed away once it became obvious that my children spoke and understood Estonian better than some of my siblings.

10.2   Some Thoughts about Multilingual Practices

My long biographic introduction serves to point out that multilingualism is relevant in terms of carrying emotional value for multilingual individuals and affecting their social locations and belonging as well as their social and political practices. While they are not fixed for life, language use and practices help to determine a person's self- and externally ascribed identification by others, and provide orientation in everyday social interactions, including the recognition as a valid and represented group member with specific rights (see Yuval-Davis 2006). Hence, the ways in which multilingual research and education policies design, use and present multilingual practices need to contribute to deepening understanding for the social and political implications as well as the psychological and individual dimension of multilingualism (see Aronin and Ó Laoire 2004; Pavlenko 2006).

Unlike in my childhood, there is now a growing broader awareness of multilingualism in recent years that favours a shift away from viewing language predominantly as a problem (Ruíz 1984). Across Europe, languages and language learning are increasingly promoted in terms of a personal and societal resource that represents linguistic plurality and cultural diversity in society in relation to various experiences of social, political and economic processes and phenomena, such as increased global interaction and mobility of people (see Conteh and Meier 2014; Meier 2018, p. 106). For instance, the objective of the EU's education policy is 'to increase individual multilingualism until every citizen has practical skills in at least two languages in addition to his or her mother tongue' (EC 2005, p. 4). However, language education policies at national and European level still combine the promotion of individual multilingualism with the idea of having one mother tongue as the norm, which puts the emphasis on making people become multilingual speakers instead of taking into consideration that multilingual practices are part of social reality (see Meier 2018; Gynne 2019; Paulsrud et al. 2020). In political discourses, language learning and multilingual practices are constructed to serve the objective of facilitating integration, social cohesion and dialogue (e.g. EC 2005; EC 2007). However, such differentiation between dominant and non-standard/minority languages continues to reiterate power imbalances and reinforce political agendas of identity-building and belonging (see also Yuval-Davis 2006; Gynne 2019; Paulsrud et al. 2020).

Next to the family home, educational institutions represent a social micro-cosmos that plays an important role for socialisation: for acquiring formal knowledge of a language, learning about structures of social interactions and for feeling accepted or rejected. They serve as an arena for knowledge transfer and production but also impart a hidden political ideology and national perspective that help to establish and convey a specific sociocultural frame-work of references, and set expectations and attitudes at the same time (see Piller 2016). Current education practices often do not acknowledge other linguistic repertoires, discursive practices and cultural knowledge as resources for meaning-making and belonging but transport unchallenged ideas about language standards, values, hierarchies and world views as the norm, including the appreciation or stigma of some (groups of) people and languages (see also Piller 2017; Meier 2018, p. 104). However, with increased migration and mobility, and the growing number of binational families, educational environ-ments need to respond to new challenges in society by creating 'spaces, where all learners, teachers and parents feel they can potentially belong as legitimate members, whatever their linguistic backgrounds' (Meier 2018, p. 113). Therefore, current and future pedagogical approaches and language practices in education need to both consider how the curriculum at school and university reflects languages and language practices in social reality and implement multilingual use and practices in such a way that both students with a different language repertoire and monolingual language learners can benefit from it.

In my view, the promotion of multilingualism and multilingual practices can indeed 'play a key role in legitimising multilingual languaging' (Gynne 2019, p. 351). However, conceptual frameworks in education need to address multi-lingual practices in the context of social inequalities and political, social and cultural power imbalances in all areas of social interaction. This includes creating awareness for the psychological dimension of multilingual practices in terms of an important individual resource but also as a legitimised means of promoting social and political recognition, representations, inclusion, empowerment, social equality and access to democratic participation (see Aronin and Ó Laoire 2004; Pavlenko 2006; Piller 2017; Paulsrud et al. 2020). Therefore, when developing and implementing new pedagogical practices and strategies, educators and researchers need to think outside the box in order to carefully integrate an understanding of language politics and a pragmatic management of learning processes in support of multifarious approaches to learning languages and uses of multilingual practices in education (see Meier 2018; Paulsrud et al. 2020). This relates to the relevance of finding a good balance between the transfer of standards, academic knowledge and skills on the one hand, and the need to strengthen self-confidence in language skills and enable social participation and complex processes of belonging on the other.

In recent years, translanguaging has been discussed as a pedagogical approach and practice that conveys to learners the ability to both differentiate between language knowledge and, at the same time, develop, strengthen and act on multiple linguistic repertoires and discursive practices inside and outside the classroom (see Conteh and Meier 2014; Meier 2018; Gynne 2019; Paulsrud et al. 2020). Planned approaches of translanguaging in education, such as collaborative strategies, project learning in foreign languages or multilingual exercises, which are not limited to foreign language acquisition, can develop and bolster the use of diverse language practices, skills and information in a variety of contexts. This makes it a promising practical approach for creating a greater sensibility towards the everyday use of multilingual practices as a legitimised part of social reality that can transform current pedagogical concepts and societal conceptualisations of multilingualism towards achieving social equality and justice in language practices and education.

REFERENCES

Applebaum, A. (2015) [1994]. *Between East and West: Across the Borderlands of Europe*. London: Penguin Book.
Aronin, L. and Ó Laoire, M. (2004). Exploring multilingualism in cultural contexts: Towards a notion of multilinguality. In C. Hoffmann and J. Ytsma, eds., *Trilingualism in Family, School and Community*. Clevedon, Toronto, Sydney: Multilingual Matters, pp. 11–29.
Ceginskas, V. (2010). Being 'the strange one' or 'like everybody else': School education and the negotiation of multilingual identity. *International Journal of Multilingualism* 7(3), 211–224.
Conteh, J. and Meier, G. (2014). *The Multilingual Turn in Languages Education: Opportunities and Challenges*. Bristol: Multilingual Matters.
EC (European Commission) (2005). Communication from the Commission to the Council, the European Parliament, the Economic and Social Committee, and the Committee of the Regions. A New Framework Strategy for Multilingualism. COM (2005) 596 final. https://ec.europa.eu/transparency/regdoc/rep/1/2005/EN/1-2005-596-EN-F1-1.Pdf [accessed 20 February 2020]

(2007). *Commission of the European Communities: Final report. High Level Group on Multilingualism*. Luxembourg: Office for Official Publications of the European Communities. http://biblioteca.esec.pt/cdi/ebooks/docs/High_level_report.pdf [accessed 20 February 2020]

Gynne, A. (2019). 'English or Swedish please, no Dari!': (Trans)languaging and language policing in upper secondary school's language introduction programme in Sweden. *Classroom Discourse* 10(3–4), 347–368, https://doi.org/10.1080/ 19463014.2019.1628791

Jessner, U. (2006). *Linguistic Awareness in Multilinguals: English as a Third Language*. Edinburgh: Edinburgh University Press.

Meier, G. (2018). Multilingual socialisation in education: Introducing the M-SOC approach. *Language Education and Multilingualism: The Landscape Journal* 1, 103–125. https://doi.org/10.18452/19034

Paulsrud, B., Zilliacus, H. and Ekberg, L. (2020). Spaces for multilingual education: Language orientations in the national curricula of Sweden and Finland. *International Multilingual Research Journal* https://doi.org/10.1080/19313152 .2020.1714158

Pavlenko, A. (2006). *Bilingual Minds. Emotional Experience, Expression and Representation*. Clevedon, Toronto, Sydney: Multilingual Matters.

Piller I. (2016). *Linguistic Diversity and Social Justice. An Introduction to Applied Sociolinguistics*. Oxford: Oxford University Press.

(2017). *Language Shaming: Enacting Linguistic Subordination*, keynote (28 August 2017). 16th International Conference in Minority Languages. Revaluing Minority Languages. University of Jyväskylä, Finland, 28–30 August 2017.

Ruíz, R. (1984). Orientations in language planning. *NABE Journal* 8(2), 15–34. https:// doi.org/10.1080/08855072.1984.10668464

Yuval-Davis, N. (2006). Belonging and the politics of belonging. *Patterns of Prejudice* 40(3), 197–214. https://doi.org/10.1080/00313220600769331

11   Some Elements of Family History and Language Biography

Daniel Coste

A language biography is, especially in our profession, not only a "history of languages" (to use a formula dear to Aude Bretegner) but also a story of encounters with men and women who help you to think and situate yourself in languages, by what they say or write or by their own way of being in languages. Colleagues, students, more or less close friends, people crossed in such and such a place ... It would be another way of retracing a biography, significantly different from this one, but where the couple of dialect speaking Alsatians would always find a place.

If we have to go further back in time to a very ordinary beginning as a child and adolescent born in Paris to Parisian parents from a very modest back-ground and growing up in a suburban commune, I had little exposure to languages other than French until my entry into secondary school (apart from the ritual formulas in a Latin mass). Diversity, in my memory, was limited to the strong Alsatian "accent" of a maternal grandmother, born in Colmar under the German regime at the very end of the nineteenth century.

But there had been an episode far from Paris, around the age of seven. A shadow in one of my lungs had earned me a medical prescription for a few months of the fresh air of a tiny village at the bottom of a Vosges valley. A farm, a couple of local farmers, and a dozen cows welcomed me. The farmers, both born well before 1918, when Alsace was German, reminded me of my grandmother, but with some more striking features: A helmet-tipped photo of a brother who died at the front during WWI adorned one of the farm's rooms and the map of Europe pinned to the wall showed a very different position of borders than the one I remembered from my primary school. Alsatian was spoken, German was read, and French was almost totally unknown in the house. I attribute to this immersion of a few months not only my healing but also my first strong experience of linguistic plurality and a certain mode of intercultural relations; and a heightened sensitivity to "accents," which earned me, on returning to the Paris region, the amusement and taunting of my peers at hearing the regionally acquired rhythm and intonation of my ways of speaking that bore a certified geographical origin.

Figure 11.1 Il était une fois … Once upon a (long) time!

The younger villagers than my Alsatian hosts with whom I had become acquainted had not only spoken the dialect (which was not promoted as a regional language nor a "Langue de France") but also used it all the more vivaciously!

I don't know if exposure to a Germanic dialect had any effect on my learning of German and then English at school in junior high and high school (in the modern sections, without Latin or Greek) but, at the time of university studies, the switch was made to English for a Bachelor's degree certificate in modern literature and for the then-new aggregation in this same discipline. The preparation of this aggregation also brought me into intensive but rudimentary contact with Latin, which had (and still has) the right, in the competition, to a separate evaluation. But English had largely prevailed, even before the aggregation, thanks to a one-year stay in England and then another year in the United States.

It was during the latter that I met the woman who was to become my wife, born in the United States to Italian parents of Calabrian origin, who had arrived via Ellis Island in the early 1920s. Philomena, declared Filomena at birth, would also be, in the United States or in France, in diachrony or in synchrony, depending on the interlocutors or correspondents: Phil, Philo, Filomena, Philomena. There were uncertainty and fluctuations in the perception of others and of oneself for someone who, as a very young immigrant girl exposed to the Calabrian dialect and Italian, was anxious above all to become Americanized and became a French teacher before becoming a young married woman "immigrant" in France. She wanted to do everything possible to integrate, as well and as quickly as possible, to the customs of this new country, even if it meant pursuing her career at the American School of Paris.

The constant practice of alternating between French and English, circles of French-speaking and/or English-speaking friends, questions and discussions about the place of English in the environment for our two children (educated throughout in the French public school system) and their level of "bilingualism" were nothing but very ordinary in a "mixed" couple. The family language policy did not go without some differences of appreciation!

Early on I was appointed to the Crédif (Centre de recherche et d'étude pour la diffusion du français) at the École normale supérieure de Saint-Cloud, and over the years I have been involved in projects, conferences, internships, and expert reports in foreign countries near and far, and have been in contact with teachers, colleagues, and various officials with whom I have had exchanges in French (and often also in English). I have very often been frustrated at not being able to practice or understand, or even, on occasion, decipher their languages, and just as often surprised to see how much most of these multilingual people explicitly showed a certain linguistic insecurity in their relationship with the "native" French speaker. These experiences have made a significant contribution to my reflection on the relationship between variation and norms in the representations, uses, and learning of French, which is mired in its overprogramming. But there has also been a gradual evolution toward the expression of, and even the demand for, diversity in the ways of appropriating and living French as a plural language. This is what, among other things, the corpus-based linguistic research carried out at Crédif had also taught me.

My long participation in Crédif's activities was also marked, in the 1980s, by an interest in the institutional history and disciplinary constitution of the field of French as a foreign language. The main focus was on the diffusion of the language and the relationship between this diffusion policy and the evolution of language sciences. Much more, at the time, than in terms of language didactics and – curiously – without any notable attention paid to the geopolitical dimensions or to the relationship with linguistic plurality and colonization, or to the political institutionalization of the Francophonie.

In my personal language biography, I owe a great deal to the few years I spent as a professor at the University of Geneva as a member of the Department of Linguistics and Director of the School of French Language and Civilization. The management of a school with a population of students of different languages and origins, with the questions of welcoming and managing individual situations and "cases," the (inter)cultural dimensions of this responsibility, the errors of appreciation committed, the involuntary successes: All of this counts. But it was also during these years that I began to intervene occasionally in Valle d'Aosta in the context of the bilingual teaching system and to take an interest in the alternation of languages in educational contexts. It was also during this period that I discovered, in meetings of the Interuniversity Commission of Applied Linguistics (CILA), with academics from German-speaking Switzerland, the pleasures of the Swiss model of plurilingual communication where each person speaks his or her own language and is supposed to understand (not always in my case) that of the other, even when, in the heat of the discussion, Hochdeutsch and Schwiizerdütsch are mixed up! And it was also during these same years that I took part, in 1991, in the Council of Europe symposium in Rüschlikon, where the CEFR (Common European Framework of Reference for Languages) and ELP (European Language Portfolio) projects were launched. The outcome of this meeting is known. If I finally add that "Towards Multilingualism? School and Language Policy" (Coste and Hébrard 1991) was published that same year, I understand better, in retrospect, how much the brief stint at the University of Geneva (1988–1992) meant to my relationship with languages, at different levels and in different contexts of reflection and intervention. I could not disentangle this range of experiences and influences in terms of their respective contributions to my personal journey and its inflections. It seems to me that these encounters have shaped the choices that I have made.

11.1   Some Singular Notes on a Plural Course

If I attempt to reconstruct my personal trajectory, I believe I can trace the moment I found plurilingualism (as one speaks of finding religion, but used here with great sarcasm) to the late 1980s and, more precisely, as the outcome of the colloquium organized by Crédif and hosted by Denis Lehmann in 1987 with the title "Didactique des langues ou didactiques de langues: Transversalités et spécificités" (see Lehmann 1988). One of the panels of that colloquium, organized by Louis-Jean Calvet and Jean Hebrard, discussed the theme "Languages policies and language teaching." Diverse circumstances following the panel led to the (late) publication of the indirectly related volume *Vers le plurilinguisme? École et politique linguistique* (Coste and Hébrard 1991).

My position on the subject of plurilingualism was not one of overwhelming enthusiasm; I saw it rather from the perspective of curriculum planning (Coste 1991). Even if the language resources of students (and not only the children of migrants) were recognized as such, the first consideration was one of the feasibility of additive plurilingualism at school, building on the diversity of languages taught and more importantly holding onto languages. The prominent question mark in the title indicated that nothing could be taken for granted and that it was time for the field of language teaching to become engaged in language policymaking, rather than continuing to be "peu encline jusqu'à présent à s'engager sur le terrain de la fréquentation et de l'utilisation plurielle des langues" ("disinclined until now to become involved in the coexistence and plural use of languages"; Coste 1991: 176). Yet it was in this same publication that, without definition, the term "plurilingual competence" appeared.

11.2   Toward the Concept of Plurilingual Competence

The movement toward a certain diversification was also a part of the stated aims of the European institutions. In 1995, the European Commission, in its *White Paper on Education and Training*, recommended knowledge of three European languages (an adjectivization that would inspire hesitation and later modification). The successive "modern languages" projects of the Council of Europe and the associated recommendations foreground the plural linguistic heritage of Europe. Thus, certain "considerings" of the preamble of Recommendation 82(18) of the Committee of Ministers concerning modern languages define the ideological orientation of the approach adopted by the Council for questions concerning languages:

> Considering that the rich heritage of diverse languages and cultures in Europe is a valuable common resource to be protected and developed, and that a major educational effort is needed to convert that diversity from a barrier to communication into a source of mutual enrichment and understanding;
>
> Considering that it is only through a better knowledge of European modern languages that it will be possible to facilitate communication and interaction among Europeans of different mother tongues in order to promote European mobility, mutual understanding, and cooperation, and overcome prejudice and discrimination;

Necessary discourse and legalese, perhaps, at the height of 1982, but a few years later, the opening of eastern and central European countries and the membership of several in the Council of Europe reinvigorated the idea of linguistic plurality, the issue of language policy, and the growing influence of English in educational systems in Europe. The 1991 Rüschlikon Symposium already mentioned, entitled "Transparence et cohérence dans l'apprentissage des langues en Europe. Objectifs, évaluation, certification," which led to the creation of the Common European Framework of Reference (CEFR) and the European Language Portfolio (ELP), noted these evolutions without quite establishing plurilingualism as such in the recommendations and conclusions of the meeting (Council of Europe 1993). The emphasis was clearly on rating scales and the comparability of certifications.

After having spent some time at the University of Geneva and been named Director of Crédif at the Ecole normale supérieure de Saint-Cloud in 1992, I also participated in the small group that wrote the CEFR (with Brian North, Joseph Sheils, and John Trim, who piloted the project) and continued to go regularly to Val d'Aoste, which I had discovered while in Geneva and where I participated in some bilingual teaching research. In this latter context, I was interested in the forms and functions of code switching in knowledge construction (Coste and Pasquier 1992; Coste 1994a, 1994b). My aim was to contextualize the switching within a process of reformulation drawing on the diversity of textual genres.

It was in this work that, for me, a certain focus emerged concerning the concept of plurilingual competence, introduced "in passing" in a piece (Coste and Hébrard, 1991) and notably taken up again in a small 1993 text entitled "Diversification linguistique, compétence plurilingue et didactique des langues" (Coste 1993). In 1995, within the context of the Council of Europe's pilot studies of the CEFR, I proposed to develop this concept with colleagues from Crédif, Danièle Moore and Geneviève Zarate. Two years later, the oft-cited *Compétence plurilingue et pluriculturelle* appeared (Coste, Moore, and Zarate 1997), which provided the first conceptual definition and operationalization of the term.

Retrospectively, at the invitation of the editors of this volume, situating this first dive into plurilingualism in terms of scientificity and epistemology has proven challenging. Although the introduction of plurilingual competence as an idea clearly served as an extension of François Grosjean's work on the capacity of bilinguals (Grosjean 1985, but also Lüdi and Py 1986), this introduction was scant on references to empirical work or clear theoretical models. We had to deal with a power grab targeting didactics and language policy rather than the implementation of a well-defined concept and problematization. When *Compétence plurilingue et pluriculturelle* appeared, the distinction (in the Francophone context) between multilingualism (applied to societies and territories) and plurilingualism (applied to individuals) was not widely agreed. It was only progressively and collectively that a more complex conceptualization, better integrated with theory, would be operationalized and therefore open to critical examination.

11.3   Plurilingual Education and Plurilingualism

Immediately following the official publication of the CEFR in 2001, the Language Policy Unit of the Council of Europe worked in other ways toward the integration of language plurality into language policy. The *Guide for the Development of Language Education Policies in Europe* (Beacco and Byram 2007), subtitled *From Linguistic Diversity to Plurilingual Education*, not only took up the concept of plurilingual competence and made it the focal point of its arguments but also brought about the passage from an aim of diversification of language offerings to a project of plurilingual and intercultural education. It was then a question of providing arguments and instruments for the implementation of language policies where the objective of promoting individual plurilingualism would fall in line with a larger educational project, with clearly articulated values where an education in language is also an education through language.

Such an orientation could only surpass (but not abandon) the unique framework of foreign language education. It encouraged taking into account the languages of schooling, focusing on an examination of arguments regarding curricula (Beacco et al. 2015), highlighting linguistic dimensions of all disciplines (Beacco, Coste, Van de Ven, and Vollmer 2010; Beacco et al., 2016), and undertaking the linguistic integration of adult migrants (Beacco, Little, and Hedges 2014). In this evolution, there was less insistence on plurilingualism itself and the platform of references and resources for a plurilingual and intercultural education was subsumed under "languages in education, languages for education."

11.4   Bi/Plurilingualism and Cultural and Linguistic Diversity

In her conclusion to the issue "Notions en question(s) en didactique des langues" on "Plurilingualisms," Véronique Castellotti broaches the idea of dropping the term plurilingualism itself, in light of its misuse and inherent ambiguities (Castellotti 2010). In fact, we have seen such formulations as "linguistic and cultural diversity" and "linguistic and cultural plurality" substituted for "plurilingualism." In the titles and texts of my own publications, the evolutions and variations in this sense can be seen (Blanchet and Coste 2010; Cavalli and Coste 2010; Coste 2011, 2012, 2013b) and are mostly a result of the use of "plurilingual and intercultural education" as part of the project "Langues dans l'éducation, langues pour l'éducation" of the Division of Language Policy of the Council of Europe. When it comes down to it, as soon as "linguistic" and "cultural" are associated with a designation, the noun "plurilingualism" has trouble fitting in, as it lacks an improbable "(inter) culturalism" in this context.

Phrases such as bi/plurilingual and bi/plurilingualism remain common in my own writing, and are temporarily and intentionally required in relation to specific situations (notably that of Val d'Aoste) or choices and evolutions of labels (as in the acronym ADEB, *Association pour le développement de l'enseignement bilingue* to *Association pour le développement de l'enseignement bi-/plurilingue*). The option in this case is to enfold the existent bilingual education within a broader perspective where it becomes possible to transcend the compartmentalized, binary polarization between two languages in bilingual education in order to emphasize the socialization of the whole child through the seamless development of plural language capacities and resources resulting from exposure to different social groups and circulation among them. Thus "bilingual" education, including schooling in a second language, is in a way joined to a prior experience of linguistic pluralism (Coste 2013; Coste and Cavalli 2015). This conception must also be instantiated throughout didactic choices and pedagogical propositions (Castellotti, Coste, and Duverger 2008; Castellotti and Candelier 2013).

11.5   Reflexive Path

These remembrances of a personal path may appear overly self-referenced (but one could say this is what was asked of contributors to this volume) and undertheorized, notably concerning the relationship between concepts and terminology. Many are the hesitations and fluctuations in the ways of indicating language plurality and linguistic diversity from the angle of how each social actor appropriates and manages language resources. No doubt this stems primarily from the circumstances of my personal trajectory since the end of the 1980s, a trajectory influenced by my belonging to different research groups, collaborating with several institutions, and consulting in different European contexts, and a particular way of thinking about engagement in teaching and language education policy.

This unique story is not very original. It is comparable in some aspects to those of other specialists who work in the same research and teaching domain and who are interested in linguistic and cultural plurality as it relates to schools, education, schooling of migrant children, and the reception and integration of migrants and their families (e.g. Auger 2008; Auger and Kervran 2011). I have attempted to characterize the last thirty years as an interplay of tensions among three paradigms: those of plurality, assessment, and alterity (Coste 2015). It seems to me that many debates and issues are located within this conflictual space. For the comparability of positionings falls far from indicating their compatibility. The work carried out under the Council of Europe and the resulting publications and instruments have been and still are the object of sometimes harsh critique from some quarters of the Francophone scholarly world and from many angles (pedagogical, ideological, scientific, political).

REFERENCES

Auger, N. (2008). Favoriser le plurilinguisme pour aider à l'insertion scolaire et sociale des élèves nouvellement arrivés (ENA). *Glottopol* 11, 126–137.

Auger, N. and Kervran, M. (2011). Construction identitaire et compétence plurilingue. *Tréma* 33–34, 41–54.

Beacco, J.-C. and Byram, M. (2003) (2007). *Guide pour l'élaboration des politiques linguistiques éducatives en Europe. De la diversité linguistique à l'éducation plurilingue.* Strasbourg: Council of Europe.

Beacco, J.-C., Little, D., and Hedges, C. (2014). *L'intégration linguistique des migrants adultes - Guide pour l'élaboration et la mise en œuvre des politiques.* Strasbourg: Council of Europe.

Beacco, J.-C., Coste, D., Van de Ven, P.-H., and Vollmer, H. (2010). *Langues et matières scolaires : dimensions linguistiques de la construction des connaissances dans les curriculums.* Strasbourg: Council of Europe. www.coe.int/t/dg4/ linguistic/langeduc/BoxD2-OtherSub_fr.asp

Beacco, J.-C., Fleming, M., Goullier, F., Thürmann, E., and Vollmer, H., with the contribution of Sheils, J. (2016). *Les dimensions linguistiques de toutes les matières scolaires. Guide pour l'élaboration des curriculums et pour la formation des enseignants.* Strasbourg: Council of Europe, Language Policy Division.

Beacco, J.-C., Byram, M., Cavalli, M., Coste, D., Egli Cuenat, M., Goullier, F., and Panthier, J. (2015). *Guide pour le développement et la mise en œuvre de curriculums pour l'éducation plurilingue et interculturelle.* Strasbourg: Council of Europe, Division des politiques linguistiques. Publié à nouveau en 2016 par le service des publications du Conseil. ISBN 978-92-871-8233-3.

Blanchet, P. and Coste, D. (2010). *Regards critiques sur la notion d' interculturalité : Pour une didactique de la pluralité linguistique et culturelle.* Paris: L'Harmattan.

Calvet, L.-J. (1999). *Pour une écologie des langues du monde.* Paris: Plon.
    (2002). *Le marché aux langues. Les effets linguistiques de la mondialisation.* Paris: Plon.

Castellotti, V. (2010). Attention! Un plurilinguisme peut en cacher un autre: Enjeux théoriques et didactiques de la notion de pluralité. *Les Cahiers de l'Acedle* 7(1), 181–207.
    (2017). *Pour une didactique de l'appropriation. Diversité, compréhension, relation.* Paris: Didier.

Castellotti, V. and Candelier, M. (2013). Didactique(s) du(des) plurilinguisme(s). *Sociolinguistique du contact. Dictionnaire des termes et concepts*, Lyon, ENS Editions, pp. 179–221.

Castellotti, V. and Moore, D. (2010). *Valoriser, mobiliser et développer les répertoires plurilingues et pluriculturels pour une meilleure intégration scolaire.* Strasbourg: Council of Europe.www.coe.int/t/dg4/linguistic/Source/Source2010_ ForumGeneva/4-ValoriserCastellottiMoore_FR.pdf
    (2011). La compétence plurilingue et pluriculturelle. Genèses et évolutions d'une notion-concept. In P. Blanchet and P. Chardenet, eds., *Guide pour la recherche en didactique des langues et des cultures. Approches contextualisées.* Paris: Editions des archives contemporaines, pp. 241–252.

Castellotti, V. and Py, B. (2002). *La notion de compétence en langue.* Lyon: ENS Editions, Collection Notions en Questions no. 6.

Castellotti, V., Coste, D., and Duverger, J. (2008). *Propositions pour une éducation au plurilinguisme en contexte scolaire.* Paris: ADEB.

Cavalli, M. (2005). *Education bilingue et plurilinguisme: Le cas du Val d'Aoste.* Paris: Didier, collection LAL.

Cavalli, M. and Coste, D. (2010). L'éducation plurilingue et interculturelle entre langues de scolarisation et pluralité linguistique. *Cahiers de Linguistique, Revue de sociolinguistique et de sociologie de la langue française* 35 (2), 145–164.

Council of Europe (1982). *Résolution (82)18 sur les langues vivantes* https://rm.coe.int/ CoERMPublicCommonSearchServices/DisplayDCTMContent?documentId= 09000016804f6367

(1993). *Transparence et cohérence dans l'apprentissage des langues en Europe. Objectifs, évaluation, certification. Rapport du Symposium de Rüschlikon de 1991.* www.coe.int/t/dg4/linguistic/Ruschlikon1991_fr.pdf

Coste, D. (1991). Diversifier, certes . . . Le Français dans le Monde. In D. Coste and J. Hébrard, eds., *Recherches et applications: Vers le plurilinguisme?* Paris: Hachette, pp. 170–176.

(1993). *Diversification linguistique, compétence plurilingue et didactique des langues, La lettre de la DFLM 13.* Paris: DFLM, 5–6.

(1994a). Conceptualisation et alternance des langues: à propos de l'expérience du Val D'Aoste. *Études de linguistique appliquée* 96, Paris: Didier Érudition, 105–119.

(1994b). L'enseignement bilingue dans tous ses états. *Études de linguistique appliquée* 96, Paris: Didier Érudition, 9–22.

(2001a). De plus d'une langue à d'autres encore. Penser les compétences plurilingues. In V. Castellotti, ed., *D'une langue à d'autres : pratiques et représentations.* Rouen: Presses universitaires de Rouen, DYALANG, pp. 191–202.

(2001b). Compétence bi/plurilingue et (in)sécurité linguistique, *L'école Valdôtaine. Valle d'Aoste regione d'Europa: L'educazione bi/plurilingue, ponte verso la cittadinanza europea,* supplément 54, pp. 10–18.

(2002). Compétence à communiquer et compétence plurilingue. In V. Castellotti and B. Py, ed., *La notion de compétence en langue,* Collection NeQ, 6, Lyon: ENS-Éditions, pp. 115–123.

(2004). De quelques déplacements opérés en didactique des langues par la notion de compétence plurilingue. In A. Auchlin et al., eds., *Structures et discours: Mélanges offerts à Eddy Roulet.* Montreal: Editions Nota bene, pp. 67–85.

(2011). Du syllabus communicationnel aux curriculums pour une éducation plurilingue et interculturelle. *Le français dans le monde. Recherches et applications* 49, 16–22.

(2012). Sur quelques aspects langagiers d'une éducation plurilingue et interculturelle. *SLI 55, Linguistica educativa.* Bulzoni: Società di Linguistica Italiana, Roma, 61–75.

(2013a). Le(s) plurilinguisme(s) entre projet de diversification scolaire des langues et objets de discours dans le champ sociolinguistique et didactique. In V. Bigot, A.

Bretegnier, and M. Vasseur, eds., *Vers le plurilinguisme ? Vingt ans après*. Paris: Editions des archives contemporaines, pp. 9–17.

(2013b). Pluralité linguistique et transmission des savoirs. Quelques remarques. In L. Gajo and M. Pamula-Behrens, eds., *Français et plurilinguisme dans la science. Synergies Europe* 8, pp. 67–82.

(2013). *Les langues au cœur de l'éducation. Principes, pratiques, propositions*, by a collection of members of the ADEB. Ferlemont: E.M.E.

(2015). Pluralité, évaluation, altérité : trois paradigmes en tension. In J.-M. Defays et al., eds., *Transversalités: 20 ans de FLES. Faits et gestes de la didactique du Français Langue Etrangère et Seconde de 1995 à 2015*. Brussells/Ferlemont: E.M.E., pp. 87–100.

(2016). Maintenir séparées les langues ou transgresser les parlers : deux thèses en tension? In P. Escudé, ed., *Autour des travaux de Jules Ronjat, 1913–2013: Unité et diversité des langues. Théorie et pratique de l'acquisition bilingue et de l'intercompréhension*. Paris: Editions des archives contemporaines.

Coste, D. and Cavalli, M. (2015). *Education, Mobility, Otherness: The Mediation Function of Schools*. Strasbourg: Council of Europe, Political Lingustics Unit. www.coe.int/t/dg4/Linguistic/Source/LE_texts_Source/LE%202015/Education-Mobility-Otherness_FR.pdf.

Coste, D. and Hébrard, J. (1991). Vers le plurilinguisme? Ecole et politique linguistique. *Le Français dans le Monde: Recherches et applications*. Paris: Edicef.

Coste, D. and Pasquier, A. (1992). *Principes et méthodologies, Langues et savoirs, Due Lingue per Sapere, Matériaux pour un apprentissage bilingue à l'école primaire de la Vallée d'Aoste, Supplément à L'École valdôtaine*, 14, Assessorat de l'Instruction publique, Aoste, pp. 13–26.

Coste, D., Moore, D., and Zarate, G. (1997). *Compétence plurilingue et pluriculturelle*. Strasbourg: Council of Europe. Repris dans *Le Français dans le Monde. Recherches et applications*, L'apprentissage des langues dans le cadre européen, July 1998.

European Commission (1995). *Livre blanc sur l'éducation et la formation « Enseigner et apprendre: Vers la société cognitive*. http://europa.eu/documents/comm/white_papers/pdf/com95_590_fr.pdf

Grosjean, F. (1985). The bilingual as a competent but specific speaker-hearer. *Journal of Multilingual and Multicultural Development* 6, 467–477.

Lehmann, D. (1988). *La didactique des langues en face-à-face*. Paris: Hatier – Crédif.

Lüdi, G. and Py, B. (1986) 2003. *Etre bilingue*. Berne: Peter Lang (revised edition).

Moore, D. (2006). *Plurilinguismes et école*. Paris: Didier, Collection Langues et Apprentissage des Langues.

Moore, D. and Castellotti, V. (2008). *La compétence plurilingue: Regards francophones*. Berne, Fribourg: Peter Lang, collection Transversales.

Stratilaki, S. (2008). Composantes, structure opératoire et dynamique de la compétence plurilingue: Modes d'articulation et formes de construction. In D. Moore and V. Castellotti, eds., *La compétence plurilingue : regards francophones*. Berne, Fribourg: Peter Lang, collection Transversales, pp. 51–82.

(2005). Vers une conception dynamique de la compétence plurilingue: quelques réflexions six ans après. In M.-A. Mochet, M.-J. Barbot, V. Castellotti, J.-L. Chiss, C. Develotte, and D. Moore, eds., *Plurilinguisme et apprentissages. Mélanges Daniel Coste*. Lyon: ENS Éditions, , pp. 155–168.

Zarate, G., Lévy, D., and Kramsch, C. (eds.) (2008). *Précis du plurilinguisme et du pluriculturalisme*. Paris: Editions des Archives contemporaines.

12 My Trajectory in Languages and Language Learning

Diane Dagenais

Growing up bilingual in Montreal in the 1950s to 1970s was an experience of learning to navigate in personal and institutional language politics. When we were young, my brothers and I spoke French and English with my mother, a francophone who knew little English before meeting my father. Our language of communication with her changed after my parents divorced in my early adulthood and we started to use only French with her. In our childhood home, we all spoke English with my father since he expressed himself better in that language, having migrated from Ontario, where he had grown up. Before moving to Montreal, he had lived in English even though his paternal grandfather was a francophone from Quebec who had raised his children as bilinguals. In contrast, English became the language of communication in my father's generation.

My brothers and I used both languages as a blend or in alternation, a practice often commented on by monolinguals around us. In kindergarten and first grade, I attended an English Protestant school where my mother taught French as a second language. Schools in Quebec were organized along confessional and linguistic lines so that both Catholic and Protestant systems offered instruction in French or English. I recall an awkward conversation my grandmother had with a relative as she attempted to explain why my parents sent me to a Protestant school over a Catholic one. At the time, the language of instruction I received was less of a concern to some around us than the confession of the school I attended. Attachments to religion in Quebec were changing radically in those years.

When we moved to another neighbourhood, my parents enrolled my brothers and I in the French stream of one of only three Protestant schools offering instruction in both French and English. The French stream was not a bilingual or a French Immersion programme; it simply provided instruction in French with a daily English second language class, and the English stream offered the inverse. Most of the students and teachers in the French stream were Jews and Muslims, some were Protestants, members of another religion or had no religious affiliation. Without a baptismal certificate, which was required for

Figure 12.1 Initiation in languages and literacies

registration in Catholic schools, their only option for French education in the public system was a Protestant school offering instruction in that language.

Many of the teachers in our school were immigrants from North Africa who taught from textbooks published in France which, as I learned later on, had been used in the former French colonies, where these teachers had previously been teachers or students. In fact, the materials and pedagogical practices privileged in our school were quite different from those in place in the neighbouring schools. At our school, students from both language streams shared the playgrounds, where French, English and other languages were heard. Many of my friends were bilingual or multilingual and we learned some words and phrases in a number of languages spoken by our classmates, though we were all expected to use only the language of instruction in class. During this period, I took on the North African and European French accents of my classmates and teachers, which contrasted noticeably with the *Québecois* accent heard in my extended family and neighbourhood. I was teased regularly about this, so I learned to shift accents at home and school to align with those around me and avoid being singled out.

Over the years, my family moved a few times, yet my brothers and I remained in the same school because the school bus service covered a large area of the city. In one neighbourhood where we lived, we were the only family who did not speak Italian at home. On Saturday mornings, my brothers and I joined our friends in the basement of the local school for Italian classes and we sometimes attended church with the locals, participating also in various religious festivals and activities organized by the parish.

When I entered Seventh Grade, my parents switched us to English classes. By then, my parents were both teachers and they knew the Quebec government was preparing a bill that was the precursor to the Charter of the French Language (1977). My father wanted to ensure we entered the English system before access to it became more limited under the Charter. Thereafter, I continued my education in English through to my MA degree and resumed studies in French during my PhD at l'Université de Montréal.

Elsewhere, I describe the dilemmas I faced when it came time for me to make decisions about the languages of instruction and pedagogies that might be most suitable for my daughter (Dagenais 1992). Recently, I observed how my daughter and her husband grappled in turn with choosing what school is best, linguistically and pedagogically, for their children who are also French–English bilinguals. Many parents who have a choice in their children's education also struggle with such decisions since they shape the life trajectories of their offspring.

On obtaining a teaching diploma in the early 1980s, my education and official language proficiency enabled me to secure a full-time teaching position even though unemployment records were at a peak. I became a teacher in a French Immersion programme in Toronto, where many of my students were from immigrant families and spoke other languages in addition to French and English. At the time, little attention was paid to students' multilingualism as teachers focused exclusively on the language of instruction.

A couple of years later, I was introduced to innovations in bilingual education in a graduate course co-taught by Jim Cummins and Gordon Wells at OISE/University of Toronto. This course opened the research path that I was to follow in the coming years. As we examined linguistic and cultural diversity in literacy education we focused on processes of meaning-making in learning activities. We were exposed to ideas such as the translinguistic construction of knowledge (Cummins 1984) and literacy as a social semiotic process (Wells 1986). We learned about Edelsky's (1982) work on bilingual writing and pedagogies such as Process Writing (Graves 1983) and Writer's Workshops (McCormick Calkins 1986).

As a course assignment, we were invited to develop teaching practices aimed at fostering students' bilingual literacies. I tried out a bilingual Writer's Workshop in my Grade 2/3 French Immersion class. After producing first drafts of stories in English, or a combination of French and English, my students then transitioned through several drafts towards a French final version, following peer and teacher feedback on meanings in writing. The stories were bound as books and added to our class library. Students generated extended first drafts and explored ideas in greater depth than I had seen before.

I pursued an interest in documenting innovations in literacy pedagogies in my graduate studies. At l'Université de Montréal, I was introduced to the French neologism *littératie* (Painchaud et al. 1993) as an equivalent for literacy in English. It was advanced as an alternative to *alphabétisation*, which was deemed too narrowly focused on learning the alphabetic code and unable to account for the social practices and ideological processes implicated in literacy.

When I assumed a faculty position at Simon Fraser University in 1992, I was approached by a consortium of language educators representing several school districts around Vancouver to conduct research on multilingual students in French Immersion programmes that could inform teachers. With increases in immigration, the programmes had seen an influx of multilingual students from immigrant families. Until then, few studies had focused on multilingual immersion students, with the exception of a case study of one child conducted by Taylor (1992). In light of this, I undertook a series of studies documenting the home and school literacy practices of multilingual French Immersion students from immigrant families (Dagenais and Day 1998, 1999) and examining why their parents had opted for this programme while maintaining family languages at home (Dagenais 2003).

Research interest in multilingualism was intensifying internationally, and in an early English book on the topic Cenoz and Genesee (1998) defined multilingualism as both individual and societal uses of more than two languages. At the same time, in a publication in French with the Council of Europe, Coste, Moore and Zarate (1997/2009) made a distinction between *multilinguisme* to reference societal multilingualism and *plurilinguisme* for individual multilingualism. In Canada, *multilinguisme* and *plurilinguisme* were used interchangeably in French for several years, though some researchers have started to use plurilingualism in English language publications (Taylor and Snoddon 2013) as an equivalent to *plurilinguisme*. Though I have used the latter in French, I am no longer convinced it makes sense to distinguish between the societal and the individual when such binaries are associated with a Cartesian logic, which is called into question today by scholars in many fields who see boundaries between the body and the environment as permeable (Barad 2003).

In the following years, I worked on projects describing how multilingual youth combined multiple languages at home but were required to conform to a monolingual norm at school. I also observed how some Immersion teachers recognized children's multilingualism, encouraging them to share what they knew about languages beyond the language of instruction. In these instances, children made spontaneous comparisons of languages and engaged playfully with similarities and differences between linguistic forms and practices.

This led me to inquire about Language Awareness approaches originating in England (Hawkins 1987). Later taken up in French projects such as *Éveil aux langues*, *Evlang* (Candelier 2003) and *Eole* (Perregaux et al. 2003), they aimed at using the school language to examine diverse languages and learn about linguistic and cultural diversity.

In 2001, Danièle Moore and I obtained funding to coordinate a research exchange between colleagues at Simon Fraser University and L'École Normale Supérieure Lettres et Sciences Humaines in Lyon to compare our approaches to the study of multilingual learning in childhood. Building on this exchange, I partnered with Françoise Armand (Université de Montréal), teachers in Montreal *classes d'accueil* (welcoming classes) and teachers in a Vancouver French Immersion programme to adapt *Éveil aux langues* approaches for Canadian classrooms (Dagenais et al. 2008).

Our research aimed at developing more open-ended and student-centred activities in keeping with interactive pedagogies in place in Canadian classrooms. In these activities, students examined what values were attributed to languages and language speakers and considered what stereotypic representations of languages, language speakers and languages learning circulated. This led to a larger partnership among researchers at Simon Fraser University, l'Université de Montréal and teachers in Montreal and Vancouver (Dagenais et al. 2009). We investigated how Language Awareness activities might expand beyond paper and pencil tasks and engage children in out-of-school explorations of their local linguistic landscape. We set up video exchanges between students in both cities so that they could share their discoveries of multilingualism in their communities. Danièle Moore and I expanded on this work in another study of the home literacy practices of students of Chinese ancestry enrolled in French Immersion programmes. Referencing research situated at the intersection of the New Literacy Studies and sociolinguistic studies of bilingualism, we proposed the term *répertoire plurilittératié* as a French neologism for multiliterate repertoire to account for all languages that multilingual learners use orally and in written and graphic forms, the diversity of their modes of expression, their contexts and learning conditions (Dagenais and Moore 2008).

Later, Kelleen Toohey and I collaborated on a series of studies focused on multimodal digital literacies and production pedagogies. We turned to theories of sociomateriality (Dagenais 2019) to investigate how young language learners, multiple languages and forms of expression as well as many other material things were bound up in the production of videos and digital stories (Toohey et al. 2015). In one project, we examined the uptake in French and English classrooms of *ScribJab* (www.scribjab.com), a free iPad application and website designed to enable users to illustrate, narrate and compose stories in French or English and any other language available on iPads or computers (Dagenais et al. 2017). We referenced research that challenges traditional understandings of languages as separate systems with impermeable boundaries, and questions the assumption that language learners develop parallel or separate competencies in the languages of their repertoires (Cenoz and Gorter 2015). In this research, translanguaging (Garcia and Li 2014) is described as one approach to the study of multilingualism that views communication as a process of moving through and beyond languages and modalities to include the full range of the performances of multilinguals. An argument we found compelling and relevant to the classrooms that we observed was Fuller's (2015) suggestion that hegemonic language ideologies in education that are based on normative monolingualism frame bilingual or multilingual discourse as deviant and in need of 'fixing'. Currently, I am working alongside Geneviève Brissson and two doctoral research assistants, Magali Forte and Gwénaëlle André, to research multilingual and multimodal story creation with *Scribjab*. Pursuing our thinking with sociomaterial theories, we are examining how human and material relationships are formed during *Scribjab* use and affect how literacy ecologies are constructed at home, school and in library workshops (Dagenais et al. 2020).

We have found that teachers and parents who are open to language diversity resist monolingual policies as they explore innovative practices aimed at supporting multilingualism. Some struggle when their commitment to French or English instruction is questioned because they enable children to include other languages in their practices. Adults might sometimes abandon multilingual practices after a while or resort to contradictory approaches, such as supporting language mixing and alternation at times and at others attempting to separate languages. In a few cases, we have observed teachers who engage students in multilingual pedagogies and language awareness activities, yet continue to respond to their productions through a monolingual lens, as they make students remove traces of language contact in their written and oral work. In other instances, we have seen teachers and parents become invigorated by multilingual pedagogies, associating them with a commitment to social justice and a desire to take an ethical stand against practices and policies that they deem inequitable and oppressive. Such teachers and parents give me hope and energy to continue working on multilingual and multimodal pedagogies, despite restrictions in schools, and join together with them in supporting their children while they explore multiple languages and forms of expression.

REFERENCES

Barad, K. (2003). Posthumanist performativity: Toward an understanding of how matter comes to matter. *Signs* 28(3), 801–831. https://doi.org/10.1086/345321
Candelier, M. (2003). *L'Éveil aux langues à l'école primaire. Evlang: Bilan d'une innovation européenne.* Brussels: De Boeck.

Cenoz, J. and Genesee, F. (1998). *Beyond Bilingualism: Multilingualism and Multilingual Education*. Clevedon: Multilingual Matters.

Cenoz, J. and Gorter, D. (2015). *Multilingual Education: Between Language Learning and Translanguaging*. Cambridge: Cambridge University Press.

Coste, D., Moore, D. and Zarate, G. (1997). *Compétence plurilingue et pluriculturelle. Vers un cadre européen commun de référence pour l'enseignement et l'apprentissage des langues vivantes : études préparatoires*. Special Issue: Apprentissage et usage des langues dans le cadre européen. Strasbourg: Council of Europe, pp. 8–67.

Cummins, J. (1984). *Bilingualism and Special Education: Issues in Assessment and Pedagogy*. Clevedon: Multilingual Matters.

Dagenais, D. (1992). Concerns about maintaining biculturalism when changing contexts. *Canadian Children* 17(2), 53–59.

(2003). Accessing imagined communities through multilingualism and immersion education. *Language, Identity and Education* 2(4), 269–283.

(2019). Identities and language teaching in classrooms. In C. A. Chapelle, ed., *The Concise Encyclopedia of Applied Linguistics*. Malden, MA: Wiley-Blackwell, pp. 557–561.

Dagenais, D. and Day, E. (1998). Classroom language experiences of trilingual children in French immersion. *The Canadian Modern Language Review* 54, 376–393.

(1999). Home language practices of trilingual children in French Immersion. *The Canadian Modern Language Review* 56, 99–123.

Dagenais, D. and Moore, D. (2008). Représentations des littératies plurilingues, de l'immersion en français et des dynamiques identitaires chez des parents en chinois. *Revue canadienne des langues vivantes* 65(1), 11–31.

Dagenais, D., Brisson, G., André, G. and Forte, M. (2020). Multiple becomings in digital story creation. *Journal of Language and Intercultural Communication*, 20 (5), 419–432.

Dagenais D., Toohey, K., Bennett Fox, A. and Singh, A. (2017). Multilingual and multimodal composition at school: *ScribJab* in action. *Language and Education* 31(3), 263–282, https://doi.org/10.1080/09500782.2016.1261893

Dagenais, D., Walsh, N., Armand, F. and Maraillet, E. (2008). Collaboration and co-construction of knowledge during language awareness activities in Canadian elementary school. *Language Awareness* 17(2), 139–155.

Dagenais, D., Moore, D., Sabatier, C., Lamarre, S. and Armand, F. (2009). Linguistic landscape and language awareness. In E. Shohamy and D. Gorter, eds., *Linguistic Landscape: Expanding the Scenery*. New York: Routledge/Taylor & Francis Group, pp. 253–269.

Edelsky, C. (1982). Writing in a bilingual program: The relation of L1 and L2 texts. *TESOL Quarterly* 16, 211–222.

Fuller, J. (2015). Language choices and ideologies in the bilingual classroom. In J. Cenoz and D. Gorter, eds., *Multilingual Education: Between Language Learning and Translanguaging*. Cambridge: Cambridge University Press, pp. 137–158.

Garcia, O. and Li, W. (2014). *Translanguaging: Language, Bilingualism and Education*. New York: Palgrave MacMillan.

Graves, D. (1983). *Writing: Teachers and Children at Work*. Exeter, NH: Heinemann and Heinemann.

Hawkins, E. (1987). *Awareness of Language. An Introduction*. Cambridge: Cambridge University Press.

Hornberger, N. (2003). *Continua of Biliteracy: An Ecological Framework for Educational Policy, Research and Practice in Multilingual Settings*. Clevedon: Multilingual Matters.

McCormick Calkins, L. (1986). *The Art of Teaching Writing*. Portsmouth, NH: Heinemann Educational Books.

Painchaud, G., d'Anglejan, A., Armand, F. and Jezak, M. (1993). Diversité culturelle et littératie. *Repères: Essais en éducation* 15, 77–94.

Perregaux, C., De Goumoëns, C., Jeannot, D. and de Pietro, J.-F. (2003). *Education et ouverture aux langues à l'école*. Neuchâtel: CIIP.

Taylor, S. K. and Snoddon, K. (2013). Plurilingualism in TESOL: Promising controversies. *TESOL Quarterly* 47(3), 439–445.

Taylor, S. (1992). Victor: A case study of a Cantonese child in Early French Immersion. *The Canadian Modern Language Review* 48, 736–759.

Toohey, K., Dagenais, D., Fodor, A., Hof, L., Nuñez-Mendez, O., Schulze, E. and Singh, A. (2015). 'That sounds so cooool': Entanglements of children, digital tools and literacy practices. *TESOL Quarterly* 49(3), 461–485. https://doi.org/10.1002/tesq.236

Wells, C. G. (1986). *The Meaning Makers*. Portsmouth, NH: Heinemann Educational Books.

13 Multilingualism as Norm
Advocating for Equity for Multilingual Learners

Ester de Jong

My language biography starts in the mid-eastern part of the Netherlands, Steenwijk, where I was born. My father came from an urban area where a more standardized form of Dutch was spoken. My mother came from a rural town closer to the German border, where she and her family used one of the Dutch "dialects" for daily communication. At home, our Dutch variety approximated the more standardized version taught in school. My mother's home language was part of our lives but on the periphery. It emerged when she was talking with her parents and siblings and others from her hometown. When we visited, my grandparents accommodated by shifting their language to be closer to our variety of Dutch. At the time, I had no idea that these choices would be explained by Howard Giles as part of his communication accommodation theories. These choices were not questioned but the use of the dialect was also not critiqued; it was part of our family.

Foreign languages were introduced for the first time in middle school. English and French in my first year; German was added in the second year of my six years in secondary school. The expectation that you would learn another language was normalized; multilingualism made pragmatic sense (communicating with neighboring countries, TV shows were in English and German) and was a sign of being educated. I enjoyed the analytics of grammar (largely the focus of instruction), and this contributed to my decision that "doing something with languages" would be a good goal for the future. However, I did not immediately gravitate to education and foreign language teaching. Instead, I chose to enroll in a program with a focus on "Language Sciences and the Sociology of Literature" at Tilburg University in the southern part of the Netherlands.

Moving to Tilburg represents the first time I became aware of my own accent. My hard northern g-sound contrasted sharply with the soft g-sound of my southern peers as did my intonation patterns. While not labelled as such, translanguaging across different modalities was the norm at the university. In addition to English language classes, we read research conducted and reported on in English, while discussing and writing in Dutch. I worked on a project on trilingualism where the research was conducted in Dutch and my supervisor

Figure 13.1 Ester de Jong

was from the United States. Our conversations would have been interesting to analyze: a mix of my speaking Dutch and her speaking English and vice versa and all the bilingual variations in between. My final research thesis was in Dutch on Dutch as a second language vocabulary learning. My capstone report for my internship was in English, however, as I went to the United States to meet this requirement. Language was a tool – a tool for learning and for communicating – and you use all the tools that you have to complete the task at hand.

The combination of sociolinguistics, language policy, and education at Tilburg University set the stage for the rest of my career. This is where I was exposed to and became interested in the languages of those who came from our former colonies, our border areas, as well as immigrants in the Netherlands (particularly those who had been recruited for labor from Turkey and Morocco). I came to realize that, even though multilingualism was expected when I was growing up, this was very much a matter of elite bilingualism. Children from Turkish or Arabic-speaking families rarely had access to their home languages and, if offered, it was rarely done in a way that validated and legitimized the use of those languages for learning in schools. Similarly, US schools demand that speakers of Spanish, Mandarin, or African American Vernacular English in the United States give up the language of their families and communities while celebrating foreign language learning for fluent English speakers. This double standard was troubling and failed to recognize the linguistic and cultural resources minoritized language speakers bring to school. I thus began to focus my work on how educators can create environments where minoritized students' home languages are valued and leveraged for teaching and learning. Bilingual education seemed an innovative approach at that time, and when it came time to choose an internship, I indicated that I would like to go abroad to visit bilingual programs. I was fortunate that this worked out and I ended up doing my internship at the Massachusetts Department of Education in the United States.

My internship and living abroad proved to be a life-changing event in many ways. Working and communicating solely in English was a novel and an initially exhausting experience. I became quickly aware of the difference between social and academic language and how little informal language proficiency I had! I did not have the vocabulary for the simplest things (household items, shopping) but could easily hold forth on bilingual education programs in English. For my internship, I was placed on a project related to two-way immersion (TWI) bilingual programs, a program type I had not heard of before, and I saw the power of these programs in action. TWI programs bring together students on a continuum of proficiency in two languages (English and a partner language) with the goal of becoming bilingual and biliterate in a program that has high academic expectations and supports the development of intercultural competence. I ultimately decided to pursue my doctoral studies in this area in the United States to better understand these programs and bilingual phenomena. As part of my doctoral program, I engaged in a study abroad experience in Niger, West Africa, where I had to use French to learn Hausa, one of the lingua francas in the area, and travelled to Sweden and Denmark. These experiences added a layer of experiences of what it means to not be fluent in the major language of communication and yet trying to engage as a professional within that context.

From this time onward, my language biography is written primarily in English with small sections in Dutch, some in Spanish, and other languages as I travel, work with dual language program teachers, present at conferences, and work with graduate students who come from around the world. Working in the Framingham Public School system after my doctoral program with ESL, bilingual and two-way immersion program teachers provided opportunities for direct engagement in Brazilian Portuguese–English and Spanish–English bilingual settings. About ten years later, formal language-related episodes occurred through participation in a Spanish immersion experience in Costa Rica and another Spanish immersion program in Mexico in an effort to bring some productive skills to complement my receptive abilities in Spanish. Trying to learn these languages formally as an adult through immersion has added new dimensions to my own repertoire and understandings of the unique nature of learning new languages.

I consider myself multilingual, while recognizing that my sense-making of the world is primarily in and through English at this juncture.

13.1   Key Concepts and Practices

Several themes have guided my scholarship to date. None of these themes have been static: they have changed over time in response to personal and professional experiences. Two themes have been particularly consistent, however, in guiding my teaching and research: taking a bilingual stance and one size does not fit all. Both are integrally connected, of course. In practice, I have grounded my classroom-based work more on the former and my advocacy and program development work more on the latter. For ease of analysis, I will discuss them separately next, introducing the concept and showing how it has influenced practices.

13.2   Taking a Bilingual Stance

In a seminal article, Francois Grosjean (1989, p. 3) noted, "bilinguals are not two monolinguals in one person." This simple sentence significantly shifted my perspective during my graduate years. Grosjean's fundamental understanding of bilingualism underscores the unique linguistic practices of multilinguals and the need to reflect bi/multilinguals' unique histories in research. His statement helped move away from a deficit view of bi/multilingual individuals to one that approached bi/multilingualism holistically across the bi/multilinguals' entire repertoire. Notions that have emerged in our field more recently, such as translanguaging (language meshing), dynamic bilingualism, and language plurality, draw from Grosjean's notion of a holistic linguistic repertoire.

As I worked with teachers, students, and parents I realized that we also need to understand Grosjean's statement in terms of identity and equity. Not only do we need to understand bilingual phenomena; we also must treat bi/multilingual individuals as bi/multilinguals. Jim Cummins and colleagues (2005, pp. 38–39) captured this well when they noted, "It is hard to argue that we are teaching the whole child when school policy dictates that students leave their language and culture at the schoolhouse door."

In practice, both dimensions of "bilinguals are bilinguals" are captured for me with the phrase "taking a bi/multilingual stance" as researchers, teachers, and teacher educators (de Jong and Freeman, 2010; de Jong, 2011). This notion has become particularly relevant as I have been working with preservice teacher preparation. By far the majority of the preservice teachers (PSTs) consider themselves monolingual in English and do not envision becoming teachers of English language learners. Yet, in Florida, preservice teachers must graduate from their initial teacher preparation program with what is called an ESOL endorsement. The PSTs' own sense of monolingualism and limited experiences with linguistic and cultural diversity growing up pose challenges to engage them in multilingual practices. Guiding our work has been two questions: (1) how can we develop a sense of efficacy and the necessary expertise in working with bilingual learners; and, in doing so, (2) how can we cultivate a multilingual stance with these preservice teachers who will be working in schools where English and monolingual hegemony reign? (e.g., de Jong, 2013; de Jong, Harper, and Coady, 2013; Coady, de Jong, and Harper, 2016). Our practices are constantly evolving but have included the following actions: provide students with a language immersion experience, the inclusion of a unit on bilingual books in the students' Children's Literature course, explicit attention to the role of students' home languages when teaching a second language, providing access to online resources in languages other than English, and explicitly integrating strategies for leveraging students' home languages in the classroom, including the use of cognates. As we experiment with activities, our understandings of what taking a bi/multilingual stance means continue to evolve and deepen. Our next steps include the development of a clearer vision of the concept, both theoretically and in practice.

13.3   One Size Does not Fit All

Working with teachers in schools has made me aware that the models (bilingual education, English as a Second Language) described in the literature are (necessarily) abstractions (de Jong, 2016). As a result, they do not always do justice to the complex realities of schools and the challenge of implementation. Yet, teachers and administrators cannot make random decisions either; their work must be grounded in our understandings of learning processes for bilingual students. This realization brought me to thinking of policies and practices as decision-making that is principled and contextual. I developed this insight more in my book *Foundations of Multilingualism in Education: From Policy to Practice*: The overarching driver is the Principle of Educational Equity and its three supporting principles, the Principle of Affirming Identities, the Principle of Additive bilingualism, and the Principle of Integration. For me, the principles framework has been helpful in stressing the importance of knowing why building on students' linguistic and cultural resources is important as well as underscoring the importance of contextual differences in aligning practices with the principles. It has helped explain why one size does not fit all and the need to allow for differences without compromising on what research shows matters for minoritized language speakers (de Jong and Freeman, 2010; de Jong, 2010, 2011; Brisk, de Jong, and Moore, 2015).

REFERENCES

Brisk, M. E., de Jong, E. J., and Moore, M. C. (2015). Primary bilingual education: Pedagogical issues and practices. In W. Wright, S. Boun, and O. García, eds., *Handbook of Bilingual and Multilingual Education*. Chichester: Wiley-Blackwell, pp. 319–335.

Coady, M. R., Harper, C. A., and de Jong. E. J. (2016). Aiming for equity: Preparing mainstream teachers for inclusion or inclusive classrooms? *TESOL Quarterly* 50 (2), 340–368.

Cummins, J. et al. (2005). Affirming identity in multilingual classrooms. *Educational Leadership* 63, 38-43.

(2011). *Foundations for Multilingualism in Education: From Principles to Practice.* Philadelphia: Caslon Inc.

(2013). Preparing mainstream teachers for multilingual classrooms. *Association of Mexican American Educators Journal* 7(2), 40–49.

(2016) Two-way immersion for the next generation: Models, policies, and principles. *International Multilingual Research Journal* 10 (1), 6–16.

de Jong, E. J. and Freeman, R. (2010). Bilingual approaches. In C. Leung and A. Creese, eds., *English as an Additional Language: Approaches to Teaching Linguistic Minority Students* (pp. 108–122). London: SAGE.

de Jong, E. J., Harper, C. A., and Coady, M. (2013). Enhanced knowledge and skills for elementary mainstream teachers of English language learners. *Theory into Practice* 52(2), 89–97.

de Jong, E. J., Li, Z., Zafar, A., and Wu, C. (2016). Language policy in multilingual contexts: Revisiting Ruiz's "language-as-resource" orientation. *Bilingual Research Journal* 39(3–4), 200–212.

14   From Patois to Inter-comprehension Issues

Pierre Escudé

14.1   First Discoveries

I was born in 1967 in Le Havre, at the mouth of the Seine, because my father
had been appointed there as a Spanish teacher for eight years. My first
memories are of Toulouse, the city where we arrived in 1969, and of
Ponsampère, the village of Astarac: those hills of the Gers in Gascony that
overlook the Pyrenees and where my grandfather had been elected mayor after
the Liberation. As a child, I saw André Dufilho – the actor as we say here –
arrive in the farmyard in a sidecar; he asked my grandfather about the process
of receiving the Agricultural Merit. There was also Ribeiro, an old farm worker
from the north of Portugal, a country he had left a long time ago. In the
kitchen, Papi and Ribeiro would talk for hours. They understood each other
perfectly, while I understood nothing. Papi spoke Gascon – the Occitan of
Gascony – and Ribeiro spoke Portuguese.

In 1975, in my third grade in the suburbs of Toulouse, I remember that we
talked about "language registers,"

People in high places, they speak a high register; people like me – said the teacher – or
like your parents, they speak the medium register; poor people like workers and
peasants, they speak a low register.

I didn't know what *register* meant: I imagined it was like a drawer in a piece of
furniture where you put the beautiful things on top and where you hide the bad
things at the bottom: Like in a chest of drawers where Sunday laundry –
"Sunday language," as Gilles Ménage called it and as Claire Benveniste
reminds us – was at the top but the drawers are totally sealed together. The
simple fact of putting these drawers in the same cabinet is a huge democratic
step in the awareness that we all have the ability to speak, to be in a language.
We dress differently but we are never naked.

In 1972, new ministerial directives had overturned an order that had been
sent from on high for schools during the period of post-Treaty of Versailles
nationalism The "Official Instructions" (1923–1972) explained to teachers the
reality of their pupils' lives and what their function as teachers should be,

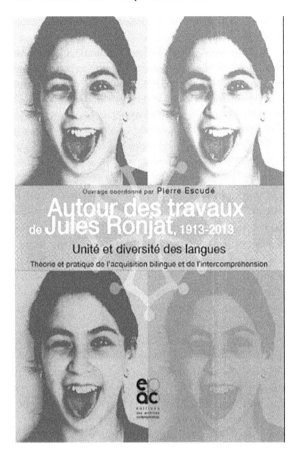

Figure 14.1 Un langage et plusieurs langues

No one is unaware of the difficulties encountered by the teacher in teaching the French language. When the children are entrusted to him, their vocabulary is poor and more often belongs to the slang of the neighbourhood, the village patois, the dialect of the province, than to the language of Racine or Voltaire. … Teaching French is not only about maintaining and expanding a beautiful language and literature, it is also about strengthening national unity.

Speaking a language other than the national language was not really French. And to speak with an accent other than the accent of television, radio, theatre, and school was to speak strangely; it was not really speaking very well. A young substitute teacher, in the third grade, spent the whole month she was with us trying to get us to pronounce "la rôse" well, and not the unworthy "la rause."

In the summer of 1975, we did not go to Spain as usual, but to Portugal. We went from roses to carnations. My father, as usual, stopped the Renault 4 at the edge of a field and went to talk to people. As a Spanish teacher, I understood why he did that in Spain. But in Portugal, I didn't understand: The language didn't make any sense. After an hour, my mother and big brother honked their horns because it was very hot under the sheet metal of the dark blue car. My father came back half an hour later, reluctantly leaving the peasants. "What were you talking about?" asked my mother. But I asked myself: "How did you manage to talk?"

When we went to Ponsampère – a journey that takes more than two and a half hours by car from Toulouse – at the end of the meal, everyone sang in Occitan. My mother, who was born in Paris, laughed at the stories told by Grandpa or Uncle Michel in Occitan. In the summer, on the farm, Grandpa and Grandma, who looked after me, had only ever spoken Occitan to each other. Around the month of May, a shared chore among neighbors brought my Papi with his shovel to the ditch that the neighbors, my uncle, and my father were cleaning together: estóssitz venguts drin mai tard, que serí arribat jo en avança! Everyone laughed. My father stopped digging, looked at me and said: "Did you hear that? It's the imperfect subjunctive." I remembered then what my third grade teacher said about the low register of peasants and workers.

My other grandfather was from Auvergne. He had no family, no cousins, and I liked him a lot, but it was much less fun to go to Brioude, on the Allier. It took six hours by car. And even more when there was snow on the road between Aubrac and Cantal. How I hoped every time we went there in winter! Pépé had left Auvergne at the age of fifteen in 1924, and all his life he was a *bougnat* in Paris: he carried coal on his shoulders, then ran a bistro in the gates. One evening in the garden, I heard him singing in a low voice: Vai, vai vai Mascarada; Vai, vai vai te lavar; Quand tornaràs Mascarada; Quand tornaràs dançaràs. "That's Occitan," my father told me, "It's a lullaby to a drunken rhythm." I thought to myself: Grandpa, too? But we were more than eight hours' drive from Ponsampère! I didn't understand what this country was, and yet I understood that there were language and accents that existed, which were what millions of people spoke, and TV, radio, and school didn't speak about at all.

I learned Occitan in high school. My father never spoke Occitan to me along the way, or else I hadn't wanted him to and had unconsciously taken precautions against it. There was a complex between us. He passed on his complex to me. He didn't want me to be stained by this language that is not a language: "the slang of the neighbourhood, the patois of the village, the dialect of the province," which created so many obstacles to reach "the beautiful language, the beautiful literature."

I learned Occitan at the Saint-Sernin high school in Toulouse. We were a class of up to a hundred students, and my father was the main teacher of this subject, which was not a recognized one yet. I later learned that the headmaster of the lycée, and some of his colleagues, did not want there to be Occitan classes: "You are against national unity," my father was told. We sang, we read, we learned how to conjugate, and at the end of the year, we danced. I overcame my complex with my father, and with my classmates. I understood that this language, this culture, its literature and history were mine. No more and no less.

In 1989, I was at university; I was preparing to pass the exam to become a French teacher, or rather, as they say, a literature teacher. My grandfather had grown old, but he could still straddle the straw chair with his back to the fire to watch television. The news was playing and a dense crowd passed in front of the camera. A sign carried by a demonstrator passed by for a short moment: "*Dictarorul a cazut.*" My grandpa turned to grandma at the stove: a *cajut lo dictator in Romania*. A few seconds later, the journalist announced the fall of Ceausescu, over there, in Bucharest. My grandfather, who left school at thirteen in 1924, could read this sign written in Romanian and that had been on TV for half a second. But me, what had I learned at school?

As a young teacher, I went abroad as a volunteer, to the Lyautey High School in Casablanca. There was an expatriate teacher from Aveyron. Together we spoke only Occitan. One evening he took me to a party of the Cercle Amical des Français, in the rather chic district of Beauséjour, near a park. It was an Auvergne-themed evening, and there were maybe 800 people present. At the end, a few people got up and sang the *Se Canta*. Little by little, the majority of the guests got up and sang *Se Canta*. This was the song that was sung, head up, at the end of meals in Ponsampère. It brought tears to my eyes. I then registered for the CAPES[1] d'Occitan, Option Literature (letters), which I took at the French embassy in Rabat. From then on, I was a professor of Occitan and Literature.

We went back during the winter holidays to Toulouse. In the heart of the city, there was a large round square with benches, a lawn, tall trees at Christmas with the red Occitan cross, and in the center of the square, a white statue, the largest statue in Toulouse: larger than Joan of Arc and even larger than Riquet, the creator of the Canal du Midi. It is a statue of the Baroque poet Pèire Godolin (1580–1649): I would eventually write my dissertation on this author. My father offered me a reprint of his works by Doctor Noulet, in 1887,

---

[1] CAPES : Le certificat d'aptitude au professorat de l'enseignement du second degré.

published by Privat in Toulouse. I would try to understand why the people of Toulouse had placed him in the center of their city, and why, at times, they turned their backs on him. I republished his complete works, with Privat, in Toulouse, in 2009.

14.2   Professor

After our two years in Casablanca, I taught with my wife for four years in Moscow. Being far from France made me feel very French. French means something very physical and embodied. For me, it immediately evokes an attachment to landscapes, people, and language and a way of being anchored in a geography that for me is Occitania, from the Gascon Pyrenees to the Massif Central: which in Occitan is known as "Massís del Nòrd." Teaching French – letters, literature, and grammar – for six years to students who were mostly not French, has taught me that you only enter French – its literature, its culture – because you can enter its language. You get into the French language through the language, or languages, as is so often the case for students from French high schools abroad, which we already have in ourselves. There is never a vacuum, we are always from somewhere, and we always carry stories.

We only enter the signified by the signifier. The signifier only has meaning through a primary referent.

We returned to Toulouse and I taught Occitan in two middle schools and two high schools. At Fermat high school, they tore down the posters that I taped up to invite students to come and follow my classes: between noon and two. I had up to a hundred students across the four schools, for an hour or two a week. How could I get them to enter into a full, natural language like the one I had come to understand that I had grown up in? I was also working at the time at the university, where I taught Occitan, language, and literature.

I spoke Occitan only to my fourth daughter. I hadn't dared with the first three, not only because of the complex with the language but also because Camille had been a baby in Morocco and as such began speaking Arabic, and Marion and Juliette had been babies in Russia and they began speaking Russian: all on par with the French we spoke at home.

My job became training students to be teachers in Occitan. Bilingualism was now possible: it was even valued by Rector De Gaudemar, who would eventually be in charge of School Education at the Ministry of National Education. He would publish the first national guidelines in favor of the languages of France. I was behind the opening of the first bilingual kindergartens in Toulouse, in the Matabiau district, a central but popular area of Toulouse. African mothers registered their children there: "bilingualism is important." "I speak six languages," said a mother from Cape Verde. And also, "If my little one speaks Occitan, he will really be French."

During one of my visits to this bilingual kindergarten, a four-year-old girl turned to me after the beginning of the class ritual where we call the students, one by one, to ask if they are present. She explained, "You see, teacher, in Occitan, we hear the –'T'." We say 'present' and we hear the final -t in Occitan. But, we say présent (in French) and we do not hear this sound, even though it is marked by the letter t. The little girl showed me "You see": at the age of four, the contact of two languages allows for observations that can prove to be metalinguistic. We understand how gender and number work in two languages.

Then, one summer, on holiday in Venice, my little Claire, aged six, read a sign in front of a restaurant: *Pizza cotta a forno di legna*. "Debon èsser bonas aicí, las pizzas, papà." "E perqué?" I asked her. "Perque son cuèitas al fuòc de lenha."[2] Italian and Occitan aren't so far apart, in the same way that Romanian and Occitan could be understood by my grandpa.

14.3   At the University

My studies led me to read the work of Friedrich Diez, of Édouard Bourciez, and closer to us of Pierre Bec, of Jacques Allières, and I came to understand what I knew confusedly: all languages that are similar – from Portuguese to Romanian – form a coherent, predictable system. I opened Frédéric Mistral's large dictionary and for each word I found the variants in the Occitan dialects, from Niçart to Gascony in the Landes, from Périgourdin to Alpine Provence, but also the forms of the great Romance languages such as Portuguese, Castilian, Catalan, Italian, and Romanian. Walter von Wartburg refers to Occitan as "the central language of the Romanesque." I understand the geography of this statement but also the history: The Troubadours are the source of the first modern European literature.

After reading the works of the Germans of EuroComRom and Claire Benveniste (Eurom4), I developed my first works in inter-comprehension. It became the European program euro-mania.org, which led to a first disciplinary learning manual in seven languages, for a school population of eight to twelve years old. Euromania is a large project (2005–2008) that proposes four integrations: between languages themselves; languages and disciplines; cross-linguistic activities (understanding and producing in written and oral form); and the most complicated finally, curricular integration in national school systems that remain stuck on the separation of languages, and the waterproofing of languages and disciplines, still nonlinguistic. The 2008 Toulouse symposium invited the Great Lady Claire Benveniste.

---

[2] "Pizza must be good here, Dad. And why?" I asked her, "and why?" "Because they're baked over a wood fire."

I discovered that the word inter-comprehension owes its origin to the Occitan novelist Jules Ronjat in 1913. Ronjat published two theses in the same year: one on the Development of language observed in a bilingual child, the first French thesis to study scientifically and without bias bilingualism (in this case French–German) and what it allows (especially plurilingualism) (republished in 2013 by Peter Lang); the other on the Syntax of Provençal, where the word inter-comprehension appears. To explain the linguistic state of a Provençal shepherd from La Crau (near Arles) who, during transhumance, leads the herds to the highest pastures in the Alps. The language changes along the way. There is variety, differences, but just as much structural unity in the language. And comprehension because of intentionality.

I suggest that this word inter-comprehension is concomitant with the concept of social intercourse used by Ferdinand de Saussure in the Cours de Linguistique Générale that Ronjat re-reads from the first edition in 1916. Saussure, in the chapter on "the propagation of linguistic waves," sums up the functioning of all human reality: and here of language.

In every human mass, two forces are constantly acting simultaneously and in opposite directions: on the one hand, the particularistic spirit, the parochial spirit; on the other, the force of intercourse, which creates communication between people.

Variety and diversity are as consubstantial with the languages of men as they are with men themselves. This does not prevent us from being human: from communicating, and thus from entering into the cognitive functions that are the true functions of abstract language. To believe that there would be "parochialism" would be to go more and more into demarcation, into communitarism. To go toward the "force of intercourse" only would be to go toward standardization. Believing that some languages are only dialectal is as foolish as believing that only some languages are universal.

Inter-comprehension has seemed to me to hold a key to enter the field of language teaching and learning, as languages are places of learning and the even more important and related field of life in society, of a healthy and serene teaching of human contact, of good politics, and good trade between human beings.

REFERENCES

Escudé, P. (2015). We can learn through Languages because we are defined by languages. In R. Dolci and A. J. Tamburri, eds., *Intercomprehension and Plurilinguism: Assets for Italian Language in the USA*. New York: John D. Calandra Italian American Institute Queens College, The City University of New York, pp. 79–101.

Escudé, P. and Janin, P. (2010). *L'intercompréhension, clef du plurilinguisme*. CLE International.

Ronjat, J. (1913a.). *La syntaxe du provençal moderne*. Protat frères.
    (2013). *Le développement du langage observé chez un enfant bilingue* [Champion, 1913b]. Scientific edition. Peter Lang.
Saussure (de), F. (1972). *Cours de Linguistique Générale*. "Propagation des ondes linguistiques," Paris, Geneva: Payot, 1972 [1916] Tullio de Mauro edition.

15   Biography, Linguistic Coexistence, and Epistemological Reflection

Carole Fleuret

15.1   A Quick Look Back

Coming from a country in which French is and always will be the language of the nation, as clearly demonstrated in the work of Auger (2013) and Spaëth (2008) highlighting the prevalence of French as the sole language of instruction, an undeniable historical residue of the colonial and postcolonial periods (p. 26), the place of other languages has always been just an illusion, a struggle, and a chimera. Blanchet (2014) speaks of historical hegemony regarding the monolingual and mononormative approach of French in schools.

I grew up in France, where only this idiom was the legitimized language and the one necessary to succeed academically and socially. Yet, I could see and, especially, hear around me, many classmates from my elementary school speaking Turkish, Arabic, Portuguese, and even Spanish: I loved it! I found it amazing and funny that people could speak a language that others did not understand!

15.2   "He Has a Strong Accent"

That said, it is mostly when I got to *collège*[1] that I realized that not everyone saw things the way I did, for various reasons. First, age drew me out of childhood and its innocence, if I can put it that way, but, rather remarkably, it was within my own family, my friends from elementary school, and those around me that I became aware of the "differences." One day, someone had me notice that my grandfather spoke with a "strong accent" or that "it was hard to understand anything he said"! I did not really fully grasp what that meant at that time because I had never really paid attention to it; he spoke and that was it. However, looking back now, I remember that the comments hurt me a lot.

---

[1] Equivalent to high school in Quebec.

Figure 15.1 I still hear my grandfather calling me Mitra

Consequently, these comments made me realize that my mother came from an exogamous home: a French mother and a Macedonian father (Macedonia was a province of the former Yugoslavia), something I had never really dwelled on before. I loved those moments I shared with my grandfather, alone, because I felt special; he taught me words, phrases, and even songs in Macedonian; I felt as though this language was ours because it was so emotional that it allowed me to enjoy exceptional moments. Actually, he never called me by my first name and until his death only called me *Mitra*. I have to admit that I miss hearing him call me that.

Now, in hindsight and with the knowledge I have acquired, I realize that my grandfather's French was tinted with lexical loans, hybrid syntactic structures and language skills that he had learned from his contact with other immigrants (Polish, Italians, etc.) on the construction sites, and Macedonian and French that he spoke with my grandmother and the family. He loved France, the country that had given him the opportunity to make a life for himself, to feel good, as he said, and I think this is why he felt indebted and wanted to speak French. He had strong ties to the host country that led him to become a citizen. Also, the various French administrations misspelled his first and last name systematically, which bugged him a lot. So, given that he had spent a number of years on the territory, he decided to become a French citizen and thereby solve all the patronym issues, which, we believe were far-reaching!

15.3   My Awareness of Languages and Their Status

What I highlighted at the beginning of this chapter made me aware, somewhat, at ten years old, that there were differences between people. This awareness, once well established and throughout the years, revealed the hidden face of difference, namely exacerbated ethnocentrism, prejudice, and racism, which I experienced during my teenage years when, during numerous identity checks, the police asked me if I was French!

Beyond the accent and phenotypes, it is really in collège that I became aware of all the symbolic violence experienced by my friends who spoke other languages. I did not understand this willingness to speak only French and only the right way, with no accent. Auger (2013) speaks of a monolingual ideology and a total denial of the variations of French in schools. This is exactly what I felt because I too did not understand this obsession with the norm, good French, which undeniably outlined otherness while totally ignoring the devastating impacts of such a choice. All in all, I did not understand why only the language spoken by the majority, in schools, for social promotion, was the legitimized one (Spaëth 2008). So, I was not surprised to see friends slowly "sinking" in school, partly because of their poor academic performance, which was well documented by teachers, and, mostly, mentioned in front of the entire class, or feeling increasingly less motivated as the academic year and their schooling progressed.

On the other hand, we had to learn other languages as part of the school curriculum, namely those that my friends spoke! For me, that was the ultimate paradox! With time, I understood that the perception of English, Spanish, or German was linked to a "foreign language" status and that these languages should never be spoken outside of class under any circumstance. The status . . . a perverse label leading to social reproduction by sowing symbolic violence to categorize languages and individuals (Bourdieu and Passeron 1964). French remained the only language used. As I write these words, I cannot help but think of Castellotti, Coste, and Duverger (2008), who mention that "for language education to emerge, it is important not to remain in skimped bilingualism, which would actually only be the product of two juxtaposed monolingualisms" (p. 29).

15.4   English as the New Language Repertoire

For me, English immersion only confirmed that I liked this language and wanted to learn to speak it. I listened to lots of Anglo-Saxon music and was frustrated because I could not understand the words. Suddenly, learning the language allowed me to grasp what the authors were saying and develop my vocabulary, and I loved it! It allowed me to read and understand the words of the songs that I listened to. The more I learned, the more I wanted to learn! I actually had two teachers who gave me books to read in addition to what we had looked at in class, because I was bored.

15.5   Another Language Repertoire: Spanish

I must have been very convincing with my mother when Spanish came into my life. My collège had actually strongly recommended German because my grades were excellent and my mother obviously wanted what was best for me. Finally, she agreed and I started Spanish. One of my closest friends was Spanish and I heard her speaking Spanish with her mother when I visited her. I was sure that I had made the right choice: I loved that language, its sound, accentuation, I loved it all. I then continued Spanish and often went on trips in Spain, Cuba, and even the Dominican Republic. I am now relatively comfortable speaking the language both professionally and personally. I used a similar approach for Spanish as I had with English, namely reading books and newspapers to expand my knowledge.

15.6   And Now

Looking back, the first thing that I am sure of is that it is my grandfather who made me love languages; for me, Macedonian is everything emotional. The second thing I am also sure of is that the injustice with which my friends were treated regarding their language repertoire troubled me a lot at that time. I would also like to add that my own experiences with racist and stereotypical comments pushed me to go beyond, to want to change things. All in all, I wanted to explore, understand, and expand my knowledge on these subjects to better grasp the issues related to them.

My curiosity and openness to the world led me to leave France more than twenty years ago to come to live in Canada. After living for twelve years in

Quebec, the only Francophone province in the country, I am now in Ontario, a largely Anglophone province, in which French is a minority and the school populations are increasingly heterogeneous given the growing number of new immigrants.

Talking about immigration also means talking about the minorization of populations and languages. Earlier in the chapter, I mentioned France's position as a hegemonic State regarding French, but Francophone Ontario adopts a similar position regarding other languages and their speakers. As reported by Gérin-Lajoie and Jacquet (2008), Allophones, for the most part, live in double or triple minorization. Actually, Canada is living a rather paradoxical situation; on the one hand, there is the policy on multiculturalism that fosters diversity and plurality, in other words, schools must account for this reality, and, on the other, the linguistic duality given that French and English are both official languages. In the Franco-Ontarian context, given the prevailing sociolinguistic situation, only French, in fact, is valued; the majority group is reproduced by making new immigrants the minority groups. And even then, not just any group; the Franco-Ontarian group totally rejects the idea of plurinormalism (Auger 2013).

This special context was a breeding ground for my research from an empirical standpoint, to better grasp the linguistic, educational, and social contexts. It now seems necessary to make teachers aware of the value of languages, namely by deconstructing the stereotypical representations unwaveringly gravitating around them, because we know that the social value given to them varies significantly; for example, some might say that English is a lot more prestigious than Arabic (Spaëth 2008). Le Ferrec (2008) is totally right when she clearly highlights the fact that academic difficulties cannot be attributed solely to language matters but also involve social, cultural, and identity aspects.

As such, our research aims to reduce social inequality by proposing that teachers go beyond a method of teaching that focuses solely on the language of the majority. This involves implementing teaching and academic practices that support, from a Bourdieusian perspective, the student's habitus to abandon the linguistic capital of the dominant group and further promote his/her access to the school's social capital. Since Cummins' seminal work in 1979 (see also his very popular work in 2000), researchers agree that the language skills gained in the first language serve as levers in learning a second language. Indeed, the students' cognitive interactions allow them to build academic knowledge. So, to abandon these practices that are deeply rooted in schools, we must think of an educational renewal.

Accordingly, our vision, regarding pedagogical practice, in our research, and regarding students' language experiences, operates through children's literature. In Europe, and within the perspective of what Candelier (2008) termed *Pluralistic approaches*, we address diversity with stories and narratives that speak to students. Children's literature helps to forge a multidimensional relationship with the world, as it leads to the building of literacy skills (reception and production) from various linguistic and cultural contexts. As such, a reading posture[2] is developed with reports that are language and culture inclusive. This type of practice fosters the development of a plurilingual and an intercultural skill and promotes communication spaces needed to highlight the students' experiences (Candelier 2003). Furthermore, peer discussions support discourse and position statements. As highlighted by Dabène (1994), the teacher is a guide, establishes the upper hand to stress the issues in the consensus to build, and, lastly, passes on the knowledge to teach. Therefore, meaning is developed through confrontations, discussions and negotiations (Bigot, Bretegnier, and Vasseur 2013). Students speak and use the language of instruction, building on their own if they feel it necessary and they are authorized to do so. All of these cognitive operations foster the development of metalinguistic skills and build equitable representations regarding the status of the languages in contact.

Through plurilingual books that are graphically staged, children's literature also raises awareness among students regarding different scripts and thus diversity of contexts, languages, and cultures (Fleuret and Sabatier 2019). It also promotes the overturning of traditional dichotomies between languages and cultures that characterize the school environment (Fleuret 2013).

In terms of the continuum model proposed by Hornberger (2003) regarding pluriliteracy repertoires, and in keeping with pluralistic approaches, we are also working on writing through invented spelling. The latter is a writing attempt that highlights students' comprehension of writing at a given time of their development. From the traces left, we value what is, build on language matters studied, and are work on the hypotheses made by the writer. In this way, by drawing closer to the student's cognitive work, we are better able to understand mistakes made and potential transfers.

In conclusion, by working both on reception and production with children's literature from an educational standpoint, we allow students to be what they are with their stories, their languages, and cultural backgrounds, while simultaneously working on content studied. This change of paradigm obviously scares teachers, as it forces them to move away from what they know, but we deem it essential to review and rethink school programs. It also seems that in Ontario,

---

[2] "By reading posture we mean a posture that fosters work (for the student) initiated from resistant texts, reluctant texts that breed cognitive conflicts created by comprehension breakdowns or proliferating texts that create interpretation issues (Tauveron 1999). In other words, a reading posture is built from problem solving that gives access to the social and cultural norms that are expected on school grounds and to specific knowhows all the while echoing the singularity of students." (Fleuret and Sabatier, 2019, p.7)

the policies are rather restrictive regarding the place given to student language on school grounds. There is still lots to be done, namely working with language representations, which is not an easy thing to do.

REFERENCES

Auger, N. (2013). Vers une prise en compte du plurilinguisme /plurinormalisme à l'Ecole française. Communication donnée dans le cadre du 19e Congrès des Linguistes. Geneva.

Bigot, V., Bretegnier, A., and Vasseur, M. (2013). *Vers le plurilinguisme? Vingt ans après*. Paris: Éditions des archives contemporaines.

Blanchet, P. (2014). Inclure une didactique du français dans une didactique de la pluralité linguistique: Repères théoriques et méthodologiques entre recherche et intervention. In J.-F. de Petro and M. Rispail, eds., *L'enseignement du français à l'heure du plurilinguisme*. Namur: Presses Universitaires de Namur, pp. 33–48.

Bourdieu, P. and Passeron, J.-C. (1964). *Les héritiers*. Paris: Les éditions de minuit.

Candelier, M. (2003). *L'éveil aux langues à l'école primaire. Evlang : bilan d'une innovation européenne*. Brussels: De Boeck.

    (2008). Approches plurielles, didactiques du plurilinguisme. *Les Cahiers de l'Acedle* V5(1), 65–90.

Castellotti, V., Coste, D., and Duverger, J. (2008). *Propositions pour une éducation au plurilinguisme en contexte scolaire*. Tours: Association pour le Développement de l'Enseignement Bi/plurilingue. Université François Rabelais de Tours.www.adeb .asso.fr/publications_adeb/ADEB_brochure_Tours_2007.pdf

Cummins, J. (1979). Cognitive/academic language proficiency, linguistic interdependence, the optimum age question and some other matters. *Working Papers on Bilingualism* 19, 121–129.

    (2000). *Language, Power and Pedagogy: Bilingual Children in the Crossfire*. Clevedon: Multilingual Matters.

Dabène, L. (1994). *Repères sociolinguistiques pour l'enseignement des langues*. Paris: Hachette.

Fleuret, C. (2013). Quand la langue d'origine devient un levier nécessaire dans la résolution de problème orthographique chez des élèves en français langue seconde en difficultés d'apprentissage. In D. Daigle, I. Montesinos-Gelet, and A. Plisson, eds., *Orthographe et populations exceptionnelles: Perspectives didactiques*. Quebec City: Presses de l'Université du Québec. pp. 81–104.

Fleuret, C. and Sabatier, C. (2019). La littérature de jeunesse en contextes pluriels: Perspectives interculturelles, enjeux didactiques et pratiques pédagogiques. *Le Français dans le Monde - Recherches et Applications*. Numéro spécial: Lectures de la littérature et appropriation des langues et cultures. [Numéro coordonné par Chiara Bemporad, Haute École Pédagogique de Lausanne et Thérèse Jeanneret, Université de Lausanne]

Gérin-Lajoie, D. and Jacquet, M. (2008). Regards croisés sur l'inclusion des minorités en contexte scolaire francophone minoritaire au Canada. *Éducation et francophonie* 36(1), 25–43. https://doi.org/10.7202/018088ar

Hornberger, N. (2003). *Continua of Biliteracy*. Clevedon: Multilingual Matters.

Le Ferrec, C. (2008). Littératie, relations à la culture scolaire et didactique de la lecture écriture en français langue seconde. In J.-L. Chiss, ed., *Immigration, école et didactique du français*. Paris: Didier, pp. 101–145.

Spaëth, V. (2008). Le français "langue de scolarisation" et les disciplines scolaires. In J.-L. Chiss, ed., *Immigration, école et didactique du français*. Paris: Didier, pp. 62–100.

16   Fighting off Zombies in France's Multilingual Education

Gilles Forlot

In this short text, I will draw the attention of the reader to the French situation, not only because it is the one I know best but also because it unveils remarkable and formidable contradictions. Language issues in France have been much influenced by post-revolutionary ideas on the unity of the Republic and the construction of the French nation-state. Hence, there is a very unified, centralized and homogenizing view of what a language should be, for instance, that of an emblem of the nation and the people. These initial comments hardly come as a novelty (see Lodge 1997).

The linguistics student I once was quickly found himself confronted by issues external to languages themselves (but involving them), such as ethno-cultural and linguistic diversity, multicultural contacts or language inequalities. My interest grew out of formal linguistics, which I found fascinating but unable to come to grips with the socio-educational situations that I was soon to face as a teacher and as a citizen as well. I chose to assert a very different kind of epistemological stance: that of a sociolinguistics of flexible multilingualism (Weber 2014) where language is a resource (Blommaert 2010; Heller and Duchêne 2011).

A particular case in point – probably not specific to France though – caught my attention: despite the fact that the French language landscape is remarkably rich and diversified (many languages are still spoken, and numerous languages are offered in secondary and college education), the institutional translation of all this is nevertheless still premised on a high level of fixed multilingualism, stemming from a long-lasting monolingual ideology (Boyer 2000).

16.1   Pedagogical Issues and 'Zombie Categories'

Like any other teacher trainee, my earlier teaching was dedicated to attempting to find pedagogical approaches that were the most efficient and adapted to my audience. But another question quickly arose: what were the actual aims of language teaching? What struck me at once was the instrumental dimension of all this: language teaching was portrayed, in my training and in my initial practice, to have two main purposes. The first explicit goal was to enable my

Figure 16.1 Gazing at the British coast on Brexit day

pupils to improve their reading and speaking skills. Fair enough. It is obvious that one learns languages in view of speaking them. But I quickly wondered why some realities of speaking languages were not taken in account. For instance, why was language variation not advised, let alone taught? How could one explain to learners that speaking a different language necessarily means handling one's multilingual repertoire, for instance making errors and resorting to code-switching/mixing? And how could one account for the fact that pupils were so rarely taught a new language with the help of those they already knew to some degree? To put it another way, how was their multilingual repertoire used in education?

The second goal of language teaching was providing access to cultural elements. Nevertheless, the approach was, to say the least, rather monocultural, drawing on the old principle of one language–one nation (or several nations/ countries in the case of English or Spanish). The issue at stake here is the way stereotypes were being reinforced for implicit ideological reasons: a given language and a given place or social construct (e.g. a community, a nation) are imagined (Anderson 1983) as co-constructing each other. This essentialist approach is both reifying of languages and cultures and takes little account of the gradual changes experienced by nation-states in recent decades.

If language teaching is to be regarded as a concrete action of language policy, then without a doubt and despite a rich scholarly literature on multilingual education, language education has been stifled by 'zombie categories', as Beck (2002, cited in Wee 2016) puts it, that is, defunct conceptions which hinder the development of theoretical approaches that are relevant to our times – that is our globalized and detraditionalized (Wee 2016) times and societies. The nation-state and homogeneousness are some of these zombie concepts which have nowadays lost their relevance for social theorists, be they sociologists (Beck 2002) or language – sociolinguistics and language education – scholars.

My experience as a sociolinguist and teacher educator has led me to share some of my colleagues' beliefs (Narcy-Combes et al. 2008) that 'institutional' teacher training in France lacks theoretical depth and inspiration, and, should we retain Beck's and Wee's criticisms, I am concerned that a series of those 'zombie' concepts are still reproduced and spread beyond academia: French language teachers and educators have long adopted zombie conceptions of language, among which one finds the necessity of language compartmentalization; the fear of 'unsuitable hybridity' (Jucquois 2003); the obsession of false cognates and the attention to exceptions in language systems; the illegitimacy of all forms of language contact; and a supposedly necessary balanced set of skills when one learns/speaks a language.

All this points to a question I still find difficult to answer with certainty. Beyond the fact that language-in-education-related matters undergo what Giddens (1987) has theorized as the 'double hermeneutic', that is, the relationship and reciprocal influence that social science and lay concepts have on each other, I wondered whether it was decades of applied linguistics training – particularly those scholars focussing on language teaching – that had perpetuated these zombie categories. Or is it because many academics, as ideologized citizens, have reproduced these images in their own scholarly views? The latter case would entail that in a French academic tradition, the concepts of unity and homogeneity would have percolated into educational thinking. Another plausible reason is offered by Wee (2016): those zombie categories are alive and kicking because they offer a simpler approach when it comes to intervention.

Nevertheless, some teachers and students are receptive to new, more plural approaches, but what has been pervasive for years is the monolingual stance. I will not dwell too long on that stance, as, first, it is not a French specificity (see Cummins 2005) and, second, because much literature has been written on that subject (on the French situation, see Coste 2001). I would argue here that the monolingual ideology is definitely a resisting zombie category in language teaching, despite the recent emergence of a series of approaches deconstructing this perception, among which are translanguaging (García and Li Wei 2014), polylanguaging (Jørgensen 2008) and metrolingualism (Pennycook and Otsuji 2010). But beyond the upsurge and complexity (and maybe the confusion) these concepts have introduced in language teaching, there are yet many conservative hurdles to overcome before these approaches can be taken up by teachers. They imply shunning away from a number of everlasting socio-linguistic representations in order to adopt a renewed stance claiming that

(a) languages are always in contact in multicultural societies and language contact does not induce decay, but reconstruction;
(b) the learning model does not have to be that of the native speaker, if we are even sure of what the latter really is (Abrahamsson and Hyltenstam 2009);
(c) the notion of difficulty in language learning is much more complex than the very structure of the language indicates on the surface (new alphabet, declensions, etc.);

and (d) learning language is not just about learning languages.

16.2   Globalization, Superdiversity and Multilingual Education: Challenges and Change

All this is certainly complex enough to deserve more than these few pages. Most educators will agree that language learning is both about having access to the structural forms of the language (its phonology, syntax, lexicon, etc.) and a way to have access to new forms of 'culture'. The common view that language and culture are inextricably linked is shared by most teachers (hence the frequent reference to language-and-culture teaching and learning). Considering that this view seems characterized by a reifying and somewhat static view of both language and culture, I find it more challenging here to approach these issues in a different way. Language learning and teaching, with its multilingual contours, is of course about communication and interaction, but since the latter and social activities are intertwined, language education is then about group cohesion and power as well.

   The common perception is that to attain cohesion, people should share some common values, such as practising the same religion, having the same cultural values and speaking the same language. If, as Blommaert (2017) aptly suggests, we are to look at social issues through the lens of language matters[1], then learning languages in the traditional L1-target paradigm is no longer very

---

[1] Which classical sociology, with a few exceptions, has failed to do, as Blommaert (2017) reminds us.

relevant. Indeed, how are we to keep this binary stance and take on board the 'vernacular globalization' (Appadurai 1996) our societies have undergone for several decades? In other words, can we as teachers invent categories of languages that are explicitly oriented while the super diverse communities we live in – thus the interactions we engage in – no longer correspond to the way we still perceive language education in mainstream school syllabi?

16.3   The Hard Sell of Theory to Language Educationists

There remain several problems for the language educator. First of all, have we got anything to offer to combat those zombie categories? As Wee puts it in reference to language policy 'dismissing these ideas as zombies when the discourse is among scholars is one thing, since this is the nature of academic theorizing and debate. Dismissing these as zombies when the focus is social intervention is very much another' (Wee 2016: 335–336). Put differently, revolutionary theoretical proposals for intervention are often a very tough sell in language teaching circles, for the reason I have expounded previously, that is, the necessity to separate language codes, the need to identify a clear-cut culture connected to a language and the call for communicative efficiency. At worst, all this – along with other scholarly sociolinguistic considerations – is even 'treated with varying degrees of baffled contempt' (Cameron 1997: 163).

I recall the sceptical reactions of my teacher candidates as I gave various unexpected presentations on new approaches to language education, focussed mostly on the possibilities of bridging languages and capitalizing on prior knowledge in order to activate new learning processes. For instance, I would insist on the fact that English as the shared language – though partially – of most students could rather easily be capitalized on, one way or another, via for instance lexical proximity or stress patterns. I would then study a unit from the 7-Romance language science school textbook *Euromania* (Escudé 2008), or excerpts from Auger (2005), a multilingual approach to the learning of French as a second language by young migrants. I would resort to other tools as well, such as Perregaud et al. (2003) or Kervran (2006), two primary school textbooks aimed at developing language awareness.

There is no doubt that my teacher candidates were interested and attracted by those tools, but they considered them to be unfit for language teaching for several reasons: (a) they claimed that language awareness was not language teaching per se; (b) they strongly believed that their mandate was to make their students reach as high a communicative performance as possible; (c) they perceived some dangers in language decompartmentalization, such as hybrid oral or written production, lexical mixing and confusion; (d) they felt they had to prioritize their teaching on language performance rather than on non-linguistic learning or this sort of new pedagogical experiment.

This leads me to another problem – or obstacle – in multilingual education as championed by some language educators: that of the perceived origins of those multilingual proposals. This is actually quite a paradox, as a positive sign that language educational theories have entered the realm of political circles is the fact that the Council of Europe hired a number of leading academics in the field. This led to the publication of educational guidelines, including the seminal *Plurilingual and Pluricultural Competence* (Coste, Moore and Zarate 2009), the original French version of which was published in 1997 and partially heralded the *Common European Framework of Reference for Language* (Council of Europe 2001). But in turn, the fact that these guidelines had originated in European institutions created an impression of (and reluctance to) supranational, top-down instructions in the area of language education.

16.4   Concluding Remarks on the Role of Language Education in a Multicultural Society

I have alluded to the multicultural question several times in this text, but it remains a complex topic. Although it is obvious in the places I investigated where official multiculturalism is explicit, such as Canada or Singapore, the link among language education, multilingualism and the development of multiculturalism is still rather set aside by social theorists and multicultural thinkers. The hypothesis would be that multicultural education would contribute to social cohesion and appease societal conflicts. But here lies another paradox, forcefully voiced by those in France who challenge any kind of decentralized education. For them, what builds cohesion can only be 'mono-focussed', not 'multi' in any way. A cohesive society requires some levelling and homogeneousness. Hence the sharp criticism that multicultural education receives in France, where it is often treated as unsuitable to the construction of equalitarian, homogeneous citizenship. For instance, some religious education was introduced in secular public schools a few years ago, aiming to give a fair presentation of religious facts and differences to students. But it was soon suspected of introducing – or at worse increasing – an ethno-cultural difference between students.

This leads me to posit that France, albeit a multicultural country de facto, is not ready, for historical and sociological reasons, to officialize its diversity, despite the fact that the latter has now become quite commonplace. Political ignorance of the pluri-ethnic composition of the French nation is quite rare, after all, and everyone prides themselves when a multiracial French national football team wins international tournaments. But more than anywhere else maybe, one element of French identity remains sacrosanct: language. Imagining a French nation with several languages is still a remote dream (or nightmare for some). And besides specific pedagogical obstacles that

I mentioned earlier and which other educational systems probably experience, fostering multilingual education in France is, to say the least, a difficult task ahead. France has not yet rid itself of its educational zombies, perhaps because to the minds of many actors in the educational field, in particular those involved in language teaching, they are not defunct at all.

REFERENCES

Abrahamsson, N. and Hyltenstam, K. (2009). Age of onset and nativelikeness in a second language: Listener perception versus linguistic scrutiny. *Language Learning* 59(2), 249–306.

Anderson, B. (1983). *Imagined Communities: Reflections on the Origins and the Spread of Nationalism*. London: Verso.

Appadurai, A. (1996). *Modernity at Large: Cultural Dimensions of Globalization*. Minneapolis: University of Minnesota Press.

Auger, N. (2005). *Comparons nos langues: Démarche d'apprentissage du français auprès d'enfants nouvellement arrivés*. Editions CNDP, collection Ressources Formation Multimédia. Fabrication: CRDP Languedoc-Roussillon/ CDDP du Gard (DVD: 26 min and pedagogical guide: 15 p.).

Beck, U. (2002). The cosmopolitan society and its enemies. *Theory, Culture and Society* 19(1–2), 17–44.

Blommaert, J. (2010). *The Sociolinguistics of Globalization*. Cambridge: Cambridge University Press.
    (2017). Society through the lens of language: A new look at social groups and integration. *Working Papers in Urban Language & Literacies* 207 (on line), Tilburg Papers in Culture Studies, No. 178.

Boyer, H. (2000). Ni concurrence, ni déviance: L'unilinguisme français dans ses œuvres. *Lengas: revue de sociolinguistique* 48, 89–101.

Cameron, D. (1997). Reply to James Milroy's review of Verbal Hygiene. *Journal of Sociolinguistics* 1(1), 163–166.

Coste, D. (2001). De plus d'une langue à d'autres encore: Penser les compétences plurilingues ? In V. Castellotti, ed., *D'une langue à d'autres: Pratiques et représentations*. Rouen: Presses Universitaires de Rouen, pp. 191–202.

Coste, D., Moore, D. and Zarate, G. (2009). *Plurilingual et pluricultural competence*. Strasbourg: Council of Europe.

Council of Europe (2001). *Common European Framework of Reference for Languages: Learning, Teaching, Assessment*. Strasbourg: Language Policy Unit.

Creese A. and Blackledge, A. (2011). Ideologies and interactions in multilingual education: What can an ecological approach tell us about bilingual pedagogy? In C. Hélot and M. Ó Laoire, eds., *Language Policy for the Multilingual Classroom: Pedagogy of the Possible*. Clevedon: Multilingual Matters. pp. 3–21.

Cummins, J. (2005). A proposal for action: Strategies for recognizing heritage language competence as a learning resource within the mainstream classroom. *Modern Language Journal* 89, 585–592.

Escudé, P. (2008). *Euro-mania, manuel d'apprentissage disciplinaire en intercompréhension des langues romanes*. IUFM & CRDP Midi-Pyrénées/ European Commission.

Forlot, G. (2013). Towards language diversity at school and a renewed role of English as a 'gateway language'. *LEND -Lingua e nuova didattica* 42(3), 18–25.

García, O. and Li Wei (2014). *Translanguaging: Language, Bilingualism, and Education*. London/New York: Palgrave Macmillan.

Giddens, A. (1987). *Social Theory and Modern Sociology*. Cambridge: Polity Press.

Heller, M. and Duchêne, A. (2011). *Language in Late Capitalism: Pride and Profit*. London: Routledge.

Jørgensen, J. N. (2008). Polylingual languaging around and among children and adolescents. *International Journal of Multilingualism* 5(3), 161–176.

Jucquois, G. (2003). Hybridité. In G. Ferréol and G. Jucquois, eds., *Dictionnaire de l'altérité et des relations interculturelles*. Paris: Armand Colin, pp.147–153.

Kervran, M. (2006). *Les langues du monde au quotidien*. Cycle 3. Rennes: CRDP Bretagne/Scérén.

Lodge, R. A. (1997). *Le français, histoire d'un dialecte devenu langue*. Paris: Fayard.

Narcy-Combes, J.-P., Tardieu, C., Le Bihan, J.-C., Aden, J., Delasalle, D., Larreya, P. and Raby, F. (2008). L'anglais à l'école élémentaire. *Les Langues Modernes* 4, 72–82.

Pennycook, A. (2016). Mobile times, mobile terms: The trans-super-poly-metro movement. In N. Coupland, ed., *Sociolinguistics: Theoretical Debates*. Cambridge: Cambridge University Press, pp. 201–216.

Pennycook, A. and Otsuji, E. (2010). *Metrolingualism: Language in the City*. London: Routledge.

Perregaux, C., de Goumoëns, C., Jeannot, D. and de Pietro, J.-F. (2003). *Éducation et ouverture aux langues à l'école (EOLE)*. Neuchâtel: SG/CIIP.

Weber, J.-J. (2014). *Flexible Multilingual Education: Putting Children's Needs First*. Bristol: Multilingual Matters.

Wee, L. (2016). Are there zombies in language policy? Theoretical interventions and the continued vitality of (apparently) defunct concepts. In N. Coupland, ed., *Sociolinguistics. Theoretical Debates*. Cambridge: Cambridge University Press, pp. 331–348.

17 From Language Planning to the Didactization of Plurilingualism

A Swiss Perspective

Laurent Gajo

17.1 Introduction

Plurilingualism and migration have spanned my education according to two dynamics: an immediate awareness (through experience) and a delayed awareness (through teaching).

In terms of experience, I grew up in a mixed family (Swiss mother and Italian father). While the dominant language of the nuclear family was French, Italian was used regularly with the extended family, during our many stays in Italy, but also with visitors and within the Italian community. Our participation in the local Italian community was structured by the organizations, social circles and work projects in which my father was very much involved, notably through delegated responsibilities from the Italian Consulate. My contact with the Italian community also took place, for some time, through my attendance at the Italian School (courses in the language and culture of origin). As a second-generation migrant, I was born at a time when in Switzerland only men transmitted their nationality. So I was born Italian (I obtained dual nationality years later) and, in my early years of schooling, I raised my hand when people asked who was a foreigner. Although I was the son of a Swiss mother and grandson of a well-known school teacher in the square, I was able to experience the feeling of being a minority. This feeling was compounded, regionally, by the feeling of belonging to a French-speaking minority community in a canton that was bilingual but with a German-speaking majority. These two feelings found political outlets and I engaged in social debates in which it was difficult not to take a position, even though my parents, as the head of a business, invited discretion. Coming from a mixed family with a rather privileged social background, the son of an émigré who had successfully integrated, I very quickly felt the importance of this integration. For example, I found it impertinent to be asked at school which passport I would sacrifice if I had to choose. Was I made up of the sum of two nationalities? I also remember a high-profile media event that my father organized: the Italian-Swiss Week, designed to bring communities together at a time when Switzerland was under pressure from an anti-foreign political force (Schwarzenbach initiatives). To bring together, not to oppose. This movement of *rapprochement*, of integration, was facilitated by my

142

Figure 17.1 Repas au bord du lac de Biel/Bienne, ville bilingue non loin de laquelle j'ai grandi. Je revenais de l'Ambassade d'Italie à Berne, où j'avais accompagné mon père, alors correspondant consulaire, à une réception en présence du président Sandro Pertini

mother's choices, as she very quickly learned Italian and became involved in community affairs. Her involvement went so far as to set up a dance group for the Italian community with an emphasis on popular Romagna music and dance ('il liscio'). My life experiences have led me, subsequently, to feel the importance of multilingualism in my travels. In particular, I remember my first big trip without my parents, which took me to California for a stay with the American branch of our family (my paternal grandmother was born near San Francisco). In New York, I was unable to get my connection to San Francisco. So I had to sleep there and reschedule a flight, all with almost no English. Noticing that Spanish seemed to be known by a number of employees, I pretended to be able to speak this language and unknowingly activated a process of inter-comprehension with Italian.

Crossing borders, the complexity of belonging, the futility of passports . . . the lessons were many.

17.2   Reflections on the Concepts

My work has led my reflection along two main paths: migration and bi-plurilingualism. Behind migration and in connection with plurilingualism, the question of interculturality arose. I entered the migration issue through two main fields, that of the school and that of the hospital. I have analysed multilingualism mainly from two angles, education and science.

In the study of the phenomena of linguistic and cultural diversity, a distinction has gradually become established in the French-speaking world and, subsequently, more widely. This is the distinction between 'pluri' and 'multi'. 'Pluricultural' and 'plurilingual' apply to the individual, while 'multicultural' and 'multilingual' are used to designate a community, a geopolitical space. In my view, this terminological specialization is welcome, because the phenomena of diversity at the collective and individual levels do not involve the same issues. At the collective level, it is above all a question of establishing diversity, recognizing it and managing it. At the individual level, it is more a question of identity and the socio-communicative resources associated with plurilingualism and/or pluriculturalism. In addition to these two levels, the phenomena of contact between languages and cultures have been widely studied within the framework of institutional projects, particularly educational projects. At this level, the prefixes 'pluri' and 'inter' dominate, because it is not simply a question of establishing a certain diversity, but of making a stake, an objective within the framework of a diversification project.

The proliferation of terminology is particularly important on the Francophone side (see Paul 2004), for at least three reasons: the social relevance of the phenomenon, the diversity of the contexts considered (in space and time) and the variety of scientific viewpoints. The term 'bilingual' is undoubtedly the most widely used and, as a result, the most loaded. In Latin, 'bilinguis' also meant 'perfidious' and, in the seventeenth century, 'bilingual' could mean 'liar' (see Py and Gajo 2013). The scientific uses of the term 'bilingualism' multiplied during the twentieth century, with a terminological explosion beginning in the 1980s. This explosion can undoubtedly be explained by a change in the social climate around questions of diversity and mobility, but also and above all by the very tools of scientific research. Indeed, technologies related to the recording of social events (conversations) allow a better understanding of what it means to speak bilingually and stimulate the development of new theoretical paradigms in sociolinguistics and psycholinguistics. We enter more precisely into the 'world of bilinguals' (see Grosjean 2015), and we accurately describe the 'bilingual speaking', the 'transcodic marks'. The latter notion has given rise to much research in a variety of theoretical and cultural traditions. One need only think of the countless studies on the phenomena of code-switching. The focus on code-switching stems not only from the challenge it presents on the theoretical level but also from the many ideologies it is subject to in the field, especially in education. In order to build a bridge between the work of scientific description and the realities of language alternation in the educational field, a process of 'didactization of alternation' has been progressively supported by research refining the opposition between micro-, macro- and meso-alternation (see Gajo and Steffen 2015). The latter makes it possible to show that forms of code alternation can be sought in the organization of certain didactic tasks, in connection with pedagogical strategies and/or institutional expectations linked to the context. For example, social contexts marked by official multilingualism bring into the classroom a 'legitimate' diversity that must be taken into account in the organization of teaching.

The proliferation of French terminology has also led to typographical marks in the articulation between 'bi' and 'pluri' ('bi-plurilingual', 'bi-/plurilingual') and to the increasingly regular use of the plural to designate 'plurilingualism' ('plurilinguismes'). The articulation between bilingualism and plurilingualism gives rise to several theoretical and epistemological positions. These include the question of whether plurilingualism can be considered to be an extension of bilingualism or whether it is only a special case of the latter.

The most recent terminological development, however, is on the Anglophone side, with the notion of 'translanguaging' (see García and Wei 2014). This is interesting, but no less problematic, in that it presents a significant polysemy, which is, moreover, insufficiently perceived. García (2008) has already shown that this notion can be understood in at least two ways, at the linguistic level and at the didactic level. Linguistically,

For us, translanguaging includes but extends what others have called language use and language contact among bilinguals. Rather than focusing on the language itself and how one or the other might relate to the way in which a monolingual standard is used and has been described, the concept of translanguaging makes obvious that there are no clear-cut boundaries between the languages of bilinguals (García 2008, p. 47).

From a didactic standpoint, Baker (2001), himself inspired by the work of Cen Williams, argues that translanguaging corresponds to a 'pedagogical practice which switches the language mode in bilingual classroom – for example, reading is done in one language, and writing in another' (García 2008, p. 45). The term 'translanguaging' is being used more and more frequently, and its relevance is becoming diluted, especially when it is used to invalidate the very notion of language, which is very much present in everyday discourse and in institutional organization. This is why I have a preference for the notion of 'plurilanguaging' (Lüdi 2013).

With Pennycook (2016), it seems more important to speak of the 'trans-metro-poly movement', which anchors the notion of 'translanguaging' in social contexts often marked by superdiversity. In this regard, I also note, in the recent evolution of studies on multi- or plurilingualism, a linking of linguistic analyses with a more general reflection on the management of diversity (Berthoud, Grin and Lüdi 2013; Yanaprasart and Lüdi 2017).

To conclude, it should also be noted that the term 'transcultural' has not met the same fate, although it too has a certain polysemy, since transculturality can be associated both with taking differences into account and overcoming them.

I have used it mainly to analyse communicative practices in the hospital environment (Gajo 2006).

17.3   Pedagogical Practices

It is clear that 'translanguaging' in certain meanings can refer to a pedagogical practice that consists in legitimizing the passage between languages in classroom interaction. I refer then to what I said previously about the didactization of language alternation. The latter is, however, only one of the mechanisms at work in pedagogical practices that promote plurilingualism.

In Europe, since the end of the 1990s, 'alternative' approaches to language teaching have emerged. What they had in common was that they did not focus exclusively on one language but on several. They work towards several languages, from several languages, in several languages, and are gradually being grouped together under the title 'didactics of plurilingualism' (Billiez 1998; Moore 2006; Gajo 2009; Troncy et al. 2014) or 'plural approaches' (Candelier 2008). In the last fifteen years, there has been an increasing amount of research on either a particular plural approach or on the didactics of plurilingualism as such. The most lively debates have focused on the margins of the paradigm, and in particular on three points: the admission of intercultural pedagogy within the didactics of plurilingualism, the admission of immersion teaching and the point of rupture between the didactics of languages and the didactics of plurilingualism. This means revisiting the links between language and culture, language and knowledge, and language and plurilingualism. On the theoretical level, discussions are continuing and are leading to a more precise analysis of the fundamental mechanisms of the didactics of plurilingualism, including integration, contrastivity and alternation (see in particular Gajo and Steffen, 2015; Fonseca and Gajo 2016). The integrative perspective is undoubtedly the threshold of entry into the didactics of plurilingualism and can serve as a point of contact with language didactics. Such a perspective can be found as soon as a teacher, although in charge of a single language, attempts to use the plural repertoire of pupils or his or her own knowledge of other languages to feed into his or her work. The founding character of the integration process is reflected in a certain terminological vagueness, which, in Switzerland for example, leads to the translation 'integrated didactics' by 'Mehrsprachigkeitsdidaktik' ("didactics of plurilingualism"). The alternation of languages, on the other hand, is primarily characteristic of bilingual education, but research is currently being carried out to show the variations. For example, the teaching material developed in the EUROMANIA project (Escudé 2008) confronts pupils with documents written in a variety of Romance languages. Thus, we are dealing with an alternation in comprehension. The languages used are indeed working languages but do not require production skills. At the same time, the alternation of languages in reading comprehension favours a work of comparison between languages (contrastivity). The shift between these different mechanisms, their greater or lesser proximity, makes it possible to return to the specificities and intersections between plural approaches, which can be expressed in various ways. Recent research on integrated intercomprehension (Fonseca 2017) shows a subtle interweaving between intercomprehension and bilingual education, as disciplinary contents (history, science, etc.) are worked on on the basis of documents formulated in various languages of the same family.

Research in the field of the didactics of plurilingualism still has great potential and needs to be continued at the theoretical level. In terms of teaching resources, there is still a long way to go, but there are some very useful materials, particularly for language awareness (EOLE – Perregaux et al. 2003; EVLANG – Candelier 2003) and integrated inter comprehension (EUROMANIA – Escudé 2008). The development of plural approaches and the densification of research on the didactics of plurilingualism have more recently led to the development of ad hoc reference frameworks. I would like to mention in particular FREMA/ CARAP (Framework of Reference for Pluralistic Approaches – Candelier 2007) and the very recent REFIC (Reference Framework of Competencies in Plurilingual Communication in Intercomprehension – De Carlo 2015) and REFDIC (Reference Framework of Competencies in the Didactics of Intercomprehension – Andrade 2015), resulting from the MIRIADI project. These frameworks have the merit of highlighting the particular skills sought and worked on by approaches that do not relate to the didactics of a single language. They resonate with a reflection on curricula, which are key places for the inclusion of plurilingualism in education and can provide for thoughtful articulation between the teaching of various languages in the curriculum, 'The school curriculum should aim at a curricular economy, coordinating the progression of skills through the different courses of study and identifying cross-cutting skills that promote coherence (longitudinal and horizontal) between learning' (Beacco et al. 2010, p. 4).

In Switzerland, a multilingual country, the adoption of approaches related to the didactics of plurilingualism can be observed in a differentiated manner, according to the following trends: integrative approaches have been explicitly and widely encouraged by intercantonal educational bodies for the past fifteen years or so, but are still struggling to establish themselves in the field; the bi-multilingual cities and/or cantons are more committed to plurilingual projects and are more quickly able to sustain them; bilingual education courses are offered almost everywhere in upper secondary school (lycée), whereas they are struggling to establish themselves in compulsory school; language awareness approaches are encouraged in primary school but remain very unevenly used depending on the region and the teachers.

There are some fine initiatives from the field but, at the same time, there is a fragility of didactic reflection and a reluctance to sustain projects. The way in which these projects are designated varies considerably, in particular because of the choice of terrain or local traditions, but it always implies a point of view.

Generally speaking, both the presence of migrant communities and national multilingualism stimulate initiatives in the area of plurilingualism. However, while the traditionally multilingual context undoubtedly favours the taking of linguistic and cultural diversity seriously, it does not guarantee a rapid regularization of alternative approaches. Perhaps even the multilingual 'naturalness' of the environment does not help us to see what is at stake in the didactization of plurilingualism. This is the case, for example, with a certain competition between bilingual education and language stays, wrongly referred to as 'immersion' and, as a result, considered to be the most successful form of bilingual education. While the stay remains an important means of experiencing otherness and building plurilingual skills, it is based primarily on individual initiative and places the pupil in a situation of 'submersion', insofar as the language is taught/used as a first language to a predominantly native audience. There is therefore no didactization of plurilingualism and a form of export of the pupils' language training. For me, the major issue lies in a tension – to be questioned, to be shifted – between naturalization and the didactization of plurilingual development. This tension can be found in teacher education, which struggles to keep up with the demands of the didactics of plurilingualism. For example, in bilingual or immersive teaching, there is a regular tendency to privilege the native character of the teacher rather than his or her training in didactics. On the other hand, when developing an early bilingual education pathway, the 'one person-one language' model should be applied as much as possible (see Gajo 2016 for a critical approach to this model). While circulation between unilingual spaces is one of the driving forces in the construction of plurilingualism in social trajectories, the school cannot be satisfied with this and benefits from using plurilingualism as a cognitive lever and as a tool for didactic work. The didactization of plurilingualism therefore goes beyond mere planning.

REFERENCES

Andrade, A. I. (2015). Un *Référentiel de compétences en didactique de l'intercompréhension* (REFDIC), Projet MIRIADI. Disponible en ligne.
Baker, C. (2001). *Foundations of Bilingual Education and Bilingualism*, 3rd ed., Clevedon: Multilingual Matters.
Beacco, J.-C. et al. (2010). *Guide pour le développement et la mise en œuvre de curriculums pour une éducation plurilingue et interculturelle.* Strasbourg: Council of Europe.
Berthoud, A.-C., Grin, F. and Lüdi, G. (2013). *Exploring the Dynamics of Multilingualism: The DYLAN Research Project.* Amsterdam: John Benjamins, DYLAN Prestige Series.
Billiez, J. (1998). *De la didactique des langues à la didactique du plurilinguisme. Hommage à Louise Dabène.* Grenoble: CDL-LIDILEM.
Candelier, M. (2003). *Evlang: L'éveil aux langues à l'école primaire. Bilan d'une innovation européenne.* Brussels: De Boeck Duculot.
    (2007). *CARAP: Cadre de Référence pour les Approches Plurielles des Langues et des Cultures.* Graz: CELV - Council of Europe.

(2008). Approches plurielles, didactiques du plurilinguisme: Le même et l'autre. *Cahiers de l'ACEDLE* 5(1), 65–90.

De Carlo, M. (2015). *Un Référentiel de compétences de communication plurilingue en intercompréhension* (REFIC). MIRIADI. Available online. www.miriadi.net/skills-framework

Escudé, P. (2008). *J'apprends par les langues: Manuel européen EURO-MANIA.* Toulouse: Centre National de Documentation Pédagogique.

Fonseca, M. (2017). *Didactique du plurilinguisme et intercompréhension intégrée: étude de pratiques en terrain catalan et occitan.* Doctoral thesis. Université de Genève: Archive ouverte. https://archive-ouverte.unige.ch/unige:96383.

Fonseca, M. and Gajo, L. (2016). Apprendre dans le plurilinguisme: Contact, intégration et alternance de langues en intercompréhension intégrée. *Domínios de Lingu@gem* 10(4), 1481–1498. https://doi.org/10.14393/DL27-v10n4a2016–13

Gajo, L. (2006). Interaction et compétence transculturelle en milieu hospitalier. *Recherche Migration et santé: Dans le cadre de la stratégie 'Migration et santé 2002–2007' de la Confédération.* Berne: Office fédéral de la santé publique.

(2009). De la DNL à la DdNL: Principes de classe et formation des enseignants. *Les langues modernes* 4, 15–24.

(2016). La méthode de Grammont-Ronjat (une personne – une langue): Définition, enjeux et limites d'une pratique fondatrice. In P. Escudé, ed., *Autour des travaux de Jules Ronjat (1913–2013): Unité et diversité des langues: Théorie et pratique de l'acquisition bilingue et de l'intercompréhension.* Paris : Editions des archives contemporaines, pp. 73–74.

Gajo, L. and Steffen, G. (2015). Didactique du plurilinguisme et alternance de codes : le cas de l'enseignement bilingue précoce. *Canadian Modern Language Review / Revue canadienne des langues vivantes* 71(4), 471–499.

García, O. (2009). *Bilingual Education in the 21st Century: A Global Perspective.* Malden, MA: Wiley-Blackwell.

García, O. and Wei, L. (2014). *Translanguaging: Language, Bilingualism, and Education.* New York: Palgrave Macmillan.

Grosjean, F. (2015). *Parler plusieurs langues: Le monde des bilingues.* Paris: Albin Michel.

Lüdi, G. (2013). Receptive multilingualism as a strategy for sharing mutual linguistic resources in the workplace in a Swiss context. *International Journal of Multilingualism* 10(2), 140–158.

Moore, D. (2006). *Plurilinguismes et école.* Paris: Éditions Didier, coll. LAL.

Paul, C. (2004). (Co)existence of one or more languages in a country or an individual: a terminological-historical overview. In G. Holtzer, ed., *Pathways to Plurilingualism.* Besançon: Presses universitaires de Franche-Comté, pp. 25–32.

Perregaux, C. et al. (2003). *Education et ouverture aux langues à l'école.* Neuchâtel: CIIP (Conférence intercantonale de l'instruction publique de la Suisse romande et du Tessin).

Py, B. and Gajo, L. (2013). Bilinguisme et plurilinguisme. In J. Simonin and S. Wharton, eds, *Sociolinguistique du contact, modèles, théories. Dictionnaire encyclopédique des termes et concepts.* Lyon: ENS Editions.

Troncy, C. (ed.), De Pietro, J.-F., Goletto, L. and Kervran, M. (2014). *Didactique du plurilinguisme: Approches plurielles des langues et des cultures. Autour de Michel Candelier.* Rennes: Presses universitaires de Rennes.

Yanaprasart, P. and Lüdi, G. (2017). Diversity and multilingual challenges in academic settings. *International Journal of Bilingual Education and Bilingualism.*

18   A Sociolinguistic Biography and Understandings of Bilingualism

Ofelia García

18.1   Yo Vengo de Todas Partes

I learned these words when I first went to school in La Habana, Cuba. The verse is from José Martí's *Versos Sencillos*. Martí was a late nineteenth-century Cuban patriot who organized the Cuban War of Independence from Spain, and a major Latin American literary figure and thinker. These verses then became part of the popular song, Guantamera, which I learned to sing in New York, where I have lived since I was eleven years old. The Guantamera that became popular in New York, that of Pete Seeger and later The Sandpipers, was different from that sung by my father in my early youth. The new music and rhythm, and even the Spanish language itself, had acquired a sense of coming "de todas partes," from everywhere. And it was finding my sense of place while surrounded by people and languages coming "de todas partes," that gave me my sense of belonging in the New York City of the early 1960s. It took a long time for me to acquire a sense of valuing my voices "de todas partes," hearing all voices "de todas partes," and especially understanding the relationship between voices heard "de todas partes" and the freedom to go, as the poem continues, "hacia todas partes," toward everywhere. My interest in bilingual speakers and communities comes from this sense of the importance of projecting different voices "de todas partes" in order to create different paths of liberation for language-minoritized speakers.

18.2   Four Scenes

There are four scenes that play in my mind as I think of what has shaped my professional interest in multilingualism in education. In the first, I am an eleven-year-old Spanish-speaking girl, newly arrived in New York. The second scene is that of that same girl in her first year of secondary school, then in her third year. In the third scene, she is now a college student in Spanish class. Finally, in the fourth scene the college student has turned into an

Figure 18.1 With my grandchildren

Figure 18.2 With my advisor Dr. Joshua A. Fishman

inexperienced young teacher standing in front of a classroom. They represent first experiences that have shaped me: the first time I understood English; the first time I realized the impact of curriculum and pedagogy in raising voices; the first time I recognized the pernicious effects of teaching only standardized language; and the first time I understood the importance of bilingualism in education.

18.2.1   Scene 1: Language and Cognition

I sat through classes in the first six months of sixth grade without understanding much of what my English-speaking teachers were saying. I had been a good student in Cuba, so I knew the classroom script. I knew how to behave in school; I copied well from the blackboard; I sat quietly; I did my homework as best I could. I soon made a couple of friends who spoke Spanish like me. One of them, Leonor, was bilingual. One day, I was waiting for Leonor after class as she was talking to the teacher. I didn't understand a word they were saying, but I did understand when Leonor told the teacher, "Don't worry, she's just a stupid Cuban girl." I then comprehended much more than the English language; I understood that speaking Spanish and being Cuban made me stupid in her eyes. At age eleven, I knew that one of my roles in life had to be to make others understand that speaking Spanish and being born in a Latin American country didn't make you foolish and unintelligent.

18.2.2   Scene 2: Testing, Teachers, Curriculum, and Pedagogy

By the time I entered the ninth grade, I spoke English, I thought, well. But the teachers in the high school who tested my English proficiency didn't think so. Of course, I didn't score well enough in the test of English language skills they administered when I entered high school. They placed me in the "slowest" English class. For a year, we did grammar exercises, vocabulary exercises, writing of short paragraphs. We did read novels, but we were encouraged to also read the "SparkNotes": summary notes of the plots of the books. We were tested on the content of the novels: Who was this character? What happened next? When did it happen? Rarely did we engage in any type of critical analysis of the novel. Once in a while a "why question" was asked, but there was little discussion of different options. There was always a right and wrong answer.

In my second year of high school, I had a wonderful teacher. Although she was required to continue the very mechanical language exercises in the curriculum for the "lowest level class," she took an interest in me. Despite what others saw as my "accent" and perhaps my "limited English," she focused on my strengths as a reader. That teacher fought for me and maybe saved me. She went to the principal and demanded that the following year I be moved to the "advanced" English class. When in my third year of high school

I was placed in the "advanced" English class, I thought that everyone was crazy. They were discussing novels as if the characters and situations were real! I had been taught to read fiction just to answer factual questions. The students wrote essays and research papers. I had never been asked for my opinion either orally or in writing. Through that experience, I learned a few things about the inaccuracy of standardized tests, the importance of teachers, and the consequences of curriculum and pedagogy.

Before I had graduated from high school I knew that standardized assessments of language skills were not valid for bilinguals and do not demonstrate what bilinguals know. I also understood that teachers make a difference; they can accept test scores or they can observe students closely and become their advocates. And finally, I knew in my own skin that curriculum and pedagogy make all the difference in learning. Robbing bilingual students of an opportunity to engage in a rich curriculum with exciting ideas and creative and critical opportunities is condemning them to silence. I was convinced then that alternative ways had to be found to assess bilingual students; that teachers had to be taught to not accept students' standardized scores blindly and to become their students' advocates; and that a curriculum and pedagogy either condemn students to silence or liberate their voices as creative and critical human beings.

18.2.3   Scene 3: Teaching the "Standard" Language

After seven years of English language instruction, I took my first Spanish language college course. Even though I lived through Spanish, my college professor told me that my Spanish was "corrupt." I was told that many of the words and ways of using Spanish we used so competently at home as a family and in my bilingual community were "wrong." "You don't say it that way," my teacher, Prof. Bonilla, used to tell me, "That's just the way people speak in the street." How could they be wrong, I asked myself, if everyone says it this way? I realized then that to succeed in teaching a minoritized language, teachers had to validate bilingual students' language practices. Successful bilingualism and biliteracy develop only when teachers can extend the language repertoire that speakers bring, not by eradicating their own linguistic practices.

18.2.4   Scene 4: Bilingualism in Education

I finished college and became a teacher in a New York City community that was heavily Puerto Rican. I was given a sixth-grade class of newly arrived students who were Spanish-speakers. I was supposed to teach all their subjects in English, as well as English as a Second Language. I tried, and failed. After the first month I marched into the principal's office and told him I was going to teach bilingually. It was 1971 and bilingual education was just beginning to emerge as an idea.

"What does that mean?" he asked me. I told him, "I don't really know. But I know what I'm doing doesn't make sense. The children don't understand me. They're not learning anything. I can do it much better if I make the learning meaningful for them by doing it through Spanish." I knew from that day forward that teaching had to be about ensuring that students made meaning. This was the beginning of my commitment to bilingualism and bilingual education.

18.3   Multilingualism/Plurilingualism/Heteroglossia: Adding Bilingualism and Translanguaging to the Mix

For those of us in the United States for whom bilingual education was a result of political struggle over the education of language-minoritized students during the Civil Rights era, the word "bilingual" carries a sign of resistance that cannot be eliminated. Dismissing it is to be complicit with the progressive silencing of "bilingualism" that has occurred in the United States as a result of conservative politics, growing xenophobia, discrimination against immigrants, and a neoliberal economy. The word "bilingual" has been silenced in the only US educational programs today that can possibly result in bilingualism: the so-called dual language programs. In accordance with neoliberal economic concerns, these programs not only omit any mention of bilingualism but also demand that they be "two-way," commodifying the language "other" than English for the benefit of English-speaking students, and robbing language-minoritized students of a way to construct a bilingual identity through their own language practices.

It is critical also to attend to the concept of *translanguaging*, as it is sometimes seen in opposition to the concept of "bilingualism." But these two concepts only acquire meaning side-by-side. Bilingualism is dynamic, not additive (García 2009). And so bilingualism cannot be solely interpreted through a "bi" lens. Bilingual individuals have a unitary linguistic repertoire, a unitary *internal* system, which goes *beyond* the *external social* construction of two named languages; that is, Spanish, English, Chinese, Russian, Haitian Creole etc. (Otheguy, García, and Reid 2015). Bilinguals are always **trans**languaging, going **beyond** the *named languages* of the "bi-." Therefore, bilingual education cannot solely strictly compartmentalize the two languages that have been designated as media of instruction. And ALL teachers need to leverage the students' translanguaging practices.

In particular, education programs that aim to produce or educate bilingual speakers (whether they are formally designated as bilingual, second language, foreign language, or heritage language programs) need to adopt translanguaging curricula and pedagogies (see García and Kleyn 2016; García, Johnson, and Seltzer 2017). A translanguaging pedagogy (www.cuny-nysieb.org) enables emergent bilingual students to incorporate new linguistic features into their existing linguistic system, as teachers leverage bilingual students' entire linguistic repertoire, at all times, so as to extend it. Translanguaging makes education more socially just by disrupting the linguistic hierarchies that exist in society and its schools.

Multilingualism in the United States is mostly interpreted as the presence of many different languages in communities and classrooms. In this way, it is similar to the way in which the Council of Europe defines it. But sometimes the concept of multilingualism is applied to students who simply speak more than two languages, a growing population in the United States. And some educators often think of "multilingual" students as simply those who speak languages other than those in which bilingual education programs commonly take place, mostly Spanish. The concept of multilingualism in education has a danger and a promise. The danger, of course, is that students' dynamic bilingualism and translanguaging is not leveraged in the "English only" English as a Second language "multilingual" classroom to which these students are mostly relegated in the United States. There are, however, teachers who are able to leverage the translanguaging of students in multilingual classrooms (see CUNY-NYSIEB, García and Kleyn 2016; García, Johnson, and Seltzer 2017). These teachers disrupt not only the "monolingual" English-only teaching in classrooms for "multilingual" students but also the static view of "two" languages in many bilingual classrooms. Most students today in bilingual classrooms are speakers of more than two named languages, and yet, bilingual teachers rarely acknowledge linguistic practices other than those of the two named languages of instruction. This is the promise enabled by a translanguaging lens in multilingual classrooms: that all teachers may see the possibility of leveraging all students' translanguaging, which goes beyond the named language(s) of instruction.

The European concept of *plurilingualism* has had little impact in US scholarship. Epistemologically, plurilingualism and translanguaging have different positions. Plurilingualism holds on to the concept of proficiency in named languages, although it defines proficiency not as something that speakers have, but as what they "do" with language in different communicative situations.

18.4   Heteroglossia and Transfer

Translanguaging rests on the Bakhtinian concept of *heteroglossia*, acknowledging linguistic practices that go beyond those that are constrained by the construct of the named language. But whereas heteroglossia acknowledges the presence of distinct varieties within a single language, translanguaging, by adopting an internalist perspective, questions both the concept of the named languages and the distinct variety.

Translanguaging also clarifies the concept of *transfer* that Jim Cummins (1981) popularized in the context of bilingual education. Cummins' interdependence hypothesis stated that the language abilities a child learned through one language could be "transferred" to another because of what Cummins posited as the Common Underlying Proficiency. There has long been confusion about what Cummins meant by "transfer," leading bilingual educators to often ask, "But if I teach them in language X, when will they 'transfer' that knowledge to their performance in language Y?" The answer is that they won't on their own. Transfer does not refer to the individual language features of "named" languages, meaning, for example, that an individual who learns the necessary vocabulary, morphology, syntax, and phonology in Spanish that enables him to speak or write about, say, photosynthesis, will necessarily have the features needed to do so in English or German. So then, what is being "transferred" in Cummins' model? General linguistic performance (García, Johnson, and Seltzer 2017) includes the ability to use the language features of the speaker's existing linguistic repertoire to think, find meaning in texts, and produce discourse both oral and written. It is this ability that Cummins might say is "transferable" because it is not "named language-specific." The Spanish-speaking child who breaks down the cycle of photosynthesis in a Spanish text has general linguistic performance knowledge because he can analyze the task, but may not have the language-specific features to perform that task if the text were in German or English.

So, if language-specific performances are not "transferable" then how should educators support emergent bilingual children's development of specific named languages? To answer this question, it is helpful to reframe Cummins' conceptualization through a translanguaging lens.

Instead of transferring, we can say that individuals *do* language (notice the singular in the word "language"), applying what they know about language, generally, to perform linguistically using new features. But since named languageS (notice the plural) are a social construction, named languages need to be experienced by new speakers, and the features that identify them as such need to be explicitly practiced and taught. The language-specific performances that require students to suppress some of the features of their repertoire and activate those that correspond to what society calls "another language" are a product of good language teaching. Only by ensuring that bilinguals appropriate the new features as their own will bilingual students feel empowered to use their full language repertoire to act in the world and participate in meaningful ways.

18.5   Language Awareness

Even with the recent focus on English language standards that the Common Core State Standards have recently promoted in the United States, there is little talk in the United States of a *Language Awareness* program of the type promoted by Eric Hawkins for both students and teachers. In the United States, language is indeed a "loaded weapon" (Bollinger 1980) and schools generally silence inquiries into language.

Because of the monolingual monoglossic ideology that pervades US life, *multilingual language awareness* systems of the type developed by Candelier and others are rare in the United States. Yet, I have argued that "*critical multilingual awareness*" (CMLA), an awareness that goes beyond named languages to the translanguaging of bilingual individuals and communities, is important in education (García 2017). CMLA would help disrupt the current hold that monolingual English language standards have in instruction and assessment in US education.

18.6   Intercultural/Pluricultural/Multicultural Education: Adding Transcultural to the Mix

From the 1960s through the end of the twentieth century, multicultural education in the United States was often seen in contrast to bilingual education. Multicultural education was understood to be what African Americans needed, an education that was culturally relevant, acknowledged the history of slavery, and was often Afrocentric. Bilingual education was understood to be what Latinos needed, an education that was always named as bilingual-bicultural. But with the globalization brought about by a neoliberal economy that encouraged immigration from diverse countries with different cultural and linguistic practices, both multicultural education and bilingual education came under attack. Around the same time, the concept of "culture" itself became questioned by those who had traditionally studied it: the anthropologists.

A generative concept of culture was encapsulated in the concept of *transculturación* proposed by Cuban ethnologist Fernando Ortiz in 1940. Ortiz referred to the cultural practices that result from blending those of enslaved Africans brought to the Americas, Europeans who came as conquerors, and Indigenous groups who were subjugated. In this blending, "a new reality emerges, compounded and complex," "a new phenomenon, original and independent" (Ortiz 1940/1978, p. 4). A truly just education for ALL must incorporate all language and cultural practices to *transform* the oppressive educational practices that minoritized groups have received. In so doing, it must disrupt linguistic and cultural hierarchies, while also sustaining home linguistic and cultural practices. This is what Paris and Alim (2014) call "culturally sustaining pedagogy." I see translanguaging as offering education a way of being transcultural.

18.7   Linguistic Repertoire/Communicative Repertoire

My use of linguistic repertoire does not refer to languages and dialects circulating in a community as in Gumperz, but to the unitary internal language system of individual speakers. A person's linguistic repertoire is made up not of languages or dialects (which are social categories), but of lexical and structural features that make up the speaker's idiolect. Translanguaging is thus defined in Otheguy, García, and Reid (2015) as "the deployment of a speaker's full linguistic repertoire without regard to the watchful adherence to the socially and politically defined boundaries of named languages" (p. 281). The idiolect, a person's own unique, personal language, the individual's linguistic repertoire, not only emerges in interaction with other speakers but also enables the person's use of language, as the speaker deploys items selectively depending on interlocutor and context, and also their history.

My use of linguistic repertoire follows Blommaert in focusing on individual speakers and not on communities as did Gumperz. Blommaert sees language as one element of a "communicative repertoire," the term preferred by Rymes (2014), which refers to the ways individuals use not only language but also other means of communication (gestures, dress, posture, accessories). Blommaert (2010) also defines repertoires as the complexes of linguistic, communicative, and semiotic resources that people possess and deploy.

I distinguish between the linguistic repertoire, which is limited to verbal and structural linguistic features, and the full semiotic repertoire. Of course, human beings make meanings through many representational and communicational resources, of which language is but one. But the strong legacy of modernist notions of language and society makes it imperative that we first deconstruct the concept of named languages, especially because it is the instrument used in schools to form subjectivities. Focusing on the linguistic repertoire in adopting a translanguaging approach has enabled me to shed the concept of named languages, while still accounting for it, and has transformed how I think about teaching bilingual children and assessing their language performances.

At the same time, the potential of translanguaging as a sociolinguistic concept, as well as an approach to pedagogy, relies on encompassing a full meaning-making semiotic perspective that focuses on all the resources with which individuals signify, including those within each of them (e.g. the linguistic features of their repertoire), those that they embody (e.g. their gestures, their posture), as well as those outside of themselves that through use become part of their bodily memory (e.g. computer technology). The fact that technology has transformed the media through which we communicate and learn, now multimodal and including, not only speech and writing but also gestures, visual images, etc. means that individual's full semiotic repertoire has to be taken into account in teaching and learning. My point, however, is that because language holds a privileged place in meaning making for individuals and because schools hold on to the modernist notion of the language of the nation-state, it is important that the linguistic repertoire receives the attention it deserves, primus inter pares, among all means of signification.

REFERENCES

Blommaert, J. (2010). *The Sociolinguistics of Globalization*. Cambridge: Cambridge University Press.

Bollinger, D. (1980). *Language: The Loaded Weapon*. New York: Routledge.

Cummins, J. (1981). The role of primary language development in promoting educational success for language minority students. In California State Department of Education, ed., *Schooling and Language Minority Students: A Theoretical Framework*. Los Angeles: Evaluation, Dissemination and Assessment Center, pp. 3–50.

García, O. (2009). *Bilingual Education in the 21st Century: A Global Perspective*. Malden, MA and Oxford: Wiley/Blackwell.

(2017). Critical Multilingual awareness and teacher education. In J. Cenoz, and D. Gorter, eds., *Language Awareness and Multilingualism. Encyclopedia of Language and Education*. Switzerland: Springer.

García, O. and Kleyn, T. (2016). *Translanguaging with Multilingual Students: Learning from Classroom Moments*. New York and London: Routledge.

García, O., Johnson, S., and Seltzer, K. (2017). *The Translanguaging Classroom: Leveraging Student Bilingualism for Learning*. Philadelphia: Caslon.

Gumperz, J. (1964). Linguistic and social interaction in two communities. *American Anthropologist* 66(6), part 2, 137–154.

Krashen, S. (1981). *Second Language Acquisition and Second Language Learning*. Oxford: Pergamon.

Ortiz, F. (1940/1978) *Contrapunteo Cubano del Tabaco y el Azúcar*. Caracas: Ayacucho.

Otheguy, R., García, O., and Reid, W. (2015). Clarifying translanguaging and deconstructing named languages: A perspective from linguistics. *Applied Linguistics Review* 6(3), 281–307.

Paris, D. and H. S. Alim (2014). What are we seeking to sustain through culturally sustaining pedagogy? *Harvard Education Review* 84(1), 85–100.

Rymes, B. (2014). Communicative repertoire. In B. Street and C. Leung, eds., *Routledge Companion to English Language Studies*. New York and London: Routledge, pp. 287–301.

Swain, M. (2000). The Output hypothesis and beyond: Mediating acquisition through collaborative dialogue. In J. Lantolf, ed., *Sociocultural Theory and Second Language Learning*. Oxford: Oxford University Press, pp. 97–114.

19 Experiential and Research Journey
Questioning Linguistic and Cultural Otherness

Cécile Goï

19.1 Childhood and Otherness

I grew up in a school. In the 1970s, my parents were teachers in the communal school of a small village and we lived in the school itself, as was the custom at that time. As soon as the bell rang, my brother and I had the empty classrooms, the schoolyard and the playground with its climbing rope as our playground. My childhood was cradled by the beautiful maps on the wall that took us on adventures, the big sponge with which we carefully erased the pictures, the inkwells that we had to fill in at night, the smells of chalk and alcohol from the copying machine whose crank we turned with application. These memories allow us to imagine the life of the child that I was: my life as a little girl was inseparable from the school, its spaces, the knowledge that was given there, the people with whom we lived there.

In a rural village, closed in on itself, one might think that there was little room for otherness. It did exist, however: social otherness, differences in status, ways of being or speaking that categorized one person from another and played a role in inter-individual and collective relations.

But this world – complex like any social group and capable of tearing itself apart internally – was nevertheless a block in the face of an otherness that arose in the village every spring and autumn. In fact, on the fairgrounds opposite the school, twice a year, the 'Gypsies', the 'Manouches', settled in. They put down their trailers, set their horses free, took out chairs and armchairs and lived there on the grass under the tall chestnut trees. The children came to school but not many of us enjoyed sitting next to them in class. Most of the time they couldn't read and they didn't always know how to count either. In stick writing, they wrote their name (only one word, both first and last name). They were dark-skinned and spoke 'funny French', with a special accent and words we didn't know.

Most of my regular classmates, like their parents, looked down on these families when they arrived and the children were shunned and laughed at.

Figure 19.1 Là où tout a commencé

What's more, my brother and I, who shared our children's games with the Gypsies, were also mocked for cozying up to these outcasts.

It was my first contact with a cultural, linguistic otherness in the school space. And it was probably my first "gesture of indignation" (Moscovici 1988) at the way these different children were considered and treated. This first contact with how people can be ostracized on the basis of cultural or linguistic difference outraged the child I was. Today, I am better able to put into words what my friends at the time meant to this village and its inhabitants: an otherness that disturbs, that worries, that sometimes frightens but that can also, in a way, fascinate.

As a child, I also experienced (without being able to name things that way at the time), linguistic and cultural otherness in my family space: a Basque mother's family, straddling France and Spain, discussions in which French, Spanish and Landes dialect were mixed. And Basque when we were getting down to business, that is to say, when it was a question of cooking or, even more so, when there was an argument in the air. A father's family, on the other hand, was a 'home-grown' family from Berry, where conversations were also full of expressions, turns of phrase and a pictorial vocabulary, which today are staged, between tenderness and irony, in shows for the general public.

Awareness of differences in language use, social codes and cultural imprints came, therefore, early on. I also understood early that the different social spaces constituted by the family, the group of friends and the school could not be lived in the same way. Otherwise, they would be marked by too great a difference; otherwise, they would be rejected or ostracized.

Each story or biographical continuum has its own set of personal fictions, a posteriori reconstructions and imaginary memories. But today I think that in my childhood story, in my first childlike connections to the otherness of others, as well as to the intrinsic otherness of my own family, the experiences shaped first my professional commitments, and then my scientific ones. Against this essential backdrop, several political events have also marked my path as a researcher, generating questions both about the substance of what was then at stake and about the pragmatic form that related institutional demands could take. I will detail some of them here.

19.2   A Researcher's Identity between Professional History and Political Event(s)

One of these events was the publication of the Social Cohesion Law in 2005. This law, which affects politics in its broadest aspects, proposed a change of perspective on education and 'equal opportunities', introducing the notion of 'educational success' when, until then, institutional discourse had been mainly concerned with 'school success'. Action-research conducted in sensitive areas and the theorization of contemporary concepts were initiated following this publication.

Then, another event took part in the conceptual deepening and social declinations of the research undertaken: the rewriting in 2012 of the Official Bulletin on the Organization of the Schooling of Newly Arrived Allophone Pupils (EANA) with a claimed aim of school inclusion. Several research projects have made it possible to work on these issues, to develop a model for analysing institutional 'realities' from this angle and to bring a scientific voice to the social field.

19.3   A Researcher's Commitment as Part of a Biographical Journey

My identity as a researcher is indeed part of a professional history as a former teacher of EANA because my entry into the thesis course was motivated by professional questions, generated by my daily encounters with students 'like no other'. Indeed, after having taught for five years in an 'ordinary' context (if there were any), from kindergarten to CM2 (French equivalent of fifth grade), in rural as well as in sensitive urban areas, I had chosen to move towards a position as a teacher of so-called newcomer students. The practice of this profession for more than twenty years led me to ask myself questions about my pupils: why was it that some migrant children, allophones or not, engaged in dynamics of academic success when others seemed not to be able to do so?

The intuition at the time led me to consider that there were processes at work here, involving phenomena of authorization: authorization to succeed that is granted to the child or that the child himself or herself grants (Goï 2005, 2015). These 'grassroots' questions echoed more general concerns expressed by others (Auger 2005, 2010) and were part of concerns about the school reception of foreign students, most often non–French-speaking.

In 2002, I was in the midst of writing my thesis when a BO on the schooling of Newly Arrived Pupils in France was published. A special competition led me to set aside six months in the thesis process to write a book on the reception of these particular pupils (Goï 2005). This first exercise in long-term writing initiated a dual path: a concern for conceptual scientific developments and critical analyses of current political events, on the one hand, and a social intervention assumed in the co-construction of research carried out with the actors and then in the dissemination and associated intervention work, on the other hand.

My path as a researcher in a professional capacity began with my recruitment as a senior lecturer. In the academic world, it is common to historicize one's positions through the 'path' and through a certain form of self-presentation, almost defining of who one is: explaining 'where one is speaking from' is an expression frequently used in round table discussions or ritual presentations of colloquia, conferences or study days.

In 2008, despite having defended a thesis in Educational Sciences, I became a teacher-researcher in a department of Sociolinguistics and Didactics of Languages (Sodilang) and attached to a multidisciplinary team (seventh and seventieth sections). The institutional scientific affiliation associated with a university department for training in language didactics strongly coloured this first professional designation and the articulation among training, research and intervention was particularly impregnated by it. As indicated by Philippe Blanchet and Patrick Chardenet,

Far from representing a simple intellectual challenge, research in the didactics of languages and cultures responds to a range of social needs in education (initial training, vocational training and lifelong learning, etc.), in support of population mobility (migration, refugees, study, work, tourism, etc.), in administration (urban centres, centres and physical and electronic communication channels, human organizations), in politics (social relations and cohesion, identities, international and intercultural exchanges, etc.). (Blanchet and Chardenet 2010 p. 2)

This orientation of the 'ends of knowledge' in the social field marks the specificity of a path based on an experiential journey.

19.4   Questioning Practices: Which Didactic Approach for the Appropriation of French for EANAs?

In terms of research themes related to practices, my biographical and professional background has made me sensitive to several scientific issues, one of which has been particularly oriented towards teaching practices and the representations associated with them: what didactics for the appropriation of French in a context of linguistic diversity?

Here again, the research orientations are eminently linked to lived experience. Indeed, as a new 'official' recruit at the university in a department of sociolinguistics and didactics, I had to introduce myself several times and, while I was comfortable enough to retrace my career path, I was rather embarrassed when I was asked, 'So, are you a sociolinguist or a didactician?'. I knew I wasn't a sociolinguist. But a pedagogue: was I? Having been a French teacher for allophone students and a teacher trainer, I had practised and taught didactics for a long time. But could I define myself scientifically as a pedagogue? This embarrassment in categorizing myself in a self-referential way gradually diminished thanks to the 'others'. In fact, although I did not consider myself a 'specialist' as a researcher, I was gradually identified by colleagues outside the team as being 'specialized' in the didactics of French in a migratory context: invitations to study days, proposals for collaboration or publication orders were the means by which this image of me as a 'French didactician' and more specifically of 'French as a second language' (now FSL) emerged and solidified what I can now claim as one of my professional identities.

As far as I am concerned, this institutional affiliation has therefore had a sort of performative function in that it has led me to be identified and to identify myself professionally and to direct my research perspectives along certain paths rather than others.

I also wondered about didactic practices, and in particular about the teaching of French in a plurilingual context. In an action-research project carried out when I was a teacher with my own allophone pupils, I sought to uncover the links between the way in which children view the languages they speak and the way in which they engage in the development of a metalinguistic awareness

Beyond the cognitive dimensions of collaborative and shared reflective work, in confrontation with the knowledge of other plurilingual pupils and accompanied by the teacher, how do children construct the passages, convergences and divergences in their own personal, linguistic and biographical continuum? (Goï 2009:1)

This research was carried out 'intuitively', in the moment of a shared pedagogical moment, with a simple tape recorder taken out of the office at an opportune moment, without having anticipated what this could initiate, neither on the didactic level (I was an FSL teacher) nor on the scientific level (I revisited this experience a posteriori to theorize it, in the service of my path as a researcher).

This article contained in substance the seeds of my future research actions; it already questioned the meaning of school work (Perrenoud 2015) and the meaning that learning in a language and a country that are not those of their ancestors can have,

Isn't it of crucial importance to enable young people to situate themselves in their country and its history, to articulate immediate history and the diversity of filiations, in order to overcome a crisis of meaning in school? ... What meaning does the child attribute to going to school and learning things there, what meaning does he or she give to what is learned there and to the ways of learning? (Charlot, Bautier and Rochex 1992: 20)

This action-research also called on symbolic dimensions and suggested that the recognition of languages and cultural imprints was essential for a rehabilitation of the meaning of learning in French schools. At the same time, I tried to show that their use on the cognitive level is also a powerful lever in the service of the pupil himself. It is these two 'weapons' – both symbolic and pragmatic – that could enable an allophone child, 'between two cultures', to construct the meaning of what he or she does at school, of what he or she learns there, of what he or she reconciles there. Thus, 'when language becomes a carrier of meaning even in another language and, more precisely, in the language of the "country of adoption", a dialogue is established in the "inner self" of the multilingual subject, between identity and otherness' (Goi 2009 p. 11).

Continuing the reflection from the cognitive to the symbolic level, a 2009 text concluded as follows,

Reflexivity about pupils' first languages, in a multicultural and multilingual context, leads the child to develop metalinguistic skills and to build a plurilingual repertoire in which social and linguistic skills are nurtured.

At a personal level, reflexivity about languages restores all its strength to the child's history, separates and reconciles, unites and connects the languages and cultural events of his or her journey. In so doing, the passage opens up between the before/there, the here/now and, probably, the after/elsewhere, ordering internally the child's biographical continuum. (Goï 2009: 8)

We have observed here some of the scientific questions whose emergence is part of a personal, professional and intellectual biographical continuum. The whole of my scientific path could be summarized by what Serge Moscovici wrote in 1988,

Thus a research, however modest, begins with a gesture of indignation. One has the impression that something in human existence is not as it should be. Or one starts from a desire whose object can be distinguished and which one wishes to satisfy. One or the other pushes us to work systematically and logically to discover what corresponds to them in the reality of things. Whether the transformation of indignation or desire takes place, our science will be more sure of itself and more anchored in the facts. (Moscovici 1988)

A 'gesture of indignation' is indeed at the root of many research concerns: indignation about the 'treatment' of linguistic and cultural diversity in schools and its effects on the dynamics of success and on the individuals of allophone students or their families. Indignation in the face of certain forms of political and institutional blindness that lead to segregation and discrimination of vulnerable children (Goï and Huver 2013). These indignations are accompanied by a desire: that of carrying the singular voice of a life experience, a voice shared with others, in the collective scientific concert.

REFERENCES

Auger, N. (2005). *Comparons nos langues: Démarche d'apprentissage du français auprès d'enfants nouvellement arrivés* (ENA) (DVD), Montpellier: Scérén-CNDP, CRDP de Montpellier.
    (2010). *Élèves nouvellement arrivés en France*. Paris: Éditions des Archives contemporaines.
Blanchet, P. and Chardenet, P. (2011). *Guide pour la recherche en didactique des langues et des cultures: Approches contextualisées*. Paris: Éditions des Archives Contemporaines.
Goï, C. (2005). *Autorisation à réussir et transculturalité en éducation: Contribution à la conceptualisation de l'entre-trois au travers du cas de trois personnes dites de 'double-culture'*, doctoral thesis, Université de Pau et des Pays de l'Adour.
    (2009). Réflexivité et plurilinguisme: De l'outil d'apprentissage à la cohérence du continuum biographique. In E. Huver and M. Molinié, eds., *Praticiens-chercheurs à l'écoute du sujet plurilingue: Réflexivité et interaction biographique en sociolinguistique et didactique*. Carnets d'Ateliers de Sociolinguistique, L'Harmattan. https://hal-univ-paris3.archives-ouvertes.fr/hal-01873622/document
    (2015). *Des élèves venus d'ailleurs*. CANOPÉ, Futuroscope. www.reseau-canope.fr/notice/des-eleves-venus-dailleurs_7383.htm

Goï, C. and Huver, E. (2013). Accueil des élèves migrants à l'école française, des pratiques et des postures ségrégatives et/ou inclusives ? In M.M. Bertucci, ed., *Glottopol*. Rouen: Université de Rouen, Laboratoire Dylis, Lieux de ségrégation sociale et urbaine: tensions linguistiques et didactiques? pp. 117–137. www.univ-rouen.fr/dyalang/glottopol/telecharger/numero_21/gpl21_08goi_huver.pdf

Moscovici, S. (1988). *La Machine à faire des dieux : sociologie et psychologie*. Paris: Fayard.

Perrenoud, P. (2015). *Métier d'élève et sens du travail scolaire*. Paris: PUF.

20 Multimodality and Multilingualism
Biographical Notes, Key Concepts, and Practices

Maureen Kendrick

20.1 Resonance 1: My Mother

20.1.1 Language Learning and Identity

I trace my earliest interests in multilingualism to my family experiences with my mother and grandparents, who emigrated from Eastern Europe. As a young child, I vividly recall visiting my grandparents on Sundays. Although my mother occasionally used Ukrainian at home with us, we never really got to hear the language spoken in dynamic conversation the way it was in my grandparents' home. I was fascinated by how when my mother spoke Ukrainian she was somehow different than she was in English – she laughed more, talked faster, and seemed more joyful. My own knowledge of Ukrainian was more limited to simple conversations with my grandparents, who struggled to learn English in a small Ukrainian farming community. In these moments of easy-talking, laughter, and family interaction, my mother became someone who was just beyond my reach. It was as though an invisible veil cloaked the space between us. A key moment for me was the realization as a child that people express aspects of their identities differently through different languages, and that ways of being, thinking, and doing were inextricably linked to language.

20.2 Resonance 2: Early Teaching Experiences

20.2.1 Reciprocal Teaching

A second resonance relates to my first teaching experiences with newcomer students in north central Alberta (Canada), in a town that in the 1980s became home to many refugee and immigrant background families. I focus on two students specifically and what they taught me about the interplay among language learning, identity, ways of knowing, and modes of expression. The first student arrived in this small town from Vietnam, reunited with his father but separated from his mother who temporarily had to remain in Vietnam. He was in grade 3 when I started working with him; I was responsible for designing individual education plans

Figure 20.1 My mother and me

for new English language learners. I remember him as a boy who was eager to share his humor along with his language and culture. We would spend several mornings a week exchanging vocabulary in English and Vietnamese, matched to objects, textures, tastes, and actions. The opportunity for him to engage me in learning Vietnamese alongside his own learning of English resulted in a recipro- cal exchange of language and a diminished power relationship between us. He would dissolve into laughter at my odd pronunciations and my facial expres- sions when I tasted the exceptionally spicy food that he would bring to class to teach me Vietnamese vocabulary. Our reciprocal teaching arrangement allowed for pedagogic creativity that made language learning much like a game. What emerged from this experience was a powerful reminder of the connections between ways of knowing and being, language learning, and resilience.

20.2.2   Investment

The second student was older and arrived from Lebanon, sent by his parents somewhat against his will to live with relatives in Canada. He was just starting grade 10 when I began teaching him English. He was highly motivated to learn and in addition to our classroom activities, he spent many hours watching English television. Within a short time, he was experimenting with English idioms and expressions that he had learned from cartoons and sitcoms, all harnessed in his efforts to relay stories about his military training in Lebanon.

His identities as "soldier," "fighter," and "revolutionary," both real and imagined, were integral to how and why he invested in English language learning, and in particular, how his language use was carefully aligned with how he wanted to represent himself to others.

Threaded across these resonances are issues of identity, power, investment, and modes of meaning making. In making sense of these issues, I draw on Norton (2013), who defines identity as, "how a person understands his or her relationship to the world, how that relationship is structured across time and space, and how the person understands possibilities for the future" (p. 45). This definition points to the role of imagined identities and communities in how and why we invest in particular futures and learner identities. What underlies my interest in multilingualism overall is how different modes of communication spotlight the human condition in unique ways, providing clues for how as researchers and educators we might proceed in a way that changes those conditions for the better.

20.3   Reflections on Key Concepts and Practices

In this section, I discuss the key concepts and practices as they relate to my research and teaching contexts.

20.3.1   On Multilingualism/Plurilingualism/Heteroglossia

In my home context of Canada, bilingualism (English/French) and multiculturalism have been official policies and ideologies for the past fifty years. Yet, in practice, it is primarily among immigrant Canadians that bilingualism and multilingualism are succeeding (Duff 2007). Multilingual education has taken a variety of forms in Canada, from what Cummins (2007) refers to as the "two solitudes" approach, whereby English and French are kept rigidly separate and taught through monolingual strategies, to more innovative language programs such as French immersion and pedagogies that build on students' multilingual resources. In my own work, I conceptualize multilingualism along with multimodality as semiotic resources for learning and communication. This pairing highlights the functional integration of both languages and modes among individuals and communities, and draws on people's use of a "multiplicity of multilingual [and multimodal] discourses" (Garcia 2009, p. 53) to interact, communicate, and make meaning. In other words, both linguistic and modal diversity are framed not as problems but as key resources for all learners, including monolinguals.

In my collaborative research in Uganda, a linguistically diverse nation, we have focused more on the concept of *plurilingualism* rather than multilingualism (see e.g. Abiria, Early, and Kendrick 2013). We draw on the work of Canagarajah and Liyanage (2012), who emphasize that plurilingualism captures the notion that "proficiency in languages is not conceptualized individually, with separate competences developed for each language. What is emphasized is the repertoire – the way the different languages constitute an integrated competence" (Canagarajah and Liyanage 2012, p. 50).

   Much like Blommaert and Rampton (2011), I think of *heteroglossia* (Bakhtin 1981) as one concept among many that has been applied to the practices language users employ to move fluidly between and among their repertoire of linguistic resources; for example, crossing (Rampton 1995), codemeshing (Canagarajah 2006), polylingual languaging (Jørgensen 2008), translanguaging (García 2009), flexible bilingualism (Blackledge and Creese 2010), and metrolingualism (Otsuji and Pennycook 2010). More recently, I have also considered *heteroglossia* as a foundation for understanding *modemeshing* (or synesthesia, see Kress 1997), which takes place as learners and creators negotiate meaning across modes in text construction (e.g. filmmaking) and experiment with and draw simultaneously on the various perspectives offered by the visual, linguistic, gestural, and audial.

20.3.2   On Intercultural/Pluricultural/Multicultural Education

Multiculturalism has been used to both describe Canada in terms of the religious and cultural influences in our culture but also in reference to official laws and policies, including *multicultural education*. Within my program of research both in Canada and in East Africa, I have turned to other terms such as *transculturalism* to capture both new ways of thinking about human relations and the increasing mobility and global instability that requires awareness that people who live in and with diversity engage in diasporic practices that vary across places and spaces. For example, we have positioned multiliteracies pedagogies as a response to transculturalism and the need to account for the intersection of local and global practices in classrooms that result from complex migration patterns and language use (see Early and Kendrick 2017). Of particular importance is the perspective that cultural and linguistic diversity in classrooms are resources for meaning making.

20.3.3   On Linguistic Repertoire/Communicative Repertoire

I think of *linguistic repertoire* as part of a larger *communicative repertoire* that includes linguistic as well as other modes of communication, such as visual, audial, and gestural. My research is more broadly in the area of multimodality, which addresses how different modes/semiotic resources work in a range of cultural contexts and the potential of different modes for creating access to new knowledge and new opportunities. As Kress (2015) notes, "The social / cultural / semiotic world of every community depends on how the senses have been and are valued, fostered, developed in a community" (p. 56). Within *communicative repertoires*, I strive to carefully consider the relationship between linguistic and multimodal resources (see e.g. Early, Kendrick, and Potts 2015).

I argue that when learners are given opportunities to draw on their full multimodal repertoires, the learning activities become generative because of the modemeshing/synesthetic opportunities inherent in negotiating meaning across languages, sign systems, and modes (see e.g. Kendrick 2016). As Kress (1997) emphasizes, different modes give rise to different ways of thinking because humans constantly translate meaning from one mode to another. For children in particular, their approach to learning is entirely synesthetic, "things are always more than one thing, and have different logics, different uses, depending on where you stand when you are looking" (Kress 1997, p. 139). In school, however, the use of written language is typically fostered over all other modes of expression; this is evident especially as children get older (see Kress 1997). Yet written language enables only one form of cognition, the visual (e.g. drawing) enables another, and sound and movement enable yet others. Kress's argument is that we need to foster this synesthetic ability in children's learning rather than suppress it. In other words, we need to encourage children to think like children.

20.3.4   On Awareness of Language/Language Awareness

Rather than focusing specifically on *awareness of language / language awareness*, I frame my work more broadly in terms of *modal awareness* such as meta-cognitive, meta/cross-linguistic, and meta-modal awareness as learners make-meaning through multiple languages, modes, and identities (see e.g., Kendrick, 2016). My interest is in how learners become aware of the nuances and meaning potentials of the semiotic resources (including linguistic) that are part of their communicative repertoires.

As an illustrative example, I draw on a year-long case study of Leticia, a young Chinese-Canadian girl (see e.g., Kendrick, 2016) to demonstrate how her linguistic awareness in combination with her modal awareness enabled her to make sense of written Chinese. Although several languages were spoken in her home (English, Vietnamese, Mandarin, Chao Chiu) and she was enrolled in a Mandarin-English bilingual kindergarten, she displayed a reluctant stance toward Mandarin, particularly when asked to read or write. In my dual role of researcher-playmate, on one occasion Leticia and I worked collaboratively to create a bilingual Chinese-English book about sea animals based on a teacher made text from school. Figure 20.2 shows one page of the book we created during an episode of playing school in which Leticia took on the identity of teacher and I played the teacher's assistant. By continually working back and forth across the visual image, the print in English and Chinese, and oral-language both in and out of role, we were able to interweave and build meaning across modes and languages, as these short excerpts demonstrate:

MAUREEN: "Now we have to draw [the killer whale]? Which parts on this picture do you want to draw?"

LETICIA: "I want to do that (the English sentence)."

Figure 20.2 Dual language book

MAUREEN: ".… Now I'll do this one (the Chinese sentence)?
MAUREEN: "…What does it say? The whole thing?"
LETICIA: *"Zhè shì yi tou **shi ren jing** (…食人鯨[1])."*
MAUREEN: "I wonder why it has 'people' (人) there?" I carefully printed the Chinese
           characters while Leticia watched. "Do you want to do the period at
           the end?"
LETICIA: "Yeah.…" As she printed, she said the sea animal names in Chinese, *"lan
           jing* (blue whale), *[shi] ren jing* (killer whale)."
MAUREEN: *"Jing* means whale?"
LETICIA: "Yep, it's whale. This is a killer whale," (reading the English sentence).

Our discussion provided an opportunity for Leticia, both as a more knowledgeable speaker of Mandarin and in her role as teacher, to become an
authority as she solidified her own understandings by shifting meanings across
Chinese, English, and the visual, both in and out of her play role. Because we
were both learning to read and write in Mandarin, we were able to talk freely
about the challenges we both faced in learning to write Chinese characters and
in learning to draw. My process in many ways paralleled Leticia's, and seeing
me struggle may have created a safety zone in which she was willing to show
her own vulnerabilities and emerging knowledge as a language learner, something I had never observed her display at school or at the kitchen table with her
printing book. It is possibly this slowing of time and collapsing of space and
movement across symbol systems in the liminal, multimodal context of play
that made visible for her (us) the similarities and strategies in our processes.

---

[1] The literal translation here is "whale that eats people."

20.3.5   On Inter-comprehension/Education for Cross-Linguistic Transfer

I think of the practice of *cross-linguistic transfer* in terms of Cummins' (2007) argument that we need to rethink monolingual instructional practices in multilingual classrooms. His premise is that when we stop relying exclusively on monolingual instructional approaches, "a wide variety of opportunities arise for teaching languages by means of bilingual instructional strategies that acknowledge the reality of, and strongly promote, two-way cross-language transfer" (p. 222). In other words, pedagogical practices in multilingual classrooms need to engage students' prior knowledge. This understanding is an underlying assumption in the design of a new research project investigating the language and literacy education of refugee-background youth in Canadian classrooms (see Kendrick et al. 2016). The project aims to support refugee-background youth, for whom limited prior schooling often presents a barrier to learning, social adjustment, and academic success. We foreground students' lives, experiences, and communicative repertoires as central to their language and literacy learning, taking into careful consideration Cummins' (2014) proposition that, "significant components of the background experiences of [marginalized groups] are transformed into actual educational disadvantages only when the school fails to respond appropriately to these background experiences . . . " (pp. 3–4).

20.3.6   On Translanguaging

In my discussion of *translanguaging*, I return to an example from my collaborative research in Uganda. In urban communities and trading towns in particular, plurilingualism (Coste, Moore, and Zarate 2009) and translanguaging (García 2009) are common. As García (2009) distinguishes, "translanguaging captures the implications of plurilingualism for one's own communicative repertoire and use" (p. 51). Most Ugandan children draw on the multiple languages of their families and communities as resources they can use to meet their communicative needs. In our research study focused on plurilingual pedagogical practices in Northern Uganda (see e.g. Abiria, Early, and Kendrick 2013), we took into consideration Blommaert and Rampton's (2011) recommendation that "rather than working with homogeneity, stability and boundedness as the starting assumptions, mobility, mixing, political dynamics and historical embedding are now central concerns in the study of languages, language groups and communication" (p. 3). Given that the terms that have been applied to the practices of language users are, "often indeterminate and contested" (Blommaert and Rampton 2011, p. 7), and because our research was undertaken in a school, we found García's (2009) concept of translanguaging, that is, the practices by which bilinguals are "accessing different linguistic features or various modes of what are described as autonomous languages, in order to maximize communicative potential" (p. 140), most helpful.

REFERENCES

Abiria, D., Early, M., and Kendrick, M. (2013). Plurilingual pedagogical practices in a policy constrained context: A rural Ugandan case study. *TESOL Quarterly* 47(3), 567–590.
Bakhtin, M. (1981). *The Dialogic Imagination*. Austin: University of Texas Press.
Blackledge, A. and Creese, A. (2010). *Multilingualism: A Critical Perspective*. London: Continuum.
Blommaert, J. and Rampton, B. (2011). Language and superdiversity. *Diversities* 13(2), 3–21.
Canagarajah, A. S. (2006). The place of World Englishes in composition: Pluralization continued. *College Composition and Communication* 57, 586–619.
Canagarajah, A. S. and Liyanage, I. (2012). Lessons from pre-colonial multilingualism. In M. Martin-Jones, A. Blackledge, and A. Creese, eds., *The Routledge Handbook of Multilingualism*. London: Routledge, pp. 49–65.
Coste, D., Moore, D., and Zarate, G. (2009). *Plurilingual and Pluricultural Competence*. Strasbourg: Council of Europe.
Cummins, J. (2014). Beyond language: Academic communication and student success. *Linguistics and Education* 26, 145–154.
  (2007). Rethinking monolingual instructional strategies in multilingual classrooms. *Canadian Journal of Applied Linguistics*, 10(2), 221–240.
Duff, P. (2007). Multilingualism in Canadian schools: Myths, realities, and possibilities. *Canadian Journal of Applied Linguistics* 10(2), 149–163.
Early, M. and Kendrick, M. (2017). 21st century literacies: Multiliteracies reconsidered. In R. Zaidi and J. Rowsell, eds., *Literacy Lives in Transcultural Times*. London: Routledge, pp. 43–57.
Early, M., Kendrick, M., and Potts, D. (2015). (Guest editors). Multimodality: Out from the margins of English language teaching, *TESOL Quarterly* 49(3), 447–622.
García, O. (2009). Education, multilingualism and translanguaging in the 21st century. In T. Skutnabb-Kangas, R. Phillipson, A. K. Mohanty, and M. Panda, eds., *Social Justice through Multilingual Education*. Clevedon, UK: Multilingual Matters, pp. 140–158.
Jørgensen, J. N. (2008). Polylingual languaging around and among children and adolescents. *International Journal of Multilingualism* 5, 161–176.
Kendrick, M., Early, M., Stille, S., and Taylor, S. (2016). Language and literacy learning among youth refugees in Canadian secondary school classrooms. Canadian Social Sciences and Humanities Research Council (SSHRC) Insight Development Grant No. FAS F16–04594.
Kendrick, M. (2016). *Literacy and Multimodality across Global Sites*. London: Routledge.
Kress, G. (1997). *Before Writing: Rethinking the Paths to Literacy*. London: Routledge.
  (2015). Semiotic work: Applied Linguistics and a social semiotic account of Multimodality. *AILA Review* 28(1), 49–71.
Norton, B. (2013). *Identity and Language Learning: Extending the Conversation*. 2nd ed. Bristol: Multilingual Matters.
Otsuji, E. and Pennycook, A. (2010). Metrolingualism: Fixity, fluidity and language in flux. *International Journal of Multilingualism* 7, 240–254.
Rampton, B. (1995). *Crossing: Language and Ethnicity among Adolescents*. London: Longman.

21 Researching Multilingualism and Language Education across Borders and over Decades

Kendall A. King

I grew up surrounded by English, and only started to learn my second language, Spanish, in high school, and then more seriously, at university. These awkward early attempts are best described as experiences of language curricularization (Valdés 2015); my classmates and I learned grammar rules as if they were math formulae, and vocabulary lists as if they were biology terms. As Valdés (2015) has argued, when a language is curricularized, it is treated not as a species-unique communicative system acquired naturally in the process of primary socialization, but as a curricular subject or skill, the elements of which can be ordered and sequenced, learned and tested in artificial contexts within which learners of the target language outnumber proficient speakers (262). And as widely noted, and was most definitely the case for my peers and for myself, this approach generally results in low levels of proficiency. My other attempts at learning additional languages through formal study resulted in varied (generally low) levels of competence, but never really felt (or have yet to feel) like natural ways of communicating, for example, one year of 'Swedish for Foreigners' classes while living in Stockholm; two months of studying Quichua at Madison; and formal and informal study of Ojibwe, one of the original languages of my now home state of Minnesota.

I only began to function as – and to feel myself to be – a bilingual person after extensive time abroad: one year in Madrid through a University of California study abroad programme, one semester in Mexico City and an internship in rural Mexico; and finally, eighteen months conducting dissertation research in highland Ecuador. While I did not have the words (or conceptual understanding) at the time, I now think that Spanish 'stuck', and has become a permanent part of my linguistic or communicative repertoire, and thus is integrated into my identity, because of my full personal investment (Peirce 1995), and in particular, the allotted time and space to build meaningful relationships in and through Spanish. While I had been a motived language learner in formal educational contexts, there were no opportunities to develop a Spanish-speaking self through routine, everyday, authentic interactions about things that mattered, and with people who mattered to me.

Figure 21.1 Kendall King in Saraguro, Ecuador in 1995

These investments, and the resulting language skills, allowed me to develop deep and lasting interpersonal relationships in and through Spanish, further propelling my language competence, and allowing me to inhabit a Spanish-speaking self. My particular circumstances, including the opportunities and obligations to interact in Spanish over extended periods of time, were of course critical here. In addition, I also benefited from the linguistic hierarchies – or what Flores and Rosa (2015) term raciolinguistic ideologies – that result in the privileging and praising of English speakers stumbling in non-perfect Spanish (while deriding Spanish speakers who use 'non-standard' dialects or Spanish as a second/heritage language as 'not being able to speak'). These up close, everyday interactions sharpened my awareness of second language learning processes, language inequities and language identity.

Nevertheless, until I was about twenty, my interests in language learning and multilingualism bent towards narcissistic concerns (e.g. How could I become more fluent? What were the keys to 'passing' as a native speaker?), and in academic pursuits, leaned towards cognitive neuroscience (e.g. What changes are evident in the brain as the result of learning?). This paradigm shifted when I took a last-minute position as an intern for UNESCO in the Mexican state of Tobasco. My task was to evaluate the impact of a UNESCO-supported art school in a Maya-Chontal community (Tamulté de las Sábanas). The art school was unexpectedly closed during my visit, leaving me with little to do other than interview students and parents, initially about the functioning of the art school, although we seldom stayed on topic. Through these home visits I had the chance to see language shift up close. At that time (the early 1990s), the community was in the midst of a rapid shift from Chontal Maya to Spanish. Even to my novice and naïve eyes, it was clear that without some sort of change in policies or practices, the community would likely be largely monolingual in Spanish within a few decades.

My time in Tamulté de las Sábanas, together with my own experiences in learning Spanish, shifted my interest from language and cognition to a focus on language in social life. In short, I became less curious about how language learning impacted brain structures, and more interested in understanding how social, cultural and economic forces impacted language learning – and crucially, what language policy and multilingual education practices could do to support minority languages and minority language speakers.

This new focus on language loss and language revitalization drove my desire to pursue a PhD in Educational Linguistics at the University of Pennsylvania, to work with Professor Nancy Hornberger, and to develop a specialization in Quichua-Spanish bilingualism, bilingual education and language policy. My training at Penn grounded me in the fields of the ethnography of communication, linguistic anthropology and the sociology of language, and I became 'fluent' in describing and analysing 'speech communities', 'communicative repertoires', 'diglossia', 'speech acts', 'events' and 'situations'.

Using many of these constructs, the early late 1980s and early 1990s saw significant expansion in theoretical and empirical work on bilingual education and language maintenance (Hornberger 1987); language loss and revitalization, in turn, were only beginning to gain the attention of scholars and policymakers (Krauss 1996). I set out to conduct my dissertation research on Quichua language revitalization in the southern Ecuadorian Andes, confident in the utility of my theoretical constructs, and certain I could address my research questions using many of the same tools that had been productive for the study of bilingual education in the previous decades. It was 1995 and I had little idea how many of the core constructs of my field would shift.

21.1   Key Concepts and Practices over Time

Tectonic theoretical shifts were of course already underway by the time I left for Ecuador, but their impact was only beginning to crack the foundations of the field of applied linguistics. The shifts, familiar and even dated to us now, include, for instance, post-structural critiques which called into question long-standing constructs in the field such as 'native speaker' (Davies 2003), motivation (Peirce 1995) and even the notion of language itself as a 'countable institution' (Pennycook and Makoni 2006, p. 2). Concurrently, the field saw the development of a distinctive tradition of critical, ethnographic and discursive research on multilingualism (Martin-Jones and Martin 2017), defined by greater attention to language ideology, power, identity and agency. These conceptual shifts, in conjunction with demographic and technology changes around the world, often referred to as globalization (Appadurai 1996) and superdiversity (Vertovec 2007; De Fina, Ikizoglu and Wegner 2017), lead applied linguistics scholars to reconsider and reconceptualize many of the field's key concepts and practices.

Over the last two decades, my research has sought to identify and analyse the policies and practices that support minority languages and their speakers. I have conducted this work across a range of national and situational contexts, in homes, schools and communities in the United States, Sweden, Chile and Ecuador. To take stock of how these concepts have evolved in applied linguistics research, here I contrast how key concepts were defined and utilized in some of my earliest research, that is my dissertation work on language revitalization in Ecuador, and in my more recent work with East African refugee adolescents with limited or interrupted formal schooling.

21.2   Multilingualism and Heteroglossia

Prior to 1995, multilingual or multilingualism was often used to describe a social context or a language policy (e.g. Alladina and Edwards 1991; Mansour 1993; Skutnabb-Kangas 1995). More recent work, in contrast, has tended to use multilingual as an adjective to describe individuals or to characterize individual practices (e.g. Wyman, McCarty and Nicholas 2013; Clark and Dervin 2014)

This shift is evident in my own work as well. While my early work examined opportunities for use of different varieties of Quichua and Spanish, and how these were utilized by community members, this analysis was driven by ethnography of communication constructs (e.g. communicative competence, speech events, speech acts) (Hymes 1980), and emphasized how two languages (Spanish or Quichua) fit into the SPEAKING mnemonic. My early work was shaped by the ethnography of communication goals of describing the rules of use, and how individual language varieties patterned systematically across domains.

My more recent research, in contrast, takes up notions of multilingualism and heteroglossia (Bakhtin 1981) as central to the description and analysis of both the context and speaker practices. More broadly, this work has also revealed how students' multilingual practices are powerful resources for literacy learning (Vanek, King and Bigelow 2018).

21.3   Intercultural/Pluricultural/Multicultural Education

Intercultural is a long-standing adjective for describing an approach to education in much of Latin America. Political movements that sparked legislative and constitutional shifts in the early 1990s in Ecuador allowed for the adaptation (and uneven implementation) of *educación intercultural bilingue*. The use of *intercultural* in this context is meant to imply two-way, reciprocal learning, that is, with Indigenous people learning a Spanish language (and Western cultural and academic norms) while Spanish speakers also learn an Indigenous language (and gain understanding of Indigenous cultural norms). This conceptual reframing and power-shifting, while clearly implied, was not consistently put into place, in large part owing to resistance among Spanish speakers. As Hornberger (2000) has noted, there is an ideological paradox inherent in transforming a standardizing education into a diversifying one, as well as in constructing a unified national identity that is also multilingual and multicultural. In my own site of research in the southern Ecuadorian Andes, there was little evidence of cross-cultural exchange or of the reciprocity implied in *intercultural*.

Conversely, in the hyper-diverse classrooms where I presently conduct my research, intercultural offers little in terms of analytical power because of its ubiquity. My current context of work is defined by cross-cultural, cross-linguistic communication, and multiculturalism permeates school policy and practice. Our research has at times asked how cross-cultural communication works (e.g. between speakers of different dialects of Somali from different regions of the country, or between Central American students and East African students in an online space). For instance, our work in using language-specific online social media groups to promote native language and literacy work often involved cross-group communication in unexpected ways: Somali students writing in Spanish to be inclusive or especially entertaining. While this analysis provided insights into students' multilingual practices, cross-cultural communication was just one narrow dimension and not particularly fruitful in our analysis here, as our data suggested that other dynamics (e.g. variable literacy levels) were more influential (Vanek, King and Bigelow 2018). Intercultural or cross-cultural are thus less useful or applicable terms in superdiverse contexts that are defined by hybridity and fluidity.

21.4   Linguistic or Communicative Repertoire

Linguistic or communicative repertoire, generally defined as the set of language varieties used in the speaking and writing practices of a speech community, has been a key concept across nearly all of my work. What has shifted more in my analytical focus is how speech community is defined and operationalized. My early work sought to identify the communicative norms and to describe the linguistic repertoires across two highland Ecuadorian Indigenous communities: one which was more geographically remote, more economically fragile and more bilingual (Tambopamba), and one which was centrally located (to the highway and main town), home to more professionals and with fewer speakers of Quichua and more Spanish monolinguals.

More recent work, in turn, has moved away from these attempts at comprehensive descriptions, and instead focused on how learners take up particular aspects of their repertoire in everyday classroom contexts, and how emergent multilingual students negotiate those stances with peers. For instance, our recent work has examined how older adolescents draw on humour and word play in English and Somali to keep each other (more or less) 'on task' while doing rather dry classroom activities (King, Bigelow and Hirsi 2018). Our analytical goal here was not so much to describe the communicative repertoire of these students (much less of the entire classroom), but rather, to analyse how students utilized aspects of their repertoire to (dis)engage from classroom tasks while in the process of acquiring both English and initial literacy skills.

21.5   Translanguaging

Finally, the field has seen dramatic shifts in the conceptualization of language alternation, code-switching and translanguaging in recent decades. While translanguaging initially referred to the 'planned and systematic' use of two languages within the same classroom lesson (Williams 1994, see Lewis, Jones and Baker 2012), the term has taken on a much broader set of meanings in the last decade or so (García 2009). Translanguaging – and related constructs such as heteroglossia, codemeshing, code-switching and multilanguaging – embrace a holistic view of bilingualism and bilinguals, emphasizing speakers' 'creative and critical construction and use of interrelated language features' (García, Ibarra Johnson and Seltzer 2017, pp. 20–21). For García and her colleagues (2017), translanguaging refers to 'both the complex language practices of multilingual individuals and communities and to the pedagogical approaches that draw on the them to build the language practices desired in formal school settings' (p. 20).

Code-switching, in turn, refers to a widely documented style of speech in which bilinguals alternate between languages; this line of research, which dates back to the 1970s, has documented the ways in which code-switching is rule-governed, systematic and pragmatically nuanced (MacSwan 2017). While code-switching research has demonstrated the ways in which bilinguals' two grammatical systems are differentiated (work that is supported by research on bilingual first language acquisition as well; see MacSwan 2017 for a helpful overview), work on translanguaging has emphasized 'the ways that bilinguals use their language repertoires, *from their own perspectives*, and not from the perspective of national or standard languages' (emphasis in the original, García, Ibarra Johnson and Seltzer 2017 p. 20).

My dissertation work was informed by this foundational work in code-switching, language contact and language borrowing. This research was in line with the work of the time, as evident, for instance, in how 'Spanish' and 'Quichua' were conceptualized as distinct, 'countable' systems, with my analysis perhaps (over)emphasizing the distinctiveness (rather than the naturalness) of these language alternation practices.

My more recent work, influenced by translanguaging approaches to pedagogical practice, has demonstrated how Somali language and literacy practices can support student identities, academic learning and multilingual/literacy development. This approach appears to be particularly well suited and productive for adolescences with emergent print skills and interrupted schooling.

While our collective theorizing on this topic has deepened and evolved, there is still work to do and points of disagreement remain. For instance, there is broad agreement that translanguaging approaches offer potentially productive contributions to our understandings of pedagogy, policy and ideologies surrounding multilingual learners. However, more controversial are translanguaging scholars' accounts of bilinguals' grammatical knowledge as undifferentiated (MacSwan 2017). As an alternative, MacSwan offers what he terms a 'multilingual perspective on translanguaging', in which multilingualism is real and universal to all humans, and wherein 'code-switching may be seen as an instance of translanguaging, alongside other bilingual phenomena such as translation, borrowing, etc.' (p. 191). How this proposal will be taken up and revised by the next generation of scholars is yet to be seen, but is sure to be interesting.

REFERENCES

Alladina, S. and Edwards, V. K. (1991). *Multilingualism in the British Isles: The Older Mother Tongues and Europe*, vol 1. Harlow: Longman Publishing Group.

Appadurai, A. (1996). *Modernity at Large: Cultural Dimensions of Globalization*, vol. 1. Minneapolis: University of Minnesota Press.

Bakhtin, M. M. (1981). In Michael Holquist, ed., *The Dialogic Imagination: Four Essays*. Austin: University of Texas Press

Bigelow, M. and King, K. (in progress). Teaching and learning language and literacy among refugee adolescents (working title). *Annual Review of Applied Linguistics*.

Bigelow, M. and King, K. A. (2015). Somali immigrant youths and the power of print literacy. *Writing Systems Research* 4–19. https://doi.org/10.1080/17586801.2014.896771

Clark, J. S. B. and Dervin, F. (2014). *Reflexivity in Language and Intercultural Education: Rethinking Multilingualism and Interculturality*, Vol. 2, New York: Routledge.

Davies, A. (2003). *The Native Speaker: Myth and Reality*, (Vol. 38). Clevedon, UK: Multilingual Matters.

De Fina, A., Ikizoglu, D. and Wegner, J. (2017). *Diversity and Super-Diversity: Sociocultural Linguistic Perspectives*. Washington, DC: Georgetown University Press.

Flores, N. and Rosa, J. (2015). Undoing appropriateness: Raciolinguistic ideologies and language diversity in education. *Harvard Educational Review* 85(2), 149–171

García, O. (2009). *Bilingual Education in the 21st Century: A Global Perspective*. Malden, MA: Basil Blackwell.

García, O., Ibarra Johnson, S. and Seltzer, J. (2017). *The Translanguaging Classroom: Leveraging Student Bilingualism for Learning*. Philadelphia: Calson, Inc.

Hornberger, N. H. (1987). Bilingual education and Quechua language maintenance in Highland Puno, Peru. *NABE Journal* 11(2), 117–140.

    (2000). Bilingual education policy and practice in the Andes: Ideological paradox and intercultural possibility. *Anthropology & Education Quarterly* 31(2), 173–201.

Hornberger, N. H. and King, K. A. (1996). Language revitalization in the Andes: Can the schools reverse language shift? *Journal of Multilingual and Multicultural Development* 17(6), 427–441.

Hornberger, N. H. and López, L. E. (1998). Policy, possibility and paradox: Indigenous multilingualism and education in Peru and Bolivia. In J. Cenoz and F. Genesee, eds., *Beyond Bilingualism: Multilingualism and Multilingual Education*. Clevedon: Multilingual Matters, pp. 206–242.

Hymes, D. (1980). *Language in Education: Ethnolinguistic Essays. Language and Ethnography Series*. Center for Applied Linguistics, 3520 Prospect Street, NW, Washington, DC 20007.

King, K. A. (2001). *Language Revitalization Processes and Prospects: Quichua in the Ecuadorian Andes*. Clevedon: Multilingual Matters Press.

King, K. A., Bigelow, M. and Hirsi, A. (2017). New to school and New to print: Everyday peer interaction among adolescent high school newcomers. *International Multilingual Research Journal* 11(3), 137–151.

Krauss, M. (1996). Status of Native American language endangerment. In J. Reyhner, ed., *Stabilizing Indigenous Languages*. Flagstaff, AZ: Northern Arizona University Center for Excellence in Education, pp. 16–21.

Lewis, G., Jones, B. and Baker, C. (2012). Translanguaging: Origins and development from school to street and beyond. *Educational Research and Evaluation* 18(7), 641–654.

MacSwan, J. (2017). A multilingual perspective on translanguaging. *American Educational Research Journal* 54(1), 167–201.

Mansour, G. (1993). *Multilingualism and Nation Building*, Vol. 91. Clevedon: Multilingual Matters.

Martin-Jones, M. and Martin, D. (2017). *Research Multilingualism*. New York: Routledge.

Peirce, B. N. (1995). Social identity, investment, and language learning. *TESOL Quarterly* 29(1), 9–31.

Pennycook, A. and Makoni, S. (2006). *Disinventing and Reconstituting Languages*. Clevedon, UK: Multilingual matters.

Skutnabb-Kangas, T. (1995). Multilingualism and the education of minority children. In O. García and C. Baker, eds., *Policy and Practice in Bilingual Education: Extending the Foundations*. Clevedon, UK: Multilingual Matters, pp. 40–62.

Valdés, G. (2015). Latin@s and the intergenerational continuity of Spanish: The challenges of curricularizing language. *International Multilingual Research Journal* 9(4), 253–273.

Vanek, J., King, K. A. and Bigelow, M. (2018). Social presence and identity: Facebook in an English language classroom. *Journal of Language, Identity and Education* 4, 236–254.

Vertovec, S. (2007). Super-diversity and its implications. *Ethnic and Racial Studies* 30 (6), 1024–1054.

Williams, C. (1994). Arfarniad o ddulliau dysgu ac addysgu yng nghyd-destun addysg uwchradd ddwyieithog [An evaluation of teaching and learning methods in the context of bilingual secondary education]. Unpublished doctoral dissertation, University of Wales, Bangor.

Wyman, L. T., McCarty, T. L. and Nicholas, S. E. (2013). *Indigenous Youth and Multilingualism: Language Identity, Ideology, and Practice in Dynamic Cultural Worlds*. New York: Routledge.

22 Possible Selves

Claire Kramsch

22.1 My Linguistic Biography

Growing up as I did at the confluence of four different languages, language was for me, from the start, always a focus of attention and a source of endless mirth. Together with my French brothers and sisters, I made fun of my English mother's anglicized French, of my French father's Gallic intonations in English, of my Polish relatives' Yiddish, and of my Hungarian grandmother's heavy Danube basin accent in whatever language she spoke. With my mother's family, misunderstandings were legion, culture was always an excuse for inappropriate behavior, and language was always an opportunity for jokes and ridicule. I longed to have a French mother like everyone else. My French relatives, on the other hand, staunchly Franco-French but fluent in German, never dared to speak English and, after three wars with the Germans, never cared to speak German, but were well versed in German music, literature, and philosophy, which they discussed: in French. I grew up during the Occupation and spent the war years down in the Dordogne with my French grandmother, while my parents stayed in Paris. Those five war years were decisive in many respects for my relation to language and culture, and for the notion of symbolic competence that I developed much later in another part of the world.

Every night, sitting in her wicker armchair in the living room, our grandmother would read to us from a thick book of German fairytales that had been given to her in 1904 by a certain Maria Braun, a German nanny she had brought back from Germany to help her raise her own children before WWI. It carried a dedication, *"Dem Andenken gewidmet"* [In memoriam]. Adjusting her reading glasses, she would follow with her finger the undecipherable signs enclosed within the golden illuminated borders of each page, and translate for us directly from German into French a magical world filled with poor but beautiful young girls, who were mistreated by cruel stepmothers and saved by wandering knights. "Alors, Mémé, raconte!" [Go on, Mémé, tell the story!]: "Mais attendez, mes enfants, il faut d'abord que je lise!" [But wait, children, I first have to read!]. My grandmother searches for the right word, the proper turn of phrase. Slowly, she goes back and forth between an unknown world of

Figure 22.1 This illustration by Gustave Doré of the famous fable Le corbeau et le renard [The crow and the fox] by Jean de La Fontaine (1668) captures my love of folklore and languages of all kind. It expresses my interest in the symbolic power games we all play to obtain through words what we need to ensure our physical and social survival

mysterious forests and romantic castles and our daily life in Vichy France. Our eyes wander toward the burlap-covered walls of the living room where our grandmother has attached a map of Europe and North Africa. Color-headed pins show the advances of the Wehrmacht and of the Allies during that terrible winter of 1942. Every night, after listening clandestinely to the BBC on our little radio, she goes and moves the pins once we have gone to bed.

Rumors abound of collaboration with the Germans, resistance, denunciations. There is the terrifying arrival in the village of an SS German unit on April 3, 1944. They set the eleventh-century old castle on fire and deported the owners to Dachau before marching on to Oradour-sur-Glane. I know nothing of the trips my grandmother made every year before the war to the Wagner festival in Bayreuth nor the music classes she took in Passau, and I don't know any of the German composers listed on the program of the piano concerts she gave in Paris. I don't know where nor when she had learned German, nor why she was so proud of speaking such good German that people took her for a native speaker. And I don't know why she insisted on having a German nanny to speak German with her children. All I know is that we are at war again with the Germans, *les Boches*, and that on August 25, 1944 sitting at that little radio, I see for the first time my grandmother cry. Paris has just been liberated.

Back in Paris, I am ten and I start learning German in school. My mother, who in the meantime has progressed so far in her mastery of the French language that she can go shopping on her own, returns home from the market one day and expresses her dismay at the exorbitant price of oranges. "I asked him: 'How much, your oranges?' He said: 'Forty francs the kilo'. And I said: 'Que-oua (quoi ?= Whaaaaaat?)'." This manner of splitting the word "Quoi" was so un-French that we burst out laughing and my father, didactic as always, exclaimed, "Mais de quoi de quoi?," expressing strong disagreement with my mother's pronunciation. She in turn makes an angry comparison between the market vendor and Napoleon, whom she hates and my father admires. There we go again and the dinner conversation moves from Austerlitz to Waterloo. I realize once again that the dialogue between cultures is full of unexpected traps. My English is most rudimentary. I understand what is said, but I have a strong French accent when I speak it and I never learned how to read and write in it. The English language evokes for me a world with which I do not wish to identify. I go to Germany in 1952 to perfect my German. I notice for the first time that my French world is seen differently on the other side of the border. My culture shock is profound. The first German I encounter is a former POW who, when I tell him about the atrocities committed by the German occupying forces in France during the war, exclaims, *"Die Franzosen hatten doch den Krieg verloren, warum haben Sie noch Widerstand geleistet? Das war unfair!"* [The French had lost the war, why did you resist? It was unfair]. The second German I encounter is an elderly woman from Silesia. As she tells me about her childhood in Breslau around WWI she suddenly says, *"An dem Tag hatten wir schulfrei, denn es war Sedantag"*[(on that day we didn't have school because it was Sedan day]. It takes a while for me to realize that from the German point of view the battle of Sedan in 1870 was not an ignominious defeat but a day of national celebration. I begin to understand that my French identity has been shaped by a certain historical discourse that in other countries is not self-evident and is not equally shared on the other side of the English Channel or the Rhine.

I was not particularly good at German, but I became obsessed with the fundamental lack of understanding between people, despite their efforts to speak each other's language. I just couldn't believe in a genetic code of nations that makes them intrinsically good or bad, as many in France seemed to think after the war. Like many of my French colleagues who studied German with me at the Sorbonne after the war and became, like me, German teachers, I thought that by learning the language of the enemy and marrying a German I was not only contributing to the building of Europe, but I was building bridges between incompatible worldviews. Moving to the United States in 1965 provided me with a third place from where to explore the momentous questions I had brought with me from war-torn Europe. However, as I was teaching German at M.I.T, I realized once again that I really did not understand my American students, nor did they really understand me. For instance, why did they always talk about having "agency" or of making good "choices"? Goethe and Schiller certainly didn't help in understanding America.

Once again, folktales and storytelling came to the rescue. Through the bedtime stories I was telling my own children at the time, I reconnected with my love of myth and fairytales of various kinds. Vladimir Propp's *Morphology of the Folktale* (1968) had just been translated into English, and I was seduced by his structural analyses of Russian folktales that formed a bridge to the structural approach I was using to teach German at the time. Through Clifford Geertz, Erwin Goffman, Emanuel Schegloff, as well as Henry Widdowson, I discovered that form and structure carried meaning and that the link between form and meaning was discourse. By sheer serendipity, I discovered at Harvard not only a treasure trove of scholarship on folklore and oral literature but also a whole research group on discourse and narrative. They opened up for me, beyond linguistic structures, the world of living speakers and writers, living storytellers as well as national narratives and ideologies. They helped me understand the social and historical discourses my students were reproducing in their attempts to learn German. For instance, when they wrote that Gregor Samsa in Kafka's *Metamorphosis* had "lost control" (*die Kontrolle verloren*) over his life, and that he now had to make "hard choices," I now recognized an American discourse of individualism and personal agency that spoke through them and that, I realized, forms the bedrock of American self-understanding. I got hooked on discourse studies and switched fields from German Literature to Applied Linguistics.

22.2   Key Concepts

My first attempts to capture my new insights into the relation of language as discourse were my two books *Discourse Analysis and Second Language Teaching*, published in the United States in 1981, and *Interaction et Discours dans la Classe de Langue*, published in France in 1984. These two books clearly lay the ground for a conception of culture as enacted through the turns-at-talk, the management of topics, and the conversational tasks of daily interactions. They were not affiliated with the intercultural movement associated with the work of Michael Byram, whose 1989 book gave the concept of culture a slightly different meaning. Coming as he did from British cultural studies and education, Byram lay the ground for a social psychological view of culture and the intercultural. My 1993 book *Context and Culture in Language Teaching* showed my interest in culture and thus was read as contributing to Byram's work, but it retained an explicit link to discourse studies and to the work of Ron Scollon and Deborah Tannen in sociolinguistics, A. L. Becker in linguistic anthropology, and Homi Bhabha in critical theory. Culture, I argued, is not a fixed set of beliefs, practices, and institutions common to members of a given community but a process negotiated through discourse and interaction between living speakers and hearers, writers, and readers (Kramsch 1985; Kramsch 1998). In other words, as Street and Thompson would say later, "culture is a verb" (Street and Thompson 1993) The concept of "third place," which I borrowed from Homi Bhabha (1994), was a convenient metaphor to characterize the subject position of the language learner who was operating, so to speak, "between languages" (MLA Report 2007; Kramsch 2009a, p. 249). Despite my sympathy toward what Byram later called "intercultural communicative competence" (Byram 1997), I never saw myself as belonging to the field of intercultural communication. Instead, I always considered myself to be in Applied Language Studies or Applied Sociolinguistics (Kramsch 2002) and have criticized the intercultural movement for its neglect of the discourse dimension (Kramsch 2009b).

By the end of the nineties, at a time when globalization was starting to pick up speed, I had not abandoned my hope to build bridges between people who don't share the same worldviews, but with the spread of English as a Lingua Franca, social media, and global media, the world seemed to become more and more homogeneous. When, in the early 2000s, global migrations and computer-mediated technologies reframed the relationship of language and culture from the intercultural/transnational to the global/multilingual, I welcomed the opportunity to coordinate with Genevieve Zarate and Daniele Levy an edited volume on plurilingualism (Zarate et al. 2008), and to espouse what Stephen May later termed "the multilingual turn" in SLA (May 2014), but I had no illusion that multilingualism was bringing about more peace and understanding around the world.

Up to that time, I had not considered myself to be multilingual. I happened to have grown up knowing and living in different languages and cultures but I remained, in my view, staunchly monolingual in each of these languages. Code-switching was not seen favorably in my family and I never thought I was teaching my students how to become bi- or multilingual. As far as I was concerned, I was trying to bring them as close as possible to the proficiency of an idealized native speaker. However, with the advent of globalization, the monolingual native speaker became less and less justified as a target of instruction, and the multilingualism of minority, immigrant, and refugee speakers became worthy of scholarly interest. At the same time, interest in late modernity made the writings of Anthony Giddens and Mikhail Bakhtin relevant to research in second language learning. In particular, Bakhtin's concept of "heteroglossia" (Holquist 1990) enriched my conceptualization of language teaching practice. I started seeing the classroom as a heteroglossic environment in which teachers and learners strive to tell the richest story possible (Kramsch 1989) by opening up spaces for as many voices as possible (Kramsch and Huffmaster 2009; Huffmaster and Kramsch 2015). Bakhtin's concepts of "dialogicality" and "answerability" (Holquist 1990) brought in the ethical dimension of multilingualism that has found its way into the more recently published Kramsch (2009c) and Kramsch and Zhang (2018).

By the early decade of the new century, it was clear that communicative language teaching had not brought about the deeper "expression, interpretation and negotiation of meaning" that it had promised in the eighties (e.g. Breen and Candlin 1980), but rather had been watered down to a mere exchange of factual information and to the "communication for communication's sake of social media" (Castells 2009). And that the lack of understanding among people and nations had increased, not decreased, as a consequence of globalization. The hopes raised by the spread of English as a global language were dampened by the realization that true understanding could only be achieved by struggling through the very languages that separate us, not through one lingua franca. This struggle was, in my mind, a struggle for symbolic power and for the survival of what Terrence Deacon has termed "the symbolic species" (Deacon 1997), that is, our uniquely human ability to make meaning. I felt that the notion of communicative competence, which Dell Hymes had coined (Hymes 1972) in contradistinction to Chomsky's competence *versus* performance, had to be reframed as "symbolic competence." Symbolic competence would include the ability to express, interpret, and negotiate the referential and pragmatic meanings of symbols, but it would also include a dimension of symbolic power: the power to understand the historical density of symbolic structures, the power to reframe the meaning of a situation or activity, and to find a satisfactory subject position between languages (Kramsch 2006). Such symbolic competence was eminently displayed in the study by Anne Whiteside of undocumented Yucatec immigrants in the Bay Area in California and of the way they used Maya, Spanish, and English in their daily interactions with Chinese and Vietnamese merchants in the Mission district of San Francisco (Kramsch and Whiteside 2008).

22.3   Symbolic Competence and Its Variations

The fate of the notion of symbolic competence became immediately intertwined with various other related notions that sprung up around that time and that all attempted to capture the multicultural and multilingual dimensions of communication across cultures. Byram's *intercultural communicative competence*, drawing from social psychology and British cultural studies, focused on attitudes and values in the dialogue between members of different national cultures (Byram 1997). The MLA's *transcultural competence* focused on linguistic, social, and historical consciousness (MLA 2007). Sharifian's *metacultural competence* was based on insights from cognitive psychology (Sharifian 2013). While these three notions maintained the national boundaries between languages and cultures, others were more radical and put into question the very integrity of individual linguistic systems. García's notion of *translanguaging* (García 2009; García and LiWei 2014) and Canagarajah's *translingual practice* (Canagarajah 2013a) redefined the very boundaries between linguistic codes and drew their inspiration from the verbal practices of bi- and multilinguals, who mesh codes according to the needs of the moment. Canagarajah's *performative competence* (Canagarajah 2013b) grew out of the observation of multilingual speakers in international encounters in a global economy.

By contrast, *symbolic competence*, with its ecological flavor and its strong critical discourse component, brings in the element of symbolic power that was missing from communicative competence (Kramsch 2020). This power is the power of history, memory, and the imagination to transform present social reality. While the other notions proposed in this chapter capture the actual processes and practices of communication across cultures in the here-and-now, symbolic competence aims at transforming the very worldview within which these other notions operate by linking it to the past and the future. In a metaphorical sense, it attempts to bring together "Sedan-as-national-defeat" and "Sedan-as-national-victory" and transform both into one of the events that lay the ground historically for the building of the united Europe we have today. It also plays a role in current attempts to resolve the tension between nationalism and neoliberal cosmopolitanism in the Europe of tomorrow.

Given the current neoliberal trends of thought that have commodified education, instrumentalized the teaching of foreign languages, and even weaponized language as psychological warfare, a notion such as symbolic competence has been difficult to operationalize. Indeed, it goes against an educational system that has associated "competence" with assessment and control procedures (see the CEFR) and with the ability of learners to regurgitate knowledge bites on worksheets and multiple choice tests. It also goes against the grain of the devaluation of language that we see in our current public life. As it seeks to make language and content inseparable, it strives to rehabilitate the reading of literature and the practice of literary translation.

Given its broad theoretical underpinnings, the notion of symbolic competence has inspired an equally broad range of scholars to rethink the epistemological, cultural, and aesthetic foundations of foreign language education. In the United Kingdom, Li Wei (2017) has recently attempted to reframe language theory in light of translanguaging and symbolic competence, and scholars in Germany are reframing the teaching of literature in language classes (Altmayer et al. 2014), to do justice to the symbolic aspects of language in literary texts (Riedner 2015). In Canada, Ryuko Kubota is rethinking Japanese language instruction in light of the critical historical consciousness that symbolic competence can bring (Kubota 2012, 2017). In the United States, Kimberly Vinall has proposed ways of using the concept for raising the political and historical consciousness of learners of Spanish at the college level (Vinall 2012, 2016); and Claire Kramsch and Lihua Zhang have recently applied the relational and transformative pedagogy implied by the concept of symbolic competence to the teaching of German and Chinese, respectively (Kramsch and Zhang 2018).

In the same way as the symbolic power of language has shaped my biography, so has it shaped the lives of many foreign language students, and showed us the many possible selves that we could be. Symbolic competence does not prescribe a course of action to bring about understanding across various levels of historicity and subjectivity; rather it gives us insights on how symbolic systems shape and in turn are shaped by who we are (Kramsch 2020). Ultimately, it enables us to manipulate symbols with greater understanding and with greater respect for their awesome symbolic power.

REFERENCES

Altmayer, C., Dobstadt, M., Riedner, R., and Schier, C. (2014). *Literatur in Deutsch als Fremdsprache und internationaler Germanistik: Konzepte, Themen, Forschungsperspektiven*. Tuebingen: Stauffenburg Verlag.
Bakhtin, M. (1981). *The Dialogic Imagination*. Austin: University of Texas Press.
Bhabha, H. (1994). *The Location of Culture*. London: Routledge
Breen, M. and Candlin, C. N. (1980). The essentials of a communicative curriculum in language teaching. *Applied Linguistics* 1(2), 89–110.
Byram, M. (1989). *Cultural Studies in Foreign Language Education*. Clevedon: Multilingual Matters
(1997). *Teaching and Assessing Intercultural Communicative Competence*. Clevedon: Multilingual Matters.
Canagarajah, S. (2013a). *Translingual Practice*. London: Routledge
(2013b). From intercultural rhetoric to cosmopolitan practice: Addressing new challenges in Lingua Franca English. In D. Belcher, and G. Nelson, eds., *Critical and Corpus-Based Approaches to Intercultural Rhetoric*. Ann Arbor: University of Michigan Press, pp. 203–226.
Castells, M. (2009). *Communication power*. Oxford: Oxford University Press.
Deacon, T. (1997). *The Symbolic Species. The Coevolution of Language and the Brain*. New York: Penguin.
García, O. (2009). *Bilingual Education in the 21st Century: A Global Perspective*. Oxford: Basil Blackwell.
García, O. and Li Wei (2014). *Translanguaging: Language, Bilingualism and Education*. New York: Palgrave Macmillan.
Holquist, M. (1990). *Dialogism: Bakhtin and His World*. London: Routledge.
Huffmaster, M. and Kramsch, C. (2015). Multilingual practices in foreign language study. In J. Cenoz and D. Gorter, eds., *Multilingual Education: New Perspectives*. London: Routledge, pp. 114–136.

Hymes, D. (1972/2006). On communicative competence. In A. Pride, J.B. & Holmes, J., eds., *Sociolinguistics*. London: Routledge, pp. 269–293.

Kramsch, C. (1981). *Discourse Analysis and Second Language Teaching*. Language in Education: Theory and Practice, Vol. 37. Washington, DC: Center for Applied Linguistics.

(1984). *Interaction et discours dans la classe de langue*. Paris: Hatier-Credif.

(1985). *Reden, Mitreden, Dazwischenreden. Managing Conversations in German*. Textbook, Instructor's manual and cassette. Boston: Heinle and Heinle.

(1989). *Discourse and Text: A Narrative View of the Foreign Language Lesson, Georgetown University Round Table on Languages and Linguistics*. Washington, DC: Georgetown University Press, pp. 69–80.

(1993). *Context and Culture in Language Teaching*. Oxford: Oxford University Press.

(1998). *Language and Culture*. Oxford: Oxford University Press.

(2002). In search of the intercultural: Review article. *Journal of Sociolinguistics* 6(2), 275–285.

(2006). From communicative competence to symbolic competence. *Modern Language Journal* 90(2), 249–252.

(2009a). Third culture and language education. In V. Cook and L. Wei, eds., *Contemporary Applied Linguistics: Vol.1 V. Cook, ed., Language Teaching and Learning*. London: Continuum, pp. 233–254.

(2009b). Discourse, the symbolic dimension of intercultural competence. In A. Hu and M. Byram, eds., *Intercultural Competence and Foreign Language Learning: Models, Empirical Studies Assessment*. Tübingen: Gunter Narr, pp. 107–122.

(2009c). *The Multilingual Subject: What Foreign Language Learners Say about Their Experience and Why It Matters*. Oxford: Oxford University Press.

(2011). The symbolic dimensions of the intercultural. *Language Teaching* 44(3), 354–367.

(2020). *Language as Symbolic Power*. Cambridge: Cambridge University Press.

Kramsch, C. and Huffmaster, M. (2008). The political promise of translation. In E. Burwitz-Melzer, ed., *Lehren und Lernen mit literarischen Texten*. Special issue of *Fremdsprachenlehren- und lernen* 37, pp. 283–297.

Kramsch, C. and Whiteside, A. (2008). Language ecology in multilingual settings: Towards a theory of symbolic competence. *Applied Linguistics* 29(4), 645–671.

Kramsch, C. and Zhang, L. (2018). *The Multilingual Instructor: What Foreign Language Teachers Say about Their Experience and Why It Matters*. Oxford: Oxford University Press.

Kubota, R. (2012). Memories of war: Exploring victim-victimizer perspectives in critical content-based instruction in Japanese. *L2 Journal* 4, 37–57.

(2017). 'We must look at both sides' – but denial of genocide, too? Difficult moments on controversial issues in the classroom. *Critical Inquiry in Language Studies* 11, 225–251.

Li Wei (2017). Rethinking language in translanguaging: Implications for learning, use, and policy. Plenary speech delivered at the AAAL Annual Meeting in Portland, OR on March 18.

May, S. (2014). *The Multilingual Turn: Implications for SLA, TESOL and Bilingual Education*. London: Routledge.

Modern Language Association (MLA) AdHoc Committee on Foreign Languages (2007). Foreign languages and higher education: New structures for a changed world. *Profession* 2007, 234–244.

Polanyi, M. (1958). *Personal Knowledge: Towards a Post-Critical Philosophy.* Chicago: University of Chicago Press.

Propp, V. (1968). *The Morphology of the Folktale.* Trsl. Lawrence Scott. Bloomington: Indiana University Press.

Riedner, R. (2015). Das Konzept der symbolic competence (Claire Kramsch) im Schnittpunkt von Linguistik, Kulturwissenschaft und Fremdsprachendidaktik. In M. Dobstadt, C. Fandrych, and R. Riedner, eds., *Linguistik und Kulturwissenschaft. Zu ihrem Verhaeltnis aus der Perspektive des Faches Deutsch als Fremd- und Zweitsprache und anderer Disziplinen.* Bern: Peter Lang, pp. 129–150.

Sharifian, F. (2013). Globalisation and developing metacultural competence in learning English as an International Language. *Multilingual Education* 3(7). https://doi.org/10.1186/2191-5059-3-7

Street, B. V. and Thompson, L. (1993). Cultural is a verb: Anthropological aspects of language and cultural process. In D. Graddol and M. Byram, eds., *Language and Culture.* Clevedon: BAAL in association with Multilingual Matters, pp. 23–43.

Vinall, K. (2012). *¿Un legado histórico?*: Symbolic competence and the construction of multiple histories. *L2 Journal* 4, 102–123.

(2016). "Got Llorona?": Teaching for the development of symbolic competence. *L2 Journal* 8(1), 1–16.

Zarate, G., Levy, D., and Kramsch, C. (2008). *Précis du plurilinguisme et du pluriculturalisme.* Paris: Éditions des Archives Contemporaines.

23 Feeling at Home across Languages, Schools and Countries

Emmanuelle Le Pichon-Vorstman

I am a linguist who works on the concepts of *language awareness*, *foreign languages*, *mother tongues*, *language of schooling*, *multilingualism* and *literacy*, and more recently, with *translanguaging*, in particular with regard to the school and higher learning education context. All of these concepts refer to a specific attitude of someone towards the society in which he/she lives. Each of us could give a different nuance to these concepts depending on his or her own linguistic and cultural backgrounds. How should the education system make sense of these diverse trajectories?

I was born and raised in France and I was exposed almost exclusively to the French language until the moment I started to learn English at school and then, subsequently, German. At that time, both English and German were *foreign languages* for me, because I heard those languages only in the context of 'the foreign language classroom'. After high school, I spent a year in a non-governmental organisation in Italy and I learned the Italian language to a reasonable level within three months only by being immersed in it every day, all day long. The common roots of the Italian language with my own facilitated *inter-comprehension* and helped me tremendously to make sense not only of the semantic, syntactic and morphologic rules but also of the pragmatic ones. After a year, I was not only fluent but also in love with the language, the country and the people; I had found my way in Italy without having set foot in a language classroom. Back to France, I met my future husband, who was Dutch. I soon came to live in the Netherlands, where I started to learn the Dutch language at the University of Amsterdam with students from all over the world. We all needed to pass the required exam at the end of the year to be able to continue our academic study or to find a suitable job. I also vividly remember my struggles with understanding the culture, politeness rules, way of socialising, management of time and space . . . it took me two years to feel at ease in The Netherlands instead of three months in Italy. This time, my native language and culture did not help me; they were more in the way. I disliked the pauses in conversations and my own conversational habits got me into situations of discomfort, accentuating the mismatch

Figure 23.1 One of my brothers, at the time a newly arrived political refugee, is in the centre. We surround him and he surrounds me with his arms. So much of what I received from my family is captured in this photo

between me and them. Perhaps consequently, my friends tended to be mainly people from abroad. Together we spoke Dutch, English, sometimes Italian, and some spoke Arabic or German. The goal was to communicate, not to impose one language and culture on the other. We were all equal, as we all had to cope with a society that we had difficulty understanding. A positive side effect was that we all opened up to other cultures, trying to understand each other and breaking through our situation of isolation, thus bridging the gap with intercultural understanding and intercultural communication and forming a little international transcultural community of students.

When my first child was born, it was for me of vital importance to raise her in the French language. Why? French was the language in which I could transfer my emotions and feelings through songs, poems, stories or kind words of which I owned all the nuances and meanings. I also believe that I wanted my daughter to be recognised by French people as French. Now, with hindsight, I dare to say that I was projecting on her my own identity. But, as these things tend to go in life, she developed her own identity, which was one firmly grounded in two languages and cultures. Two languages? Quite early in our marriage, our oldest had just turned six, we went to live in the United States for a couple of years. When we came back, the oldest had learned to speak, write and read in English and French at school and I had discovered the cognitive benefits of multilingual education. The topic even became the subject of my PhD thesis. My daughter felt confident in the three languages even though her competences in these languages were unequally developed. In 2009, Moore proposed that if teachers make use of the interrelation of the languages, if they reflect on these languages and if the languages are imbedded into the classroom routine, then multilingualism becomes an asset (Moore 2009; see also Cummins 1991; Benson 2002; Herzog-Punzenberger, Le Pichon-Vorstman and Siarova, 2017). After we moved back to the Netherlands, I witnessed up close how she just needed to transfer the skills she had acquired in French and English to the Dutch language. One doesn't learn to read twice: once you have learned a skill in one language, you just transfer that skill to the other. So, let me describe my daughter at age nine: three unequal competences, in three languages and cultures. So here is my question: Which one is her *mother tongue*? The experience of my own children has suggested an answer to me: these three languages simply all belong to her.

At the moment, the concept of *inclusion* is going viral. This is understandable; we all want our schools and our societies to be inclusive. There is also a more strategic aspect to this attitude; at the higher education level, we all desperately try to find ways to attract more and more international students. So, on the one hand, we embrace the *internationalisation* that we see as an enrichment of our societies and institutions. The term 'enrichment' can be interpreted both in a figurative and in a literal way: the richness of multiple cultures but also more international students means a stable economy and the possibility of growing. Both aspects are important, justified in their own right and motivate policymakers to act. On the other hand, *internationalisation* also means that we have an obligation to include students from all over the world. It implies that we have to organise our systems in such a way that different language repertoires are adequately accommodated. This is not always easy. In the Netherlands for instance, university teachers are required to be able to teach in English, if needed. For instance, even if only one student in the course did not understand Dutch, I was required to switch to the English language. This represents an important change in policy. When I entered Utrecht University in 2006, it was not yet a requirement. One was supposed to be able to give a course in one's own language of speciality and in the official language (i.e. Dutch). Thus, what appeared quite recently is the notion of bilateral effort (teacher and student) as opposed to monolateral. Internationalisation means that teachers and students work together to facilitate communication in order to reach a higher level of literacy and, little by little, together, they change the identity of the university. Thus, education in literacy and communication seem to be the emergent key concepts which are somehow dethroning the concept of education in the national language. This development in education shows that the use of languages is in essence dynamic and that the education system should reflect this dynamism. Gogolin and her colleagues suggested that the education system should follow a biographical, thematic and plurilingual continuity (Gogolin et al. 2011, pp. 55–59) in order to foster the student's development. However, this approach implies a whole school and consistent multilingual pedagogy across all subjects taught.

Let's continue the story of my daughter. At the age of twelve, she started secondary school and had to learn two foreign languages: English and French. Foreign? These languages were not foreign for her. All of a sudden something very strange happened: when she would have been legitimate in either a French schooling system or in an English schooling system, she became illegitimate in the French foreign language classroom within the Dutch school system. She was bored. She was also perceived as a threat by some teachers as they found it difficult to have a student with better skills than they had themselves in the target language. However, luckily enough, she also got to learn German, and there she was legitimate. She could work hard for it and learned the language fast, an advantage that also partly depended on her plurilingualism. The enhanced *metacognitive awareness* only needed to be supported by the environment to flourish (O'Laoire 2005; Le Pichon-Vorstman et al. 2009; Kim et al. 2015). Conversely, and at the same time, I was approached by a psychologist who was treating children suffering from selective mutism. These children are unable to speak in social environments but speak normally in the home context. Strangely enough, a large number of them were plurilingual, that is, were exposed to different languages in the home than at school (Le Pichon and de Jonge 2015). The questions that we had then were: why don't these children speak in the school context in particular and to which extent is the silence related to their individual plurilingualism? We cannot firmly answer these questions yet and more interdisciplinary research is surely needed. However, I believe that the attitude towards multilingualism within the school context may play a key role in the extent to which a child may engage in interaction. Teachers should be encouraged to recognise the plurilingualism in their students and label it positively instead of identifying it as a threat to the teacher's authority and/or to the child's ability to learn. They should view that as an asset while giving the necessary support to improve language skills and nourish thirst to learn more not only about the language but also about the people, their habits and their history, a curiosity which is specific to plurilingual and multi-country children: they link the languages to people, to communication

situated in a specific social, cultural, historical and economic context and
dependent on the participants in the exchange (Beerkens et al. 2020);
language is not foreign, rather the language is a tool to know how other people
live and think around the world here and now.

Being a plurilingual person suggests more metacognitive awareness. The
implication is that we should start thinking about encouraging the use of
transferable skills instead of discouraging the use of other languages in the
classroom. Such radical change in attitude is bound to have far reaching
implications for language learning and planning. A couple of years ago, in
my university, I started a project in which I asked students from abroad to give
feedback to our students in the languages that they were learning (French,
English, German, Italian, Spanish, Chinese, Dutch). At the end of her internship, one of the students from France wrote,

My parents were both Portuguese and I was 8 when I arrived in France. I don't have
French nationality. The institute in France refused me as a teacher of *French as a
second language*, because of that: I wasn't French. You have given me the chance to be
legitimate in a language that is mine: the French language. Thank you.

These words raised an important question: which conditions render belonging
to a particular language and community legitimate? It seems to me that the
individuals in this institute were very much reasoning from their own perspective; it is very likely that they have had an upbringing closely resembling my
own; one language, one culture and everything else in the context of foreign
language learning in a school. I strongly doubt that someone who himself grew
up in a multilingual, multicultural environment would have refused this bril-
liant student as a teacher of French as a second language. To quote Thomas
Riccento, 'normativity is the biggest enemy of social change' (Riccento 2017),
to which I would like to add that the normativity of the educational institution
is in contradiction with the process of globalisation.

However, I am beginning to see that the theme 'teaching languages in
Europe in schools' has definitively left the limits drawn by the traditional
language classrooms (Le Pichon, Siarova and Szőnyi 2020). Indeed, teaching a
language has quickly become a concept that can be relevant to different kinds
of classes, not only to the foreign classroom, but virtually to all classes where
the school language is still a language to be learned. And precisely because the
population is more and more plurilingual every class becomes a language
classroom. Currently, most of my research is on the inclusion of minority
language students in the school context. One of the current difficulties of our
schooling systems related to the inclusion of newly arrived students is the
incapacity to assess their previous learning. Examples that we have come
across in our studies include, 'language: Moroccan', or: 'the child speaks

Chinese', which show that the fact that there are different languages spoken in Morocco and China is completely ignored. In the case of the child from Moroccan parents, the child was born in Spain and had been schooled in a Spanish-speaking school. There was no mention of that language nor of his literacy in the Spanish language. Most of the students coming from abroad and entering the Dutch classroom have a complicated history of migration and, thus, of languages and cultures. The only mention of the country of provenance of this child's parents will not sufficiently help the teacher to build knowledge on previously acquired literacy.

Furthermore, guided by our own monolinguistic experiences, we invariably focus on teaching the student the language spoken at school. While this is important, in doing so we not only forget to appreciate the sometimes impressive linguistic repertoires these children already have but also the fact that they are thirsty to learn the things children want to learn at school. A too narrow focus on teaching children the school language may come at the expense of the broad array of topics (maths, geography, biology, history, etc.) the by nature curious child is longing to learn more about. One of the young students that we interviewed put it like this, 'the problem with the school here is that I had to relearn everything that I already know'. Thus, there is still a perceived conviction, deeply rooted in our ideological and political beliefs, that there is an *advantageous* bilingualism and a *disadvantageous* one, some languages being more advantageous than others. Individual plurilingualism is still perceived as partial competence in languages, with no reconfiguration over time possible, rather than a balance in skills in different languages. However, in my research, I see that schools are seeking new ways of teaching, that they are differentiating more and more and that the concept of differentiation is intrinsically linked to individual migration paths. It focuses on the linguistic and social results of contacts and also seeks alternative paths for language planning in the classroom.

A major challenge to the translation of these facts into policies is our inability to make sense of the dynamic complexity of social and linguistic representations, beliefs and practices, as well as of their effects on language planning. Further, as our awareness of the complexity of sociolinguistic phenomena has risen, we have developed new ways of thinking about and describing language and identity. However, we as scholars are often still unable to completely shed our old ways of representing, believing and practising because many of us were born and raised ourselves in a more or less monolingual and monocultural way of life (Le Pichon et al. 2020). In today's society, the borders of languages are increasingly blurred by increased mobility. It is by taking into account all these considerations that my colleague Dr Ellen-Rose Kambel and I created the Language Friendly School: our ambition is to reach beyond respect for students' languages by proactively celebrating the diversity of linguistic and cultural assets that a student brings to school (Le Pichon 2020).

REFERENCES

Beerkens, R., Le Pichon-Vorstman, E., Supheert, R., and ten Thije, J. D. (eds.). (2020). *Enhancing Intercultural Communication in Organizations: Insights from Project Advisers* (1st ed.). New York: Routledge, pp. 1–166.

Benson, C. (2002). Real and potential benefits of bilingual programmes in developing countries. *International Journal of Bilingual Education and Bilingualism* 5(6), 303–317.

Cummins, J. (1991). Interdependence of first- and second-language proficiency in bilingual children. In E. Bialystok, ed., *Language Processing in Bilingual Children*. Cambridge: Cambridge University Press, pp. 70–89.

Gogolin, I., Dirim, I., Klinger, T., Lange, I., Lengyel, D., Michael, U., Neumann, U., Reich, H., Roth, H. and Schwippert, K. (2011). *Förderung von Kindern und Jugendlichen mit Migrationshintergrund FÖRMIG: Bilanz und Perspektiven eines Modellprogramms*. Berlin: Waxmann.

Herzog-Punzenberger, B., Le Pichon-Vorstman, E. and Siarova, H. (2017). Multilingual education in the light of diversity: Lessons learned. *NESET II Report*. Luxembourg: Publications Office of the European Union. http://nesetweb.eu/wp-content/uploads/2015/08/Multilingualism-Report.pdf

Kim, T. J., Kuo, L-J., Ramirez, G., Wu, S., Ku, Y-M., de Marin, S., Ball, A., and Eslami, Z. (2015). The relationship between bilingual experience and the development of morphological and morpho-syntactic awareness: a cross-linguistic study of classroom discourse. *Language Awareness* 24(4), 332–354. https://doi.org/10.1080/09658416.2015.1113983

Le Pichon, E. (2020). Digital literacies and language-friendly pedagogies: where are we now? www.schooleducationgateway.eu/en/pub/viewpoints/experts/digital-literacies-pedagogies.htm

Le Pichon, E. and De Jonge, M. (2015). Linguistic and psychological perspectives on prolonged periods of silence in dual language learners. *International Journal of Bilingual Education and Bilingualism* 19(4), 426–441.

Le Pichon, E., Siarova, H. and Szőnyi, E. (2020). The future of language education in Europe: Case-Studies of innovative practices. *NESET II report*. Luxembourg: Publications Office of the European Union.

Le Pichon-Vorstman, E., de Swart, H., Ceginskas, V., and van den Bergh, H. (2009). Language Learning Experience in school context and metacognitive awareness of multilingual children. *International Journal of Multilingualism* 6(3), 256–280.

Le Pichon, E., Cole, D., Baauw, S., Steffens, M., van den Brink, M. and Dekker, S. (2020). Transcultural itineraries and new literacies: How migration memories could reshape school systems, In. L. Passerini, G. Proglio and M. Trakilović, eds., *The Mobility of Memory: Migrations and Diasporas across European Borders*. Berghahn, New-York. Oxford.

Moore, D. (2009). *Plurilinguismes et école*. Paris: Éditions Didier, collection LAL (Langues et apprentissage des langues).

O'Laoire, M. (2005). Three languages in the schools in Ireland. *International Journal of the Sociology of Language*. 171, 95–113.

Riccento, T. (2017). *Language Policy and Planning: The Nature and Goals of a Scholarly Tradition with Multiple Roots and Multiple Functions*. Unpublished personal communication. LPP conference 2017, Toronto.

24 From Monolingual Habitus to Plurilingual Education

David Little

24.1 My Language Biography

I was born in 1942 and brought up and educated in a monolingual environment. I began to learn French in 1953, when I started at grammar school; we were taught according to a particularly unforgiving version of the grammar/translation method. In my fourth year of learning French I took part in a two-week school visit to France during which we had little contact with native speakers. I took O-level German in the Lower Sixth and A-level German as well as French in the Upper Sixth, stayed on at school for an extra year to prepare for university entrance, and was admitted to the University of Oxford to read modern languages (French and German) in 1961.

At Oxford we were 'taught' French and German via weekly classes in 'prose composition' (translation from English into French/German); and although we were expected to read French and German literature in the original, lectures were given in English, which was also the language in which we wrote our weekly essays. By the time I graduated I had decided, with some encouragement from my French and German tutors, to become a university teacher. Staying on at Oxford to write a B.Litt. thesis on Goethe and Novalis, I was painfully aware that I needed to improve my spoken German, so I took a one-year post as *Lektor* at the *Auslands- und Dolmetscherinstitut* (Institute for Foreign Studies and Interpreting) of the University of Mainz in Germersheim (1965–1966). My conversational German did indeed improve, though my capacity to speak and write academic German remained seriously underdeveloped.

In January 1967 I was appointed to a junior lectureship in German at Trinity College Dublin. To begin with, I was required to teach two English–German translation classes (more 'prose composition'), two classes in Middle High German and two German literature classes for students in the third and fourth years of the General Studies degree. The approach was closely similar to what I had experienced at Oxford except that students were required to read many

Figure 24.1 Already beginning to worry about language

fewer books and spared the weekly tutorial essay. I had learned rather little French and German from 'prose composition', so I soon took advantage of the autonomy available to me to change my language classes, replacing translation by project work based on a German text that I chose in consultation with my students.

In 1979 I was appointed director of the newly established Centre for Language and Communication Studies (CLCS) at Trinity College. CLCS combined the functions of a university language centre with those of a linguistics department and a research institute. As director I was supposed to know how to teach and learn languages, but there were still embarrassingly large gaps in my theoretical knowledge and practical expertise. Around 1980 a group of second- and third-level language teachers got together to explore ways of making language teaching at school more communicative. Our project produced a best-selling textbook for French, and some of the proceeds were used to bring various language teaching gurus to Dublin. Most of them were no more convincing than I was. The exception, Leni Dam, preached the gospel of learner autonomy and presented us with ample evidence that her mixed-ability Danish teenagers were impressively fluent in English; their proficiency was clearly an integral part of their developing identity.

I first heard Leni Dam speak about learner autonomy in 1985 and soon afterwards began the process of deriving general principles from her practice in order to apply them to my own context. I also began to publish on learner autonomy and by the mid-1990s was regularly being invited to speak at conferences and to give talks at universities. As a result, I spent a lot of time in Germany and found that I could speak German quite fluently (though I mostly gave talks in English). What was more, membership of various Council of Europe working groups brought me into regular contact with French, which I discovered I could still speak, though less fluently than German.

By the end of the 1990s I was firmly convinced that the language learning programmes most apt to develop high levels of target language (TL) proficiency and integrated plurilingual repertoires are those in which, from the beginning, learners' agency is channelled through the TL. This entails that they use the TL individually and collaboratively to plan, execute, monitor and evaluate their own learning. I followed this approach when, in 1993, it fell to me to design and implement an Institution-Wide Language Programme for Trinity College students who were not taking a foreign language as part of their degree studies.

In 1998 I founded Integrate Ireland Language and Training (IILT), a not-for-profit campus company that was funded by the Irish government to provide intensive English language courses for adult refugees and to support the teaching of English as an Additional Language (EAL) in primary and post-primary schools. We set out to implement the principles of learner autonomy in our courses for adult refugees and used regular in-service seminars to encourage teachers of EAL to do the same. We believed that plurilingual repertoires should be cherished not only for their own sake but also because they play a vital role in their owners' formal learning. Accordingly, we devised versions of the European Language Portfolio that encouraged teachers and learners to explore linguistic and cultural similarities and differences.

Ireland's immigrant population is not spread uniformly across the school system; some schools have a linguistically diverse population and others do not. Scoil Bhríde (Cailíní), Blanchardstown, belongs to the first category. In 2015–2016 there were about 320 pupils on the roll; 80 per cent of them had a home language other than English or Irish; most of the 80 per cent had little or no English when they started school at the age of four and a half; and there were fifty-two home languages, not counting English (the school had no Irish-speaking pupils).

Déirdre Kirwan was principal of Scoil Bhríde until her retirement in 2015. In 2004 she embarked on PhD research under my supervision as a way of documenting and exploring the linguistic development of her immigrant pupils. Her research informed the evolution of Scoil Bhríde's highly innovative approach to language education, which places no restrictions on pupils' use of their home languages inside or outside the classroom. From the beginning, pupils are encouraged to volunteer comparisons between English, Irish (the obligatory second language of the curriculum) and their home language (if it isn't English or Irish); French is added to the mix in the last two years, when the pupils are aged eleven and twelve. Perhaps most important of all, with help from their parents, pupils from immigrant families transfer the literacy skills they are acquiring in English and Irish to their home language, writing parallel texts in two or three languages from an early age. Scoil Bhríde's pupils achieve unusually high levels of literacy in all their languages and unusually high levels of metalinguistic awareness. The school regularly performs above the national average in standardized tests. Since 2013, Déirdre Kirwan and I have been engaged on an extensive theoretical and practical exploration of Scoil Bhríde's approach, which we believe should be easily replicable in other contexts (Little and Kirwan 2019). This is my first research involvement with multilingualism, and it began four years after my retirement.

24.2   Reflection on Key Concepts and Practices of Multilingualism in Education

My understanding of the role of multilingualism in education is shaped by my work on learner autonomy. Autonomous learners use their target language individually and collaboratively to plan, implement, monitor and evaluate their own learning; their target language use is thus both communicative and metacognitive. In my publications (for example, Little 1991, 2004, 2007, 2009, 2021; Little, Dam and Legenhausen 2017) I have supported this view with reference to language learning procedures and their outcomes in primary, post-primary, university and adult immigrant education. In each of these contexts autonomous learners have achieved a capacity to communicate spontaneously, fluently and effectively in their target language, in speech and in writing. Requiring learners to share responsibility and control helps to overcome motivational problems; and because they channel their agency through the target language, their emergent proficiency is a fully integrated component of their linguistic repertoire.

24.3   Key Concepts

24.3.1   Multilingualism/Plurilingualism/Heteroglossia

As I have explained, my own foreign language learning took place in a monolingual environment. Growing up in southern England in the 1940s and 1950s I rarely encountered multilingual individuals; and travel abroad during my teens brought me into contact with speakers of other languages whose education had mostly been shaped by the same assumptions as my own. They thought of themselves as monolinguals, and this self-concept was mostly confirmed by their everyday communicative experience.

I have always been concerned to help the learners I am responsible for to become as proficient as possible in their TL(s). The standard language and educated native speakers have provided the model, especially with regard to writing skills, though most learners fall a long way short of educated native speaker proficiency. In recent years it has become fashionable to deprecate the 'monolingual habitus' and to contest the status of native speakers, but much of what is written on these topics seems to me exaggerated and misguided. It is undeniable that the populations of many large cities are dizzyingly diverse and that in an age of mass migration many people use more than one language to navigate the world in which they find themselves. But even the most diverse multilingual cities (London is a good example) have large numbers of monolingual inhabitants, and within fifty kilometres of most large cities there are populations that remain as unapologetically monolingual as they ever were. Also, when a language is learnt in a formal educational context, the proficiency that is acquired adds to the individual learner's cultural capital to the extent that it enables him or her to participate in one of the literate cultures whose medium is the language in question. It is difficult to see how this goal can be achieved if the standard language and native speaker models are not in focus.

I find the Council of Europe's distinction between multilingual communities and plurilingual individuals useful; and the 'plurilingual approach' advocated by the *Common European Framework of Reference for Languages* certainly challenges us to rethink the conceptual basis and goals of language education (CEFR; Council of Europe 2001, p. 5). But the CEFR's definition of plurilingualism as 'a communicative competence to which all knowledge and experience of language contributes and in which languages interrelate and interact' (Council of Europe 2001, p. 4) seems to me problematic. What precise meaning should we attach to the verbs 'interrelate' and 'interact'? Are they intended to denote a capacity to switch between languages and to recognize and exploit the relations between them? Or do they imply belief in a 'multi-competence' in which the boundaries between languages are dissolved? If the latter, this definition flies in the face of a substantial body of psycholinguistic evidence to the contrary (Singleton 2016).

I have only ever used the term 'heteroglossia' when teaching introductory sociolinguistics courses to undergraduate students. It has not been a feature of any community I have lived in for an extended period of time or of individuals with whom I have had extensive contact.

24.3.2 Intercultural/Pluricultural/Multicultural Education

I understand 'culture' to mean the body of beliefs, behaviour, social practices and artefacts (including linguistic artefacts) by which we recognize and define societies and communities. Languages play a key role in the development, preservation and mediation of cultures, which explains why language is never culture-free. When we learn a new language, we necessarily become familiar with some of its pragmalinguistic and socio-pragmatic functions (Leech 1983), but we do not thereby learn a new culture. Rather, we acquire the means to navigate a new culture, of which we may or may not become temporary or permanent members in due course.

24.3.3 Linguistic Repertoire/Communicative Repertoire

I began to use the term 'repertoire' in the 1980s when I first engaged with the Council of Europe's *Threshold Level* (van Ek 1975). I have never attempted to distinguish systematically between 'linguistic' and 'communicative' repertoires. In the language learning programmes for which I have been responsible, the concept of repertoire has had the advantage that it facilitates a focus on linguistic or communicative behaviour rather than linguistic knowledge. This has proved helpful in promoting a needs-based approach to the specification of curricula and syllabuses and communicative methods in the classroom.

24.4 Key Practices

24.4.1 Awareness of Language/Language Awareness

I first became aware of the concept of language awareness in the 1980s thanks to the work of Eric Hawkins (e.g. Hawkins 1984), who proposed language awareness as a new curriculum subject. For Hawkins, language awareness was a product of the individual's explicit knowledge about language. From the perspective of my work on learner autonomy, I became interested in the relation between this explicit knowledge and 'the "awareness" that learners have of language, *independently of conscious reflection on language*' (Nicholas 1991, p. 78; italics in original): the relation between language awareness as an educational goal and language awareness as part of our innate capacity for acquiring and processing language. In an article published in 1997 I argued that the communicative and reflective writing tasks typical of the autonomy classroom create an interface between the two kinds of language awareness (Little 1997).

Language awareness plays a central role in the approach to language education developed by Scoil Bhríde (Cailíní), which is the focus of my current research. From an early age, pupils from immigrant families are encouraged to talk about and explore similarities and differences between their home language, English, Irish and (in the last two primary grades) French. As a result, they develop unusually high levels of language awareness, including sensitivity to linguistic form (Little and Kirwan 2019).

24.4.2   Inter-comprehension/Education for Cross-Linguistic Transfer

I have never engaged in or been responsible for language teaching that seeks to exploit cross-linguistic transfer. I have, however, experienced inter-comprehension as a spontaneous phenomenon among Scoil Bhríde's multilingual pupil cohort. Girls whose home languages belong to the same language family – for example, Polish and Ukrainian – quickly learn to exploit this fact in informal communication and are keen to demonstrate its potential to their teachers. The practice of inter-comprehension undoubtedly helps to enhance their language awareness.

24.4.3   Translanguaging

The term 'translanguaging' was originally used in Welsh–English bilingual education to refer to the practice of providing learners with input in Welsh and requiring output in English and vice versa (Williams 2002). Its meaning has since been extended to embrace a variety of pedagogical procedures in which two or more languages are used as well as communication via two or more languages outside the classroom (García 2009). Translanguaging occurs spontaneously in any educational context in which learners from immigrant families are encouraged to use their home languages to support their learning, whether of the language of schooling or curriculum content. To judge by the literature, the paradigm case is one in which a teacher who is bilingual in the language of schooling and a minority language uses the latter to mediate the language of schooling and curriculum content to learners from the minority language community. This version of translanguaging is not an option, however, in a school like Scoil Bhríde, where many home languages are present and the teacher is proficient in none of them. In such a situation, translanguaging in classroom communication is necessarily pupil-led and takes two forms. Pupils with a home language other than the language of schooling contribute information about their home language, including comparisons between it and other languages, to the discourse of the classroom; and when performing collaborative learning tasks, they translanguage between their home language, other pupils' home languages if they are related to their own, and the language of schooling. I assume that such practices are shadowed and supported by psycholinguistic processes that also entail translanguaging.

As I noted previously, some of the literature seems to assume that there are no boundaries between languages in linguistic multi-competence. Similarly, much discussion of translanguaging seems to imply that the traditional learning outcome of proficiency in specific languages should be replaced by some kind of hybrid proficiency. I find this implication incoherent because it is unclear how exactly such proficiency is to be achieved, and irresponsible because educational capital attaches to literate proficiency in standard languages.

REFERENCES

Council of Europe (2001). *Common European Framework of Reference for Languages: Learning, Teaching, Assessment*. Cambridge: Cambridge University Press.

García, O. (2009). *Bilingual Education in the 21st Century: A Global Perspective*. Chichester: Wiley-Blackwell.

Hawkins, E. (1984). *Awareness of Language: An Introduction*. Cambridge: Cambridge University Press.

Leech, G. (1983). *Principles of Pragmatics*. London: Longman.

Little, D. (1991). *Learner Autonomy 1: Definitions, Issues and Problems*. Dublin: Authentik.

  (1997). Language awareness and the autonomous language learner. *Language Awareness* 6(2), 163–172.

  (2004). Democracy, discourse and learner autonomy in the foreign language classroom. *Utbildning & Demokrati* 13(3), 105–126.

  (2007). Language learner autonomy: Some fundamental considerations revisited. *Innovation in Language Learning and Teaching* 1(1), 14–29.

  (2009). Learner autonomy in action: Adult immigrants learning English in Ireland. In F. Kjisik, P. Voller, N. Aoki and Y. Nakata, eds., *Mapping the Terrain of Learner Autonomy: Learning Environments, Learning Communities and Identities*. Tampere: Tampere University Press, pp. 51–85.

  (2021). Language learner autonomy: Rethinking language teaching. Language Teaching 54(4), 64–73.

Little, D. and Kirwan, D. (2019). *Engaging with Linguistic Diversity: A Study of Educational Inclusion in an Irish Primary School*. London: Bloomsbury Academic.

Little, D., Dam, L. and Legenhausen, L. (2017). *Language Learner Autonomy: Theory, Practice and Research*. Bristol: Multilingual Matters.

Nicholas, H. (1991). Language awareness and second language development. In C. James and P. Garrett, eds., *Language Awareness in the Classroom*. London: Longman, pp. 78–95.

Singleton, D. (2016). A critical reaction from second language acquisition research. In V. Cook and Li Wei, eds., *The Cambridge Handbook of Linguistic Multi-Competence*. Cambridge: Cambridge University Press, pp. 502–520.

van Ek, J. A. (1975). *The Threshold Level*. Strasbourg: Council of Europe.

Williams, C. (2002). *A Language Gained: A Study of Language Immersion at 11–16 Years of Age*. Bangor: University of Wales Bangor, School of Education.

25   My Path toward Awareness of Languages and Linguistic Diversity

Marie-Paule Lory

25.1   Language Biography

I was born in France in the late 1970s. I come from a monolingual and monocultural environment (or rooted in a "Monolingual Habitus," Gogolin 1997): my family is from a francophone background and when I was a child, because we couldn't afford long-distance trips, we spent most of our holidays in France or in an adjacent francophone country. Therefore, my first language is French and I was mostly surrounded by French language throughout my youth. My first "exposure" to another language was at elementary school. One of my classmates was from Morocco. I never heard him speaking a single word of Arabic at school even though I knew it was the language he used at home with his parents and his brother and sisters. At the age of ten, I went to Belgium, where I heard people talking in Flemish. There, I was exposed for the first time to the relations of power between languages (Fairclough 1989). A French speaker from Belgium explained to me that she couldn't speak Flemish, and the Flemish language was sometimes purposely used by her colleagues at work to exclude her from a conversation. I subsequently started learning English at secondary school: English was taught to me as a "foreign" language. Languages had never been a strength of mine and the only memory I have of that time was failing an English test because I was too annoyed to learn a list of irregular verbs. A few years later, I started learning my second "foreign" language, Spanish. I experienced a similar situation, learning by heart vocabulary lists did not seem to engage me in learning languages. These early social experiences with languages and in learning them shaped, for a long time, my representations on languages (Moore 2006). I struggled to learn them and I felt, at that time, that linguistic and cultural diversity were not part of my daily life.

After a first job in the marketing department of a bank in France, I decided to expand my job possibilities by learning English in an anglophone environment. I wanted to live the popular "Canadian experience." I enrolled in an English school in Toronto (Canada), where I spent one semester.

Figure 25.1 Lake Ontario and the CN Tower

This language school gave me opportunities to meet with people from all over the world with the same goal: learning English. Unlike my previous learning experiences, where grammar was the core of the learning process, the communicative approach was mostly used and I was surrounded by English, so I could practise my new language in a concrete environment. I felt that after just a few weeks, I could easily communicate and live in English. This is not an uncommon situation in second language acquisition where, through immersion and with motivation, one develops a language faster than in a classroom. With my learning experience being so positively different from the one I had during my youth, I decided to reorient my professional aspirations to become a French teacher. I returned to France to enrol in a master's program at Paris V University, where I would discover the world "foreign language pedagogy." During my masters, I decided to be part of an exchange program (CREPUQ) with Montreal (Canada). I travelled back and forth between the two countries, and I was able to graduate while I was working as a research assistant on an Awareness of Language project (ELODiL) in Montreal. From there, I started a PhD in Montreal, and I worked with elementary and secondary school students on the implementation of the ELODiL project. The students I was working with implementing the program allowed me to travel the world. Their stories, their lives, and their languages were shared with me with enthusiasm and so much engagement. This is when it became clear to me that school has to be the place where students' languages and experiences are totally embraced. It was also at that time that I started to reflect on my own communicative repertoire, and I began feeling more at ease to speak, even partially, other languages.

My social representations on languages (Castellotti and Moore 2002) were first shaped by personal experiences but evolved mostly because of others' experiences and stories that have been generously shared with me. Through time, I gained more confidence in being exposed to other languages, in learning about these languages even though I may not speak a word of them. Today, I enjoy being able to talk in English without questioning myself on a list of irregular verbs. I'm curious when people explain to me how an expression is different in another language, and when I hear languages I don't know, I try to catch some cognates or guess the meanings of the sentences.

After ten years in Montreal, I am now in Toronto, where English is part of my daily life, I teach mostly in French, and I'm doing research in French and English. Collaborating with researchers in other languages represents sometimes a challenge but, mostly, it has been a great opportunity to question and think through another lens. In one of my latest research experiences, I was asking a friend and colleague of mine to verify a translation from French to English for a conference paper. Our discussions on the subtleties of words and their connotations made us both reflect more deeply on key concepts of our own research in both languages. I like to think that, finally, our exchanges are not lost in translation but found in "traduction." Through our discussions mobilizing our communicative repertoires, drawing on french-language and English-language scholarship and working across English, French immersion, French-language, and Spanish bilingual schools, we have collaboratively come to define the notion of Linguistic and Cultural Collaboration (Prasad and Lory 2019/Collaboration Linguistique et Culturelle; Lory and Prasad 2020).

25.1.1   *Multilingualism and Plurilingualism in Education*

For the past ten years, my research interest has been in promoting linguistic and cultural diversity in schools through the implementation of an Awareness of Language project (ELODiL and ELODiL Ontario) in two provinces of Canada: Quebec, in the city of Montreal; and more recently, in Ontario, in the cities of Ottawa and Toronto. Quebec and Ontario together welcome the majority of immigrants to Canada (Statistics Canada 2017). These two provinces are then defined by their linguistic and cultural diversity. However,

Quebec is a francophone province, while Ontario is an anglophone province. In Quebec, most of the students are schooled in French, and in Ontario, in English. Because of the Canadian Charter of Rights and Freedoms (S.23[1]), some students may be able to enroll in an English school in Quebec or in a French school in Ontario. In both contexts, I am/was working with schools where French is the language of schooling. In Montreal, French is a majority language, while in Toronto and Ottawa, French is a minority language. The implementation of pluralistic approaches in schools implied the evolution of social representation from teachers and, more largely, the school system, moving from a monolingual paradigm to a plurilingual paradigm (Prasad 2012, 2015). To support this change of paradigm, I found that a sociolinguistic perspective helps us to reconsider the way that, in school, plurilinguism and multilingualism could be seen as an asset. Blommaert, Collins and Slembrouck (2005) explained that the lack of competence to communicate is not "a problem of the speaker, but [as] a problem for the speaker, lodged not in individual forms of deficit or inability but in the connection between individual communicative potential and requirements produced by the environment" (p. 198). In research conducted in Montreal during the implementation of a Plurilingual Drama-Based project with academically challenged students from immigrant backgrounds (Armand, Lory and Rousseau 2013), a teacher participant explained how before the implementation of the project, she had the tendency to see what was lacking in French from her students and not how their previous knowledge could become an asset in their new environment. Therefore, in today's world where we cannot deny the prevalence of cultural and linguistic diversity, it should not be about how students can adapt to one monolingual and monocultural school system but rather how the school, as a microcosm of the society, can adapt to the multilingualism of the society and the plurilingualism of our students. If the school system could see beyond the culture and language of instruction and leverage the plurilingualism of students and of their teachers, we could uncover so many hidden competences. Linguistic and cultural collaboration among students and teachers from different language backgrounds within a shared learning environment can support all actors to mobilize the full extent of their communicative repertoires such that hidden competences become visible as resources for all. Further, LCC then empowers students to be language models for one another as all students gain from becoming aware and curious about languages and cultures in the world.

Today, working in French schools in an anglophone environment in collaboration with teachers, pedagogical consultants and agents from the Ministry of

---

[1] http://laws-lois.justice.gc.ca/eng/Const/page-15.html

Education, it is a challenge to promote languages when the language of instruction is in a minority context. Teachers are mostly aware of the diversity of languages spoken by their students. But, because languages are seen as a "threat" for the sustainability of French language and culture, they put the students in an environment where their abilities in other languages are restrained. Once again, I found that in this specific context, using a sociolinguistic perspective to start reflecting on plurilingualism helps us to consider holistically the linguistic and cultural repertoire of students in order to leverage students' skills, regardless of the language.

In my research and classroom practices, I support the implementation of pedagogical Pluralistic Approaches to Languages and Cultures (FREPA 2012) and in my research, mostly through an Awareness of Language program (ELODiL and ELODiL Ontario[2]). After being the coordinator of ELODiL in Montreal, I'm adapting the project for the French schools of Ontario. To expand ELODiL in this new context, I decided to work from a top-down approach as well as from a bottom-up approach. Therefore, I'm currently collaborating with the Ministry of Education on new markers in the curriculum for French Schools in Ontario that will explicitly promote linguistic and cultural diversity[3], and I'm training in-service teachers and pre-service teacher candidates to use the Pluralistic Approach. I'm also supporting the implementation and documenting the effect of such approaches through a community of practice on students and their teachers' social representation on languages. My research in Montreal, Ottawa, and Toronto highlights the necessity to consider the specificities of each environment in the implementation of such approaches. For example, in Ontario, once convinced, teachers are more willing to use students' home languages in classroom practices than English because English is seen as the "enemy." It has been only a few decades since the French school system in Ontario came into being, and for a long time the sustainability of the French language and culture was seen as possible only by the exclusion of the language of the majority: English. With time and training, practices evolve, but it seems critical that in implementing Pluralistic Approaches that strive to rethink the way we teach, we are aware of the different factors that could impact the implementation and that we shape our approaches while considering these factors. It has been several years since I began collaborating closely with the Ministry of Education. Today, I find that my greatest success has been when teachers decide to take the risk of changing their practice and make projects like ELODiL their own.

---

[2] ELODiL: www.elodil.umontreal.ca
ELODiL Ontario: www.elodilontario.com
[3] https://edusourceontario.com/res/guide-approches-plurilingues

REFERENCES

Armand, F., Lory, M.-P. and Rousseau, C. (2013). Les histoires, ça montre les personnes dedans, les feelings. Pas possible si pas de théâtre (Tahina). *Revue de linguistique et de didactique des langues* 48, 37–55.

Blommaert, J., Collins, J. and Slembrouck, S. (2005). Spaces of multilingualism. *Language & Communication* 25(3), 197–206.

Castellotti, V. and Moore, D. (2002). *Représentations sociales des langues et enseignement, Guide pour l'élaboration des politiques linguistiques éducatives en Europe: De la diversité linguistique à l'éducation plurilingue.* Strasbourg: Council of Europe, political Linguistics Division.

European Center for Modern Languages (2012). FREPA (CARAP): A Framework of Reference for Pluralistic Approaches. www.ecml.at/ECMLtrainingandconsultancyformemberstates/CARAP/tabid/1160/language/en-GB/Default.aspx

Fairclough, N. L. (1989). *Language and Power.* London: Longman.

Gogolin, I. (1997). The "monolingual habitus" as the common feature in teaching in the language of the majority in different countries. *Per linguam* 13(2), 38–49.

Lory, M.-P. and Prasad, G. (2020). Instaurer un espace de collaboration linguistique et culturelle dans les écoles de l'Ontario. In C. Fleuret and J. Thiebault, eds., *Didactique du français en contextes minoritaires : entre normes scolaires et plurilinguismes.* Ottawa: University of Ottawa Press.

Moore, D. (2006). *Plurilinguismes et école.* Paris: Éditions Didier, collection LAL (Langues et apprentissage des langues).

Prasad, G. (2015). *The Prism of Children's Plurilingualism: A Multi-site Inquiry with Children as Co-researchers across English and French Schools.* (PhD), Toronto: Ontario Institute for Studies in Education at the University of Toronto (OISE/UT). https://tspace.library.utoronto.ca/handle/1807/71458

   (2012). Multiple minorities or culturally and linguistically diverse (CLD) plurilingual learners? Re-envisioning Allophone immigrant children and their inclusion in French-language schools in Ontario. *Canadian Modern Language Review* 68(2), 190–215.

Prasad, G. and Lory, M.-P. (2019). Linguistic and Cultural Collaboration in Schools: Reconciling Majority and Minoritized Language Users. TESOL Quarterly. https://doi.org/10.1002/tesq.560

Statistics Canada (2017). Census, 2016. Les enfants issus de l'immigration: Un pont entre les cultures. www12.statcan.gc.ca/census-recensement/2016/as-sa/98-200-x/2016015/98–200-x2016015-fra.cfm

26   A Personal Journey
School, Social Class, and Language

Jeff MacSwan

Academics don't talk much about their personal stories. We're socialized, in fact, to keep those tightly under wraps, hidden from view as we dispassionately report rigorous scientific research and scholarship. That's because our personal stories should not affect the outcomes of good research. But they can, and typically do, affect our commitments and interests. Gail Prasad, Nathalie Auger, and Emmanuelle Le Pichon's project, *Multilingualism and Education*, catalogues the personal stories of scholars in multilingualism to understand how these have situated their work and the questions they ask. My own interest in multilingualism and schooling arose in large part from my personal experience in school: not as a multilingual speaker, but as a working class kid socialized into a particular role for economic production. As my academic interests took shape as an education researcher around language and linguistics, I was attracted to multilingualism and language education because I believed I could use insights from research to inform issues of fairness and social justice for underprivileged children and families. Because of my own experience and family history, I understood schooling not as a benign institution that sought to lift the socioeconomically disadvantaged up to a level playing field, but as a social and political tool which served to indoctrinate the poor into accepting meritocratic dogma, and to justify the concentration of wealth and power in the hands of "more deserving" social elites. For me, education research was about demonstrating the inherent talents and strengths of the underprivileged, with whom I identified, and showing how these strengths could be used as leverage for them to acquire new knowledge.

My father grew up in Paisley, Scotland, where his father worked as a shoe salesman in a local shop, and his mother managed the affairs of the home. His family of five lived in a cramped three-room apartment – not three bedrooms, but three rooms: A living room, kitchen, and bathroom. He often recounted the images of extreme wealth inequality growing up in Paisley, which was home to the Coats family, among the richest industrialists in the world, employing men, women, and children in thread and textile manufacturing. At the age of twelve, my father was offered an apprenticeship as an electrician; shortly after completing it, he was drafted to fight in World War II, then returned home to take care of his aging

Figure 26.1 Bell Gardens Elementary School, about 1972 (age 11)

parents. After they passed, he immigrated to the United States, eventually settling in California, where he became a US citizen in 1956.

My mother's father and brothers worked in the steel mills of Pennsylvania. She graduated from high school and briefly attended the University of Pennsylvania. She recounted how a classmate questioned her legitimacy as a student, telling her that her family could not afford for her to attend there. Convinced her classmate was right, she quietly dropped out, telling her parents she had changed her mind about going to college. She moved to California in search of a new adventure, where she met and married my father.

They settled in Bell Gardens, where my father got a job as an industrial electrician. We never bought a home but mostly lived in single-family rented houses that were roomy enough for our family of six. Bell Gardens was racially and linguistically diverse but economically homogenous; its families, mainly white and Latino, were predominantly poor and working class, and mostly lived in multifamily housing. Bell Gardens was multilingual in those days, mainly representing English and Spanish speakers. Latinos spoke Chicano English, and whites mostly spoke what dialectologists call working class American English. Street fights were common, and the police were violent and abusive. Attending school in Bell Gardens in the 1970s, my three older brothers, who were challenging to teachers and school administrators, were each encouraged to drop out early, and did.

I was expelled from elementary school as incorrigible, and spent my years before and after that in the "opportunity room." There we quietly completed worksheets and demonstrated punctuality and compliance with authority. A few years later I found myself in Vail Continuation School in Montebello, California: a schoolwide opportunity room, as it were, where teachers were generally kind but did little or no actual teaching. If we arrived on time, kept our heads down and completed our "contract" work in a timely manner, we could keep coming back and eventually transition to the next grade.

As I began my junior year of high school, something remarkable happened. My family moved from Bell Gardens to the working class side of the neighboring town of Downey, called South Downey. We lived just close enough to the northern boundary to be in the geographical region assigned to Downey High School, which catered to the wealty and middle class families of the North. Although my family's financial situation had not changed at all, school was now a radically different place. Here teachers treated students with respect, and helped them succeed when challenged. The overwhelming focus on control and compliance shifted to one focused on engagement, understanding, and respect. In the new setting, influenced by new peers and supportive teachers, I squeaked by to become the first and only of four boys in my family to graduate from high school. While most of my new Downey friends had big plans to attend major universities, I enrolled at nearby Cerritos Community College, and later transferred to California State University, Long Beach, assisted by the Equal Opportunity Program.

In later years in graduate school, I'd come to see my own school experiences in critical work on education such as Paulo Freire's (1972) *Pedagogy of the Oppressed* and Paul Willis' (1977) *Learning to Labor: How Working Class Kids Get Working Class Jobs*. As Linda McNeil (1986) noted, schools frequently focus on control and obedience to authority, with relatively little attention paid to actual academic learning. I came to see it as the responsibility of educational researchers concerned with issues of social justice to develop a knowledge base which would assist teachers, parents, and communities to create schools which foster greater respect for students and their communities, including their home language and cultural resources, and which build a foundation for the development of tools for intellectual self-defense.

Just as I was finishing my undergraduate degree, Los Angeles Unified School District began a massive recruitment effort to address its teacher shortage, offering to hire new graduates without traditional teaching credentials. I accepted an offer to teach ESL at Le Conte Junior High School in Los Angeles, and enrolled in a teacher education program at night while also pursuing a master's degree in linguistics. I later taught ESL at Los Angeles

High School for a few years, then returned to graduate school to get a PhD in Education. My interests by then had coalesced around multilingual education; I wanted to further develop my disciplinary expertise in linguistics to inform important questions about language education for multilingual students. I was an Education major, but spent substantial time in the Linguistics Department too – working as a graduate assistant in the Psycholinguistics Lab and taking essentially all the same courses as Linguistics PhD students were required to take, in addition to those required in Education.

As a student, I developed a strong interest in the mental representation of language; but because of my focus on education, I was more specifically focused on how our understanding of language as a cognitive system interacted with the social and political context of children and their communities. Chomsky's work was front and center for me as a linguistics student, as it grappled with important questions of how an organism, such as a human, could acquire so rich and complex a system as human language from such impoverished linguistic input as children encounter in daily life. Chomsky's solution was elegant: Much of what human beings know about language is given as part of their genetic makeup, with complex linguistic knowledge simply triggered by linguistic experience.[1] This basic idea, that human nature is rich and highly capable, underlies Chomsky's core political beliefs as well:

> I believe that the study of human cognitive structures and human intellectual achievements reveals a high degree of genetically determined innate structure that lies at the basis of the creative aspect of human intellectual achievement, which is easily perceived in ... the acquisition and free use of the systems of language, which permit the free expression of thought over an unbounded range. Similarly, I think ... that related aspects of human nature lie at the core of the continuing human search for freedom from authoritarian rule, from external restriction, from repressive structures, what might be called an instinct for freedom. (Chomsky 1988, pp. 250–251)

In other words, *by their nature*, humans are rich, capable, and creative beings, and their innate capacity is evident in their acquisition of systems of knowledge, like language, and their impulse to freely create and express themselves without external restrictions. Chomsky sees schools, like other systems of propaganda, as serving in part to restrict intellectual independence and justify meritocratic distinctions, and thus a part of the external restrictions imposed on the human instinct for freedom.

My own scholarship is concerned with drawing out and affirming the linguistic talents and capabilities of students whose language is viewed or treated in a disparaging manner in school, and is primarily focused on multilingual students. These negative views of children's language, often termed "linguistic deficit theories" or simply "deficit thinking," take for granted "... that the student who fails in school does so because of his/her internal deficits ... manifested in limited intellectual abilities, linguistic shortcomings"

---

[1] For discussion of this work, see Berwick, Chomsky, and Piattelli-Palmarini (2012).

or other natural limitations (Valencia 2010, p. 14). In my view, by critiquing explicit or implicit linguistic deficit theories, we disrupt institutionalized propaganda guiding school policy, curriculum, and instruction, potentially improving conditions for politically oppressed communities.

My first effort pertained to the study of language mixing, or codeswitching, which is often viewed as a crutch or a sign of linguistic confusion. As Rampton (2007) noted, codeswitching research " . . . has waged a war on deficit models of bilingualism and on pejorative views of syncretic language use by insisting on the integrity of language mixing and by examining it for its grammatical systematicity and pragmatic coherence" (p. 306). My interest was to reconceptualize the underlying grammatical theory of language mixing using the tools of recent research on linguistic structure, positing no codeswitching-specific rules. The work showed that bilinguals who codeswitch are exquisitely sensitive to the underlying grammatical requirements of both their languages, just as monolinguals are, dispelling conceptions of language mixing as evidence of semilingualism (e.g. MacSwan 1999, 2000a).

I extended this same critical perspective to accepted dichotomies of bilingual proficiency in language education such as the BICS/CALP distinction and the notion of "limited bilingualism" embedded in the Threshold Hypothesis (e.g. MacSwan 2000b) and common language tests which identify children as "non-nons," that is, nonproficient in both English and Spanish (e.g. MacSwan and Rolstad 2006).

I have supported children's right to access their home language in educational settings in the United States. The attack on bilingual education is an attack on diversity, an effort to ban children's most critical and useful resources when and where they need them most. I conducted a number of studies in Arizona, where language education policy is perhaps more regressive than anywhere else in the United States, which found that the state-mandated English-only instructional policy was ineffective. Working with graduate students and colleagues, I organized research to show that conservative and media claims about the effectiveness of language restrictive policies in California were false (Thompson et al. 2002); that bilingual education programs were effective at teaching children English reasonably quickly, countering the rhetoric of English-only proponents in Arizona (MacSwan and Pray 2005); and that Arizona's claims of effectiveness for its language education policy were almost exactly wrong, with fewer than 11 percent of children achieving English language proficiency in one year's time (Mahoney, MacSwan, and Thompson 2005). We publicized these research results through press releases, press conferences, letters to editors, and editorial contributions to local newspapers.

My experience in school in the "opportunity room" and continuation high school left me with a deep personal connection with children whom school is designed to sort for exclusion. Although I am a full professor at a major research university, my identity is still that of an incorrigible working class kid, now fighting from within to reduce the negative impact of schooling as a mechanism of social control and socioeconomic reproduction. Good schools, for me, are those which fit, affirm, and respect children and their communities, drawing out their talents and capabilities and building on them as resources to advance knowledge and understanding. I hope to continue to contribute to this important effort for as long as I am able.

REFERENCES

Berwick, R. C., Chomsky, N., and Piattelli-Palmarini, M. (2012). Poverty of the stimulus stands: Why recent challenges fail. In M. Piattelli-Palmarini and R. C. Berwick, eds., *Rich Languages from Poor Inputs*. Oxford: Oxford University Press, pp. 19–42.

Chomsky, N. (1988). *Language and Politics*. Edited by C. P. Otero. 2nd ed. Oakland, CA: AK Press.

Freire, P. (1972). *Pedagogy of the Oppressed*. New York: Herder and Herder.

MacSwan, J. (1999). *A Minimalist Approach to Intrasentential Code Switching*. New York: Garland.

   (2000a). The architecture of the bilingual language faculty: Evidence from codeswitching. *Bilingualism: Language and Cognition* 3(1), 37–54.

   (2000b). The threshold hypothesis, semilingualism, and other contributions to a deficit view of linguistic minorities. *Hispanic Journal of Behavioral Sciences* 20 (1), 3–45.

MacSwan, J. and Pray, L. (2005). Learning English bilingually: Age of onset of exposure and rate of acquisition of English among children in a bilingual education program. *Bilingual Research Journal* 29(3), 687–712.

MacSwan, J. and Rolstad, K. (2006). How language tests mislead us about children's abilities: Implications for special education placements. *Teachers College Record* 108(11), 2304–2328.

MacSwan, J., Thompson, M., Rolstad, K., McAlister, K., and Lobo, G. (2017). Three theories of the effects of language education programs: An empirical evaluation of bilingual and English-only policies. *Annual Review of Applied Linguistics* 37, 218–240. https://doi.org/10.1017/S0267190517000137

Mahoney, K., MacSwan, J. and Thompson, M. (2005). The condition of English Language Learners in Arizona. In D. Garcia and A. Molnar, eds., *The Condition of PreK-12 Education in Arizona*. Tempe, AZ: Education Policy Research Laboratory, Arizona State University, pp. 1–24.

McNeil, L. M. (1986). *Contradictions of Control: School Structure and School Knowledge*. New York: Routledge.

Rampton, B. (2007). Language crossing and redefining reality. In P. Auer, ed., *Code-Switching in Conversation: Language, Interaction and Identity*. New York: Routledge.

Thompson, M. S., DiCerbo, K., Mahoney, K. S. and MacSwan, J. (2002). ¿Éxito en California? A validity critique of language program evaluations and analysis of English learner test scores. *Education Policy Analysis Archives* 10(7). https://doi .org/10.14507/epaa.v10n7.2002

Valencia, R. (2010). *Dismantling Contemporary Deficit Thinking in Educational Thought and Practice*. New York: Routledge.

Willis, P. (1977), *Learning to Labor: How Working Class Kids Get Working Class Jobs*. Farnborough: Saxon House.

27   Cultivating Plurilingual Gardens

Enrica Piccardo

27.1   A Multifaceted Journey: My Language Biography

I grew up in Italy, in a diglossic environment, with a father talking his beloved
Ligurian dialect and a mother answering in standard Italian, proud as she was
of her Tuscan origins, that same Tuscany that gave birth to Dante, the father of
the Italian language. My parents' was a clear identity choice as both could
speak fluently each other's language. For me it was the bare normality,
something so natural that I hardly noticed it. I would reflect much later on its
peculiarity, and later again on the fertile ground that this situation had represented for me as an applied linguist. But their personal choices were not the
only stimuli that my parents provided and that would nourish my future
language biography and professional choices. The second element was the
choice of the first and second foreign languages I would learn. In my junior
secondary my parents convinced me to choose French as a foreign language,
whereas I would have gone for English, in line with the choice of the majority
of my school friends, with the promise that I would be sent to England to learn
English in a more naturalistic way.

   In retrospective, I can say that they really had a vision, understanding that
I would probably not learn French as an elective out-of-school subject if I had
been enrolled in the English class. In this way, not only was I initiated into
both languages just a few years apart but I also came to appreciate French at
least as much as if not more than English, since the French border was only
130 kilometres away and I had several opportunities to come into contact with
speakers of that language, kids and then teenagers like me. In fact, and this is
the third seed that my parents sowed, as a family we spent a series of summer
holidays abroad on campsites in France, Spain and Portugal, and later Austria.
The exposure to the respective languages of these countries, and also of others
spoken by other children and teenagers on the campsites with whom I played
for hours in multilingual and multicultural groups, was an extremely rich and
stimulating experience that would provide a unique nourishment to my future
personal plurilingualism and my research in the field.

Als das Kind Kind war,
wußte es nicht, daß es Kind war,
alles war ihm beseelt,
und alle Seelen waren eins.
From:
Peter Handke
"Als das Kind Kind war"

Italian translation:
Quando il bambino era bambino,
non sapeva di essere un bambino,
per lui tutto aveva un'anima
e tutte le anime erano un tutt'uno.
Figure 27.1 Quando il bambino era bambino, non sapeva di essere un
bambino, per lui tutto aveva un'anima e tutte le anime erano un tutt'uno

By the age of 16, I had thus experienced a great linguistic diversity on top of
acquiring a functional proficiency in two foreign languages. It was at that same

age though that my engagement with modern languages was put on hold and my attention turned mainly towards improving my knowledge of classical languages, Latin and ancient Greek, as foreseen by the curriculum of the last three years of the secondary school I attended. It was also at that time that my interest in the German language and culture grew exponentially, especially in German philosophy. Thus, my decision to take German, English and French at university, precisely in that order, appeared to me as a natural choice: from the language I mastered the least when I was admitted to university – German – as my focal one, to my strongest one – French – as the third on the list.

Among the seeds planted by my parents' vision, was one that would germinate much later once I started being involved in language teaching and language teacher development. My early stays in England as a young teenager would allow me to experience a totally different way of approaching the study of a foreign language as a quasi-beginner, an immersive way, which on one side was very similar to that of a little child and, on the other, represented the stressful scary challenge of being confronted with the need to get by in the language to communicate every day's needs, in a word to 'sink or swim'. Thus, I had experienced on one side a good solid learning process in French as a foreign language through school and on the other hand the naturalistic learning of English. Exactly like in landscape architecture, my plurilingual trajectory was thus enriched with two different and complementary gardens, the French garden, well-planned, structured and neatly organized, and the English garden, wilder, unstructured and spontaneous. Needless to say, these two experiences – opposite but complementary – would nurture my later reflection on language education and pedagogy. Furthermore, these gardens did not grow in the desert; the ground they were rooted in was a very fertile one, the Italian language, which was not only my mother tongue but also the language I had had the chance to study through the skilful and careful teaching of exceptional educators since my youngest age. Another milestone for my future reflection as an applied linguist.

It was at university that my plurilingualism started to emerge as a way of being and thinking, and later to bear fruits. It all started with a battle against the institution in order to be allowed to study three languages instead of the two that were foreseen. Instinctively, I knew that languages do not live in isolation and that language learning is a holistic and complex endeavour where the entire linguistic, personal and cultural trajectory of an individual is reshaped. It is not just a question of how fluent one is in any of these languages but also, and even more, how the different elements of the palimpsest that constitutes our personal trajectory come into play during the process. I felt that my strong background in classical languages and in my mother tongue together with my life experience would allow me to succeed in the challenge. I was right, as I finished the first of my cohort, in spite of not having started university with a high proficiency level in any of the chosen languages, as many other students had done. My Latin and Greek together with my multilingual background and my plurilingual upbringing boosted my ability to learn languages, and made my language biography richer and more rounded. It was this strong personal experience that made me reject the expression 'langues mortes' that is very often used when referring to classical languages. Far from being dead, these languages offer a lively humus to nurture the roots of living languages, in the same way that in a wood the undergrowth plays a pivotal role in the healthy ecosystem of the wood by nurturing and sustaining plants and animals. Far from being dead, they resurrect like a phoenix into other linguistic forms to which they provide sense and continuity. For me they provided a first solid pillar through etymology: not only was I able to understand the path that words of Greek or Latin origin had followed during their journey but also I could observe and reflect on the words that had other origins and opened on other spaces, all free to be explored. Classical languages also provided me with a second, more subtle, pillar: grammar, and particularly morphology and syntax. It was a sort of template, a form of scaffolding in which other languages' structures could insert themselves harmoniously, thus becoming more access-ible or – vice versa – against which they proved their fundamental difference, which triggered my curiosity towards new ways of conceiving the relationship between words and concepts and eventually a new way of seeing the world.

27.2   Juggling with Concepts: A Repertoire of Plurality

A language biography is something that unfolds naturally as one progresses through life, something that grows and is shaped by the different events, contacts and experiences that characterize our existence as human beings. It is another thing, however, to make sense of this process, or even be aware of the very existence of a language biography. In my case, and in the context where I grew up and later started my career – not very linguistically and culturally diverse – this awareness was not automatic. It needed some concep-tual framing, some categories that would make the invisible visible. One intrinsic characteristic of our human nature is in fact the need to come up with concepts that help us make sense of what we experience and what is happening in the world around us.

In my case, plurilingualism has been such a concept. The first time I met it was in 1996 when I first discovered and started to study the Common European Framework of Reference for Languages (CEFR) that had just appeared in its preliminary version. In particular, what was eye-opening was

the explicit definition of multilingualism and plurilingualism as two complementary but distinct concepts. Plurilingualism is not a self-explanatory concept; it is a broad and deep concept, one that calls for reflection on and
attention to different phenomena and developments that are not necessarily
self-explanatory. Thus, my own understanding of the depth and potential of
this concept has required time and dedication. Like many of my colleagues,
I initially underestimated the real mental paradigm shift that is required to
embrace the depth of plurilingualism. While the functional distinction between
multilingualism and plurilingualism was clear, the former being the coexistence of a certain number of languages both at the societal and individual level
with no attention to interconnections between them and the latter stressing a
holistic, integrationist perspective, especially at the individual level where all
languages are inevitably interconnected and interdependent,[1] the practical
transposition of such a distinction to the language class was seen as quasi-
automatic, as if the fact of opting for the term plurilingualism would be
sufficient per se to shape a new mentality among students: one of curiosity
towards differences and of empowerment in the use of multiple languages.
Alas, this is not at all the case. Plurilingualism is a frame of mind, an attitude
vis-à-vis language learning and use that involves individuals' different facets:
cognitive, emotional, relational . . .

In these last two decades, the advances in reflection on the language learning
process, informed by insights from different sciences, have been key to
shaping our understanding of the tenets of plurilingualism. Plurilingualism
embeds both sociocultural and cognitive dimensions of language learning and
use, and thus it conveys a much broader view than other terms. What I found
intriguing and inspiring for my conceptual research was the Bakhtinian notion
of heteroglossia and its relationship with multilingualism and plurilingualism.
While multilingualism focuses on the coexistence of multiple languages and
heteroglossia on the multiple nature of each single language with the coexistence of multiple varieties of languages within the same text and possibly even
utterance – from social dialects to jargons to targeted types of discourse –
plurilingualism as a notion adopts a holistic framework and goes beyond both
multilingualism and heteroglossia, as it focuses precisely on the dynamics of
the whole process of using and acquiring languages. The idea behind it is
really to capture the complex and dynamic nature of humans' relationship
to languages as a phenomenon, as the ensemble of linguistic, cultural and
semiotic means that allows them to find their place in the world and to interact
with each other and the context.

---

[1] This distinction is proposed to highlight two different perspectives of seeing linguistic and
cultural diversity. Some scholars have not embraced this distinction but rather they use multilingualism to cover both semantic fields (of multilingualism and plurilingualism).

My research has focused on the exploration of this concept and thus on the discovery of all its facets. It has been a conceptual research on one side and an applied research on the other. The former has led me to produce several papers in which I was able to highlight and explain the conceptual density of plurilingualism (e.g. Piccardo 2013, 2017, 2018, 2020; Piccardo and Galante 2018, Piccardo and Puozzo 2015; Piccardo, Germain Rutherford and Lawrence 2021), and the latter refers to the creation of targeted descriptors for plurilingual and pluricultural competence within the four-year Council of Europe project that preceded the publication of the CEFR Companion Volume (CEFRCV) (Council of Europe 2020), of which I am one of the authors.

My move from a French-speaking research context to an English-speaking one constituted both an obstacle and an opportunity in my path towards the conceptual investigation of plurilingualism and its implications. I experienced, in fact, quite strong resistance in the latter context not only towards adopting a term that had originated in a non-English-speaking context but also towards capturing the depth and potential of the concept itself. I noticed, on the contrary, an endless quest for the best possible term, which came up with extended versions of multilingualism, for example, *holistic multilingualism* (Cenoz 2013), with new terms, for example, *polylingualism* (Jørgensen et al. 2011), *metrolingualism* (Otsuji and Pennycook 2010) and with an attempt to relocate innovative plurilingual pedagogies and practices at the level of over-arching concepts, for example, translanguaging (García 2009; Otheguy, García and Reid 2015).

This resistance, though, was also an asset, as it fuelled my investigation of the nature and innovation potential of plurilingualism, and guided my conceptual research all the way to the conceptualization of how plurilingualism as a concept can inform plurilingual practice. The term 'plurilanguaging' was instrumental in this process. I borrowed the term from Lüdi (2015), who used it to refer to the discourse co-construction of speakers of different languages in a multilingual context. I reinterpreted the term in the light of a complex and sociocultural view of the process of language learning and use, coming up with a definition which, building on and extending Swain's (2006) definition of *languaging*, sees plur-ilanguaging as 'a dynamic, never-ending process to make meaning using different linguistic and semiotic resources' (Piccardo 2018: 9), and calls for a broader declination of the concept in its components and implications. Thus, I identify five features of plurilanguaging: (1) a cyclical process of exploring and constructing; (2) an agentic process of selecting and (self) organizing; (3) a process of dealing with chaos; (4) an ability to enhance perception in an awareness-raising process; and (5) an empowering process in relation to norms (Piccardo 2017: 16).

Within this view, the notions of linguistic trajectory and communicative repertoire take all their sense as individuals construct, nurture and develop their resources in the process of plurilanguaging. Needless to say, the cultural aspect is always implied, as languages are interconnected with and shaped by cultures, in a reciprocal movement. Even though this area has not been at the forefront of my research, these concepts have nurtured my reflection on plurilingualism and plurilanguaging, especially when it came to developing tools for practical implementation of the plurilingual vision.

27.3   From Conceptualizing to Applying: Supporting Practitioners

Needless to say, the conceptual research was crucial in informing the applied one, as the complex and dynamic nature of plurilingualism needed to be translated into a form accessible to practitioners.

Thus, the applied part of my research consisted in supporting practitioners to realize the plurilingual paradigm shift. On one side, this translated into the creation, calibration and validation of practical tools in the form of scales of descriptors for plurilingual and pluricultural competence, as part of the CEFRCV project. On the other, it informed the conceptualization and creation of pedagogic materials for plurilingual action-oriented scenarios alongside an online tool (Language Integration Through E-Portfolio – LITE) as part of a wide-ranging project, LINCDIRE (www.lincdireproject.org; Piccardo et al. 2022). Both projects involved numerous practitioners, something which allowed us to observe how attitudes and practices towards linguistic and cultural diversity have been evolving over the past few decades.

A plurilingual perspective goes beyond the need to acknowledge existing multilingualism; it fosters an agentic attitude towards linguistic and cultural diversity,

A multilingual classroom is a classroom in which there are children who speak different mother tongues. A plurilingual classroom is one in which teachers and students pursue an educational strategy of embracing and exploiting the linguistic diversity present in order to maximize communication and hence both subject learning and plurilingual/ pluricultural awareness. (Piccardo 2018: 7)

While the strong influence of behaviourism is still powerfully felt in the classroom through the idea of keeping the classroom space pure and uncontaminated by linguistic diversity or code-switching, and a certain vision of immersion as a magical practice that by itself automatically enables language acquisition is also still powerful, practitioners increasingly see the limitations of these perspective. Language awareness starts to be seen as being almost as important as knowledge of the language itself. In the European context, where the CEFRCV research was mostly carried out, the CEFR has in the last two decades played a crucial role in bringing to the fore language awareness as an asset. During the CEFRCV project, practitioners welcomed descriptors that would help them make the invisible part of the learning process visible, that is, the reflective, metacognitive and metalinguistic dimension. The series of projects and studies on intercomprehension, especially among Romance languages, from Galatea, Galanet (Degache 2003), all the way to Miriadi (Del Barrio 2015; De Carlo and Garbarino 2021), also greatly contributed to broadening practices and breaking down walls between languages. The idea of exploiting all resources to engage in a comprehension process, or to build plurilingual and pluricultural repertoires, has thus been enthusiastically welcomed by practitioners.

Taken together, the geographical proximity of linguistically and culturally diverse contexts and traditions that characterizes Europe, with their consequent permeability, and an emerging critical perspective vis-à-vis increasing English linguistic and cultural hegemony, tend to embolden practitioners when it comes to challenging linguistic and cultural barriers.

Our choice in the latter research project I mentioned, LINCDIRE, has been to support participating teachers to realize the shift in vision that plurilingualism represents and requires, as we consider that this new vision is a necessary prerequisite for more flexible and open pedagogical practices. The results of the first round of data collection seem very encouraging, with both language and teachers realizing the value of reflecting on and building on personal trajectories and repertoires, and using real-life action-oriented scenarios to provide a space for learner agency and development both linguistically and personally.

The monolingual mindset is still very dominant in our societies. Thus, any attempt to overcome this powerful barrier is welcome. However, in the same way that the mere introduction of games was seen as sufficient to stimulate communication in communicative language teaching (CTL), the mere introduction of translingual practices is now often being seen as the golden key to plurilingualism. Alas, this is not the case since such a linear (IF...THEN) vision is far from being a guarantee of success. Plurilingualism, as we said, is an attitude, a way of thinking and living. It implies the capacity to embrace complexity, to live with imbalance, a dynamic, creative and transformative imbalance, both in research and in pedagogic practices.

REFERENCES

Cenoz, J. (2013). Defining Multilingualism. *Annual Review of Applied Linguistics* 33, 3–18.

Council of Europe (2020) *Common European Framework of Reference for Languages: Learning, Teaching, Assessment. Companion Volume.* Strasbourg: Council of Europe. https://rm.coe.int/common-european-framework-of-reference-for-languages-learning-teaching/16809ea0d4

De Carlo, M. and Garbarino, S. (2021). Intercomprehension: strengths and opportunities of a pluralistic approach. In E. Piccardo, A. Germain-Rutherford and G. Lawrence, G. (eds.), *The Routledge handbook of plurilingualism* (pp. 337–359). New York: Routledge.

Degache, C. (2003) Intercompréhension en langues romanes: Du développement des compétences de compréhension aux interactions plurilingues, de Galatea à Galanet [Intercomprehension in Romance languages: From the development of comprehension competences to plurilingual interactions: from Galatea to Galanet]. *Lidil 28.*

Del Barrio, M. M. (2015). *La enseñanza de la intercomprensión a distancia [Distance Teaching of Intercomprehension].* Madrid: Universidad Complutense de Madrid. http://eprints.ucm.es/35033/1/ense%C3%B1anza%20valido.pdf

García, O. (2009). *Bilingual Education in the 21st Century: A Global Perspective.* Oxford: Wiley-Blackwell.

Jørgensen, J. N., Karrebaek, M. S., Maden, L. M. and Møller, J. S. (2011). Polylanguaging in superdiversity, *Diversities* 13 (2), 24–37. www.unesco.org/shs/diversities/vol13/issue2/art2

Lüdi, G. (2015). Monolingualism and multilingualism in the construction and dissemination of scientific knowledge. In U. Jessner-Schmid & C. Kramsch (Eds.), *The multilingual challenge: Cross-disciplinary perspectives* (pp. 213–238). Berlin: Mouton de Gruyter.

Otheguy, R., García, O. and Reid, W. (2015). Clarifying translanguaging and deconstructing named languages: A perspective from linguistics. *Applied Linguistics Review* 6(3), 281–307.

Otsuji, E. and Pennycook, A. (2010). Metrolingualism: Fixity, fluidity and language in flux. *International Journal of Multilingualism* 7(3), 240–254.

Piccardo, E. (2013). Plurilingualism and curriculum design: Towards a synergic vision. *TESOL Quarterly* 47(3), 600–614.

(2017). Plurilingualism as a catalyst for creativity in superdiverse societies: A systemic analysis. *Frontiers in Psychology* 8, 2169. https://doi.org/10.3389/fpsyg.2017.02169

(2018). Plurilingualism: Vision, conceptualization, and practices. In P. Trifonas and T. Aravossitas, eds., *Springer International Handbooks of Education: Handbook of Research and Practice in Heritage Language Education.* New York: Springer International Publishing, pp. 1–19. doi:10.1007/978-3-319-38893-9_47-1

(2020). Rethinking plurality on our liquid societies. In F. Bangou, D. Fleming and M. Waterhouse, eds., *Deterritorializing Language, Teaching, and Learning: Deleuzo-Guattarian Perspectives on Second Language Education.* Ottawa: University of Ottawa Press.

Piccardo, E. and Galante, A. (2018). Plurilingualism and agency in language education: The role of dramatic action-oriented tasks. In J. Choi and S. Ollerhead, eds., *Plurilingualism in Teaching and Learning.* New York: Routledge, pp. 147–164.

Piccardo, E. and Puozzo, I. (2015). Introduction. From second language pedagogy to the pedagogy of 'plurilingualism': a possible paradigm shift?/De la didactique des langues à la didactique du plurilinguisme: un changement de paradigme possible? *The Canadian Modern Language Review/La revue canadienne des langues vivantes* 71(4), 317–323.

Piccardo, E., Germain Rutherford A. & Lawrence, G. (2021). *The Routledge Handbook of Plurilingual language Education.* London: Routledge.

Piccardo, E., Lawrence, G., Germain Rutherford, A. and Galante A. (2022). *Activating Linguistic and Cultural Diversity in the Language Classroom.* New York, NY: Springer International Publishing.

Swain, M. (2006). Languaging, agency and collaboration in advanced second language learning. In Heidi Byrnes, ed., *Advanced Language Learning: The Contributions of Halliday and Vygotsky.* London: Continuum, pp. 95–108.

Gail Prasad

I was born into a family where a plurality of languages, cultures and religious practices were woven into the fabric of our daily lives. Originally from India, my father, Chandreswar Prasad, had immigrated to Canada after completing an apprenticeship in Germany. He spoke and understood a variety of Indian languages, as well German, which he learned during his time in Stuttgart, and English, as a result of his schooling in English-medium schools while growing up in India. My mother, Marty Toyoko Yasunaka, was born in Canada, not long before the Second World War began. Shortly thereafter, my mother's family was moved to Tashme, the largest Japanese Canadian internment camp, known today as Sunshine Valley Ski Resort. After the war, my mother's family was relocated to Farnham, Quebec, far away from the West Coast. Her family then resettled in Montreal. While they spoke Japanese at home, she and her siblings learned English and my mom also studied French at school.

In the sixties, my parents might have been considered ahead of their times as far as inter-racial, cultural, linguistic and religious marriages went. While issues of cultural and religious practice were often hotly contested in our home, I don't recall questions of language sparking much debate. It wasn't that issues related to language weren't uncontroversial but rather that English was the common language shared across my parents' linguistic repertoires. In fact, my mother often reminded me that my parents had originally moved from Montreal to Toronto because my dad had already learned German and English and he said didn't want to learn French, too. As first and second generation immigrants who had made great sacrifices to build their lives in Canada, my parents understood acutely the importance not only of being able to speak English but also of speaking it well. My parents, both visible minorities and 'English' learners, were resolute in their venture to raise English-speaking daughters so that we would have access to greater opportunities than they had.

When I reached school age, I remember my best friends from daycare went off to French immersion schools. My parents, however, had been told that it would be difficult enough for me to learn in English at school. The school recommended against enrolling me in French immersion. In retrospect, I've often wondered whether the person dolling out such advice had first asked

232

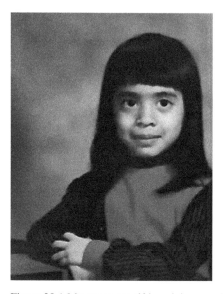

Figure 28.1 My younger self imagining a serious life as a professor of language education

about my parents' linguistic backgrounds. Perhaps the colour of my parents' skin was enough of a visible marker of their immigrant status to shut down any discussion of my enrollment before it had an opportunity to be entertained. The irony was that my mom had by that point obtained her Bachelor of Arts degree in French and was herself certified as a French-as-a-second-language teacher. She, however, knew only too well what it was like to experience racism and exclusion following the Japanese internment in Canada, so she didn't dare argue with the official directive from the school. To the extent possible, she wanted to protect her daughters from feelings of illegitimacy and unbelonging. So, off I went to English school.

Just before I turned eight, my family took our first trip back 'home' to India to visit our extended family. While I enjoyed meeting my grandmother, aunts and uncles, and all my cousins, this trip made tangible that it wasn't just the distance that separated me from our family in India. My aunts in India did not speak English, nor did my Grandmother, so our conversations had to happen through translation, often by a male family member. As a sensitive child familiar with navigating multilingual interactions, I perceived that what I wanted to communicate in English was only ever paraphrased in translation. Most of the time, my sister and I remained silently at the margins of adult conversation. Children, particularly girl children, were, after all, to be seen and not heard.

We returned to Canada with a new desire to learn Hindi, so my sister and I were enrolled in heritage language classes on Saturday mornings. After a few weeks of colouring pictures of Hindu gods and tracing the Hindi alphabet in the Devanagari script, my sister and I began to recognize that if we were going to make any progress with 'Hindi school', we would need to use the language at home. We struggled with the singular vision of a Hindi speaker promoted through the language classes. As much as we wanted to learn Hindi, many of the cultural and religious aspects of the classes didn't map onto our lived experience in a mixed family. Shortly thereafter, we dropped out of Hindi school, taking with us an even greater sense of cultural illegitimacy as a result of our linguistic inadequacy.

As I continued growing up, I often found myself trying to listen in on conversations during family gatherings that unfolded in different languages. Multilingualism was the norm in the worlds in which I lived – and as a self-proclaimed monolingual Anglophone at the time, I often felt like an outsider looking in. I didn't recognize that I was actually developing my capacity as a multilingual listener – making meaning even in contexts where I couldn't communicate through a shared language. Instead, I often felt that I was neither wholly Indian nor wholly Japanese because I couldn't speak either language. I wasn't even sure that I would ever be wholly 'Canadian', or Canadian *enough*. At school, I was conscious that I was a visible minority and an immigrant, even though I had been born in Canada. I remember thinking as a child that my parents spoke other languages because of where their families came from and that they spoke English as a sign that they had also become Canadian, at least in part.

As a child surrounded by languages, I wanted to learn French so I could become an officially bilingual Canadian. My child-like logic led me to believe that speaking both of Canada's official languages might make me 'fully' Canadian. At the time, the fact that my mom actually understood both English and French didn't enter into my calculation. As the daughter of immigrants, I couldn't change the colour of my skin or other visible signs of my difference, but I reasoned that becoming proficient in French might make me a legitimate Canadian. Despite all my efforts to learn French via the 'drip' method, the brief but unrelenting daily dose of French as a Second Language from grade 3 to grade 13 did not produce a bilingual Canadian: only a monolingual Anglophone with a severe, seemingly incurable case of linguistic insecurity whenever someone started speaking French.

I went on to pursue my Bachelor of Arts in English Literature and my Bachelor of Education at Queen's University. My parents were baffled by how they could have possibly raised a daughter who so loved the language of Shakespeare! While I joked that they had succeeded in raising a monolingual Anglophone *par excellence*, I lived with regret that I couldn't speak Hindi or Japanese and that I was just barely making it through French electives that I was still trying to take. Through my undergraduate studies in English Literature, I became captivated by writings of post-colonial authors. Reading Arundati Roy, who played with the English language, literally and figuratively in ways that made power visible, challenged me to wrestle with my often-fraught relationship with language(s). Roy's play with capitalization and parenthetical thought struck a chord with me as I realized that even in my monolingualism, I could make both creative and critical choices in how I used English either as a practice of assimilation or as an act of resistance and decolonization. Creativity and criticality have since been woven throughout my work as an educator and as a university-based researcher. I've been mindful through my personal experience and my academic training that language practices are always tied up with power and identity/ies. Whereas criticality works to make visible and dismantle hegemonic systems of power, creativity offers the possibility to build collaborative relations of power that can amplify voices and perspectives that have historically been marginalized.

I took up my first full-time teaching position as an elementary English teacher in a French international school. Soon after, I was baffled by my Kindergarteners who were learning to read, write, speak and create in multiple languages (French, English, Spanish, Mandarin plus their home languages). Thirty years earlier my parents had been counselled that their multilingualism would be an impediment to my own learning and academic success. How could multilingualism be a resource for some and a liability for others? Could teachers, particularly in public schools with increasingly diversified student populations, also support students' multilingualism? I left my classroom to pursue graduate study initially to explore my questions about language, power and multilingual literacy development. That year has turned into more than a decade of studying children and youth's social representations of multilingualism, plurilingualism and linguistic diversity. I've been invested in exploring how teachers can leverage students' plurilingualism as a resource for learning in multilingual school contexts in Canada, Burkina Faso, France and the United States.

As a former elementary teacher, and in alignment with the shift in New Childhood Studies, I became convinced that if I was serious about contributing to culturally and linguistically expansive child-centred pedagogy, the perspectives of children, particularly those from culturally and linguistically diverse backgrounds, needed not just to be included in my research but rather children's voices needed to be centred. Consequently, during my doctoral work, I engaged with children as co-investigators of their plurilingualism using arts-informed research methods, including drawing (Prasad 2018), language portraits (Prasad 2013), multimodal book-making (Prasad 2015) and collage (Prasad 2020). Adopting creative research methods in this collaborative applied linguistics inquiry enabled children to make their emic perspectives visible while showcasing their expertise and multi-competence across language(s) and modalities (Prasad 2021).

Despite my professed *insecurité linguistique en français*, my PhD advisor, Prof. Normand Labrie, encouraged me to engage with both English-language and French-language scholarship related to linguistic diversity in education. It felt daunting but through his gentle and continual nudging, a fortuitous research assistantship with Prof. Diane Farmer at the Centre de Recherche en Éducation Franco-Ontarienne and a teaching assistantship with Prof. Enrica

Piccardo within the teacher education programme for middle and high school French-as-a-Second-Language teachers, I gradually found myself immersed in French and learning to tread water. It was through my reading in French that I first encountered the notion of *plurilinguisme*. The term began appearing in French-language scholarship in the 1990s with the publication of a French journal entitled *Plurilinguismes* under the editorship of Louis-Jean Calvet. The notion of plurilingualism that focused on how individuals developed a dynamic linguistic repertoire over the scope of their lives that they could draw on according to need and context was a seismic shift in my thinking. The idea that a plurilingual individual could possess uneven (unfinished and evolving) competence across different languages and their varieties caused me to question many of my beliefs about who and what 'counted' as being bilingual or multilingual. Rather than seeing myself as a monolingual Anglophone daughter of multilingual immigrant parents, or a failed Canadian bilingual, I began considering that I might in fact be plurilingual. Could the limited knowledge I had in Hindi (family titles, foods and locations) count for something? Could I reframe my (broken) French as part of my growing plurilingual repertoire as a Canadian researcher?

I began reading French-language scholarship voraciously and French conceptualizations of *la didactique du* plurilinguisme [Plurilingual Teaching & Learning] (Coste 2010), *les approches plurielles* [pluralistic approaches to languages and cultures] (Candelier et al. 2010), *l'eveil aux langues* [language awareness] (Candelier 2003) and l'intércomprehension [intercomprehension] (Escudé 2014) began to shape my research imagination about what could be possible multilingual school settings. I wondered how the theorization of plurilingualism translated into practice (or not) in schools in France. With the support of a Weston Doctoral fellowship from the University of Toronto, I was able to spend a year in France working with Prof. Nathalie Auger at the Université Paul-Valéry III. During my stay, I extended my data generation with students and teachers in two schools in Montpellier and Sète. My time in Southern France was invigorating in many ways: I began to feel like I could swim more comfortably in French; I had opportunities to meet many of the scholars whose work I had been reading; and, I had extended, unhurried conversations with Nathalie, in particular, about her work and my own related to plurilingualism and education. While the theory of plurilingualism had appeared interesting through my reading in Toronto, words became flesh in France as I discussed theory, concepts and practice with researchers, teachers and students. I returned to Toronto with greater confidence in French (even if my *linguistique insecurité* has never fully subsided), tools to pursue Language Awareness (Candelier 2003) and Language Comparison (Auger, 2005) work that I had witnessed in practice (Prasad and Auger, 2015), and with a plurilingual lens in focus as I finished writing up my dissertation.

I hadn't ever planned to leave Canada to pursue an academic career but my positive experience in France perhaps made me more inclined to believe I could make another international move. I accepted a position at a predominantly white research-intensive university in the US Midwest immediately following my doctoral defense. I quickly came to realize, however, that before I ever opened my mouth to introduce myself on my own terms, I would first (and always) be seen as brown, – an assumed non-(native) English speaker on account of the colo(u)r of my skin, an immigrant indelibly marked as an outsider. It mattered not how I saw myself, only how I was seen and positioned by others. Early on, I remember sharing with a colleague my fatigue from dealing with the daily barrage of micro-aggressions on campus and off. Her response to me was that even though it felt awful to be a junior faculty woman of colour (WOC), my awareness and experience of systemic racism in such an acute way would sharpen my scholarship to be much more critical.

I initially held fast to using the term plurilingualism in talking about the Research-Practice Partnership I developed with a local school district (Prasad and Lory 2020), in part because I found it easier for teachers to grasp the Multilingual Turn (May 2014) and the paradigm shift from seeing monolingualism as the norm to understanding that all students (and teachers) develop and navigate dynamic and complex communicative repertoires over their lives. Using the English neologism 'plurilingualism' rather than 'dynamic bi/multilingualism' was helpful because of prevailing social representations of the multilingual individual being a polyglot who can speak multiple different languages proficiently. My use of the term plurilingualism also reflected my orientation and training for our collaborative research.

While my attention had hitherto focused rather singularly on language(s) and their use in schools, I came to witness and experience firsthand how issues of language intersect with the politics of race, gender and social class. In retrospect, I have come to understand some of the resistance to my use of theories of plurilingualism in the United States not as a rejection of my plurilingual work with teachers and students but rather as a political commitment to centre the systemic minoritization and racialization of bilingual learners. Battles for the Bilingual Education Act in the United States and on-going divisions between English-only states and those which offer different forms of bilingual education to serve minoritized and racialized children have resonance with the arduous political battles francophone minorities across Canada fought to win governance of French-language schools (Behiels 2004). While I have admittedly dismissed at times intramural scholarly debates around disciplinary nomenclature (multilingual, plurilingual, translanguaging, heteroglossia, etc.) as a distraction from moving practice forward, I recognize the need to adapt our use of terminology to particular contexts so that we don't (however unintentionally) erase the political memory of how language rights have been won often through costly activism.

We cannot dislocate our scholarship from our bodies: particularly as scholars of colo(u)r working with minoritized students and families (Mignolo and Tlostanova 2006). Theories of intersectionality and raciolinguistics have drawn attention to how race operates in relation to Language (Rosa and Flores 2017; Rosa 2019). I conclude my reflection on my own language biography and research trajectory by returning to the notion of multilingual listening. Working in multilingual classrooms and contexts, I have found it helpful to be able to distinguish between multilingual speakers and multilingual listeners in documenting and analyzing the complex languaging that we observe in classrooms today. In my recent work, I have been engaging teachers in designing their teaching for critical multilingual language awareness (García 2017) through Collaborative Learning through Multilingual Inquiry (Prasad and Lory 2020). CLMI posits that collaborative multilingual projects open up spaces of encounter for students of different linguistic backgrounds to recognize their own dynamic communicative repertoires (Rymes 2014) and literacy expertise (Cummins 2009), as well as those of their peers. Collaborative multilingual projects provide an authentic purpose for students to work together to pool their communicative resources rather than to hide them. Take for example, a group of students working to create a multilingual poster about science content: students of minoritized language backgrounds may each contribute by translating key vocabulary into minoritized languages. When they do so, they act as multilingual speakers who draw from their repertoires to translate the poster from English into their languages. The other students in the group then act as multilingual listeners who draw from and/or expand their repertoires in order to make meaning of the translated text. The (re)positioning of the multilingual speaker and the multilingual listener through Linguistic and Cultural Collaboration can disrupt expected roles and coercitive relations of power between minoritized language speakers and English dominant speakers. Everyone participates in multilingual interaction. The design parameters of Collaborative Learning through Multilingual Inquiry offer a transformative pedagogical space of encounter for all students and teachers to learn to be attentive multilingual speakers and listeners. They, by design, become invested in supporting one another to accomplish academic work that they could not do alone.

At a time that often feels like the world is fracturing along fault lines of race, language, class, gender and indigeneity, schools can become protected spaces in which to imagine and build new equitable societies. If we can't do it within public school classrooms where children are required to mix with others who are different from them, all bets are surely off that they will be able to do so productively when they leave school. Our current world provides empirical evidence that the current order is not working. We need everyone on deck, multilingual speakers, multilingual listeners and plurilingual allies and activists, to bring about sustaining change.

REFERENCES

Auger, N. (2005). *Comparons nos langues* (DVD et livret pédagogique). Montpellier: CRDP Académie de Montpellier.

Behiels, M. D. (2004). *Canada's Francophone Minority Communities: Constitutional Renewal and the Winning of School Governance*. Montreal, Canada: McGill-Queen's Press-MQUP.

Candelier, M. (dir.) (2003). *L'éveil aux langues à l'école primaire : Evlang, bilan d'une innovation européenne*. Brussels: De Boek–Duculot.

Candelier, M., Camilleri-Grima, A., Castellotti, V., de Pietro, J. F., Lörincz, I., Meissner, F. J. and Noguerol, A. (2010). *FREPA/CARAP: Framework of*

Reference for Pluralistic Approaches of Languages and Cultures. Strasbourg: European Centre for Modern Languages: Council of Europe.

Coste, D. (2010). Diversité des plurilinguismes et formes de l'éducation plurilingue et interculturelle. *Recherches en didactique des langues et des cultures: les Cahiers De l'Acedle* [numéro thématique: Notions en questions – les plurilinguismes], 7, 1–19. https://doi.org/10.4000/rdlc.2031

Cummins, J. (2009). Transformative multiliteracies pedagogy: School-based strategies for closing the achievement gap. *Multiple Voices for Ethnically Diverse Exceptional Learners* 11(2), 38–56.

De Pietro, J. F. (2009). Pour une approche plurielle des langues, quelles qu'elles soient. *Babylonia* 4(9), 54–60.

Escudé, P. (2014). De l'intercompréhension comme moteur d'activités en classe. *Tréma* (42), 46–53.

García, O. (2017). Critical multilingual language awareness and teacher education. *Language Awareness and Multilingualism* 263, 280.

Mignolo, W. D. and Tlostanova, M. V. (2006). Theorizing from the borders: Shifting to geo- and body-politics of knowledge. *European Journal of Social Theory* 9(2), 205–221.

Prasad, G. (2013). Plurilingual children as co-ethnographers of their own language and literacy practices: An exploratory case study. *Language & Literacy: an e -journal* 15(3), 4–30. https://doi.org/10.20360/G2901N

  (2015). Beyond the mirror towards a plurilingual prism: Exploring the creation of plurilingual 'identity texts' in English and French classrooms in Toronto and Montpellier, *Intercultural Education* 26(6), 497–514, DOI: 10.1080/14675986.2015.1109775

  (2018). 'But do monolingual people really exist?' Analysing elementary students' contrasting representations of plurilingualism through sequential reflexive drawing, *Language and Intercultural Communication* 18(3), 315–334, DOI: 10 .1080/14708477.2018.1425412

  (2020). 'How does it look and feel to be plurilingual?': Analyzing children's representations of plurilingualism through collage. *International Journal of Bilingual Education and Bilingualism*. 23:8, 902-924, https://doi.org/10.1080/13670050.2017.1420033

  (2021). Reframing expertise: Learning with and from children as co- investigators of their plurilingual practices and experiences. In A. Pinter and H. Kuchah, eds., *Ethical and Methodological Issues in Researching Young Language Learners in School Contexts*. Bristol: Multilingual Matters, pp. 106–125.

Prasad, G. and Auger, N. (2015). « Mais est-ce que ça existe une personne monolingue ? » Plurilinguisme des élèves au Canada et en France, pratiques artistiques et langagières et apprentissage du français. In P. Prescod and J-M. Robert, eds., *La langue seconde de l'école à l'université: État des lieux. Carnets d'Ateliers de Sociolinguistique*. Paris: L'Harmattan, pp. 65–86.

Prasad, G. and Lory, M.-P. (2020). Linguistic and cultural collaboration in schools: Reconciling majority and minoritized language users. *TESOL Quarterly* 54, 797–822. https://doi.org/10.1002/tesq.560

Rosa, J. (2019). *Looking Like a Language, Sounding Like a Race: Raciolinguistic Ideologies and the Learning of Latinidad*. Oxford: Oxford University Press.

Rosa, J. and Flores, N. (2017). Unsettling race and language: Toward a raciolinguistic perspective. *Language in Society* 46(5), 621–647. https://doi.org/10.1017/S0047404517000562

Rymes, B. (2014). Communicative repertoire. In B. Street and C. Leung, eds., *The Routledge Companion to English Studies*. New York: Routledge, pp. 287–301.

29 From Plurilingual Experiences to Pluri-Artistic Practices

Elatiana Razafimandimbimanana

29.1 Introduction

Articulating the process of becoming a teacher-researcher in relation to the theme of plurilingualism is like talking about the moments when my biographical journey turned into a professional one. It is a difficult exercise. Not only does it involve retracing excursus routes but it also requires identifying pivotal events. Rather than celebrating plurilingualism itself, it is more a question of making sense out of experiences that are situated and reinvesting them according to a plurilingual perspective.

Selectively, I will first go back to how I have experienced plurilingualism within the French education system and the (un)learning process it represents. I will then discuss the construction of a 'plurilingual consciousness'. The implications are mainly conceptual and discursive. On the pedagogical level, it gives rise to pluri-artistic practices. This will be put into perspective through the New Caledonian terrain.

29.2 (Un)Learning to Become Plurilingual within the French Education System

My aim is not to describe the system but to share a subjective experience within the French education system in France. I arrived in France in the 1990s and had 2 years of high school to complete. Beforehand, I had already migrated several times (Madagascar, Kenya, Canada). Belongingness and linguistic norms therefore resonated to me as something relative as in a social construct. The succession of different educational systems made collaboration, creation as well as trial and error my main access to knowledge. With these dynamic representations of the knowledge continuum, the French education system seemed regressive to me. The learner's (in)actions are limited to a series of injunctions: keep quiet, listen, copy, spit out. At the university level, my accent with plural influences (African, British, North American) was subject to mononormative corrections in the English faculty: 'You have to adopt a pure accent, on the other hand, I can only evaluate you if you use the Received Pronunciation(comment made by a teacher in Phonetics)'. My equally 'impure' French has caused me to be interrupted by the teacher during a presentation, 'It's obvious that you're not from here! but go on … '.

In parallel to purist discourses, I became aware of the stakes of plurilingualism. Meeting Philippe Blanchet was decisive in that his discourse, a minority discourse, rejected mononormative approaches in order to place languages in a continuum of linguistic practices (see also Blanchet 2012). Thus he historicized monolingual ideology in the Republican narrative. The 'normative project' of the French school (Fabre, 2003) is effectively modelled on a 'republican melting pot' where imperative is the erasure or marginalization of differences (Meunier 2013, p. 90). Of course, all systems can be improved. I am particularly interested in questioning the discourse that values homogeneous language practice: what does it reveal of the French education system? From what I experienced in metropolitan France as well as in Kanaky New Caledonia, there seems to be an underlying ideal based on mononormative perspectives. I call this the *mónos*.

By *mónos*, I refer above all to an ideal in teaching that is characterized by,

> a monolithic vision of knowledge to be taught under the control of a centralized bureaucracy;
>
> a monolingual ideology with the injunction to 'all speak French and all speak the same French' (excerpt from a course, Blanchet 2004);
>
> a monopoly of transmissive, standardized pedagogy, breaking with the resources already existing among learners;
>
> a homogenized conception of learners and the skills to be attained through mononormative practices and monomodal approaches (reign of academic writing).

This idealization partly explains the secularity of institutional resistance to plurilingualism in France (Fillol and Vernaudon 2011; Escudé 2013, pp. 47–48; Moro 2013; Goï 2013). By understanding this, I was able to build my own legitimacy as a multilingual researcher (Razafimandimbimanana 2008; Razafimandimbimanana and Forlot 2013). This also made me see how voicing alternative standpoints helps contribute to a more inclusive society.

29.3   The Implications of a Multilingual Consciousness

The words we use to name social groups are not neutral: it impacts people's feelings and behaviours. There is a subtle frontier between wording and labelling. As a teacher, researcher and writer, my discursive choices can either empower social minorities or emphasize social minorization. For example, I have never been comfortable with the expression 'allophone'. Whether in the past as a child migrant or today as a teacher, researcher or writer. I'd rather use the words 'bilingual' or 'plurilingual' for they focus on existing linguistic resources instead of pointing at those considered absent (often the official languages in the given country of residence) (Razafimandimbimanana and Traisnel 2017; 2019) Also, what place do we give to the very people we are naming when we are the ones speaking in their behalf? A plurilingual consciousness thus implies taking an interest in 'plurilingual realities' (Goï 2013) but also working to counter the fact that plurilingualism is denied as a reality.

During a new migration in the South Pacific (2016), I noticed how the expression 'native speaker' was widespread among students. This is not the result of a lack of awareness of the social criticisms of the concept. Nor is it simply a fact of language convenience. Rather, the idea is to refer to the sacred link to the land, which structures and unifies collective identities in Oceania,

Through the relationship to the land, collective identities are elaborated and expressed. The Kanaks make the link to the land the main language of social hierarchy and morphology. (Bensa 1992, p. 108).

The students' accounts make me aware of the extent to which, for them, the land founds a sense of authenticity without this being comparable to Chomsky's theory of the ideal native speaker. Land also serves to legitimize a historical and political raison d'être,

Traditional land logic works on the Kanak independence discourse; it is also a response to the settlement colony imposed by France. (Bensa 1992: 130).

How can the specific relationship between the Kanak people and the concept of land be translated without importing expressions like 'native speaker' that convey purist ideologies? An interesting solution came from one of the Kanak languages : Drehu, spoken on the island of Lifou. In Drehu, the word 'badei' refers to a sense of belonging based on territory but not necessarily on nativity.

We borrow here the drehu expression "badei Numea" (literally "Noumea band") with which speakers identify a drehu speaker residing mainly in Noumea in contrast to "badei Drehu", the one residing mainly on the island of Lifou. (Razafimandimbimanana and Wacalie, 2019)

Plurilingual consciousness, coherent with an epistemology of 'polyphony' (Bakhtine 1984), does not fit well with *mónos*. Pedagogically, it is similarly opposed to the standardization of learner's individualities, skills and methods of access to knowledge.

29.4   Multi-Artistic Practices

For me, teaching means 'making social practices and social needs the goals of language teaching' (Blanchet 2004). And in Kanaky New Caledonia, this means socially valorizing plurilingual identities. The history of linguistic plurality in Kanaky New Caledonia is made up of prohibitions, invisibilities and devalorizing standardization, hence the vulnerability of plurilingual identities (Salaün

2009; Colombel and Fillol 2012; Razafimandimbimanana and Favard 2018; Razafimandimbimanana and Wacalie 2019; Frain et al. 2019):

> Colonial trauma is also narrated through linguistic forms of oppression. Indeed, 'linguistic insecurity', low self-esteem as plurilingual individuals are still prevalent among speakers of minority or indigenous languages (Razafimandimbimanana, 2021, p. 111).

Indigenous voices thus describe the French school in Oceania as the public space 'where one has learned to be ashamed of oneself' (Gorodey 2005). Several young people encountered in Kanaky New Caledonia similarly equate their plurilingualism with a 'handicap' that deprives as much as it disturbs. When I arrived, my ambition was to create an educational space that was inclusive of the sociolinguistic background of the learners. Since then, I have redefined my purpose by trying to help students rebuild their plurilingual self-esteem. This has led me to opt for reflexive and pluri-artistic pedagogical approaches.

Creativity and artistic skills are mainstream amongst students in Kanaky New Caledonians. This encouraged me to see a continuum between art and university programs. It significantly helps students succeed in a plurilingual and postcolonial context (Razafimandimbimanana 2019). The pluri-artsistic projects designed with them promote linguistic plurality through, the production of dance choreographies (Razafimandimbimanana and Karim, 2019), Street Art displays (Razafimandimbimanana and Wacalie 2019; Frain et al. 2019), advertising posters, art exhibitions (Razafimandimbimanana 2019) and workshops dedicated to local arts (see Appendix 29.1). Here, the pluri-artistic approach is a form of social mediation contributing to the circulation of knowledge. In a 2020 class project for example, students were asked to conduct sociolinguistic research then to write journalistic articles on their findings order to reach a wider audience. Their articles provided insightful information on a reality many plurilingual families feel but talk little of: the non-transmission of minority languages and the widespread feeling of 'linguistic guilt'.

While it allows plurilingual students to become producers of knowledge, educational pluralism remains dominated by the ideal of the *mónos* in the French system. Various reflexive accounts urge us to think this (Razafimandimbimanana and Goï 2014; Razafimandimbimanana 2019). A multilingual woman who recently graduated from the University of New Caledonia illustrates the weight of homogenizing practices within the French education system. She is currently preparing for national competitive examinations to become a teacher and reflects:

> I spent 3 years overcoming the idea that plurilingualism was a handicap and it only took a few minutes to relapse!

29.5   Perspectives

Interestingly, when it comes to the 'broken' education system in France (Cytermann 2007, p. 31; Delahaye 2007, p. 5; CNESCO 2016, p. 25), it is

Figure 29.1 The local indigenous environment becomes our classroom
(University of New Caledonia, 2019)

often believed that the students are to blame considering their low motivation
or general disengagement. I find it insightful that learners' lack of interest or
involvement is attributed to be the major problem. At least, this is what
throughout long-term within the French education system in several regions
(Brittany, Tours, Kanaky New Caledonia, Martinique) where teachers

commonly point at three main barriers to education: 'flagrant lack of parental authority', 'deficits in government funding' and 'a demotivated generation'. Sometimes racist representations resurface e.g. beliefs some students come from 'lazy communities'. In turn, many parents share a negative representation of teachers who are considered to be 'out of touch with the real world'. As for students, they tend to put the blame on teachers' who lack pedagogical skills. In short, it always seems as though education failures are associated to *the others*. Yet reluctance to self-questioning acts as a hindrance to systemic improvements. In this perspective, a better integration of plurilingual experiences within educational systems stems from individual reflexivity.

A collective project only makes sense if it admits the plurality of point of views, experiences, stories, ideals and analyses. This polyphony refers in some ways to the 'collaboration of cultures' defended by Lévi-Strauss'

The real contribution of cultures does not consist in the list of their particular inventions, but in the differential gap they offer between them. The sense of gratitude and humility that each member of a given culture can and must feel towards all the others can only be based on a conviction: that other cultures are different from his own, in the most varied ways; and this, even if the ultimate nature of these differences escapes him or if, despite his best efforts, he can only imperfectly penetrate them. (Levi-Strauss 1952, pp. 76–77)

We can also speak of a 'differential gap' between scientific cultures hence the need for more creativity in our pluridisciplinary actions. Futhermore, promoting plurilingual experiences calls for holistic institutional spaces that empower all the other forms of social, ethnic and gender minorities.

REFERENCES

Bakhtine, M. (1984). *Esthétique de la création verbale*. Paris: Gallimard.

Bélanger, N. (2007). Une école, des langues... ? L'enseignement du français en milieu minoritaire en Ontario. *Le français aujourd'hui* 158, 49–57. https://doi.org/10.3917/lfa.158.0049

Bensa, A. (1992). Terre kanak: Enjeu politique d'hier et d'aujourd'hui. *Esquisse d'un modèle comparatif. Etudes rurales* 127-128, 107–131.

Blanchet, P. (2004). *De la didactique des langues à la didactique du plurilinguisme*. www.canal-u.tv/video/universite_rennes_2_crea_cim/de_la_didactique_des_langues_a_la_didactique_du_plurilinguisme.14786

(2012). L'identification des langues: Une question clé pour une politique scientifique et linguistique efficiente. *Modèles linguistiques* 66, 17–25. https://doi.org/10.4000/ml.282

CNESCO (Conseil national d'évaluation du système scolaire) (2016). *Inégalités sociales et migratoires: Comment l'école amplifie-t-elle les inégalités?* Paris: CNESCO. www.cnesco.fr/wp-content/uploads/2016/09/160927Dossier_synthese_inegalites.pdf

Colombel, C. and Fillol, V. (2012). Enjeux des langues d'enseignement dans la construction d'une identité scolaire des jeunes océaniens francophones. In F. Demougin and J. Sauvage, eds., *La construction identitaire à l'école: Perspectives linguistiques et plurielles*. Paris: L'Harmattan, pp. 113–120.

Cytermann, J. (2007). Les choix budgétaires en matière d'éducation. *Pouvoirs* 122(3), 31–44.

Delahaye, J. (2007). Le collège unique, miroir grossissant des difficultés de gouverner l'éducation. *Pouvoirs* 122(3), 5–17.

Escudé, P. (2013). Intégrer les langues au cœur des apprentissages: Politique, économie et didactique de l'intercompréhension. *Passages de Paris* 8, 42–61.

Fabre, M. (2003). L'école peut-elle encore former l'esprit? *Revue française de pédagogie* 143, 7–15.

Fillol, V. and Vernaudon, J. (2011). Toutes les langues à l'école: Enseignement des langues kanak et éveil aux langues de la région Asie-Pacifique à l'école calédonienne. In Foued Laroussi and Fabien Liénard, eds., *Plurilinguisme, politique linguistique et éducation: Quels éclairages pour Mayotte ?* Rouen: Presses universitaires de Rouen et du Havre, pp. 203–213.

Frain, S., Razafimandimbimanana, E. and Wacalie, F. (2019). Speaking back: Challenging linguistic microaggressions in New Caledonia through street art. *Pasifika Rising*. www.pasifikarising.org/speaking-back-challenging-linguistic-microaggressions-in-new-caledonia-through-street-art/

Goï, C. (2013). Les langues à l'école, les langues et l'école: Tentation monolingue versus réalités plurilingues. *Diversité* 176, 33–38.

Gorodey, D. (2005). Discours d'ouverture au 17th colloque CORAIL. In V. Fillol and J. Vernaudon, eds., *Stéréotypes et représentations en Océanie: Actes du 17th Colloque CORAIL*. Nouméa: Corail, pp. 13–15.

Lévi-Strauss, C. (1952). *Race et histoire*. Paris: Denoël.

Meunier, O. (2013). Un rapport difficile à la diversité dans l'école de la République. *Revue internationale d'éducation de Sèvres* 63. https://doi.org/10.4000/ries.3486

Moro, M-R. (2012). *Enfants de l'immigration, une chance pour l'école: Entretiens avec Joanna Peiron et Denis Peiron*. Montrouge: Bayard.

Razafimandimbimanana, E. (2019). Voix/voies pluriartistiques de l' 'interKulturel': Les coulisses d'une exposition par des étudiants en Nouvelle-Calédonie. Dans N. Auger et F. Dervin. *Les nouvelles voix/voies de l'interculturel: Revue Le langage et l'homme* 1, 159–178.

(2021). La diversité linguistique à l'école: représentations d'élèves en Nouvelle-Calédonie. In R. Ailincai et S. Ferrière, eds., *École et famille, Langues et cultures en Océanie: Regards croisés*. Nouméa: PUNC, pp. 102–116.

Razafimandimbimanana, E. and Favard, N. (2018). *Les élèves aux besoins éducatifs particuliers se mettent en représentation: « On parle plusieurs langues pour progresser ». Actes du séminaire de recherche régional. CREFAP/OIF. Enseignement et formation du/en français en contexte plurilingue*. Hanoi: Edition de l'Université nationale du Vietnam, pp. 311–335.

Razafimandimbimanana, E. and Forlot, G. (2013). Des chercheurs plurilingues et plurimigrants en français : des recherches *anéoué* différentes ?. In V. Castellotti, ed., *Le(s) français dans la mondialisation*. Brussels: Editions modulaires européennes, pp. 333–348.

Razafimandimbimanana, E. and Goï, C. (2014). Retour sur une expérience formative à et par la réflexivité: Lieu de "mobilités réflexivesthe." *Glottopol* 24. http://glottopol.univ-rouen.fr/numero_24.html#res_razafi

Razafimandimbimanana, E. and Karim, S. (2021). Freeze sur le Http-Hop à l'Université en. In S. Geneix-Rabault and M. Stern, eds., *La musique dans le Pacifique sud. Quand l'industrie s'en mêle. Création musicale et dynamiques sociales*. Paris: l'Harmattan. Cahiers du Pacifique sud contemporain. pp. 189–212

Razafimandimbimanana, E. and Traisnel, C. (2017). Dire les minorités linguistiques en sciences sociales : les notions de 'vitalité' et d''allophone' dans les contextes canadien et français. *Mots. Les langages du politique* 3(3), 111–126. https://doi .org/10.4000/mots.22888

    (2019). La non-neutralité du chercheur au prisme de deux concepts usités en matière de minorités linguistiques: 'vitalité' et 'allophone'. In K. Gauvin and I. Violette, eds., *Minorisation linguistique et inégalités sociales*. Brussels: Peter Lang. pp. 15-43

Razafimandimbimanana, E. and Wacalie, F. (2019). Les micro-agressions linguistiques. *Hermès, La Revue* 1(1), 156–157. https://doi.org/10.3917/herm.083.0156

Salaün, M. (2009). *L'école indigène: Nouvelle-Calédonie 1885–1945*. Rennes: PUR.

APPENDIX 29.2

Figure 29.2 Aperçu des projets pluriartistiques

30   A Personal and Professional Journey to Multilingualism

Nikolay Slavkov (Николай Славков)

30.1   Language Biography

I was born in 1976 in Sofia, Bulgaria, and was raised in what I now realize was an ethnically, culturally and linguistically homogeneous environment, with an easily and clearly identifiable native language: Bulgarian. However, by growing up in Bulgaria, at that time part of the Soviet Bloc and a strong ally of the Soviet Union, I was naturally exposed to some Russian, a close cognate language of Bulgarian. In my early childhood there were often, if not mostly, Russian movies on TV. As far as I can recall, these were not dubbed into Bulgarian (unlike some other foreign programming) and had subtitles instead; thus, I heard the Russian language with some degree of frequency and regularity at that time. In addition, once a week, the main channel of the Bulgarian national television (one of only two channels available to Bulgarians back then) tuned in to the Soviet state television's prime-time newscast in Russian, without subtitles or dubbing, for an hour or so. I cannot imagine being interested in the content of the news at that early stage of my life, but I do remember developing a fascination with the sounds of the language and with the news anchors: people from a different country and culture.

Subsequently, I started learning Russian in third grade as a school subject which was taught in a traditional and curricularized way (Valdés 2015; see also King, this volume). One of my first memories of this type of language instruction was a quiz in which I performed poorly in the first few weeks of school that year. I had missed a previous class where the difference between animate (living) and inanimate (non-living) objects had been explained. This is an important concept for learners of Russian, at least from a grammarian's point of view, as case endings on Russian nouns can vary based on this distinction. Not knowing what was required of me on the quiz, I randomly classified balloons and trucks in the same category as people and animals, on what I think was some sort of picture matching task, and thus received an unforgiving *Очень плохо!* "Very bad!" mark written in red on my quiz. I then had to work hard to redeem myself in the eyes of the strict teacher.

Figure 30.1 After a number of years of professional and personal experiences with languages, I'm happy with my own linguistic identity

This happened quickly since I quite liked memorizing case endings, prepositions and grammar rules. I was intrigued by the discovery that a language whose words were so similar to those of my own language had a very different phonological and morpho-syntactic system (for example, modern Bulgarian, unlike Russian, has lost its rich noun case-marking system almost entirely). Unfortunately, later on in school I developed a distaste for the Russian language, as the method seemed too strict and too focused on rote memorization rather than on learning to communicate well in this language.

Learning English, the next foreign language I was exposed to in the Bulgarian school system, was quite a different story. English instruction started a bit later than Russian, in fifth grade, and I loved it from the beginning. The approach was still quite traditional but I believe it was more in line with some of the then current language teaching practices around the world. It was a four skills approach, with a reading and writing emphasis, and involved comprehending and analyzing texts, taking dictations, memorization of vocabulary, explanations of grammar rules and follow-up practice exercises in a Present Produce Practice (PPP) fashion, some dialogues and some teacher–class interactions (e.g. answering comprehension questions). Learning this language must have been more difficult than learning Russian, as English is typologically more distant from Bulgarian. It also entailed learning a new writing system (Bulgarian uses the Cyrillic alphabet). Yet my enthusiasm for English and the somewhat more interesting instructional approach, compared to what I had seen in Russian, helped me excel in this subject and want to become an English teacher one day.

I also remember having teacher trainees come to English class during the first year I took this subject. Apart from being young and enthusiastic about teaching, these pre-service teachers exposed us for the first time to what must have been a communicative approach. They spoke to us primarily in the target language, acted out new vocabulary for us instead of translating it, and tried to set up a more interactive classroom, which was a great novelty and comple-mented nicely our regular teacher's instruction. For a twelve–year-old who was quickly developing a passion for the English language, and language teaching and learning in general, this was a privileged early exposure to different methods. (I would get to read about and reflect on these much later in life, as a Master's student in Canada, and later on as a professor trying to make sense of such methods so I can discuss them with my students.)

As clichéd as it may sound, English in my childhood also represented a way of reaching beyond the Iron Curtain of the Cold War, both economically and culturally. I came to associate English (and other languages of the West) with colourful clothes, high-quality chocolate and 'new' technology such as the Sony Walkman portable cassette player. I imagined that one day I would be able to visit or even immigrate to the West and indulge in a world of colourful consumerism (I did not see anything problematic in this idea at that point).

In high school and university I took a few other language classes, including German, Italian and even Norwegian for a term, and thus became exposed to additional languages. I worked as an English language teacher in my home country and later on in China, where I learned to get by in the markets or find my way around a very large city using a few words of Mandarin. I did not become proficient in any of these languages, though, partly because of the short exposure and changing life circumstances, and partly because I was already quite fluent in English and enjoyed one of the main privileges (and also a plight) of a user of a global language: being able to be understood and understand others, without necessarily having to use the local language.

30.2   The Evolution of Key Concepts and Practices in My Career and My Personal Life

30.2.1   *Multilingualism, Plurilingualism, Heteroglossia, Language Repertoires and Multilingual Education*

Although at present I am perhaps most interested in researching multilingual-ism from family, societal and educational perspectives, I discovered this interest quite late in my career. For a long time I shied away from the concept of multilingualism as it seemed daunting to me, both personally and from a scholarly perspective. On a personal level, I used to consider myself bilingual (at most), as I spoke Bulgarian and English fluently and frequently, but not multilingual, since I had various lower proficiencies in other languages, and thus did not think I was worthy of calling myself multilingual. I used to see multilingualism as multiple monolingual proficiencies.

This also had an impact on my research, where I was initially interested in second language acquisition (SLA), using a somewhat strict definition of the term *second*. As a graduate student I was exposed to Chomskyan generative linguistics and my views of language, even a few years after I received my doctorate, were still strongly influenced by this (fascinating but not very relevant to language teaching and learning) paradigm. Thus, I used to rely on the notion of an idealized native speaker as a reference point and compared language learners to that norm both theoretically and in experimental work (Slavkov 2009, 2014). For example, I would look at Bulgarian speakers who were learning English, or French speakers who were learning English, and focus on the abstract linguistic properties of their native language as well as the abstract linguistic properties of the target language (perhaps an abstract instantiation of earlier notions of contrastive linguistics in L2 acquisition). Then I would make predictions about what might happen in the process of acquisition and try to verify those predictions using a learner group and a native-speaking control group. Native speaker norms served as a useful basis for comparison and a source of explanation of second language phenomena, within a general theory of language. However, there was little room for multilingualism in my work within this tradition because multilingualism seemed too messy; it was already a challenge to try to take account of two languages (native and L2) to introduce extra factors that might confound the picture further.

While the messiness of multilingualism was something that I wanted to avoid both in my personal life and in my research for some time, my thinking eventually evolved. I came across Vivian Cook's (1991, 1999) work on multicompetence and was introduced to the concept of plurilingualism and language repertoires (Coste, Moore and Zarate, 1997, and various subsequent work), where uneven proficiencies in various languages are embraced and valorized. I also came across some work that questioned the fundamental assumptions, both theoretical and methodological, of the notion of a (monolingual) native speaker as a reference norm (Davies 1991; Singh 2010; among others). I started seeing the not-so-positive social and educational implications of native speaker paradigms in my immediate surroundings (Slavkov, Melo-Pfeifer and Kerschhofer-Puhalo 2021). For example, a bilingual school where one of my daughters was being educated, ironically, could not classify her as a bilingual from birth speaker because the forms and the computer database only allowed for a single native language to be entered in her record. This triggered a series of research studies on the language background profiling undertaken at public schools across Canada (Slavkov 2016a, 2018) showing how difficult it is to capture the complex realities of today's heteroglossic children and youth.

Changing my perspective of native speaker norms also made me feel liberated on a personal level. Discovering plurilingualism helped me to not feel guilty about not having learned languages other than English fluently; I became more comfortable with my own linguistic repertoire and started seeing myself as a plurilingual speaker. This also inspired me to propose a new language teaching initiative, called the Linguistic Risk-Taking Initiative (Slavkov and Séror 2019), at the University of Ottawa. One of the main goals of this initiative is to encourage learners to take risks in using their second official language (English or French) and speak it in a variety of new contexts across our bilingual campus, outside of the language classroom where they may be acquiring it.

My shift from monolingual native-speaker oriented approaches towards multilingual or plurilingual approaches was also facilitated by raising my children as bilingual (English-Bulgarian) at home and subsequently adding a third language through schooling (French). The unequal and uneven use and proficiencies of these three languages in their repertoires further put things into perspective for me and pushed me into indulging in the 'messiness' of multilingualism, instead of avoiding it. I also became much more interested in issues of language transmission, maintenance, shift and loss, and alternations of dominant languages in bilingual children's early development (Slavkov 2015). While these revolve around phenomena that have long been discussed in the literature (e.g. Fishman 1991; De Houwer 2009; among others), some newer conceptualizations such as family language policy (King et al. 2008) and multilingual education helped inject new energy into my research on the relationships between home and school languages (Slavkov 2016b) and offered additional angles into my teaching and in my family language practices.

In terms of research methodology, I became favourably disposed to case studies, questionnaires, qualitative interviews, language portraits, etc., where individual and personal experiences were valid and important, rather than being seen as flawed by the lack of generalizability and missing baselines or comparison groups (something that I had been preoccupied with in the past). I came to realize that the native speaker norm, the idea of speaking a language like an idealized (monolingual) individual or a homogenious group of speakers, had become less and less relevant to me as a person, and also as a professional who teaches, researches and thinks about language in an increasingly globalized, heterogeneous and heteroglossic world.

30.2.2 Translanguaging and Language Awareness

The relatively recent construct of translanguaging has captured the imagination of researchers and teachers around the world. Initially developed in a school context (Williams 1994; 2002) but subsequently extended to other settings, such as the family, the community and society in general (García 2009 and subsequent work), the ideology behind this construct has influenced my thinking a great deal. In my personal and professional journey, I have seen the benefit of popularizing a concept that valorizes and empowers the complex and hybrid language use of bilingual or multilingual speakers (beyond more traditional concepts such as code-switching, which are, of course, well known and widely researched). Legitimizing the practice of drawing on two or more languages as a communicative resource, and indeed encouraging individuals, communities and even institutions to (continue to) engage in this practice without stigma, has tremendous implications in terms of language democratization and equality on a global scale.

To give just a few examples, translanslanguaging allows immigrant children (or minority language speakers) who are placed in a new (majority) school environment to not be silenced while acquiring a new school language, and indeed affords a new perspective on and new source of pride in the diversity brought by minority languages. As a pedagogical resource, translanguaging may offer creative and potentially far-reaching tools. Translanguaging practices can be employed in multilingual classrooms where teachers do not necessarily speak students' minority languages, to still foster environments where these languages can flourish alongside the majority ones. As such, translanguaging can offer both new pedagogical advances in multilingualism and new perspectives in our thinking on language policy and language ideology (see also King, this volume). In addition, explicitly allowing or encouraging speakers to translanguage may result in general destigmatization of bilingual and multilingual practices and a higher level of language awareness on the individual, family and societal levels, thus further integrating communicative, emotional, symbolic and other functions of language. Of course, translanguaging has generated a great deal of debate, and some authors have argued against its benefits and transformative power (Jaspers 2018) or called for careful consideration and possibly limited use in minority language settings (Cenoz and Gorter 2017). As more research in this direction emerges, the evolution of the concept will undoubtedly continue.

30.3 Conclusion

Self-ethnographic approaches such as language biographies and general reflection on one's language learning journey on the one hand and evolution as a researcher on the other are not particularly common in the language teaching and learning literature. This newly emerging mixed genre poses interesting questions regarding who the target audiences are, what interests they may have in reading such work or what benefits they may be able to derive from it. This chapter has certainly helped me pause and reflect on my own language repertoire and the circumstances under which it was developed as well as on the influences it has had on me as a researcher and on my perspectives on recent methodological and conceptual developments in applied linguistics and language education. I conclude with the hope that the chapter and the other contributions in this volume will be useful to language teachers and learners and to applied linguists and educators in general.

REFERENCES

Cenoz, J. and Gorter, D. (2017). Minority languages and sustainable translanguaging: Threat or opportunity? *Journal of Multilingual and Multicultural Development.* https://doi.org/10.1080/01434632.2017.1284855

Cook, V. J. (1991). The poverty-of-the-stimulus argument and multicompetence. *Second Language Research* 7(2), 103–117.

  (1999). Going beyond the native speaker in language teaching. *TESOL Quarterly* 33 (2), 185–209.

Coste, D., Moore, D. and Zarate, G. (1997). *Compétence plurilingue et pluriculturelle: Vers un cadre européen commun de référence pour l'enseignement et l'apprentissage des langues vivantes: Études préparatoires* [Plurilingual and Pluricultural Competence: Toward a Common European Reference Framework for Teaching and Learning Living Languages: Preparatory Studies]. Strasbourg: Editions du Conseil de l'Europe.

Davies, A. (1991). *The Native Speaker in Applied Linguistics.* Edinburgh: Edinburgh University Press.

De Houwer, A. (2009). *Bilingual First Language Acquisition.* Tonawanda, NY: Multilingual Matters.

Fishman, J. A. (1991). *Reversing Language Shift: Theoretical and Empirical Foundations of Assistance to Threatened Languages.* Philadelphia: Multilingual Matters.

García, O. (2009). *Bilingual Education in the 21st Century: A Global Perspective.* Malden, MA: Basil/Blackwell.

Jaspers, J. (2018). The transformative limits of translanguaging. *Language & Communication* 58, 1–10.

King, K. A., Fogle, L. and Logan-Terry, A. (2008). Family language policy. *Language and Linguistics Compass* 2(5), 907–922.

Singh, R. (2010). Multilingualism, sociolinguistics and theories of linguistic form: Some unfinished reflections. *Language Sciences* 32(6), 624–637.

Slavkov, N. (2009). The acquisition of complex wh- questions in the L2 English of Canadian French and Bulgarian speakers: Medial wh- constructions, inversion phenomena, and avoidance strategies. Doctoral Dissertation, University of Ottawa.

(2014). Long-distance wh- movement and long-distance wh- movement avoidance in L2 English: Evidence from French and Bulgarian speakers. *Second Language Research* 31, 179–210. https://doi.org/10.1177/0267658314554939

(2015). Language attrition and reactivation in the context of bilingual first language acquisition. *International Journal of Bilingual Education and Bilingualism* 18(6), 715–734.

(2016a). In Search of the Right Questions: Language Background Profiling at Ontario Public Schools. *Canadian Journal of Applied Linguistics* 19(1), 22–45.

(2016b). Family language policy and school language choice: Pathways to bilingualism and multilingualism in a Canadian context. *International Journal of Multilingualism* 14(4), 378–400. https://doi.org/10.1080/14790718.2016.1229319

(2018). What is your 'first' language in bilingual Canada? A study of language background profiling at publicly-funded elementary schools across three provinces. *International Journal of Bilingual Education and Bilingualism* 21(1), 20–37. https://doi.org/10.1080/13670050.2015.1126217

Slavkov, N., Melo-Pfeifer, S. and Kerschhofer-Puhalo, N. (2021). *The Changing Face of the "Native Speaker": Perspectives from Multilingualism and Globalization, Berlin,* Boston: De Gruyter Mouton. https://doi.org/10.1515/9781501512353

Slavkov, N. and Séror, J. (2019). The development of the linguistic risk-taking initiative at a bilingual post-secondary institution in Canada, *Canadian Modern Language Review* 75(3), 254–272. https://doi.org/10.3138/cmlr.2018-0202

Valdés, G. (2015). Latin@s and the intergenerational continuity of Spanish: The challenges of curricularizing language. *International Multilingual Research Journal* 9(4), 253–273.

Williams, C. (1994). Arfarniad o ddulliau dysgu ac addysgu yng nghyd-destun addysg uwchradd ddwyieithog [An evaluation of teaching and learning methods in the context of bilingual secondary education]. Doctoral dissertation, University of Wales, Bangor.

(2002). *A Language Gained: A Study of Language Immersion at 11–16 Years of Age.* Bangor: University of Wales Bangor, School of Education.

31 Journey towards a Translanguaging Pedagogy for Social Justice

From School French to Critical Race Theory

Heather Jane Smith

My interaction with languages and languaging is best described in four phases: very early childhood; formal schooling; work and travels; and new understandings. It has been a sort of bumping into languaging for different purposes, audiences and contexts over time.

31.1 Early Childhood

When I was only a few months old my family immigrated to Toronto, Canada. We lived there until I was five years old. I have only vague impressions of happy memories. We lived together with families from many countries: a sort of global village in an immigrant area of the city. At kindergarten (school didn't start until the age of six) I played happily with friends and was under no pressure to learn to read or write. Our family was best friends with a family from Germany, and my friend Yvonne and I spoke to each other in Canadian English, while her parents spoke to her predominantly in German and to me in a mixture of German and English. We left Canada to return to North-East England when I was five. I spoke Canadian English and the sort of basic everyday German a five-year-old might speak.

31.2 Formal Schooling

Schooling in England was a shock to me, and between the ages of five and six I first experienced being bullied. I was treated by both pupils and teachers alike as different because of my accent, and stupid as I didn't yet read or write English. I felt a sharp sense of isolation and despair and I can still vividly recall certain critical incidents. Eventually, we settled down in a small mining village, where I was incredibly lucky to have teachers who were interested in the world beyond England, and hence in me too. Within a year I had lost my Canadian accent, and learned the 'proper' words for things, as I appropriated standard English (as opposed to Canadian English) and Geordie, a dialect only spoken in the North-East region of England. Geordie is marked by a particular grammar and lexis largely unused outside of the region, which appear to have

Figure 31.1 Me and my Canadian poncho in 1970s England

originated from the early appearance of the Angles from Denmark. So, for me, sidewalk became pavement, throw became hoy (Geordie) and pop (soft drink) remained pop, a term shared by Canadian English and Geordie. By the age of six I was a fully fledged Geordie speaker and I no longer recalled German, or so I thought.

I didn't bump into new languaging practices again until I learnt German and French as school subjects in secondary school. I loved the feel of French on my tongue, but German came more easily to my thinking. My teachers said I had a surprisingly good German accent. It took years for me to understand this was probably because of my early childhood interaction with German! I enjoyed learning languages in school, far more than *English* language and literature, but not as much as maths and science, which were the subjects I pursued to 'A' level.[1] But I never quite lost my interest in languages and when studying for a

---

[1] 'A' level: approximation of Advanced Placement exams in North America.

maths degree, I found myself choosing the module 'Russian for mathematicians', to support access to maths papers written in Russian. Again, I enjoyed the experience, but I was left with very little applicable knowledge, and this language too faded from memory.

31.3   Work and Travels

On leaving university aged twenty-one, I went straight to Zimbabwe as a VSO (voluntary service overseas) maths teacher. Although English is the official language of Zimbabwe, and is used to teach subjects at secondary level, as part of our training beforehand and in country, we were taught basic Shona (the Zimbabwean language spoken in the area where we were teaching). I found Shona full of beautiful and unfamiliar sounds, which I enjoyed playing with, but my focus was largely elsewhere and I learnt little beyond formulaic phrases and simple sentence constructions, many of which I recall to this day! It was unusual for a white person to know Shona (or any of the Zimbabwean languages), and so I used my knowledge of Shona to distinguish myself from the normalised constructions of a Murungu (white man, with connotative meanings around wealth and power, but also sometimes employed to denigrate). Only much later in life did I understand this as an act of the very privilege I wanted to deny. But I learnt other things in Zimbabwe; most significantly, I learnt the impact of racism on children's education.

   After completing a teaching qualification (Primary PGCE) and teaching as a primary class teacher back in the North-East of England, I set off to teach in New Zealand as part of my continued quest to learn about race, racism and power. I worked first in a Te Reo Maori class, wherein the teaching of the curriculum, or at least some part thereof, ought to be in Maori. At first I was taught Maori by a colleague, and later attended official evening classes, but the same pattern emerged: I learnt a little for personal gain, but not sufficient to effectively support pupils' learning.

   In both contexts my focus of attention was race and power, but I lacked sufficient awareness of the role of language status and the global domination of English in the maintenance of unequal power relations.

   On returning to England, I maintained an interest in multilingualism by becoming a 'section 11' teacher, employed to support pupils with English as an additional language. While I cannot pinpoint particular critical incidents, working with pupils and teachers soon taught me how pupils' languages are operationalised by pupils and teachers as an 'othering' device to act against pupils with EAL within the education system. This became a rationale for my PhD research (Smith 2004), following which I became a university lecturer.

31.4   New Understandings

In my role as teacher educator preparing student teachers to enter the profession, I quickly learned how entrenched societal attitudes are, even among a group of young individuals genuinely open to change. Over the years I have developed a curriculum and pedagogical approach similar to Boler's (1999) pedagogy of discomfort, which encompasses notions of multilingualism within a framework of critical race theory (Smith and Lander 2012; Smith 2014). More recent research, however, introduced the concept of translanguaging, which more comfortably positions multilingualism within a transformative agenda. Of course, this won't be my final interaction with languages and languaging, but is the point at which I have now arrived and from which I write the rest of this chapter, as learner, teacher and researcher (of pupils' learning and teacher education).

31.4.1   Multilingualism/Plurilingualism/Heteroglossia

Bilingual/ism was the terminology I first encountered professionally in my role as specialist teacher of pupils with English as an additional language (EAL), and is the terminology I employed in my doctoral thesis. Indeed, in schools and hence also on teacher education courses in England, the terms bilingual and EAL are ubiquitous and are often conflated. They are employed in England as a shorthand for multilingual/ism, as it is acknowledged that pupils often use more than two languages in their daily lives in and outside of school; one of the reasons for changing the term English as a second language to English as an *additional* language. Levine (1990, p. 5) explains the trajectory towards use of the term 'bilingual' in England from classifications such as 'beginner learners' or 'English as a second language children', as a means of avoiding concomitant prevailing prejudiced attitudes, which 'so diminishes [pupils'] status, abilities, and talents, which has so directly affected the educational provision that has been made for them, and hence, has so negatively affected their chances of achievement'. What I have found over the years, however, is that the term EAL has become pejorative in the very sense which Levine argued as long ago as 1990 was to be avoided. Student teachers and teachers often refer to pupils with EAL as 'having no language', or as 'lacking proficiency', affecting construction of pupils' learning needs. Incidents of pupils with EAL being placed into 'lower ability' groups remains a prevalent feature in the classrooms I and my students visit, even when teachers publicly denounce assumptions of cognitive deficiency in relation to EAL.

Because of the close relationship between the terms EAL and bilingual in education discourse in England, and attendant notions of deficit, as well as residual traces of judgements of unequal proficiency in relation to understandings of bilingualism (e.g. 'balanced bilingualism'), I gradually moved towards use of the term multilingualism in both my teaching and research. As the term EAL is still used in governmental and policy discourse, and appears in the teacher standards in England, however, it is therefore essential that student teachers are introduced to it. Consequently, I began to purposely distinguish my use of the terms when working with student teachers: I use the term bi/multilingual as a descriptor for individual pupils to afford status to their multilingualism, whereas I use the term EAL when describing the process or learning conditions for bi/multilingual pupils, stressing the distinction between cognitive difficulties and experience in English. I strenuously avoid the phrase 'EAL pupil' to interrupt the tendency of student teachers to define a pupil wholly in terms of their experience in learning languages as opposed to the myriad ways a pupil might think about him/herself.

In interacting with French colleagues in a European research project (ROMtels at: https://research.ncl.ac.uk/romtels/), most notably Dr Nathalie Auger, I have been persuaded by the term plurilingual/ism given the particular definition employed in the Common European Framework of Reference for Languages (Council of Europe 2001, p. 4), which distinguished plurilingualism beyond knowledge of a number of languages to an understanding which

emphasises the fact that as an individual person's experience of language in its cultural contexts expands, ... he or she does not keep these languages and cultures in strictly separated mental compartments, but rather builds up a communicative competence to which all knowledge and experience of language contributes and in which languages interrelate and interact.

The ROMtels team argue that this construction is better aligned to the concept of translanguaging (as below), which we also draw on (Smith, Robertson, Auger et al. 2017).

Shifting the words used to describe pupils and their learning on its own, however, although important and well intentioned, has proven largely ineffective in my role as teacher educator. There is more for student teachers to learn, or rather unlearn, in terms of learned prejudices, before use of new terminology becomes meaningful to transformed practice, as exemplified in the discourse of multicultural education.

The discourse of multicultural education forms a far greater part of the everyday social and political fabric of UK culture and national politics than intercultural education, a term more prevalent in the academic study of education. For example, our undergraduates study intercultural education as part of a study on the global dimensions of education, investigating relations between culture, identity and communication. Multiculturalism (and related polices including therefore multicultural education) on the other hand, is a prevalent concept in the UK, and is disparaged from both the right and left of British politics: the right (including neoliberal New Labour) presume it is the *cause* of social segregation, whereas the left critique related policies as superficial, ineffective in bringing about race equity (Gillborn 2008). Recently, the right have more overtly positioned multilingualism alongside religious affiliation (particularly Islam) as part of the construct of multiculturalism in a process of 'othering' some communities as a threat to British values and national security (Smith 2016). The consequent effect on education policies has been to effectively erase concerns for race equality (Smith 2013), replacing this with the overtly assimilationist agenda of British values, while simultaneously sidelining policies which promote multilingualism in schools. In a recent project, I argue this shift as demonstrative of a burgeoning racist nativist discourse in English media and political representations. In working with student teachers, therefore, I have learned to acknowledge their likely prior interactions with and prevailing negative preconceptions of multicultural education, including multilingualism, and the possibility of their naivety to the associated politics. To recognise and begin to 'unlearn' prejudices around race and language is a necessary first step in teacher education.

31.4.2   *Linguistic Repertoire/Communicative Repertoire*

As part of a first step in teacher education towards unlearning prejudices, I draw loosely on the concept of a linguistic repertoire in terms of the language varieties of particular communities within the UK; mostly in terms of communities who speak what is commonly referred to as 'community languages' but also more recently in terms of Eastern European Roma families. In order to shift students' thinking in relation to the status of pupils and their languages, I find it useful to begin by considering Geordie as just one of the many varieties of English with a distinct history and of equal worth to other varieties. I then introduce the plurilingual everyday lives of pupils in their class.

I conclude this section by reiterating a recurring theme, important to the subsequent consideration of key practices. Over time, as teacher and researcher, I have learnt that changing terminology when working with teachers and students, even when the rationale is made explicit, does not in itself effect the essential transformation of attitude, understandings or pedagogy. I have therefore concluded that one cannot separate the study and teaching of bi/multi/plurilingualism and multiculturalism from race equality: they are intertwined politically and historically as I have already indicated, thereby influencing teachers' pedagogical choices.

1) Awareness of Language/Language Awareness

   This is not a practice I regularly employ with student teachers, nor do I witness it in Primary schools in England. It became more present in my thinking, however, as a result of the ROMtels project, as a mechanism to illuminate comparisons between languages. The French partners demonstrated how this practice mobilised 'pupils' languages as resources to support the development of their proficiency in the language of schooling' (Smith et al. 2017, p. 21).

2) Intercomprehension/Education for Cross-Linguistic Transfer

I would suggest the previously mentioned two practices relate more to language teachers and teaching, rather than the practice of teaching *all subjects*, including English, to pupils with English as an additional language. It is the everyday messy reality of this context and educating student teachers and teachers to develop equitable practices within this context which continues to concern me most. Very recently, I have begun to examine translanguaging as a concept and pedagogy as a way forward. Here languaging is a verb, a social act people do, rather than a linguistic object that is possessed and learnt independent of its use (e.g. Garcia 2009).

3) Translanguaging

During the ROMtels project, we searched for a way to encapsulate the pedagogical approach we were advocating which assumes,

- The lived reality of languaging for purposeful meaning making in plurilingual discursive practice as a normal everyday occurrence for pupils who live and learn in two or more languages;
- An understanding that enabling such plurilingual purposeful talk in classrooms is hugely beneficial to pupils' learning;
- Differential power relations between interlocutors and between languages in terms of their perceived relative status, of which teachers are often unaware;
- A recognition that parents and families are languaging experts: they know what languages and forms of languages their children use, and when, and with whom and why,
- A recognition that teachers are the experts of pedagogical and curriculum knowledge.

We also recognised, as discussed earlier, that teachers often object to plurilingual practices partly because of misunderstandings about language learning per se but also, and crucially, because of socio-political positions which must be addressed in order to enable such an approach. Given this, the critical aspect for us in drawing on the notion of translanguaging was that it combined a concern for naturalistic usage-based plurilingual norms and subsequent opportunities for learning, with an awareness of and concern for inequitable power relations, in seeking to challenge the status quo.

Keeping a sharp focus on these dual aspects of translanguaging in informing the production of plurilingual education resources which require parent–teacher collaboration revealed an emancipatory impact on pupils and teachers in schools, on parents' involvement with schools and on the overall school community. Pupils were able to draw on all of their languaging practices as resources for learning (for video evidence see http://research.ncl.ac.uk/romtels/resources/video/), which we viewed as their *right*. Moreover, the raised status of pupils' and parents' plurilingualism, and particularly for those languages which are assigned a lower status in society, indexed a shift in pupils' identity as languaging experts in the eyes of all concerned: the pupils themselves and their peers, their families and teachers. At the same time, families became more knowledgeable about institutionalised education, and parent–school relations were transformed. In short, we found a translanguaging pedagogy has the potential to be truly transformational in its insistence on maintaining the gaze firmly on the dialectic between languaging *and* equality, in both designing educational resources and monitoring their impact in practice.

REFERENCES

Boler, M. (1999). *Feeling Power: Emotions and Education*. New York: Routledge.
García, O. (2009). *Bilingual Education in the 21st Century: Global Perspectives*. Malden, MA: Blackwell.
Gillborn, D. (2008). Policy: Changing language, constant inequality. In D. Gillbord, ed., *Racism and Education Coincidence or Conspiracy?* London: Routledge, pp. 70–89.
Levine, J. (1990). *Bilingual Learners and the Mainstream Curriculum*. Basingstoke: The Falmer Press.
Smith, H. J. (2004). Analysis of Pupil-pupil Talk During Game Playing: A Tool in the Formative Assessment of Bilingual Pupils. PhD Thesis. Newcastle University. Available at http://theses.ncl.ac.uk/jspui/handle/10443/751
      (2013). A critique of the teaching standards in England (1984–2012): Discourses of equality and maintaining the status quo. *Journal of Education Policy* 28(4), 427–448.
      (2014). Emotional responses to documentary viewing and the potential for transformative teaching. *Teaching Education* 25(2), 217–238.
      (2016) Britishness as racist nativism: A case of the unnamed 'other'. *Journal of Education for Teaching* 42(3), 298–313.
Smith, H. J. and Lander, V. (2012). Collusion or collision: Effects of teacher ethnicity in the teaching of critical whiteness. *Race Ethnicity and Education* 15(3), 331–351.
Smith, H. J., Robertson, L., Auger, N., Azaoui, B., Dervin, D., Gal, N., Layne, H. and Wysocki, L. (2017). *ROMtels handbook 1: A Pedagogy for Bi/plurilingual pupils: Translanguaging*. https://research.ncl.ac.uk/media/sites/researchwebsites/romtels/HB1_English_Translanguaging-Handbook1.pdf
Smith, H.J., Robertson, L.H., Auger, N., and Wysocki, L., (2020). Translanguaging as a political act with Roma: carving a path between pluralism and collectivism for transformation. *Journal for Critical Education Policy Studies*, 18(1), 98–135.

32   From Language Biography to a Research Life's Journey

Shelley K. Taylor

My language biography and key concepts and practices have influenced my interest in multilingualism in education systems internationally.

32.1   Language Biography

A practical way to frame my language biography is according to whether I learned a second or foreign language (L2/FL) in a naturally occurring or an instructed language learning environment; that is, practical until the lines blur. Whereas the former refers to language learning that occurs throughout the course of children and adults going along their social paths with no attempt to manipulate conditions or surroundings to promote language learning, instructed second/(foreign) language acquisition (ISLA) primarily involves formal language learning (e.g. within the four walls of a classroom); however, ISLA also pertains to study abroad and summer 'immersion' programmes since they involve 'some systematic attempt to manipulate the L2 learning process' (Loewen 2014, p. 143). I initially experienced ISLA in French and later in Spanish, Italian, Russian, German, Turkish and Irish (which I learned though synchronous teaching delivered via Zoom while under quarantine for COVID-19). I later learned French in naturally occurring contexts even within the four walls of a classroom (i.e. as a French immersion teacher). The lines blur even more regarding my experiences learning Danish. Therefore, the natural/ISLA distinction serves as a good frame until it does not. As is apparent in many current debates, many challenges relating to multilingualism defy categorization.

I always had a fascination for languages. I spent the first part of my life as the monolingual child of multilingual parents in a highly multilingual environment. Many migrants settled in my city after WW II, and for a long time it was home to the highest population of Finnish speakers outside of Finland. In my extended family setting, my grandparents only spoke English and it was an English-speaking household. Whenever I accompanied my grandfather on errands, we always took the bus. I heard so many people speaking different languages on the bus that I thought they were all speaking their own language.

Figure 32.1 Shelley K. Taylor

As a university student, I met someone from the same city who told me he thought the same thing as a child growing up in that environment. Therefore, I grew up amid a high degree of linguistic diversity at a time when Canada was viewed as mainly English- or French-speaking. From a young age, I wanted to speak my own (secret) language like the people on the bus. It was the beginning of my language awareness. (Years later, I had breakthroughs when, after learning Hebrew in an Ulpan [immersion] program in Israel, I was able to eavesdrop on people speaking Hebrew on a bus).

32.1.1 Learning French

Canadian language policy played a strong role in my ISLA in French. The Royal Commission on Bilingualism and Biculturalism ushered in changes to federal and provincial language policies on the role and delivery of French as a second language (FSL) programmes across Canada, including the introduction of FSL at the elementary level (Dunton, Laurendeau and Gagnon 1967). So began my ISLA in French. Not all Boards of Education, or even schools within the same city, introduced FSL the same year. I changed schools several times around then and was either a year behind or ahead of my classmates in French.

When I was behind, my mother tutored me. The same mother that had raised me in a monolingual English-speaking household had learned English, Ojibwe and Finnish in a natural setting (an isolated northern community) before her family moved into a city so she could attend high school. She had excelled in French and Latin and tutored me in French whenever I needed to catch up.

After living over 1,000 kilometres away from my hometown for several years, we moved back midway through my high school studies. It seemed like I was one of the only students whose home language was English. I had enough awareness of the challenges of ISLA from learning FSL to be envious of my classmates' 'home language advantage' as they were already natural bilinguals (in English and a heritage language) becoming multilingual (e.g. learning French in ISLA). I sought out 'natural' French experiences, including participating in a six-week homestay in Quebec the summer I turned sixteen. I had never heard or spoken French in an authentic situation before and was in awe of Québécois culture, which I had not even known existed (music, movies, etc.). My time in that naturalistic language learning environment enabled me to breeze through Gr. 12 French as I had already (incidentally) learned all the new grammar rules (e.g. I could not tell my host family not to use the *plus-que-parfait* because I had not learned that tense formally yet).

I later completed my HBA and MA in French literature, blending and blurring natural and ISLA learning contexts (as the only non-francophone studying French literature in a small university in Quebec while living with Quebecois roommates; teaching English in a *collège* in France and only having a French-speaking friendship network; later teaching ESL in a CEGEP in Quebec; learning new vocabulary while using French with students and colleagues as a bilingual education teacher; only using French socially when I accompanied high school students to France during summer holidays as an emergency contact person and lived in homestays; and teaching BEd and graduate courses, supervising theses and publishing *en français* as a professor).

32.1.2 Learning Danish

After my high school graduation, I moved to Denmark as my school's 'Danish exchange student'. Once there, I enrolled in the modern languages stream at *gymnasium* (preparatory college). With no prior ISLA background in Danish, it was daunting and life changing.

Except for during my English, French and Russian courses, all instruction was through the medium of Danish (Danish literature, biology, religion and social sciences) and I understood nothing for hours on end. My strategy was to ignore most things going on around me during class time and use a tiny Langenscheidt's "Lilliput" Danish–English dictionary to translate Danish words unless I heard laughter, in which case I would look up and try to figure out what was going on from facial expressions or sometimes a classmate sitting next to me might whisper a short synopsis in English. At first, I might just get through translating one sentence over the course of an hour-long lesson because I did not even know words like 'if' or 'and' in Danish yet (whereas I had gradually built up to reading novels in my French and Spanish high school courses in Canada). I had no awareness before going into the Danish educational situation of what total naturalistic crash-immersion (submersion) would be like as a rank beginner. While I was technically in an ISLA setting (four school walls) and there were some instances of translanguaging in the FL courses (e.g. Danish/French; Danish/Russian), Danish-medium instruction in non-language courses did not constitute ISLA. Lily Wong Fillmore (1991) has observed that while schooling has the potential to be the ideal setting for minoritized language students to acquire an L2, it is not a given. I experienced first-hand her description of proficient speakers not engaging with rank beginners in naturalistic settings (located in schools).

Compared to young children in submersion settings, I already saw myself as a strong student and good language learner. I concur with Cummins (2020), García (this volume) and Wong Fillmore (1991) about how disempowering it is for young children with no history of academic success to be in submersion settings. Krashen's (1981) notion of language exploding after a 'silent period' held true, and by the end of the year I completed my *studenter eksamen* in Danish and fulfilled my personal goal of reading Hans Christian Andersen's fairy tales in Danish. During my MA studies in French, Dr Gurli Ågård Woods, a professor in Comparative Literature originally from Denmark, taught me a Reading course in Danish literature. The latter was my only formal ISLA in Danish.

After teaching bilingual education for several years, I began my PhD and gained deeper understanding of naturalistic and ISLA journeys. I returned to Denmark and spent eighteen months conducting a school-based ethnography for my dissertation. In terms of my language biography, I learned more Danish in a naturalistic manner, but in an ISLA setting (observing in a Danish/Turkish bilingual/bicultural education programme); thus, again blurring the lines between naturalistic settings for language learning and ISLA. Ever since, I have continued to do academic reading, to conduct research and to publish in Danish (Taylor 2016), and my investment in the language has never waned.

Discrepancies between the evolution of my language biography and that of my minority language participants have heightened my interest in constraints on multilingual development in education systems and I have sought to deepen my insights into affordances available to me to learn French and Danish that have not been available to them (e.g. links between societal inclusion/ exclusion and academic achievement; why individual investment levels must be buttressed by supportive language learning policies, programmes, environments and practices for multilingual repertoires to develop, let alone thrive).

My work not only questions who can board the multilingual bus, but whose languages are heard even if everyone can board.

32.2   Key Concepts

32.2.1   *Multilingualism/Plurilingualism/Heteroglossia*

In my early work, I used terms such as 'multilingualism' and 'bi-/trilingualism' when discussing models of 'bi-/multilingual' education (Taylor 1992). My gaze shifted to a more plurilingual lens as a result of my exposure to complex societal multilingualism in Nepal and the multilingual language education model adopted there (Taylor 2014), and my collaboration with David Little, who introduced me to the Council of Europe's (2001) notion of 'plurilingualism' (Little and Taylor 2013). The timing was fortuitous because, I was involved in longitudinal research on immigrant background youths' language development in French immersion just then (Taylor 2015) and L1-based multilingual language education in Nepal (Taylor 2014). By adopting a *plurilingual* lens and framing my participants as social agents with varying degrees of proficiency in several languages (Council of Europe 2001), I gained a clearer picture of their full linguistic repertoires as the notion valorizes multicompetence gained in various domains. That lens magnified the inadequacy of looking at rich linguistic repertoires in deficit perspective by underrating their multicompetence based on monolingual norms and ideologies (Cummins 2007). This interest, coupled with Kristin Snoddon's interest in Deaf parents' competences in American Sign Language, prompted us to guest edit a special issue of *TESOL Quarterly* on plurilingualism (Taylor and Snoddon 2013). While I do not frame my work in terms of heteroglossia, metrolingualism or polylingualism per se, recent forays into these and related constructs are pushing the boundaries of multilingual practices (Moore, Bradley and Simpson 2020).

32.2.2   *Linguistic Repertoire/Communicative Repertoire*

I have only recently begun to frame my work in terms of linguistic, pedagogical and communicative repertoires, and primarily discuss linguistic and pedagogical repertoires

32.2.3   *Intercultural/Pluricultural/Multicultural Education*

My work has not focussed on the above per se, though the European literature on 'culturalism', which is located in intercultural education, pertained to my doctoral research. *Culturalism* found its niche in post WW II Europe after Eugenic views of racial superiority and inferiority (biological racism) were no longer acceptable (Taylor 2019). My doctoral research was framed in

Cummins' (2001) and Skutnabb-Kangas' (2000) work on language and power, along with Schierup's (1993) work on the social ostracization of minorities deemed 'too culturally different' to 'integrate' into Nordic society. In the context of my study, cultural racism (or Islamophobia) was expressed as, *'They' should 'go home' because they are too different to fit in.* Hate crimes and exclusionary sentiments permeated educator and classroom discourses, and my participants' educational experiences (Taylor 2009; Taylor and Skutnabb-Kangas 2009). My subsequent research has touched on aspects of intercultural/pluricultural/multicultural education, as my overarching goal has been to identify and address inequities.

32.3   Practices

In my own plurilingual/multicompetent mix, I have eavesdropped on a casual conversation in Dutch without having learned it by ISLA or having been extensively exposed to it naturally, but rather just by drawing on my knowledge of Danish and German – a common phenomenon in the global south (Taylor and Mohanty 2021). Similarly, I have got the gist of written Catalan by drawing on my French and (rusty) Spanish, and navigated my way through Finland by being able to read the Swedish part of bilingual signage owing to similarities between Danish and Swedish. Referring to Cook's (2007) work, Scott (2016) stresses that educators need heightened awareness of the implications of their students' multicompetences since 'A second language is not just adding rooms to your house by building an extension at the back: it is rebuilding all the internal walls' (p. 445). Learning one language does not mean turning another one off; their wiring shares the same circuits. Educators must draw on student plurilingualism and multicompetences in ISLA and content-based instruction to promote their engagement, identity affirmation and academic success (Cummins 2020).

Scott (2016) further stresses that educators must adopt a 'multilingual stance' to legitimize all languages in the classroom; a sentiment echoed by Menken and Sánchez (2019) but referred to as a 'translingual stance'. Mohanty's (2018) and Jørgensen's (2010) work documents students performing what may be described as multi- or 'polylingual' feats by navigating turns between different language families with syntactic accuracy and ease in real time; yet their linguistic capital may be invisible to teachers with limited awareness of plurilingualism. My work has touched on translingual practices that support the development of student plurilingualism and multicompetences and challenge educators' monolingual mindsets (Taylor 2014; Taylor and Cutler 2016). Regardless of the construct researchers draw on (e.g. a pluri-, trans- or multilingual stance), they concur that educators must overcome their fear of the unknown and animosity towards dealing with multilingualism and multilinguals, abandon deficit perspectives, and adopt practices that promote academic achievement and multilingual development (Taylor, Despagne and Faez 2018).

270   *Shelley K. Taylor*

REFERENCES

Cook, V. J. (2007). Multicompetence: Black hole or wormhole for SLA research? In Z.-H. Han, ed., *Understanding Second Language Process*. Clevedon: Multilingual Matters, pp. 16–26.

Council of Europe (2001). *A Common European Framework of Reference for Languages: Learning, Teaching, Assessment*. Cambridge: Cambridge University Press.

Cummins, J. (2001). *Negotiating Identities: Education for Empowerment in a Diverse Society*. (2nd ed.). Los Angeles: California Association for Bilingual Education.

(2007). Rethinking monolingual instructional strategies in multilingual classrooms. *Canadian Journal of Applied Linguistics* 10(2), 221–240.

(2020, May). *Reversing underachievement among multilingual students: Whole school instructional strategies for identity affirmation and academic success*. Plenary presented at the New Perspectives on Language Education Joint Symposium, online.

Dunton, A. Davidson, Laurendeau, A. and Gagnon, J.-L. (1967). *Royal Commission on Bilingualism and Biculturalism*. (Vol I). *The Official languages*. Ottawa: Privy Council.

García. O. (this volume). A sociolinguistic biography and understandings of bilingualism. In G. Prasad, N. Auger and E. Le Pichon-Vorstman, eds., *Multilingualism and Education: Key Concepts and Practices in Education*. Cambridge: Cambridge University Press.

Jørgensen, J. N. (2010). *Languaging: Nine years of poly-lingual development of young Turkish-Danish grade school students*. (Vol. I-II). *Københavnerstudier i tosprogethed, Køge 15-16* [Copenhagen Studies in Bilingualism, the Køge Series, K15–K16].

Krashen, S. D. (1981). *Second Language Acquisition and Second Language Learning*. (1st ed.). Oxford: Pergamon Press.

Little, D. and Taylor, S. K. (2013). Introduction: Implementing the Common European Framework of Reference for Languages and the European Language Portfolio: Lessons for future research/Introduction : Tirer des leçons des recherches empiriques sur la mise en œuvre du Cadre européen commun de référence pour les langues et du Portfolio européen des langues pour les recherches futures. *Canadian Modern Language Review/La Revue canadienne des langues vivantes*. 69(4), 1–6.

Loewen, S. (2014). Chapter 9: Contexts of instructed second language acquisition. In *Introduction to Instructed Second Language Acquisition*. New York: Routledge/Taylor & Francis, pp. 143–162.

Menken, K. and Sánchez, M. T. (2019). Translanguaging in English-Only schools: From pedagogy to stance in the disruption of monolingual policies and practices. *TESOL Quarterly* 53(3), 741–767.

Mohanty, A. K. (2018). *The Multilingual Reality: Living with Languages*. Bristol: Multilingual Matters.

Moore, E., Bradley, J. and Simpson, J. (2020). *Translanguaging as Transformation: The Collaborative Construction of New Linguistic Realities*. Clevedon: Multilingual Matters.

Schierup, C.-U. (1993). *På kulturens slagmark: Mindretal og størretal taler om Danmark* [On the battlefields of culture: Minorities and majorities talk about Denmark]. Esbjerg: Sydjysk Universitetsforlag [University of Southern Jutland Press].

Scott, Virginia M. (2016). Multi-competence and language teaching. In V. Cook and L. Wei, eds., *The Cambridge Handbook of Linguistic Multi-Competence*. Cambridge: Cambridge University Press, pp. 445–460.

Skutnabb-Kangas, T. (2000). *Linguistic Genocide in Education - or Worldwide Diversity and Human Rights?* London: Lawrence Erlbaum Associates.

Taylor, S. (1992). Victor: A case study of a Cantonese child in early French immersion. *Canadian Modern Language Review* 48(4), 736–759.

Taylor, S. K. (2009). Right pedagogy, wrong language and caring in times of fear: Issues in the schooling of ethnic Kurdish children in Denmark. *The International Journal of Bilingual Education and Bilingualism* 12(3), 291–307.

(2014). From 'monolingual' multilingual classrooms to 'multilingual' multilingual classrooms: Managing cultural and linguistic diversity in the Nepali educational system. In D. Little, C. Leung and P. Van Avermaet, eds., *Managing Diversity in Education: Key Issues and Some Responses*. Clevedon: Multilingual Matters, pp. 259–274.

(2015). Conformists & mavericks: Plurilingual pedagogy in secondary French immersion content-based instruction. *Intercultural Education* 26(6), 515–529.

(2016). Sproglige og kulturelle vidensfonde i klasseværelset [Linguistic & cultural "funds of knowledge" in worlds-in-a-classroom]. *Sprogforum [Journal of Language & Culture Pedagogy]* 62, 37–44.

(2019). Multilingualism. In N. Schmitt & M. P. H. Rodgers, eds., *An Introduction to Applied Linguistics*, 3rd ed. London and New York: Routledge/Taylor & Francis, pp. 205–220.

Taylor, S. K., Faez, F. and Despagne, C. (2018). Critical language awareness. In John I. Liontas, Editor in Chief (Project Editor: Margo DelliCarpini; Vol. Ed.: Shahid Abrar-ul-Hassan), *The TESOL Encyclopedia of English Language Teaching: Teaching Speaking and Pronunciation in TESOL*, Hoboken, NJ: John Wiley & Sons, pp. 73–86.

Taylor, S. K. and Cutler, C. (2016). Introduction: Showcasing the translingual FL/SL: Strategies, practices & beliefs. *Canadian Modern Language Review/Revue canadienne des langues modernes* 72(4), 389–404.

Taylor, S. K. and Mohanty, A. K. (2021). Chapter 18: A multi-perspective tour of best practices: Challenges to implementing best practices in complex plurilingual contexts: The case of South Asia. In E. Piccardo, A. Germain-Rutherford and G. Lawrence, eds., *The Routledge Handbook of Plurilingual Language Education*. New York: Routledge, pp. 385–393

Taylor, S. K. and Skutnabb-Kangas, T. (2009). The educational language rights of Kurdish children in Turkey, Denmark and Kurdistan (Iraq). In W. Ayers, T. Quinn and D. Stovall, eds., *Handbook for Social Justice in Education*. In Section 3, *Race and ethnicity and seeking social justice in education* Mahwah, NJ: Lawrence Erlbaum, pp. 171–190.

Taylor, S. K. and Snoddon, K. (2013). Plurilingualism in TESOL: Promising controversies. *TESOL Quarterly*, *47*(3), 439-445.

Wong Fillmore, L. (1991). Second-language learning in children: A model of language learning in social context. In E. Bialystok, ed., *Language Processing in Bilingual Children*. Cambridge: Cambridge University Press, pp. 49–69.

33   My Linguistic Biography

Kelleen Toohey

I currently live and work in and around Vancouver, British Columbia, but I was born and lived until my late 20s on the Canadian prairies. My family was Anglophone, and the only bilinguals I knew from school were some Ukrainian-Canadian classmates. However, my family had a lake cottage in northern Alberta, where we spent most of the school summer vacation. The cottage was located near the edge of a Métis colony in which Plains Cree was the language of the community. We played with children from the community, using English, but we attended Mass there every Sunday in a tiny log cabin, and the priest and most of the other parishioners spoke Cree. The service and the hymns were in Cree, and as a child, I was fascinated by the specialness of this.

My elementary school in Edmonton started French instruction in Grade 4 and I had been excited about learning French, but that excitement waned as we were audio-visualed (watching filmstrips and listening to tape-recorders) through M. et Mme. Thibaut and their strikingly boring lives for six years. In secondary school, French instruction continued, and we were finally allowed to write in French (the audio-visual method we had had in elementary school did not permit students to write anything). I continued with French but also took Latin from a gifted teacher who wrote stories about members of the class in Latin for us to translate. We all loved this teacher and tried to share his love for Latin. French was grammar/translation; this was also the age of the language lab, and we spent about one out of five classes in little cubicles with headphones trying to imitate the recorded voice. Again, too dull to engage at least this teenager. I did not come out of high school with any oral fluency in French or Latin, but I had a sprinkling of French, and quite good Latin, vocabulary and grammar. A post-bacc trip to Europe re-ignited my enthusiasm for language learning, and while what I could do with the French I knew was very minimal, it was exciting to have people understand me and me them even a little.

Another strong influence on my interest in multilingualism and cultural diversity was a school-wide team-taught unit in our Religion high school classes, which focused on understanding and combating racism. This was the time of the Civil Rights movement in the United States, and films and books portraying and condemning racism were everywhere available. The innovative

Figure 33.1 Kelleen Toohey

teaching and its subject made a strong impression on me, and I think, on my classmates. However, I do in hindsight wonder why examples of racism in our Canadian context weren't discussed, so that we didn't think racism just happened elsewhere.

My first teaching job was in a school in a small town in northern Alberta. In the 'streamed' elementary school in which I taught, there were three Grade 4 classes. My assignment was to teach Language Arts, Social Studies, Physical Education and Health to each of the three classes. There was one Cree-speaking girl in the advanced class, with all the other twenty-five or so children being Anglophone. In the middle group about half the students were Cree speakers, half Anglophone, and in the 'bottom' class, almost all children were Cree speakers. I soon discovered that few Cree children in the 'bottom' class could read or write in ways the English Language Arts or Social Studies curriculum mandated; the children in the middle group had varied capabilities to deal with the curriculum; and the top class had no difficulty at all coping with the curriculum. My fellow teachers did not take up my questions about how this streaming coincided with racial and linguistic gulfs in the community, but it worried me, and I was not at all sure how to teach Grade 4 Social Studies to children who could not read. I decided that all three streams of students in my Social Studies classes would study Cree culture and language, with modifications for each class' capabilities in English literacy. I didn't know much myself about Cree culture and language, but I enlisted help from members of the reserve not far from the school, and we made materials, and found resources that would be accessible for beginning readers of English. I started to read professional literature about linguistically and culturally relevant education. This literature was new to me, as it had not featured in my teacher education, and I found it very interesting as it contradicted so many of the everyday practices in the school and community where I taught.

All these experiences led me to want to explore these matters further, to leave the small northern town and to move to the city and the university to embark on my Master's degree. Learning about Cree culture and language and the richness of anthropological writing convinced me of the relevance of anthropological research in education, and in language teaching. Dr. Carl Urion, a Métis scholar, was my academic advisor and all his students read UNESCO's (1953) *The Use of Vernacular Languages in Education* and Nancy Modiano's (1973) *Indian Education in the Chiapas Highlands*. These now-old texts, which argued and showed the benefits of educating children first in their first languages, and my previous experiences continue to influence my interest in and commitment to multilingualism and educational equity.

After my Master's degree, I started a PhD at the Ontario Institute for Studies in Education, where the approach to second language teaching and learning research at the time was the hybrid field of psycholinguistics: language learning was seen as an 'interface between learners' mental processes and the grammatical system of the target language' (Breen, 2001, p. 173), and as Long (1997, p. 319) claimed, 'social and affective factors ... [were seen as] important but relatively minor in impact ... in both naturalistic and classroom settings'. I found psycholinguistic methods and analyses interesting, but I was also convinced that an anthropological approach to the social and cultural aspects of language learning could contribute to our understandings of these matters. This was not a common approach to language education scholarship in the late 1970s and 1980s, and I struggled to find colleagues who shared my interests. However, during my studies, I was a collaborator on a commissioned report on language use in Northern Indigenous communities and schools (with Barbara Burnaby and John Nichols). We travelled throughout northern Ontario, talking to teachers and community leaders about language use, and this led to my making connections to a community on James Bay where I did the research for my dissertation about Swampy Cree-speaking students learning English at school.

33.1   Key Concepts

Beginning in the late 1970s and through the 1990s, another hybrid field, sociolinguistics, became better known, and anthropological linguist Dell Hymes began to develop theory and describe research methods capable of cataloguing the diversity of means of communication among groups. Noting that anthropology had a long history of documenting diverse cultural practices through ethnography, he advocated an 'ethnography of communication' so that the range of communicative practices in human societies could be better understood. At about the same time, some language and literacy education researchers began to widen the disciplinary scope of their work and think about how language learning takes place in social contexts in which particular discourse patterns of various learners shape their school learning (Michaels

1981; Heath 1983; Philips 1983). Anthropologist Shirley Brice Heath's (1983) *Ways with Words* documented diversity in discourse practices within three geographically close communities, and argued that the practices of some communities aligned better with those valued in school, and thus students whose 'ways with words' were more similar to the discourse patterns of school would be advantaged there and vice versa. Other researchers interested in social aspects of language use and learning drew on the work of sociologist Pierre Bourdieu (1977), who pointed out that the 'right to speak' is not distributed equally to all, and that social power is important in determining what opportunities diverse learners have for language use and learning (Norton 2000, 2014). Another current in the social turn in language and literacy education scholarship was increasing attention to the work of L.S. Vygotsky (1978) and M.M. Bakhtin (1981) and 'sociocultural' theory and research that investigated how people, practices and resources interacted with one another in producing learning outcomes (Wertsch 1991, 1998).

Sociocultural theories coordinated well with my previous education and experiences, and in my first major research project I investigated the English language learning of immigrant children in a Canadian school to show how identity, social relations and classroom practices were interwoven and implicated in individual children's learning. Drawing on postmodern concepts of identity as explicated by language education scholar Bonny Norton (2000, 2014) as fragmented, contradictory, changing, dependent on social and material settings and expressed through discourse (Weedon 1997), I came to see that who children 'became' at school and who they 'became' in different social settings, with different learning resources, and with different pedagogical practices, had consequences for their learning. My explorations of the relationships of identity with social setting, pedagogical practices and the use of classroom resources were reported in the first edition of *Learning English at School: Identity, Social Relations and Classroom Practice* (Toohey 2000, 2nd edition 2018). In this book, I examined how student identities became formed at school and how those identities had consequences for students' opportunities to access classroom resources, and to engage in conversations and practices that might further their language learning.

In Toohey (1998) I focused on material resources (or 'things' like crayons, scissors and other classroom tools) and space (i.e. where children were located in a classroom and what constrictions were on their movements there). I found in the interactional data I had collected in a Grade 1 classroom that the distribution of material resources and children spatially, and regulation of access to movement and other children, had effects on what kinds of language were available to learners, and thus on their language learning.

In later research with language learners using digital video-making tools in schools, the importance of material resources in language learning became even more apparent to us (Toohey and Dagenais 2015; Toohey et al. 2015). We were struck by how tools like video cameras, tripods, storyboards, video editing software and so on seemed to become inextricably bound up with children's school identities and social relations, and by how these tools seemed to change classroom practices. Our research team explored concepts from actor-network theory (Latour 2005) as ways to theorize what these material tools were changing or enacting in classrooms (Dagenais et al. 2013). The concept of networks as assemblies of human and non-human actors seemed useful to us in conceptualizing what we termed 'School-as-Usual', with desks, children's bodies, teacher's bodies, distinct subjects, defined times, curriculum documents and so on joined in very durable networks (Smythe, Toohey and Dagenais 2014).

More recently, we have been what feels like *captured* by some of the recent theoretical concepts of feminist techno-science, process philosophy, anthropology, posthumanism, new materialities and the 'new ontologies', which have similarities to, but important differences from, actor-network theory (Smythe et al. 2017). For example, New Materialisms trouble the concept of identity. This work invites us to refrain from positing *a priori* individuations between things, such as people, tools, furniture, languages and so on. Rather, things are what they are in terms of how they are in relation with other things. Toohey et al. (2015) analysed the relationships involving an English language learner, an iPad, a themed piece of music, space, furniture, children's bodies, the video script, children's memories of newcasts (stored, of course, in their bodies) and myriad other entities (which are what they are because they are in relation with other 'entities'). In a particular episode these entanglements meant that the English language learner was able to participate in the group's discussion and to persuade her classmates to adopt one of her ideas. In other entanglements of people, material things, space and so on, such might not have been (and wasn't) the case. This alerted us to the complexity of phenomena in classrooms, and urged our attention to how humans and the non-human are co-participants in shifting flows of activity.

I think it is interesting to speculate about how verbal communication is also an in-the-moment kind of activity, so that speakers are creating meanings with speakers and listeners with different communicative histories. If speakers are not maintaining the distinctness of languages that language teachers and linguists have traditionally perceived, and taught, and if boundaries between languages are coming to be seen as unclear, it may be that we will see that positing language boundaries (identification) is a social process which benefits some speakers over others. Instead of prizing speakers/writers of a standard language with no 'negative transfer' from another less prestigious language, we may begin to investigate the communicative wealth of multilinguals who have many linguistic resources on which to draw. We might also see language learners as desiring to extend their possibilities to language with others, and *creating* language as they do so. This might change our jobs as language teachers from trying to transmit to, and instill grammar, vocabulary and meaning in a different language code in, language learners. Rather, our aim might be to join with learners as they navigate their lives with many speakers, in many places, and as new materialists emphasize, with many different non-human objects. Language learners are thus seen as creators of language as they engage in the many diverse activities of their lives, with other speakers and other things (places, objects, times, ideas and so on).

33.2   Key Practices

I have recently been thinking and writing about how research practices might be approached from a new materialist stance (Toohey 2019, 2021). Much of my and other observers' methods for researching language learning and teaching derive from the central anthropological practice of participant observation, an interpretive method that tries to examine people's actions and behaviours in naturalistic settings, in an attempt to determine what is going on in those settings. Participant observation might entail collecting photographs, observational field notes, artifacts and/or videos to document phenomena. New Materialism, which troubles boundaries of all sorts, reminds us that we as researchers are also 'always and already entangled with the very apparatuses (cameras, recordings, software, etc.) we use to record, or rather re-present, the phenomena in question' (Bhatt and de Roock 2013, para. 27). Feminist philosopher and physicist Karen Barad (2003) similarly argued that 'apparatuses are not mere static arrangements in the world but rather... are dynamic "(re)configurings of the world" and therefore "are themselves phenomena"' (Barad 2003, p. 816).

Taking into account the multimodality and materiality of our recording devices as well as the materiality of our bodies and our voices and choices about what to attend to as we observe further complicates how we come to represent that which we observe.

Those of us who work with novice (and not only novice) teachers know that it is often the stories we tell about classroom practice that stay in their minds, and that stimulate further thought. The stories we tell from the research in which we engage do not, therefore, purport to 'represent' learning or others in any stable or permanent way, but rather are stimuli for others to raise questions and to explore their own problems and issues. Conversations that teachers have with one another and with learners about researchers' learning and language stories will, one hopes, 'not to know with certainty but instead to wonder, to inquire with grace' (Wien et al. 2011) about possible next courses of action.

Diane Dagenais' and my recent work with child learners of English and various digital technologies has been aimed at trying to expand our gaze, to 'educate our attention' to see 'learning occur[ing] as people make their way through their daily lives, developing skills in perceiving and attending to . . . their sociomaterial . . . surroundings . . . and improvising new solutions to new problems and ecologies' (Ingold 2001, p. 152). As researchers, we are interested in investigating practices and learning activities that have promise for engaging not only the children who have always been so engaged but also those who have not been served well by schools in the past (Dagenais et al. 2017). We are encouraged by how multimodal and multilingual learning objects and activities appear to capture the attention of such children and how these objects and activities might offer more equitable opportunities for more children than they have had heretofore.

REFERENCES

Bahktin, M. M. (1981). *The Dialogic Imagination: Four Essays*. Austin: University of Texas Press.
Barad, K. (2003). Posthumanist performativity: Toward an understanding of how matter comes to matter. *Signs: Journal of Women in Culture and Society* 28(3), 801–831.
  (2007). *Meeting the Universe Halfway: Quantum Physics and the Entanglement of Matter and Meaning*. Durham, NC: Duke University Press.
Bhatt, I. and deRoock, R. (2013). Capturing the sociomateriality of digital learning events. *Research in Learning Technology* 21. http://dx.doi.org/10.3402/rlt.v21.21281
Bourdieu, P. (1977). The economics of linguistic exchanges. *Social Science Information* 16, 645–668.
Breen, M. (2001). *Learner Contributions to Language Learning: New Directions in Research*. Harlow: England: Pearson Education.
Dagenais, D., Fodor, A., Schulze, E., Toohey, K. (2013). Charting new directions: The potential of actor-network theory for analyzing children's videomaking. *Language and Literacy* 15(1), 93–108.
Dagenais, D., Toohey, K., Fox, A. and Singh, A. (2017). Multilingual and multimodal composition at school: *ScribJab* in action. *Language and Education* 31, 263–282.
Heath, S. B. (1983). *Ways with Words: Language, Life and Work in Communities and Classrooms*. Cambridge: Cambridge University Press.
Ingold, T. (2001). From the transmission of representation to the education of attention. In H. Whitehouse, ed., *The Debated Mind: Evolutionary Psychology versus Ethnography*. New York: Berg, pp. 113–153.
Latour, B. (2005). *Reassembling the Social: An Introduction to Actor-Network Theory*. Oxford: Oxford University Press.
Long, M. H. (1997). Construct validity in SLA research: A response to Firth and Wagner. *The Modern Language Journal* 81(3), 318–323.
Michaels, S. (1981) 'Sharing time': Children's narrative styles and differential access to literacy. *Language in Society* 10(3), 423–442.

Modiano, N. (1973). *Indian Education in the Chiapas Highlands*. New York: Holt, Rinehart & Winston.

Norton, B. (2000). *Identity and Language Learning: Gender, Ethnicity and Educational Change*. London: Longman.

(2014). *Identity and Language Learning: Gender, Ethnicity and Educational Change* (2nd edition). London: Longman.

Philips, S. (1983). *The Invisible Culture: Communication in Classroom and Community on the Warm Springs Indian Reservation*. Long Grove, IL: Waveland Press.

Smythe, S., Hill, C., MacDonald, M., Dagenais, D., Sinclair, N. and Toohey, K. (2017). *Disrupting Boundaries in Education and Research*. Cambridge: Cambridge University Press.

Smythe, S., Toohey, K. and Dagenais, D. (2014). Video making, production pedagogies and educational policy. *Journal of Educational Policy* 30(5), 740–770.

Toohey, K. (1998). 'Breaking them up; taking them away': ESL students in grade one. *TESOL Quarterly* 32, 61–84.

(2000). *Learning English at school: Identity, social relations and classroom practice*. Bristol: Multilingual Matters.

(2018). *Learning English at School: Identity, Socio-Material Relations and Classroom Practice*, 2nd Edition. Bristol: Multilingual Matters.

(2019). The Onto-Epistemologies of New Materialism: Implications for Applied Linguistics Pedagogies and Research. *Applied Linguistics* 40(6), 937–956.

(2021). Observant participation and representation in New Materialistic research. In C. Porter and R. Griffo eds., *The matter of Practice: Exploring New Materialisms in the Research and Teaching of Languages and Literacies*. Charolotte, NC: Information Age Publishing, pp. 31–47.

Toohey, K. and Dagenais, D. (2015). Videomaking as sociomaterial assemblage. *Language and Education* 29(4), 302–316.

Toohey, K., Dagenais, D., Fodor, A., Hof, L., Schulze, E. and Singh, A. (2015). "That sounds so cool": Entanglements of children, digital tools and literacy practices. *TESOL Quarterly* 49(3), 461–485.

UNESCO (1953). *The Use of Vernacular Languages in Education*. Paris: I.F.M.P.P.

Vygotsky, L. S. (1978). *Mind in Society: The Development of Higher Psychological Processes*. Cambridge, MA: Harvard University Press.

Weedon, C. (1997). *Feminist Practice and Poststructural Theory*. Oxford: Blackwell.

Wertsch, J. (1991). *Voices of the Mind: A Sociocultural Approach to Mediated Action*. Cambridge, MA: Harvard University Press.

(1998). *Mind as Action*. New York: Oxford University Press.

Wien, C. A., Guyevsky, V., and Berdoussis, N. (2011). Learning to document in Reggio-inspired education. *ECRP Early Childhood Research & Practice*, 13(2), 1–2.

34   Travelling Back and Forth between Local Language Variation and Global Multilingualism

Piet van Avermaet and Sven Sierens

34.1   Guiding Questions

34.1.1   Piet van Avermaet

34.1.1.1 Linguistic Repertoire My mother tongue is 'Dutch' but this label comprises several varieties, meaning that my repertoire is 'multiglossic'. It contains, first of all, standard Dutch, which is the prestigious variety used in formal contexts in Flemish Belgium. In informal contexts though, I am usually speaking a mixture of Flemish *Tussentaal* and the local dialect of the semi-rural municipality where I was born and still live. I also have mastered a number of foreign languages, which I acquired through formal education, and use mostly in my professional life. These are French (speaking, reading and writing), English (speaking, reading and writing), German (receptive), Spanish (simple conversations; i.e. A1 level attained through an independent study course) and Italian (some notions).

34.1.1.2 Elements That Influenced My Interest in Multilingualism in Education Systems When I was in primary school, there was a Moroccan boy in my classroom with whom I had frequent contact both at school and outside school. I was intrigued by this boy and his different background: how he lived at home, the cultural differences, the 'incomprehensible languages' that were spoken (a mix of Berber and French), also the poor living conditions (most immigrant families lived in a *cité*, where poor working class people were housed). My mother, who, motivated by a sense of charity, wanted to help this family, also came into contact with it and spoke French with the boy's parents. It pleasantly surprised me that my mother was capable of communicating with the parents and could build some kind of a rapport, which was usually absent between immigrant and native Flemish families.

Between 1976 and 1978, I studied in a teacher trainer college, where I participated in a voluntary project with immigrant families. I offered

Figure 34.1 Piet van Avermaet

homework assistance to the children, who mostly struggled with the acquisition of Dutch as the language of schooling. I became fascinated by the multilingual realities in education and the challenges of acquiring Dutch. Since then and throughout my entire professional (academic) career, I have been (and still am) interested in the complex dynamics of language ideology, monolingual versus multilingual discourses, policies and practices (including curricula), how policies and practices on social inequality, equity and excellence in education interact with discourses.

34.1.2   Sven Sierens

34.1.2.1 Linguistic Repertoire My mother tongue (Dutch) is very similar to Piet's and shows the same multiglossic features. However, in my childhood, standard Dutch was not that frequently spoken at home. A mixture of *Tussentaal* and the urban dialect of the city where I was born and lived all my life characterised daily communication in my family. Today, my wife and

Figure 34.2 Sven Sierens

I predominantly speak *Tussentaal* with one another. With relatives and intimate friends originating from my home town, my language use varies or switches on a 'dialect – *Tussentaal* – standard Dutch' continuum.

Also, I acquired additional languages in much the same way as Piet. I have learnt French (speaking, reading and writing), English (speaking, reading and writing), German (receptive), Modern Standard Arabic (A2 level), Turkish (receptive yet now a little rusty), Italian (notions) and Moroccan Arabic (notions).

34.1.2.2 Elements That Influenced My Interest in Multilingualism in Education Systems I grew up in a neighbourhood which was to some degree socially mixed: mainly working class and a minority of lower middle class families (including mine). When immigrants from the Mediterranean area started to settle in the 1960s in my neighbourhood, it gradually became ethnically and linguistically mixed. In the street where I lived my entire youth, most immigrant families were of Moroccan (Berber) origin. The children of these families were part of my ethnically mixed group of playmates in the street, with which I had almost daily contact and spoke *Tussentaal* (and a few 'dirty' words of Moroccan or Turkish that I had picked up). My parents spoke French with some of the Moroccan parents and showed a friendly, open-minded and helpful attitude towards neighbours of other ethnic groups. My Moroccan friends simply told me that they spoke 'Moroccan' at home, and that was fine for me. After quite a few years, it dawned on me that this term veiled, in fact, various complicated multilingual repertoires in Moroccan families.

After having obtained a Master's degree in Communication Science, I decided to follow a special post-graduate programme in Social and Cultural Anthropology: an interest that was definitely aroused by the multicultural experience in my youth. Immediately thereafter, I started my professional career at the university, conducting ethnographic research on the school careers of immigrant youth. This led me to subjects such as migrant culture, intercultural education, minority language and culture teaching, social and ethnic inequalities in the education system and so on. My interest in linguistics and multilingualism came in an indirect way, namely via studying Modern Standard Arabic as an adult. This led me to delve into the scholarly literature on Arabic linguistics and sociolinguistics. I got to know concepts such as 'diglossia', 'multiglossia', 'codeswitching' etc., and became familiar with the theories on linguistic variation in the Arabic language. However, it was only about ten years ago that I began empirically investigating practices of migration-induced multilingualism in education.

34.2   Key Concepts and Practices

34.2.1   Key Concepts

34.2.1.1 Multilingualism/Plurilingualism/Heteroglossia In the Dutch language, the common term in scientific and practical discourse is *meertaligheid*, which covers 'multilingualism' and 'plurilingualism' in English. In our English-language work we use the two terms interchangeably.

As an alternative to 'multilingual(ism)', we tend to use more and more in our work the notion of 'linguistic diversity' to describe societies, as well as the linguistic repertoire of a person or a group. In this sense, 'linguistic diversity' can be a more apt umbrella concept than 'multilingualism'. It is well known that 'multilingual' seen as a competence of an individual speaker is fraught with misconceptions, such as multilingual equals fluency in different languages or languages are separate units in the mind or in communication. These ideas show the persistent influence of a monolingual mindset, as has been expressed, for instance, through Cummins' (2007) notion of the 'two solitudes assumption' of bilingualism; the concept of multilingualism as 'parallel monolingualisms' (Heller 1999) or the 'monoglossic perspective' (García 2009).

What about 'heteroglossia' then? The concept was introduced by Bakhtin. It describes the coexistence of and conflict between different language varieties within a single 'language'. In Bakhtin's view, any language (or speech) stratifies into many 'voices', such as social dialects, characteristic group behaviour, professional jargons, generic languages and so on. Blommaert and Van Avermaet (2008) clarified a similar critical sociolinguist perspective on language. Although the term 'heteroglossia' as such is not used, the 'heteroglossic' nature of language is implicitly present throughout its contents:

languages as packages of genres, styles, registers; looking at repertoire instead of language; language as synonymous with multilingualism; the multimodal character of literacy; the polycentric, hierarchic order of linguistic markers. That being said, it is clear that for us the notion of 'linguistic repertoire' self-evidently presupposes the diverse, complex, variable and multi-voiced nature of languages. In sum, saying that a linguistic repertoire is 'diverse' refers to both the 'multilingual' and the 'heteroglossic' dimension.

34.2.1.2 Intercultural/Pluricultural/Multicultural Education When the Centre for Intercultural Education (*Steunpunt Intercultureel Onderwijs = SICO*), the precursor of the current Centre for Diversity & Learning (CDL), was established at Ghent University in 1995, the concept of 'multicultural education' was never really considered an option. They would have called it a misnomer in any case. For that matter, the term 'pluricultural' exists indeed in the Dutch language (*pluricultureel*), but it is not common in scientific or societal discourse: unless perhaps as a nice sounding synonym for multicultural'.

The notion 'intercultural education' had already been proposed in the 1980s as a better alternative for 'multicultural education'. It should highlight more specifically the dynamic, multidimensional and contextual nature of interactions between persons from different cultural and ethnic backgrounds. The concept 'multicultural' is seen by scholars as problematic for three reasons. The first reason is that the term has both a descriptive and prescriptive purpose: 'multicultural' is what 'is' and what 'ought to be'. The second reason is that 'multicultural' implies a notion of culture that is considered outdated in postmodern and postcolonial anthropology as it evolved in the 1960s. Anthropologists have frequently alerted us to the almost invariably committed sin of 'cultural essentialism': culture is viewed and experienced as a static, homogeneous, bounded, totalising entity. A culture therefore coincides with an ethnic group, if not a society or country, and a multicultural society is basically regarded as a 'multi-ethnic society', which is represented as a mosaic or juxtaposition of various separate 'cultures' or 'ethnic groups'. A third reason has to do with the observation that a (positive) perception of 'multicultural' tends to idealise intercultural relations and to celebrate cultural differences, while downplaying negative realities such as socioeconomic inequalities, social exclusion, discrimination and racism. In the 1970s and 1980s, anti-racist education emerged largely in opposition to multicultural education (Sleeter and Delgado Bernal 2004).

Nevertheless, SICO also had issues with the term 'intercultural' (Verlot et al. 2000). From the outset, it seemed that in practice intercultural education kept its ethnic bias, being narrowed to 'interethnic education' and unilaterally focussing on the division in society between the 'native' majority and 'non-native' minorities. So, all the criticisms aimed at multicultural education equally apply to intercultural education: perhaps not in its theoretical approach, but certainly in its practical development in classrooms and schools.

For theoretical and practical reasons alike, SICO changed its name in 2005 to Centre for Diversity & Learning. The use of 'diversity' instead of

culture is meant to broaden and differentiate the perspective on social interaction by turning away from a narrow focus on culture-as-ethnicity and,
instead, highlighting the complex, intersectional, multi-layered and contextual
framework of diversity and inequality in society. Also, diversity is given a
central place in the educational process, both as education 'for' and 'in'
diversity. Education-for-diversity stands for learning to handle diversity as
part of becoming a citizen in a democratic society; education-in-education
emphasises the potential didactic benefits of exploiting the diversity that is
present in extant groups and contexts (Sierens 2007).

34.2.1.3 Linguistic Repertoire/Communicative Repertoire Brigitta Busch (2012)
has noted that, as a sociolinguistic concept, linguistic repertoire can be traced
back to the work of John Gumperz in the early 1960s (he called it initially 'verbal
repertoire'). For us, a reference point is the paper entitled 'Spaces of multilingualism' authored by Blommaert, Collins and Slembrouck (2005). We noted earlier in
this chapter that 'linguistic repertoire' is a useful concept to denote the multilingual
and heteroglossic nature of sociolinguistic practices of individuals and groups (see
De Backer, Van Avermaet, and Slembrouck 2019). In addition, our work
regarding Functional Multilingual Learning (FML, Sierens and Van Avermaet
2014) has been a stimulus to increasingly promote among educational practitioners the notion of a pupil's 'linguistic repertoire' as a functional tool for learning.
The notion can indeed help transcend the uncritical binaries in education between
'first language' versus 'second language', 'monolingual' versus 'bilingual'
speakers and 'native' versus 'non-native' students. This is in line with
Kramsch's (2009) conception of 'third culture', which 'does not propose to
eliminate these dichotomies, but suggests focusing on the relation itself and on
the heteroglossia within each of the poles. It is a symbolic place that is by no
means unitary, stable, permanent and homogeneous' (p. 238). We define FML as
the strategic use in education of the (emergent) multilingual learners' language
resources. These resources function as a mediating, facilitating tool in powerful
learning environments in the mainstream classroom to improve learning of both
the language of schooling and curricular content. In essence, FML aims beyond
the binary and combines the functional approach to first language use in second
language acquisition (SLA) and pedagogical translanguaging. More specifically,
FML is tailored to mainstream learning settings where the second language is
predominantly used as medium of instruction, while the learners use various
linguistic repertoires, including marginalised languages or language varieties.

34.2.2   Key Practices

34.2.2.1 Awareness of Language/Language Awareness The first time we came
across the concept of 'Language Awareness' (LA) in Flanders was through the
work of the regional Foyer centre in Brussels, which, among other things,
develops and supports initiatives promoting plurilingualism. The term LA was

translated into Dutch as *talensensibilisering*, which is in fact an adapted translation of the French *éveil aux langues*. The LA approach and materials at the time developed by Foyer staff members were inspired by various language programmes supported by the European Union and the Council of Europe (e.g. Evlang). The LA concept was picked up during the preparation of the Home Language in Education (HLiE, *Thuistaal in onderwijs*) project, which was initiated by the educational department of the city of Ghent. This project was subject to an evaluation study conducted by the CDL in collaboration with the Centre for Language and Education at the University of Leuven (Ramaut et al. 2013). One of the two major objectives of this local trial project, carried out between 2008 and 2013 in four primary schools in Ghent, was to implement LA. However, the pre-study revealed contradictions in teachers' observed classroom behaviour. While a teacher sometimes enacted spontaneous LA moments, by showing an interest in or praising children's home languages ('What a beautiful language Turkish is!'), the same teacher would also reprimand children's use of home languages at other moments, particularly during arithmetic or language lessons ('Hey, are you speaking Turkish again?'). On the basis of this finding, we proposed to extend the project aim of LA and add to it the 'functional' use of home languages in mainstream classroom learning (Bultynck et al. 2008). The evaluation study itself revealed that using existing LA materials often was restricted to doing nice things with languages, often during peripheral classroom activities. Some teachers didn't like working with ready-made LA lesson packages, finding them 'artificial' and preferring spontaneous LA moments popping up in classroom interaction (Ramaut et al. 2013). This experience with LA was one of the stepping stones in our coinage of the concept of Functional Multilingual Learning (Sierens and Van Avermaet 2014; see earlier). In the meantime, the concept of LA (*talensensibilisering*) also began to turn up in policy documents at the Flemish national level. However, the notion was novel, and gave rise to some confusion and misunderstanding among both policymakers and practitioners. Commissioned by the Flemish Education Council, we carried out, together with colleagues from the University of Leuven, a literature study in order to clarify the concept of LA and its implementation in Flemish schools (Frijns et al. 2018). The study resulted, among other things, in a guidebook for educational practitioners (teachers, coordinators, school managers) in primary and secondary education (Devlieger et al. 2012). Another outcome of our conceptual and theoretical work was the first systematic review of LA interventions in educational contexts, which examined effects on learners, teachers and parents (Sierens et al. 2018). Finally, collaboration with Christine Hélot also led us to endorse a critical multilingual approach to LA (Hélot et al. 2018).

34.2.2.2 Translanguaging In the past decade or so, the notion of (pedagogical) translanguaging has spread like a forest fire around the international literature about multilingualism. Given its widespread use, to the point of its becoming a

mere container concept, translanguaging has been subject to different interpretations and discussions. Much of the current discussion revolves in essence
around the nature or definition of 'language'. In accordance with Cummins
(2017) and García and Lin (2017), a distinction can be made between a
'strong' and a 'weak' version of translanguaging. García and Li Wei (2014)
support a 'strong version' of translanguaging, asserting that it assumes per
definition that students' whole linguistic repertoires are dynamically used
without a clear-cut distinction between languages. They even go so far to
argue that the construct of 'a language' is illegitimate and that there is only one
linguistic system with features that are totally integrated rather than being
associated with any one language. This reflects a critical perspective which
does not take the category of 'language' for granted, but treats it as an
ideological construct, an 'invention' or discourse that is selective, partial,
interested, situated and political (see Jaffe 2011).

In response, Cummins (2017) critically points out that although the construct of separate languages indeed lacks 'objective' linguistic reality, one can
still maintain that in social reality languages clearly exist as constructions with
arbitrary and fluid boundaries, which generate an immense material and
symbolic reality. Cummins concludes that it is 'legitimate to distinguish
languages in certain contexts and for certain purposes in order to make sense
of and act on our worlds' (2017, p. 112). Furthermore, the fact that languages
are real autonomous systems does not rule out that they are connected, have
permeable boundaries and are prone to influence by other languages. In short,
softening the boundaries between languages is not the same as imagining a
merged, hybridised linguistic system.

So where do we position ourselves in this discussion? We recognise the
materiality as well as psychological and affective realities of language/linguis-
tic identities where there continue to be clear distinctions between languages.
With Slembrouck and Rosiers (2018) we believe that translanguaging is not
inextricably bound up with linguistic hybridity and, therefore, does not
exclude the pedagogically effective use of two or more named languages,
'side-by-side'. In our opinion, strong translanguaging, which views languages
as a single 'hybridised linguistic system', runs the risk of turning into a new
norm, replacing the old norm of languages as 'compartmentalised units'.
Paraphrasing Vogel and García (2017), we argue that both approaches are
valuable theoretical lenses that offer a different view of bilingualism and
multilingualism. And coming back to our concept of FML, we advocate to
go beyond the binary and normative discussion of 'language hybridity' versus
'language as compartmentalised unit'. The concept of 'linguistic repertoire'
can be helpful here. In education, pupils need to acquire the 'language of
schooling'. Their multilingual repertoire – in addition to its value in itself –
functions as didactic capital, as scaffold for learning the language of schooling
and for learning in general.

REFERENCES

Blommaert, J. and Van Avermaet, P. (2008). *Taal, onderwijs en de samenleving: De kloof tussen beleid en realiteit* [Language, education and society: The gap between policy and practice]. Berchem: Epo.

Blommaert, J., Collins, J. and Slembrouck, S. (2005). Spaces of multilingualism. *Language & Communication* 25, 197–216.

Bultynck, K., Sierens, S, Van Avermaet, P., Slembrouck, S. and Verhelst, M. (2008). *Vooronderzoek m.b.t. de plaats van de thuistalen van de allochtone kinderen binnen onderwijs en opvang in vier scholen van het project 'Thuistaal in onderwijs': Eindrapport* [Preliminary investigation into the role of the home languages of immigrant children in education and care in four schools of the 'Home Language in Education' project: Final report]. Ghent University and University of Leuven.

Busch, B. (2012). The linguistic repertoire revisited. *Applied Linguistics* 33, 505–523.

Cummins, J. (2007). Rethinking monolingual instructional strategies in multilingual classrooms. *The Canadian Journal of Applied Linguistics* 10, 221–240.

(2017). Teaching for transfer in multilingual school contexts. In O. García, A. M. Y. Lin and S. May, eds., *Bilingual and Multilingual Education*, 3rd Edition. New York: Springer, pp. 103–115.

De Backer, F., Van Avermaet, P. and Slembrouck, S. (2019). Language passports: Unraveling the complex and multi-layered linguistic repertoires of multilingual pupils in Flanders (Belgium). In S. D. Brunn and R. Kehrein, eds., *Handbook of the Changing World Language Map*. New York: Springer.

Delarue, S. (2016). Bridging the policy-practice gap: How Flemish teachers' standard language perceptions navigate between monovarietal policy and multivarietal practice (unpublished doctoral dissertation). Ghent University.

Devlieger, M., Frijns, C., Sierens, S. and Van Gorp, K. (2012). *Is die taal van ver of van hier? Wegwijs in talensensibilisering van kleuters tot adolescenten* [Is that language from far or from here? Becoming familiar with language awareness from preschoolers to adolescents]. Leuven: Acco.

Frijns, C., Sierens, S., Van Avermaet, P., Sercu, L. and Van Gorp, M. (2018). Serving policy or people? Towards an evidence-based, coherent concept of language awareness for all learners. In C. Hélot, C. Frijns, K. Van Gorp and S. Sierens, eds., *Language Awareness in Multilingual Classrooms in Europe: From Theory to Practice*. Berlin: De Gruyter Mouton, pp. 87–115.

García, O. (2009). Education, multilingualism and translanguaging in the 21st century. In A. Mohanty, M. Panda, R. Phillipson and T. Skutnabb-Kangas, eds., *Multilingual Education for Social Justice: Globalizing the Local*. New Delhi: Orient Blackswan, pp. 140–158.

Garcia, O. and Li Wei (2014). *Translanguaging: Language, Bilingualism and Education*. New York: Palgrave MacMillan.

García, O. and Lin, A. M. Y. (2017). Translanguaging in bilingual education. In O. García, A. M. Y. Lin and S. May, eds., *Bilingual and Multilingual Education*, 3rd Edition. New York: Springer, pp. 117–130.

Gielen, S., Padmos, T., Philips, I. and Truyts, I. (2012). *Talensensibilisering in het kleuter- en lager onderwijs: Tips voor de klas- en schoolpraktijk* [Language awareness in preschool and primary education: Tips for classroom and school practice]. Leuven and Ghent: University of Leuven and Ghent University.

Heller, M. (1999). *Linguistic Minorities and Modernity: A Sociolinguistic Ethnography*. London: Longman.

Hélot, C., Van Gorp, K., Frijns, C. and Sierens, S. (2018). Introduction: Towards critical multilingual language awareness for 21st century. In C. Hélot, C. Frijns, K. Van Gorp and S. Sierens, eds., *Language Awareness in Multilingual Classrooms in Europe: From Theory to Practice*. Berlin: De Gruyter Mouton, pp. 1–20.

Jaffe, A. (2011). Language-in-education policy: The Corsican example. In T. McCarty, ed., *Ethnography and Language Policy*. New York: Routledge, pp. 205–229.

Kramsch, C. (2009). Third culture and language education. In Li Wei and V. Cook, eds., *Contemporary Applied Linguistics. Vol. 1: Language Teaching and Learning*. London: Continuum, pp. 233–254.

Ramaut, G., Sierens, S., Bultinck, K., Van Avermaet, P., Slembrouck, S., Van Gorp, K. and Verhelst, M. (2013). *Evaluatieonderzoek van het project 'Thuistaal in onderwijs' (2009-2012): Eindrapport* [Evaluation research into the 'Home Language in Education' project (2009-2012): Final report]. Ghent: Ghent University.

Sierens, S. (2007). *Leren voor diversiteit – leren in diversiteit. Burgerschapsvorming en gelijke leerkansen in een pluriforme samenleving: Een referentiekader [Learning for diversity – learning in diversity* [Citizenship education and equal learning opportunities in a pluriform society: A framework]. Ghent: Ghent University, Centre for Diversity & Learning.

Sierens, S. and Ramaut G. (2018). Breaking out of L2-exclusive pedagogies: Teachers valorizing immigrant pupils' multilingual repertoire in urban Dutch-medium classrooms. In P. Van Avermaet, S. Slembrouck, K. Van Gorp, S. Sierens and K. Maryns, eds., *The Multilingual Edge of Education*. London: Palgrave Macmillan, pp. 285–312.

Sierens, S. and Van Avermaet, P. (2014). Language diversity in education: Evolving from multilingual education to functional multilingual learning. In D. Little, C. Leung and P. Van Avermaet, eds., *Managing Diversity in Education: Languages, Policies, Pedagogies*. Bristol: Multilingual Matters, pp. 204–222.

Sierens, S., Frijns, C., Van Gorp, K., Sercu, L. and Van Avermaet, P. (2018). Effects of raising language awareness in mainstream and language classrooms: A literature review (1995–2013). In C. Hélot, C. Frijns, K. Van Gorp & S. Sierens, eds., *Language Awareness in Multilingual Classrooms in Europe: From Theory to Practice*. Boston: De Gruyter Mouton, pp. 21–85.

Sleeter, C. E. and Delgado Bernal, D. (2004). Critical pedagogy, critical race theory and antiracist education. In J. A. Banks and C. A. McGee Banks, eds., *Handbook of Research on Multicultural Education*, 2nd Edition. San Francisco: Jossey-Bass, pp. 240–238.

Slembrouck, S. and Rosiers, K. (2018). Translanguaging: A matter of sociolinguistics, pedagogics and interaction? In P. Van Avermaet, S. Slembrouck, K. Van Gorp, S. Sierens and K. Maryns, eds., *The Multilingual Edge of Education*. London: Palgrave Macmillan, pp. 165–187.

Verlot, M., Sierens, S., Soenen, R. and Suijs, S. (2000). *Intercultureel onderwijs: Leren in verscheidenheid* [Intercultural education: Learning in diversity]. Ghent: Ghent University, Steunpunt ICO.

Vogel, S. and García, O. (2017). Translanguaging. In *Oxford Research Encyclopedia of Education*. Online publication. https://doi.org/10.1093/acrefore/9780190264093.013.181

35   A Reflection on Generational Diaspora and Resulting Linguistic Acclimatization

Rahat Zaidi

I come from a family that has experienced three generations of migration across the subcontinent, North America and Europe, with relocation and displacement, in some cases marked by necessity and in others by choice. Some of my earliest memories emerge from my upbringing in a trilingual environment in Shiraz, Iran. My individual multilingualism grew as a direct consequence of having parents who spoke to me mixing Urdu and English. My grandmother only spoke to me in Urdu, I attended a strictly Farsi school and I also spoke to my neighbours in this language. In effect, I began to unconsciously practise translanguaging at a very young age, using my personal repertoire of language skills to develop a hybrid form of communication and establish myself as a default communicator between community and family members. This resulted in a deep understanding, both linguistically and culturally, of the community around me as I continually transitioned back and forth between community and family languages. I learned very quickly how to engage plurilingualism in my daily activities, easily switching between languages, depending on with whom I was conversing at the time.

Translanguaging became part of my daily routine as I learned to think in a blend of Urdu and English and use both languages to express my thoughts and emotions. While I lived and attended school in Pakistan, I was a student in classrooms where we read a great deal of literature handed down as a legacy of the British Empire, and this served to reinforce the cultural background of my English language use. This post-colonial legacy gave me the opportunity to become familiar with works from Shakespeare and other British literary influences. Further into my education, I began to understand both the linguistic and cultural ramifications of colonialism, especially hearing my grandparents‘ context, which often included sacrificial and bloody perspectives of the British influence on India. It was within this context that I was living a classic example of a person bound by the societal norms of the day; norms that recognized the English language as the power broker. As a result, I began to use English more and more with my parents, a typical behaviour of many children who were in similar circumstances as myself. The other language I spoke, Urdu, was really a young language, created out of the consequences of

Figure 35.1 Sankofa: 'it is not taboo to fetch what is at risk of being left behind'

independence, and helped me formulate an amalgamated cultural understanding of the languages I knew how to speak.

Since my youth, I have always considered myself a cultural boundary crosser of some sort or another. As such, I have learned a great deal about other people and the world around me, in part owing to my openness to other cultures. This openness has also helped to broaden my perspective and better understand culture-specific behaviour. It has also opened doors to research opportunities and professional engagement. Today, I perceive the stages of my life as having come together into moulding the person I am and the career path I have chosen to follow: a mother of two daughters and a professor in a Canadian university.

My adult life has been characterized by a divide between my public and private life in that at home I always wanted to encourage my daughters to be proud of their heritage and language (speaking Urdu to them). In my public life, on the other hand, my own identity has had to be submerged to accommodate the demands of my career. In other words, living in a primarily Judaeo/Christian/English culture has presented interesting challenges and opportunities, particularly with my children's questioning of their placement and identity within the Canadian culture. For example, I remember one Christmas in particular when my eldest daughter wanted to know why we did not have a Christmas tree in our house. This event caused me to think deeply about my own identity and how to safeguard what was precious to me and counterbalance that with the desire to integrate into Canadian society. In the beginning, I resisted this pressure to integrate; however, as the years passed I saw through my children the need to counterbalance the mainstream culture with my own heritage and identity. Therefore a Christmas tree is now included as part of our winter celebrations. For me this was a significant marker of what I was experiencing and witnessing through my daughters' eyes. Their education was so much different from mine, in that they attended a monolingual institution with few opportunities for sharing and exploring the various facets of identity at home and within the community. In fact, community identity was largely shaped by Pakistani immigrant families living in our city. When I was able to look back at the education systems around the world of which I had been part (Iran, Pakistan, United States and France), it was at this point that I began developing a much clearer understanding of how these experiences shaped my understanding of language, culture and identity.

Throughout the course of my career, my research has affirmed much of how I feel regarding my own identity. It is no secret that post-colonial Canada in particular has strived over many years to secure national unity and loyalty among its peoples. Its multilingual/multicultural makeup has been the cornerstone of its nation building ideology and yet I, along with so many others, have yet to feel this sense of unity. Today, I still struggle with the identity that I have created for myself: an identity that is rooted in a variety of locales and spaces, punctuated by linguistic and cultural variety and the push-pull mechanisms that are created as a result of the choices I have made over the years. Consequently, this hybrid sense of who I am has influenced key concepts that underpin my interest in the issue of multilingualism/plurilingualism/identity in educational systems. These key concepts have been a driving force in both my personal and professional life and have helped form much of my research agenda over the span of a decade.

35.1   Key Concepts and Practices

The lived experiences described here have formed the foundation for the kinds of research questions I have decided to develop. My own personal trajectory mirrors that of many Canadians today. Within this country, we face an interesting reality in the current system with the rise of a different kind of bilingualism that disrupts the traditional English and French of recent history (Baluja and Bradshaw 2012). The 2016 Canadian census confirmed earlier trends of expanding home languages and mother tongue diversity nationwide (Statistics Canada 2017), with an increase of 910,400 people (13.3%) who speak a language other than English at home (Statistics Canada 2015, 2017).

My understanding of and interest in multilingualism have largely propelled my research around successful integration of newcomer families into mainstream society and the role that their language plays in the development of strong multicultural/multilingual individuals. I locate my work within a paradigm that recognizes the intimate relation between language, culture and identity. People today live in a world where borders are being crossed in a variety of changing and accelerated ways, with special emphasis on geopolitics, culture, linguistics and literacy. My research focus initially began with the development of pre-service teacher training programmes in which I recognized a number of perspectives. These included placing an emphasis on understanding how families and students can best function together and within the school system. My work valued the plurilingual nature of Canadian society and also recognized the new paradigm in which teachers were finding themselves: a classroom filled with a rich, strong variety of students who carried cultural and linguistic capital that needed to be tapped. My interest in multilingualism stemmed from the educational context of schools where this phenomenon was taking a new shape and form. Through my work in schools with educators, students and families I joined researchers (Orellana 2017; Gutiérrez et al. 2011, 2009, 2003) who reiterated the importance of tapping into the transcultural capital of immigrant children, encouraging and inspiring diverse ways of thinking, doing, acting and being, all to prepare future citizens to co-exist in a global society.

Over the last decade I have aimed at highlighting Hall's (2004) 'cultural flows' that occur as people and practices transcend time and cultural spaces. The learning ecology of multicultural classrooms in present day schools is characterized by hybrid language practices, digital modes, social media and identity markers that form a backdrop to the mainstream programme of studies with which teachers are mandated to work. I have been inspired by some of the basic principles defined by Cummins and others, who acknowledge that (a) the boundaries between languages/dialects are fluid and socially constructed, (b) as emergent bilinguals gain access to their two languages, these languages become fused into a single integrated system (common underlying proficiency), (c) languages and languaging are socially contested sites and encounters where the legitimacy of cultures and identities are negotiated, and (d) school programmes serving emergent bilingual students should connect instruction with students' lives, including their multilingual repertoires, and teach for transfer and greater integration across languages. I have worked closely with schools, families, students and teachers to develop instructional strategies within multicultural classrooms focusing on multilingual resources. One of these strategies has involved the use of dual language books where classroom teachers and invited guest readers have engaged young students in a form of dialogic reading in several languages (Naqvi et al. 2012, Zaidi 2020;

2013). Modelling good reading strategies, these activities have progressively aligned with the programme of studies for Language Arts. Through extensive textual analysis of books published in several languages, I have identified characteristics of effective and usable multilingual literature. Analysis and usage have underlined the importance of authentic stories, often written by immigrants that represent the hybrid characteristics of modern immigrant communities. Many of the storylines are contextualized in the actual lives of families living in North America and Europe and capture the essence of a hybrid existence. (For more information go to www.rahatzaidi.com).

As an example of this philosophy, one of my projects involved the use of a dual language book entitled *Grandma's Saturday Soup*. The book takes us on a week-long story in which the central character, Mimi (a young Jamaican girl living in a new country), reminisces about her Grandmother's Saturday soup. She is reminded of the soup wherever she goes, including the fluffy white clouds in the sky that recall the dumplings in the soup and the fresh fallen snow that conjures up memories of soft Jamaican sand. Working with younger children in Grade 1 and 2 classrooms, this book was used by the teachers to introduce students to different languages where guest readers were invited into the classroom to read in several different languages (Urdu, Punjabi, French, Tagalog, Spanish and English). The story was always read page by page, first in a language other than English, followed by the same page read in English. During the course of the reading, I encouraged both the guest readers and the teachers to emphasize the dialogic nature of the reading approach. This was characterized by shifting traditional reader/listener roles (teachers reads, student listens) and opening up the conversation to allow children to actively participate through questions, adding information both culturally and linguistically, and encouraging them to describe more. As a result, the children were more engaged and more aware of the linguistic components of the books and also gained considerable insight into the pluralistic and multicultural nature of the books and their own identities. There was rich discussion around food, clothing, head gear, religious icons and language, all of which leant a great amount of credibility to the languages and cultures represented in the classroom at the time. Such scaffolding ensures that the child is actively engaged in the reading process and helps him/her move towards new skills, concepts and levels of understanding. Moreover, this shared reading between adult and child supports linguistic development in general and the development of decontextualized language in particular (Senechal and LeFevre 2002; Jimenez, Filippini and Gerber 2006). Thus, dialogic reading is seen as an especially appropriate tool for fostering the multiliteracy skills of multilingual students.

I have witnessed the power educators have to affect their students' identity construction and the significant role DLBs have played to encourage students to move beyond their assumed limitations into a new, hybrid identity. This identity enables them to redefine who they are in terms of their talents and accomplishments, both linguistic and intellectual. In addition, my research has also reaffirmed the need for pre-service teacher programmes to allow the development of new teachers to stop the institutional labelling of their students and seek the potential that lies within them, steering them away from structures that devalue their identities and endorsing the legitimacy of dynamic hetero-glossic conceptions of bi/multilingualism (Cummins 2017).

Over the years, my interest in this arena has evolved, as has the culture in which my investigations have taken place. We know that throughout history, people have immigrated to different lands, learning how to integrate and mediate local and global identities whenever they began their new life in any given country. My research has examined what happens when people project their languages and identities through a framework that is being transplanted in a country like Canada. Affiliations with the mother country change and new affiliations begin, and this happens both with parents and with children born into the family. While Canada has always been a nation of immigrants, more recent immigration from other than European countries has raised new questions which cannot simply be contained in the passive language of multiculturalism. As a result, my work moves beyond the plurilingualism/multiculturalism arena, and I have been forced to think about how things are being constructed and reconstructed in a time when immigration looks similar to but is also very different from previous waves. In my initial years of research, I adhered to concepts such as interculturalism, and multiculturalism to characterize some of the things I was witnessing as strong themes in my work. Multiculturalism stood out as the phenomenon that has historically characterized Canadian culture, referring to a society promoting a range of lifestyles, philosophies, religions and codes (Zaidi 2017). Interculturalism helped me understand the nuances that existed within the larger concept of multiculturalism, building on the definition of a community in which there is a deep understanding and respect of all cultures. I have looked at how new immigrants are affected by plurilingualism and multiculturalism, and I have come to the conclusion that it is not interculturalism nor multiculturalism; in essence, what I am witnessing now has brought me into a new stance in research where I am working with notions of transculturalism. This refers to migrational flows that have taken place over decades and how countries around the world have become more linguistically and culturally complex. Being local matters as much as being global; it involves navigating transcultural spaces as much as forging dynamic identities. Some of these dispositions are inherited; some are acquired through the public education system, keeping in mind that the hegemonic mainstream culture still carries power and weight (Zaidi and Rowsell 2017). The question becomes important in the sense that someone like myself is interested in the notion as to how transculturalism can be used as a theoretical tool in the lives of students and educators. Migration and plural identities are consequences or characteristics of these transnational movements, and in order to understand local and global dynamics, we need to pay attention to cultural flows. We need to think about schools as compositions of places of learning, characterized by linguistic and cultural diversity, and multiple identities. The bigger picture now involves more questions: How does the face of multiculturalism embrace change as it strives to integrate religious differences as well as cultural dynamics? How can cultural, linguistic and religious integration succeed without isolating the cultures themselves? Should a culture be permitted to maintain its structure to the point of segregation? These types of questions now propel my research into the next decade. The imperative to educate for cultural understanding and the need to nurture our receptive side also require sound knowledge and forms of information that can contribute to not simply learning about the other but offering language and tools for meeting at the boundaries in engaging and meaningful ways. Education is not the domain of any one subject in school but is something that can and should be woven into the fabric of teaching and learning across the curriculum.

REFERENCES

Baluja, T. and Bradshaw, J. (2012). Is bilingualism still relevant? *The Globe and Mail.* A.12. www.theglobeandmail.com/news/national/is-bilingualism-still-relevant-in-canada/article4365620/

Cummins, J. (2017). Teaching minoritized students: Are Additive Approaches Legitimate? *Harvard Educational Review* 87(3), 404–425. https://doi.org/10.17763/1943-5045-87.3.404

Fraser, S. (2005). *Grandma's Saturday Soup.* London: Mantra Lingua.

Gutiérrez, K. and Rogoff, B. (2003). Cultural ways of learning: individual traits or repertoires of practice. *Educational Researcher* 32(5), 19–25.

Gutiérrez, K., Morales, P. L. and Martinez, D. (2009). Re-mediating literacy: Culture, difference, and learning for students from non-dominant communities. *Review of Research in Educational Research* 33, 212–245.

Gutiérrez, K. D., Bien, A. C., Selland, M. K. and Pierce, D. M. (2011). Polylingual and polycultural learning ecologies: Mediating emergent academic literacies for dual language learners. *Journal of Early Childhood Literacy* 11(2), 232–261. https://doi.org/10.1177/1468798411399273

Hall, K. (2004). The ethnography of imagined communities: The cultural production of Sikh ethnicity in Britain. *ANNALS* 595, 108–120.

Jimenez, T. C., Filippini, A. L. and Gerber, M. (2006). Shared reading within latino families: An analysis of reading interactions and language use. *Bilingual Research Journal* 30(2), 431–452.

Naqvi, R., Thorne, K., Pfitscher. C. and McKeough, A. (2012). Dual language books as an emergent-literacy resource: Culturally and linguistically responsive teaching and learning. *Journal of Early Childhood Literacy* 13(4), 501–528. https://doi.org/10.1177/1468798412442886

Naqvi, R., Thorne, K., Pfitscher, C., Nordstokke, D. and McKeough, A. (2013). Reading dual language books: Improving early literacy skills in linguistically diverse classrooms. *Journal of Early Childhood Research* 11(1), 3–15. https://doi.org/10.1177/1476718X12449453

Orellana, M. F. (2017). Solidarity, transculturality, educational anthropology, and (the modest goal of) transforming the world. *Anthropology & Education Quarterly* 48 (3), 210–220.

Senechal, M. and LeFevre, J. (2002). Parental involvement in the development of children's reading skill: A five-year longitudinal study. *Child Development* 73(2), 445–460.

Statistics Canada (2015). Proportion of the school-age population (aged 5 to 24) with non-official home language, Canada and jurisdictions, in and out of census metropolitan areas (CMAs), 2011 [Data table]. www150.statcan.gc.ca/n1/pub/81-582-x/2015002/tbl/tbla2.3-eng.htm

    (2017). Linguistic diversity and multilingualism in Canadian homes. www12.statcan.gc.ca/census-recensement/2016/as-sa/98-200-x/2016010/98–200-x2016010-eng.pdf

Zaidi, R. (2017). *Anti-Islamophobic Curriculums*. New York: Peter Lang.

    (2020). Dual-language books: Enhancing engagement and language awareness. *Journal of Literacy Research* 52(3), 269–292. https://doi.org/10.1177/1086296X20939559

Zaidi, R. and Rowsell, J. (2017). *Literacy Lives in Transcultural Times*. New York: Routledge.

36   On Language(s), Education and Dynamic Language Users
Final Words and Future Directions

Nathalie Auger, Gail Prasad and Emmanuelle
Le Pichon-Vorstman

In the pages of this volume, authors have generously shared stories and perspectives – personal and professional – about their experiences at the intersections of Multilingualism and Education. While contributors have undoubtedly been privy to their students' and their research participants' language biographies, it has not been common in academic publications for researchers to also disclose their own language biographies. While some authors shared that they were uncomfortable with this exercise, we remain grateful for each individual who rose to the challenge. We invited a variety of researchers to take a singular look at crucial notions in our fields of research and pedagogical action. By bringing them together, we have chosen to lay the groundwork for a conversation that will lead researchers, educators and students to greater understanding of our use of these concepts, based on the acceptance and recognition of a fluid and changing reality that adapts and requires adjustments over time. This collection of papers makes visible how concepts and practices emerge and take shape differently across contexts. When we adopt an embodied listening posture, we can begin to imagine futures for our field that allow us to move forward, building knowledge and transforming practice together.

From the beginning, and as the title 'Multilingualism and Education' indicates, this book had a two-fold objective.

The first goal was to explore how, through both personal and professional embodied reflection, possibilities might emerge to advance our understanding of working with learners in multilingual educational contexts around the world. The second goal was to foster collective reflection for further directions for teacher preparation and training in language teaching and learning in a Post-Multilingual world.

In Chapter 1, we introduced each individual contributor. To conclude, rather than citing the perspectives of contributors by name, we foreground the polysemic nature of notions that emerge across contributions. While individual contributors hold different perspectives, the personal narratives in this volume provide context to help us understand that different approaches to common themes do not necessarily imply an inherent contradiction.

These differences invite conversation among the various texts considering their specific contexts. We believe that, on the contrary, they can invite a dialogue, and help to better understand, at a general level, how concepts have been formed and used in each of our research areas.

The aim is to generate, for readers who so wish, the possibility of pursuing an individual or specific analysis beyond our own. To facilitate this, we organized contributions at the outset by author in alphabetical order and we have included an index by concept to allow readers to easily return to specific concepts addressed across contributions.

What became particularly interesting in editing this volume is that much like the multilingual people we study – children, youth, educators, and/or families – researchers traverse multiple contexts on an ongoing basis, often beginning in childhood. Multilingualism is not stable or stagnant. Its dynamic flow is captured through the narratives that make up this volume – and that is a key message in and of itself. As we look to the future of multilingualism and education in research and practice, we hear through the lives and research trajectories of those invested in this field that there is a need to find ways to facilitate reciprocal and responsive flows of ideas, concepts and theories that help build knowledge collectively rather than in silos or in opposition. However, what also emerges is that this ideal is not easy to reach: each of us has a complex history filled with multiple trajectories that rarely show up in academic publications but undoubtedly influence our unique meaning-making.

The aim of this volume was not only to highlight individual subjectivities but also to cultivate nuanced understandings of the different paths of researchers, their choices and interests. We sought to invite a range of perspectives to the table. In review of the different perspectives presented across this volume and after reflecting on the results of a word cloud generated from this volume based on word count, we were drawn to three notions: language/s, education and dynamic language users.

The recurrence of certain words led us to think about the multiple configurations of each term throughout this volume and the richness of the multiplicity of definitions proposed throughout the contributions. We have chosen to highlight this plurality of interpretation by reflecting on the three main word categories presented in Figure 36.1 and to consider how such plurality can inform teacher education. We hope that readers in turn will engage in further reflection on various notions presented in this volume and enter into dialogue about how they manifest within their own contexts.

Figure 36.1 Multilingualism and Education Word Cloud

36.1   On Language/s/ing

> **LANGUAGE**: acquisition, alternation, and cultural repertoire, and knowledge,
> and plurilingualism, appropriation, as a barrier for full participation in social and
> academic life, attrition, awakening' approaches, awareness, biography, borrowing,
> boundaries, choice, compartmentalization contact, of *schooling, coursework,*
> curricula, democratization, Dynamics, and Management of Diversity, education,
> Educator Awareness, identity, ideology, in social life, inequalities, interdependence
> hypothesis, learners, learning programmes, maintenance, mastery, mixing, of
> instruction, of the majority, of the Nation, of the oppressor, planning, policy,
> policy-making, norms, regulations, portraits, practices in education, proficiency,
> learning, repertoire, representations of teachers, resources of students, rights,
> separation, skills, pronunciation, standards, values, hierarchies, status, teacher,
> educator, researcher, teaching, transmission, maintenance, shift, loss, use and
> practices, varieties, Awareness, plurilingualism, identities, and cultural practices,
> separate units, cultural events, dialects, sacrosanct, family, languaging, equality, as
> the assemblage of movements, bodies, objects, experts, langues mortes

Unsurprisingly, the notion that occurs with greatest frequency across contributions is that of 'language'. In reviewing contributions in English and in French, the term 'language' in English is far from transparent. Language can be used both to refer to a single or discrete language and to reference the phenomenon of 'language' and languaging in general that encompasses the practices associated with a speech community and/or speech event. In French, this polysemic difference is clearly distinguished through the use of separate terms: *langue, langage, pratiques langagières* and *discours*. *Langue* refers to a specific language, while *langage* or *pratiques langagières* and *discours* can be expressed in English as language, discourse and/or speech, particularly as related to the practices and norms of a community. That is, a speech community is characterized by a set of norms for language interactions. As Blommaert (2009) describes, the diversity of individuals who form an imperfect group, constituted of '(ab)normal' individuals (p. 421), situated and limited in time and space. The language, then, of a particular group concerns not only possible named languages or language variations but also the norms that govern language use in such ways that identify members who belong to a given speech community and those who fall outside its boundaries. Metalinguistic reflections or epilinguistic reflections participate in building awareness of one's language experience and learning phenomena in situations of linguistic diversity experience. A number of authors raise questions regarding the nature of language and draw attention to the fact that languages are not necessarily stable and discrete but rather they are socially constructed, hybridized.

The question becomes then: what are the consequences for language teaching and learning? What emerges across the chapters of this book is that even if one adopts a fluid perspective about language(s), there is value in certain contexts to describing a language in relation to how it obeys social orders. It also follows syntactic, lexical and pragmatic regularities, even if, of course, these boundaries are socially constructed.

What we see across authors' contributions is an attention not just to language in the singular, albeit with multiple meanings, but also to languages in the plural. The Multilingual Turn (May, 2014) has disrupted the ideology of the uniform, monolithic language that defines the nation state. In a Post-Multilingual world, authors have highlighted a shift in focus from singular, discrete, named languages towards trans-visions of languages and languaging in the plural. Authors who have worked with the Council of Europe, in particular, have tended to draw on theories of plurilingualism. For all authors, relationships to languages and language reflect different theories of language. These theories of language are fundamental to considerations and questions concerning multilingualism and education. Indeed, these theories of language index the different sociopolitical contexts that authors have lived in and worked in, as well as the literatures on which they draw.

As theories of language emerge from different contexts, they in turn inform how researchers position themselves in and through their research, how we train teachers and how teachers design authentic learning activities for their students and learners. Clearly then, it is critical that teacher education engages teacher candidates in interrogating theories of language as a foundation for making pedagogical and political decisions about how they support learners' language development and languaging practices. Rather than approaching these theories in opposition, teacher education could focus instead on fostering understanding of how theories evolve across contexts as our understanding of practice deepens and vice versa. This approach positions teachers as knowledge-generators (Cummins, 2021) whose practice with multilingual learners in language-rich classrooms contributes powerfully to theory building.

Contributions in this volume discuss a range of theories of language including but not limited to translanguaging, plurilingualism, repertoires, variation and micro-/meso- and macro-alternation. The vast nomenclature concerning multilingual languaging practices signals how concepts emerge in context and then travel and evolve, often in deterritorialized ways which lead undoubtedly to reinterpretation. Teachers need to encounter these concepts and their conceptual roots and routes in order to make informed choices about their instructional design for their specific context. The capacity to make informed choices implies knowing the epistemology of one's choice, that is to say how these theories and concepts are constituted in order to understand their *raison d'être* and avoid the semantic loss of a concept. Languaging practices can be seen as an actualization of theories of language, as well as the foundation for building new theories. What is responsive to one context may not necessarily meet the needs of another: different histories and contexts do not necessarily cancel the validity or relevance of a given theory of language but rather highlight the complexity and nuance required to foster conditions for multilingual thriving in and through education.

36.2 On Education

> **EDUCATION/AL**: policies, design, system, capital, and health professionals; equity, institutions, practices, projects, Sciences, space, success systems; **SCHOOL (S)/ING:** as a political instrument, through the official language, curriculum, inclusion, of the twenty-first century, policy and practice, programs, reception of foreign students, space, success, teachers with monolingual and monocultural backgrounds; **CLASSROOM:** interaction, practices; **FOREIGN:** language classes, status, language, offered at school; **formal** contexts; **elementary** and secondary school, students; **inclusion, inclusive** educational practices in contexts of diversity; **institutional** 'realities', expectations, regulations, **institutionalised** education, propaganda; **institutional** policies; **instructional** strategies; **teacher** autonomy, training, **teachers'** feelings, pedagogical choices, social representation on languages, teaching and learning second/foreign languages in schools, culturally diverse students, experiences with newcomer, practices, learning languages

This brings us to the second concept that emerges across contributions, that of 'education'. Again, the notion of education is multidimensional and under its rubric we can also include a variety of related notions. Discussions of education naturally pervade this collection by design as teaching and learning in whatever context occurs in and through the double entendre of language/s. The adage 'Every teacher is a language teacher' has become popularized in recent years to reflect the role that all teachers play in supporting all students in the development of their linguistic competence. What becomes clear across this volume, however, is that *all education is a form of language education*. In some contexts, education as a field of research is separate from language teaching; language didactics, for example, fall into the field of language sciences. Despite this disciplinary separation, these two fields are critically interrelated. When we consider the intersections of multilingualism and education, we see that language education not only takes places in the classroom but also, of course, through the family and across a whole range of situations that can be classified as informal or non-formal: such as in community-based associations, in professional contexts, in person-to-person social interactions, etc. As much as formal language education has historically been characterized by monoglossic orientations that have kept languages separate, authors' reflections on multilingualism and education suggest the need not only to soften boundaries between languages through pedagogies that take this pluricity into account but also the need for an integrative approach to multilingualism across the triptych of formal, informal education and non-formal situations. Interestingly, scholars in this volume are all individuals who have themselves crossed languages and often countries both personally and professionally. Further, all of the authors have been students themselves and many of the authors also have been/are teachers, parents or even grandparents. Experiences as and with practitioners animate their reflections and imagination of education beyond languages, borders and boundaries.

Teachers play a critical role when it comes to mobilizing multilingualism as a resource, particularly in formal education settings. They are the ones who have the keys to change the face of language education across our multilingual and multicultural contexts. Contributions in this volume raise questions of and for teachers: what are their experiences with multilingualism? What posture or stance do they need to develop towards multilingualism and multilingual learners? What is the role of the school and teachers supporting students across formal, informal and non-formal learning contexts? These questions warrant further study across contexts in order to build nuanced understanding of the support necessary for teachers and their students as they teach and learn in multilingual and multicultural schools and communities.

The concept of 'school' emerges quite prominently across contributions: school as a place of socialization and formal learning of a language or different languages with norms that can sometimes be experienced as oppressive or subversive. Indeed, through all contributions, it becomes clear that the school is a very important parameter in promoting value judgements related to how languages are spoken, how languages are learned or about the languages in the students' repertoire. It is not possible to consider the schooling without considering the teacher preparation. Teacher candidates who will go on to work in schools have a decisive role to play in cultivating an inclusive and welcoming language ethos within schools. Teachers, therefore, have a crucial role to play in citizenship education, particularly through the multilingual approach. Across contexts, authors call for the need for a range of alternative approaches in schools, including more equitable approaches, inclusive approaches, and critical and creative approaches, etc. These alternatives counter the traditional doxa associated with monoglossic orientations to teaching, learning and language hierarchies naturalized in schools.

36.3   On Language Users

> **LANGUAGE USERS**: bi-national families; children; citizen; elementary and
> secondary school, students, emergent bilinguals, multilingual students, emerging
> bilingual; family; father; generations; interpreter; learner, majority; nation and
> people; majority; Métis colony; migrant, minority children, communities, mother;
> native-speaker; newcomer families; parents; politically oppressed communities;
> refugees, stateless; second and third generation pupils from immigrant families;
> raising trilingual children; settlement colony; siblings; teachers; transnational and
> transcultural families; underprivileged children and families; working class people

While the term 'language users' is not immediately visible in the word cloud
in this section, several concepts could be regrouped under the rubric of this
category. Concepts such as people, family, children, students and teachers
suggest a shift in the focus of the study of multilingualism from specific
languages to the ways in which languages become embodied in individuals
and the ways in which we use languages as we traverse time and space across
various spheres like home, school, work and community. As with shifts from a
singular view of language to multiple perspectives, the need to adopt an
integrative view of formal and informal language education is clear. It is
language users themselves who navigate across varieties of language(s)
and contexts.

Interestingly, children and youth became a central node for reflection across
authors' contributions, whether in relation to their own childhoods growing up
with languages at home and learning languages at school; whether in relation
to their own children, the challenges and joys of raising multilingual children
and/or grandchildren; or whether in relation to their function as teachers or
teacher educators. Children and youth occupy a prominent place in the question of multilingualism and education. Of course, one begins as a child and one
becomes an adult through languages and languaging. Experiences as a child
have a major impact on the social representations we form of languages,
learning and the world in general. All the contributors to this book take a
holistic approach to multilingualism and education, seeing students as having
to navigate with different languages in complex and changing socio-cultural
spaces. All contributors denounce deficit approaches to languages and language repertoires and see languages as tools for engaging in a variety of
learning activities. They advocate that educational programmes should be
designed with the greatest care, especially for this youngest group.
Moreover, through their biographies, we see how important the issue of
children is, since the life trajectories show how, as children, they have been
marked by their experiences with languages, experiences that have shaped

their social representations of language learning. Teacher education must prepare teachers to design multilingual instruction with great care and openness, particularly for the youngest of students. It also becomes very clear that becoming aware of one's own language biography and trajectory, as well as listening to the experiences of others, is critical to becoming more empathetic language users, teachers and learners.

Indeed, this shift to focus on people as dynamic language users must also include consideration of the notion of otherness. Indeed, language learners are the constituents of a certain otherness inherent in the relationship of the learner to the language community to which they are seeking to gain membership by developing their language competence. The issues of otherness and difference raise questions related to developing an intercultural framework for multilingual education. Understanding culture(s) and co-fostering understanding and appreciation of linguistic and cultural diversity is central to the work of language teaching and learning. Authors' language biographies speak poignantly to the harmful impact of rigid, deterministic visions of culture that assign individuals to categories with which they themselves may or may not identify. Just as we have sought to foster a space for listening to diverse perspectives across contexts, authors' reflections and research perspectives highlight the need to envision more expansive cultural frameworks based on heterogeneity and a humanism of the diverse.

Diversity is constitutive of all the situations of our authors, and constitutive of all the teaching and learning situations they describe. Too often, in the collective imagination that, for example, continues to define school curricula, homogeneity is still emblematic of the norm, of the rule that is expected of a school situation. We can see in the authors' texts that it is this battle for recognition of linguistic and/or cultural differences as an enrichment for the class that they wish to win with their work. All of them are hyper-conscious of the variability of norms based on their own experiences with school or university. They see that, too often, it is the search for homogeneity that is targeted through the resolution of the 'problem of heterogeneity' of classroom situations. In the paradigm that emerges from this work, heterogeneity and diversity are the new norms. The question is therefore how to prepare educators and to design activities for students based on the fact that diversity is the norm (intra or inter languages). Rather than mourning the loss of homogeneity, how do we find ways to address our heterogeneous realities and find ways to center and amplify diverse perspectives.

In this final chapter, we have discussed how the multiple perspectives presented across this volume can be read side-by-side as a way of exploring pathways for designing more expansive approaches to teaching, learning and researching at the intersections of multilingualism and education. Although they are far from exhaustive, we offer these concluding thoughts to spark further discussion and dialogue among researchers, educators and students who share similar contexts, as well as those across different contexts. What Multilingualism and Education has taught us is that in holding space and taking time to listen to one another's experiences, we can find points of convergence on which to build and points of divergence on which we can enter into critical embodied dialogue that honours individual subjectivities and values contextualized understandings.

All authors of this volume are researchers, but beyond this research posture is a shared posture of inquiry. The reflexive posture that these authors take is noteworthy. We have seen through authors' self-reflexive personal and professional texts that this practice of reflexivity may also be essential for teachers. This reflexive biographical approach holds promise for language teachers and for teacher preparation as a strategy to help teacher candidates conceptualize their life courses via their language biographies. Teacher educators could further pose questions concerning intersections with multilingualism or diversity in their classrooms and in relation to the activities they propose to students. A critical self-reflexive inquiry about the self as a dynamic language user, learner and teacher in a Post-Multilingual world can be the starting point for developing a critical multi-language aware educator stance.

REFERENCES

Blommaert, J. (2009). Language, asylum, and the national order. *Current Anthropology* 50(4), 415–441.

Cummins, P. J. (2021). *Rethinking the Education of Multilingual Learners: A Critical Analysis of Theoretical Concepts*. Bristol: Multilingual Matters.

Index

Milton Keynes UK
Ingram Content Group UK Ltd.
UKHW031444290224
438440UK00022B/177